# FOR THE
# LOVE OF
# IRELAND

# BY SUSAN CAHILL

*NONFICTION*

*A LITERARY GUIDE TO IRELAND*
(with Thomas Cahill)

*DESIRING ITALY:*
Women Writers Celebrate a Country

*FOR THE LOVE OF IRELAND:*
A Literary Companion for Readers and Travelers

*THE SMILES OF ROME*
A Literary Companion for Readers and Travelers

*FICTION*

*EARTH ANGELS*

*ANTHOLOGIES*

*WISE WOMEN:*
Two Thousand Years of Spiritual Writing by Women

*WRITING WOMEN'S LIVES:*
Autobiographical Narratives by 20th-Century American Women Writers

*GROWING UP FEMALE:*
Stories by Women Writers from the American Mosaic

*MOTHERS:*
Memories, Dreams, & Reflections by Literary Daughters

*NEW WOMEN AND NEW FICTION:*
Contemporary Short Stories by and about Women

*WOMEN AND FICTION*

# FOR THE
# LOVE OF
# IRELAND

*A Literary Companion for*
*Readers and Travelers*

EDITED AND WITH AN
INTRODUCTION BY

## SUSAN CAHILL

BALLANTINE BOOKS · NEW YORK

A Ballantine Book
Published by The Random House Publishing Group

Published in the United States by Ballantine Books, an imprint of The Random
House Publishing Group, a division of Random House, Inc., New York, and
simultaneously in Canada by Random House of Canada Limited, Toronto.

www.ballantinebooks.com

Library of Congress Cataloging-in-Publication Data
For the love of Ireland : a literary companion for readers and travelers /
edited and with an introduction by Susan Cahill.—1st ed.
p.   cm.
Includes bibliographical references.
ISBN 978-0-345-43419-7
1. English literature—Irish authors. 2. Irish literature—Translations
into English. 3. Ireland—Literary collections. I. Cahill, Susan Neunzig.
PR8835 .F67   2001
820.8'09417—dc21                                        00-066753

Interior design by Ann Gold

Cover photo © HP Mereten/The Stock Market

Manufactured in the United States of America

10

*For Tom, Kristin, Joey,*
*and our new fellow traveler, Dan Garcia*


*In Ireland,*
*For Nancy Marlborough of Quin*

# Contents

INTRODUCTION     xi

OVERTURES     xiv
George Bernard Shaw, Kate O'Brien, Pete Hamill, Oscar Wilde, Brendan Kennelly, W. B. Yeats, Edna O'Brien, John Hume, St. Brigid, James Joyce


## THE PROVINCE OF LEINSTER

DUBLIN
Jonathan Swift   From "The Legion Club" • The Description of an Irish Feast • From The Drapier's Fourth Letter   3
Sean O'Casey   From *The Shadow of the Gunman*   15
James Joyce   From *A Portrait of the Artist as a Young Man* • 21
From *Ulysses*
Samuel Beckett   Ding Dong from *More Pricks than Kicks*   42
Eavan Boland   Anna Liffey   58
Nuala O'Faolain   From *Are You Somebody?*   67
Roddy Doyle   From *The Commitments*   75

KILDARE
James Joyce   From *A Portrait of the Artist as a Young Man*   85

MEATH
Cormac Mac Airt    Cormac Mac Airt Presiding at Tara        90
Thomas Cahill    From *How the Irish Saved Civilization:*
    Patrick's Breastplate                                   92
Mary Lavin    In the Middle of the Fields                  98

WICKLOW
John Millington Synge    In Glencullen • To The Oaks
    of Glencree • Prelude • Is It a Month                   117
Seamus Heaney    St. Kevin and the Blackbird                126

# THE PROVINCE OF MUNSTER

TIPPERARY
Jan Morris    From *Ireland: Your Only Place*              133

TIPPERARY AND WATERFORD
William Trevor    From *Excursions in the Real World:*
    *Memoirs*                                              138
Dervla Murphy    From *Wheels Within Wheels*               147

CORK
Sean O'Faolain    The Talking Trees                        156
Frank O'Connor    The Drunkard                             173
Lorrie Moore    Which Is More than I Can Say About
    Some People                                            187
Elizabeth Bowen    From *Bowen's Court*                    208
Eileen O'Connell    The Lament for Art O'Leary             212
Anonymous    The Hag of Beara                              223

KERRY
Liam Dall O'hlfearnáin    Kathaleen Ny-Houlahan            229
John Millington Synge    From *In West Kerry*              240
Nuala Ní Dhomhnaill    Oileán (Island)                     249

## LIMERICK

Mary Carbery    From *The Farm by Lough Gur*                       252
Kate O'Brien    From *My Ireland*                                  257
Frank McCourt    From *Angela's Ashes*                             263

## CLARE

Sean O'Faolain    From *An Irish Journey*                          274
Brian Merriman    From *The Midnight Court*                        294
Edna O'Brien    From *Mother Ireland*                              302

# THE PROVINCE OF CONNACHT

## GALWAY

Lady Augusta Gregory    The Rising of the Moon                     313
William Butler Yeats    To Be Carved on a Stone at Thoor
    Ballylee • A Prayer for My Daughter                            324
James Joyce    She Weeps over Rahoon                               332
Rita Ann Higgins    Ode to Rahoon Flats • The Did-You-
    Come-Yets of the Western World                                 335
John Millington Synge    From *The Aran Islands*                   339
Maria Edgeworth    From *Adventures in Connemara*                  348

## MAYO

Michael Longley    On Mweelrea                                     361
John Millington Synge    From *The Playboy of the
    Western World*                                                 365

## SLIGO

William Butler Yeats    Who Goes With Fergus? • Down by the
    Salley Gardens • The Hosting of the Sidhe • From *Auto-
    biographies* • The Lake Isle of Innisfree • The Fiddler of
    Dooney • The Song of Wandering Aengus • From The
    Stolen Child • Towards Break of Day • From In Memory
    of Eva Gore-Booth and Con Markiewicz • From Under
    Ben Bulben                                                     370

# THE PROVINCE OF ULSTER

DONEGAL
Brian Friel   From *Dancing at Lughnasa*                     391
Éilís Ní Dhuibhne   Blood and Water                          397
Joyce Cary   From *A House of Children*                      412

DONEGAL AND DERRY
Seamus Deane   From *Reading in the Dark*                    420

DERRY
Seamus Heaney  Digging • Mossbawn Sunlight •
The Strand at Lough Beg • Anahorish
From *Sweeney in Flight*                                     427

ANTRIM
Brian Moore   Going Home                                     436
Medbh McGuckian   The Society of the Bomb •
On Ballycastle Beach                                         445

FOR FUTHER READING                                           450
PERMISSIONS ACKNOWLEDGMENTS                                  455

# Introduction

The clichés that obscure Ireland's richly layered complexity resurrect themselves regularly in Saint Patrick's Day hype and Hollywood reruns. But you're not on Irish soil for ten minutes before you see the fraud of the shamrock-and-leprechaun approach to one of Europe's most ancient and mysterious cultures. To visit Ireland is to encounter the Irish imagination. And the best guide to that haunting and fertile landscape is the words of its writers. Many readers, including Celtophiles, unreconstructed English majors, and some of the forty million Americans of Irish descent, are familiar with the literary art of this little place which on a map of the world looks like an elbow of England. With the recent acclaim—the Bookers, the Tonys, the Pulitzers, the National Book Awards, the Nobel Prize for Literature—given to both Irish writers and American writers of the Irish diaspora, the word has spread to a growing general audience. In the twentieth century Ireland produced—and after the turn of that century continues to produce—as many major writers in the English-speaking world as the United States and Britain.

Reading, writing, and travel are creative acts. The poet Yeats believed the act of writing entails a lifelong creation of the self. Travel writer Paul Theroux compares writing a novel with traveling in a strange country since both rely on the discoveries of the imagination to amount to anything significant. No wonder, then, William Zinsser's observation in *They Went: The Art and Craft of Travel*

*Writing*: "Some of the best travel writing turns up in novels and short stories." Reading *Ulysses*, you see, hear, and taste Dublin.

Because they enliven the imagination, good books and interesting travel are, for more and more people, a kind of food, basic requirements for the fullness of life. At the feast of life's fullness, both the landscape of Ireland and Irish writing command attention. Between the two, there is an intimacy, a symbiotic presence. Traveling in Ireland, you feel the spirit of place as almost palpable, yielding a kind of revelation. Again and again Irish writers locate in the hills and valleys that are never far from the sea a mortal happiness. Many places come thick with legends and history, a layered past that inspires a writer like Seamus Heaney to break through to great depths of insight. In Ireland the material world is charged with a beauty that under certain lights the tragedies of her history—invasions, famine, emigration—only intensify.

To read and to follow these witnesses is to see their luminous sources: the mountains of Donegal that within such short distances give way to seascapes, the rocky cliffs of Clare suddenly giving over to green plains, the brooding mists of Kerry and Cork to sun and rainbows, the mix-up of faces and voices in towns and cities that are never just one thing coming through in one key. Joyce's Dublin, for instance—hilarious, eccentric, pedantic, bawdy, cruel, kind—exemplifies Ireland as the never monotonous, despite the surface monotonies of rain and bog.

With the armchair and the on-the-road traveler in mind, *For The Love of Ireland* is both an anthology of engaging primary sources in which the writers evoke a particular place and a travel guide to the places and contexts that these writers bring to life. Having walked, climbed, driven, and lived in Ireland, I've found out for myself how closely the writers' descriptions match the places travelers can still discover today. The short commentaries following each selection will help you find the specific world each writer creates and loves.

In a country so roiling with contradictions, the attempt to say anything definite about its cultural contexts is as challenging as, say, finding William Trevor's Nire Valley under a hailstorm in June throughout which the sun still shines and the road signs get blown in the wrong direction. *("Now why would you say 'wrong,' missus?")* Up to a point, the writers in this book make things easy. Knowing Ireland's multiple identities, the writers represent a full range of them. In a wide range of moods, swinging from delight to cool-eyed criticism to rejection, these visionaries and incomparable wits alert you to any foolish generalizations; they also communicate their often comic acceptance of Ireland's instabilities. Their poems, short stories, and memoirs resound with multiple sensibilities, ancient and modern, fierce and gentle, a pagan and Christian mix— the ground, I think, of Ireland's seductiveness.

On-the-road travelers will appreciate that the writings highlight Ireland's most dramatic settings—the Dingle Peninsula, the Cliffs of Moher, the North Antrim Coast (or Giant's Causeway), Connemara. But the plain places are here, too, thanks to the extraordinary writers who've found gold amidst the ordinariness—McCourt's Limerick, Brian Moore's Belfast. Where would Swift, O'Casey, and Joyce have been without their "dear dirty Dublin"? Some hidden places—the lush and tranquil Blackwater Valley, southwest Mayo—are personal favorites (the former loved as well by Elizabeth Bowen and Dervla Murphy, the latter by Grace O'Malley, the rebel Pirate Queen and Michael Longley). Red flags of warning are applied to some destinations, glutted with coaches and tourists in high season. For the most part, though, overcrowding (except in pubs) is not yet an Irish problem. Many areas are so sparsely populated (except for the sheep) the calendar might have been put back a century.

To attempt to name a unifying theme among the writers in this book is to risk exhaustion or absurdity or both. As critics have observed voluminously of Samuel Beckett, there is, in centuries of Irish poetry and prose, a counterbalancing of the comic and pathetic, the yes and the no, hope and despair. ("Almost always," Yeats believed, "truth and lies are mixed together.") Representing Ireland's high tolerance for ambiguity, Irish writers, male and female, allow neither the comedy nor the tragedy of life, neither optimism nor pessimism to become an absolute. Until recently, the harsh fact of Irish poverty, with all its consequent suffering and failure, showed itself in every county, in all four provinces. Yet always the writers, taking a cue from their magical landscape (where rain and sun pour forth simultaneously) perform a kind of magic on their unpromising material: they transform the bitter facts by the power of their poetry. In the plays of Sean O'Casey, Brian Friel, and Sebastian Barry, this pattern of redemption by language might pass as a unifying theme. Clearly it passes the test of longevity. From the beginning, literature, above all other arts, has flourished here.

In contrast to movies and songs that reduce Ireland to a sentimental cartoon, the Ireland of the writers—especially the new Irish writers—reads at times like a lament or a curse. Since joining the European Union (EU) in 1972, the country has begun to overcome the insularity that made it ban the very books that have made it famous. The tone of the new Irish writing has been described as irreverent, anti-tradition, post-everything, and above all, free of the burden of the mythic and national past. But Irish iconoclasts are nothing new. While Ireland was still a colony of the British Empire, the savage indignation of Swift and the wild iconoclasm of Joyce figured boldly on her literary map. And long before Heisenberg's principle of uncertainty, Irish writers (like the Russians with whom they're often compared) saw that nothing in this life is certain.

What is new in literary Ireland is the proliferation of first-rate women writers. For years underpublished and underrepresented in anthologies, in the last twenty years or so they've found an audience in Ireland and Britain and increasingly in the States. Memoirist/journalist/first-time novelist Nuala O'Faolain made the American best-seller lists with her *Are You Somebody: The Accidental Memoir of a Dublin Woman*. Dublin poet Eavan Boland directs the creative writing program at Stanford University. *For The Love of Ireland* includes many more women writers—and their points of view—than you'll find in either out-of-print or current books about Ireland's literary landscape. With stunning force, contemporary women writers are resisting the idealization of women so prevalent in romantic Ireland, a form of cultural silencing they once had few opportunities to challenge. Their writing also expresses an exuberant sensuality and an equally passionate love of their respective landscapes. Both the Irish earth and the bodies of lovers are sites of gratified desire. Some might say that fiction writer Edna O'Brien, with her sexy girl narrators and poetic feeling for rural Clare, led the way for these women. But O'Brien had little choice other than to exile herself to England, whereas in the new and still evolving Ireland, women writers are free to stay at home and write what they please. And long before any of these bold contemporary women, there was the passionate voice of Eileen O'Connell's "The Lament for Art O'Leary," the finest love poem in Irish literature.

This book is unique, for there is no other reader's companion or traveler's guide currently available that offers both a generous sampling of the best writing of Ireland's men and women—the country's most rare and celebrated artistic treasure—and helps you find the places that inspired it. The tour starts off in Dublin and then continues in a more or less clockwise direction, ending in Belfast.

A few things I've learned from many Irish journeys: when in Ireland, slow down, get lost, ask questions. That's how I began— going slow (it poured torrentially, fog rolled in like waves from the sea); lost (well, detoured); and clueless. At the tail end of a honeymoon in Italy (recalled in the travel collection *Desiring Italy*), my husband Tom and I tried and failed to catch a flight to Dublin. (A Joyce fanatic and recent English major, I thought Dublin *was* Ireland.) Instead we landed in Cork and headed in the wrong direction. (Wrong, in a very Irish manner, turned out to be utterly right.) Corkscrewing over the peninsulas of the southwest, I remember being speechless most of the time. The landscape was so wild and beautiful that the word *paradise* didn't feel an exaggeration. (Crossing the Beara's Healy Pass and Dingle's Conor Pass was more terrifying than my first drive on the Pacific Coast Highway, in a hurricane.) After three days of a robust wind and rain, we drove at twilight into the village of Quin where the sky opened a rainbow over Quin Abbey. We made friends in Quin, a friendship I still see in the light of that rainbow.

Prolonging the honeymoon, we came back to Ireland a few years later, our love of the place intact and a contract from Scribner's to keep us focused (and eating well after daily walks through Dublin's Moore Street markets). The book we wrote—*A Literary Guide to Ireland*—is out of print now and very different from this one. And though the memory of living in Ireland still shines and makes us laugh, comparing life on the road in the Ireland of 1970 with our more current Irish travels makes me feel idolatrous toward the phenomenon of change.

Wherever you go in Ireland these days—unlike before she joined the EU—you can find central heating, a shower, food in pubs and plenty of good restaurants, though one of our children—she's not fussy—backpacked the island, choosing a tent and campfire grub over bed-and-breakfasts. Choosier travelers, however, now have the certainty that at the end of the day, with or without reservations (recommended in high season in busy places) creature comforts exist. Names and addresses are available in several helpful books which suit a range of budgets: *Ireland's Blue Book: Irish Country Houses and Restaurants* (expensive); *Be Our Guest: Hotels and Guesthouses Illustrated Guide* (pricey, moderate, cheap), available from the Irish Tourist Board—345 Park Ave. New York, N.Y. 10154; tel (212) 418-0800; *The Bridgestone 100 Best Restaurants in Ireland*; *The Rough Guide to Ireland* and *Let's Go Ireland* (both good on pubs, bed-and-breakfasts, and places to hear music). For walkers and hikers, Lonely Planet's *Walking in Ireland*, Joss Lynam's *Best Irish Walks*, and *Walking Ireland: The Waymarket Ways* are excellent. *The Blue Guide to Ireland* describes architecture and antiquities.

Last year I made part of this book's circuit by myself, curious about how traveling alone as a woman would feel in Ireland. For whatever reason, I encountered more friendliness and spontaneous conversation than I remembered from previous trips. I met a man who claimed to know who killed Michael "Mick" Collins and took an hour and a half to tell me *there are some things, missus, that can never never be revealed*. Concealing the name of the assassin, he told me the story of his childhood during the civil war. At the site of Michael Collins's birthplace, I picked up priceless oral histories of Mick's Clonakilty, Bandon, and Sam's Cross from Irish people who still debate whether Mick was a ruthless killer or a national hero. People everywhere offered me useful information and clear directions. Picking up a puncture on the Wicklow Way—it's high, it's remote, daylight was fading—I stood helplessly next to my car for less than ten minutes. A man with bright red hair and brighter cheeks pulled over, changed my tire, wouldn't let me pay. "In the morning you'll need to go for a real repair to Rathdrum." Giving me the name of the nearest bed-and-breakfast in Laragh, he took off down the mountain, his sheepdog dancing and barking with doggy happiness in the back of his truck. Women were as friendly as men. No one seemed to think it was peculiar for a woman to be driving around on her own. Of if they did, they didn't show it. The Irish know their manners.

The richness of the Ireland of the writers has a downside. There are hundreds of pages of first-rate writing I've had to leave out. These include Mary Beckett's "A Belfast Woman," Nell McCafferty's "All Our Yesterdays," the hypnotic Leitrim/Roscommon countryside of that fine novelist John McGahern and of David Thomson's *Woodbrook* (a masterpiece of the literature of place), the Monaghan poems of Patrick Kavanagh and Mary O'Donnell, excerpts from Thomas Flanagan's *The Year of the French* and from *Tain Bo Cuailnge* (The Cattle Raid of Cooley) and other favorites such as Paula Meehan, Maeve Brennan, Bernard MacLaverty and Jennifer Johnston. Some writers don't appear because their writing doesn't particularize a landscape that travelers can see for themselves. Or they do it brilliantly but either at such length or with such bleakness (certain stories by William Trevor, Neil Jordan, Joseph O'Connor)—well, the weather's bad enough.

Despite these regrets, the point of the collection is clearly not to serve as a complete literary history or travel guide. It's not a textbook, though students of Irish literature will find it useful. *For The Love of Ireland* is an invitation to a select feast of writing and landscape. And as with most of life's pleasures, less is often more.

—Susan Cahill
New York City, 2000

# Overtures

*An Irishman's heart is nothing but his imagination.*
                    —G. B. Shaw, *John Bull's Other Island*

*In any light, in any weather, any smallest piece of Ireland, hideous
or ordinary or lovely, looks only like Ireland, and like nothing else at
all. For the real beauty of Ireland is much more than skin-deep. And
it can hide itself. And I truly think that Ireland at its best is still a
secret for connoisseurs.*          —Kate O'Brien, *My Ireland*

*The Irish, like the Jews or the Armenians, are a people To Whom
Things Were Done. They did not launch armies against other
nations; their fleets did not land on foreign shores. They were a
people warred against, a people invaded, a nation shredded by the
iron will of others. And so today . . . the visitor listens to the blarney
of the tour guide, the shamrocking of history, the weaving of
gossamer inventions; some Irishmen hear the dark murmur of an
antique past, when the Irish learned to lie in order to live,
convincing the English tax collectors that a cow was a rabbit,
disguising feeling, using charm and double-talk to live another hour.
The men and women who deal with tourists are decent and skillful
and take delight in the performance, but they have the skills of
actors, and those skills were fashioned to protect a people against a
crime.*          —Pete Hamill, *Ireland: Presences*

*We Irish are too poetical to be poets; we are a nation of brilliant*
*failures, but we are the greatest talkers since the Greeks.*
     —Oscar Wilde, at a London table dinner, quoted by W. B. Yeats

*If you asked me to name one factor that makes Ireland the quietly*
*irresistible land it is, I would reply that time has failed to establish its*
*customary tyranny over the lives of many of the people and so they are*
*free to develop their personalities, indulge their natural inclination*
*toward talk and animated story-telling. . . . Ireland is a place where*
*character and personality are cherished far ahead of theory and*
*abstraction. This generates a special warmth in the social*
*atmosphere. . . . Everywhere you go in Ireland you meet beautiful*
*children. I fondly cherish the thought that they too will grow to be*
*people-lovers, nature-lovers and story-lovers like so many of those it*
*has been my privilege to meet, travelling in this old land that has*
*preserved a startling youthfulness through all its trials and tribulations.*
                         —Brendan Kennelly, "Being Irish"

          *Out of Ireland have we come.*
          *Great hatred, little room,*
          *Maimed us at the start.*
          *I carry from my mother's womb*
          *A fanatic heart.*
          —W. B. Yeats, "Remorse for Intemperate Speech"

*Ireland may have cost me a few sleepless nights, but it has given me*
*a lot as well. [Am I] Irish? In truth I would not want to be anything*
*else. . . . At least it does not leave one pusillanimous.*
                         —Edna O'Brien, *Mother Ireland*

*One of my first political lessons was learned from my father when I*
*was a child. He took me to a nationalist meeting, where they were*
*waving the tricolor and whipping up emotions. My father put his*
*hand on my shoulder and said, "Listen son, you see all that there." I*
*said, "Yes, Daddy." He said, "Just you remember one thing. You can*
*never eat a flag."*            —John Hume, "My Education"

*I should like a great lake of finest ale*
*For the King of kings.*
*I should like a table of the choicest food*
*For the family of heaven.*
*Let the ale be made from the fruits of faith,*
*And the food be forgiving love.*

*I should welcome the poor to my feast.*
*For they are God's children.*
*I should welcome the sick to my feast,*
*For they are God's joy.*
*Let the poor sit with Jesus at the highest place,*
*And the sick dance with angels.*

*God bless the poor,*
*God bless the sick,*
*And bless our human race.*
*God bless our food,*
*God bless our drink,*
*All homes, O God, embrace.*

                              —St. Brigid's Feast (tenth century)


"In risu veritas." *In laughter, truth.*

                                        —James Joyce

# THE
## PROVINCE OF
# LEINSTER

---

DUBLIN
KILDARE
MEATH
WICKLOW

---

Jonathan Swift • Sean O'Casey

James Joyce • Samuel Beckett

Eavan Boland • Nuala O'Faolain

Roddy Doyle • Cormac Mac Airt

Thomas Cahill • Mary Lavin

John Millington Synge

Seamus Heaney

# Jonathan Swift

## 1667–1745

*The first great Irish writer to work in English, Jonathan Swift was born and died a Dubliner. He never knew his father, who died before he was born. Separated from his mother as a baby, he was supported by a stingy uncle who paid his fees at Trinity College, where he reacted against what he considered the pedantry of the curriculum and a foolishly authoritarian discipline. Known as a rebel, he earned his degree "by special grace." For the next twenty-five years, he went back and forth between Ireland and England, playing a variety of roles: antiwar journalist, participant in Whig and Tory political intrigues, advocate for the Church of Ireland (the Irish branch of the Anglican Church, in which he'd been ordained in 1694), London wit and writer who hoped to rise into a bishopric in the Church of England. Instead, he was made the dean of Saint Patrick's Cathedral in his native Dublin. The appointment horrified him. As he wrote to his friend Alexander Pope, he'd been sentenced to exile, "to die like a poisoned rat in a hole." But as the following writings show, the Irish exile had a change of heart. Disappointment and despair were overcome by the dean's passionate commitment to justice on behalf of the Irish people and the Dublin poor in particular. Later on he wrote again to Pope, inviting him to take up residence with him in his deanery where daily life offered contentment (as well as an outlet for his sense of humor). By this time, Swift himself (he failed to mention) had become a popular hero in Dublin city.*

*D*ublin is a walker's city and Swift on foot was a famous Dublin
sight. "I walk the streets in peace ... and am reputed the
best walker in this Town and 5 miles around. ... I seldom walk less
than 4 miles, sometimes 6 or 8 or 10 or more, never beyond my own
limits." Hearty literary travelers, equipped with a few of his writings as well as a street map, will find Swift's Dublin. (And Joyce and
Beckett's, too, who also walked the length and breadth of it, at all
hours, in any weather.)

### FROM THE LEGION CLUB*

As I stroll the city, oft I
Spy a building large and lofty,
Not a bow-shot from the College,
Half the globe from sense and knowledge.
By the prudent architect
Placed against the church direct;
Making good my grandam's jest,
Near the church—*you know the rest.*

  Tell us what this pile contains?
Many a head that holds no brains.
These demoniacs let me dub
With the name of 'Legion Club.'
Such assemblies, you might swear,
Meet when butchers bait a bear;
Such a noise, and such haranguing,
When a brother thief is hanging.
Such a rout and such a rabble
Run to hear jack-pudding gabble;
Such a crowd their ordure throws
On a far less villain's nose. ...

---

* The title of this savage attack on the Irish Parliament as a pack of politicians from
hell comes from the Bible: "And Jesus asked him, What is thy name? And he said,
Legion, because many devils were entered into him" (Luke 8:30).

*Could I from the building's top*
*Hear the rattling thunder drop,*
*While the Devil upon the roof,*
*If the Devil be thunder-proof,*
*Should with poker fiery red*
*Crack the stones, and melt the lead;*
*Drive them down on every skull,*
*While the den of thieves is full;*
*Quite destroy that harpies' nest,*
*How might then our isle be blessed? . . .*

*Yet should Swift endow the schools*
*For his lunatics and fools,*
*With a rood or two of land,*
*I allow the pile may stand.*
*You perhaps will ask me, why so?*
*But it is with this proviso,*
*Since the House is like to last,*
*Let a royal grant be passed,*
*That the club have right to dwell*
*Each within his proper cell;*
*With a passage left to creep in,*
*And a hole above for peeping.*

*Let them, when they once get in,*
*Sell the nation for a pin;*
*While they sit a-picking straws,*
*Let them rave of making laws;*
*While they never hold their tongue,*
*Let them dabble in their dung;*
*Let them form a grand committee,*
*How to plague and starve the city;*
*Let them stare, and storm, and frown,*
*When they see a clergy-gown.*
*Let them, 'ere they crack a louse,*
*Call for the orders of the House;*
*Let them with their gosling quills,*
*Scribble senseless heads of bills;*

*We may, while they strain their throats,*
*Wipe our arses with their votes. . . .*

▭◈▭

## For the Literary Traveler

"The College" in "The Legion Club" refers to TRINITY COLLEGE DUBLIN, on the south side of the River Liffey and the east flank of College Green. This was the original hub of the city: the tenth-century Viking thingmote, or public assembly mound, and the burial mounds of the kings. Founded by Queen Elizabeth in 1591 "for the reformation of the barbarism of this rude people," whose university education on the continent had contaminated them with popery, the college includes among its alumni the brightest stars of the Protestant Anglo-Irish cultural firmament: Swift (who cut classes and missed evening roll call, and whose bust by Roubiliac stands in the majestic LONG ROOM of the OLD LIBRARY), Edmund Burke and Oliver Goldsmith (whose statues stand on the lawn outside the entrance), George Farquhar, William Congreve, Bishop Berkeley, Bram Stoker, Thomas Moore, Wolfe Tone, Robert Emmet, Thomas Davis, Isaac Butt, Oscar Wilde, John Millington Synge, Elizabeth Bowen (Trinity admitted women in 1903, long before Oxford and Cambridge), Samuel Beckett, William Trevor, Derek Mahon, Michael Longley, Mary Robinson, and Eavan Boland.

Inside, the campus is an oasis of cobblestones, quads, bright green lawns, a graceful campanile, huge beech trees, sculptures, and fine buildings. The OLD LIBRARY (1712), facing the south side of Library Square, is the home of the BOOK OF KELLS, a Latin gospel book made in an Irish monastery about the year 800. One of the most beautiful illuminated manuscripts in the world, it is, in the words of James Joyce, "the most purely Irish thing we have." (Mon.–Sat. 9:30–5; Sun., noon–4:30).

Just across the traffic intersection at College Green, "not a bowshot" from Trinity, is the old PARLIAMENT HOUSE (now the Bank of Ireland), the "building large and lofty" whose governance Swift scorns. Begun in 1728 and completed in 1739, the old Parliament was known to Swift as the seat of the political power of the Anglo-Irish Ascendancy, a group he considered as self-serving and useless to the Irish people as the English, whose Parliament he called "a den of thieves" infested with "harpies." It was considered one of the most beautiful buildings of the early eighteenth century in Europe, "incomparably the most splendid Parliament House in the Empire, even eclipsing Westminster," according to some. Visitors may visit the elegant interior during banking hours. The LORDS CHAMBER remains as it was in Swift's time, complete with ornate ceilings, chandeliers, and two tapestries celebrating the Protestant victors of the Siege of Derry and the Battle of the Boyne (guided tours Tues. 10:30, 11:30, 1:45).

On foot and on horseback, Swift moved through the medieval streets of Dublin, talking to his parishioners, noting their accents. Continuing west from College Green along Dame Street, you turn right into the narrow cobbled streets that descend to the Liffey. You've entered the TEMPLE BAR (Dublin's "Left Bank"), in Swift's time a district of brothels, pubs, and the homes of the working poor. It was named for a seventeenth-century diplomat, Sir William Temple, for whom Swift worked as a secretary after graduating from Trinity. (He arranged the marriage of the Dutch Protestant William of Orange—King Billy of the Boyne—and Mary, the daughter of James II, the Catholic Stuart king defeated by Billy.) A man of literary taste, Temple was an important influence on the young Swift (some scholars say Swift was his bastard son) who was left free to read ten hours a day in his large library when he wasn't tutoring young Esther Johnson (Stella), the daughter of Temple's housekeeper, who grew up to be the woman he would always love.

Today Temple's old real estate, after centuries of neglect, is frantic with commerce, tourism, and all-night partying. Through the maze of Temple Bar roams the progeny of the Celtic Tiger, the symbolic name for the strong Irish economy of the 1990s that Swift dared, during a time of Ireland's deepest poverty, to imagine as a possibility. The most impressive destinations within these medieval streets are artistic. PROJECT (in East Essex Street), an artists' cooperative of gallery spaces and a black-box theater, has brought progressive visual and performance art to Ireland. U2, Liam Neeson, and Gabriel Byrne trained here. THE IRISH FILM CENTER (6 Eustace Street) is an enterprise that would have appealed to Swift's practical heart. The clergyman whose proposals

were ignored by the "Legion Club" (the Irish Parliament)—he advocated the encouragement of Irish industries and the taxation of absentee
landlords—would no doubt admire the center's cluster of screening
theaters, as well as a film bookshop, pub, and restaurant, plus film
archives, and a thriving cooperative of internationally respected Irish
filmmakers who include Neil Jordan, Jim Sheridan, Pat O'Connor, and
Terry George.

## THE DESCRIPTION OF AN IRISH FEAST

*Translated almost literally out of
the original Irish*

O'Rourk's noble fare
　Will ne'er be forgot,
By those who were there,
　Or those who were not.
His revels to keep,
　We sup and we dine,
On seven score sheep,
　Fat bullocks and swine.
Usquebagh* to our feast
　In pails was brought up,
An hundred at least,
　And a madder** our cup.
O there is the sport,
　We rise with the light,
In disorderly sort,
　From snoring all night.
O how was I tricked,
　My pipe it was broke,
My pocket was picked,
　I lost my new cloak.
I'm rifled, quoth Nell,
　Of mantle and kercher,

*Whiskey
**A wooden vessel

*Why then fare them well,*
 *The de'il take the searcher.*
*Come, harper, strike up,*
 *But first by your favour,*
*Boy, give us a cup;*
 *Ay, this has some savour:*
*O'Rourk's jolly boys*
 *Ne'er dreamt of the matter,*
*Till roused by the noise,*
 *And musical clatter,*
*They bounce from their nest,*
 *No longer will tarry,*
*They rise ready dressed,*
 *Without one* Ave Mary.
*They dance in a round,*
 *Cutting capers and ramping,*
*A mercy the ground*
 *Did not burst with their stamping,*
*The floor is all wet*
 *With leaps and with jumps,*
*While the water and sweat,*
 *Splish, splash in their pumps.*
*Bless you late and early,*
 *Laughlin O' Enagin,*
*By my hand, you dance rarely,*
 *Margery Grinagin.*
*Bring straw for our bed,*
 *Shake it down to the feet,*
*Then over us spread,*
 *The winnowing sheet.*
*To show, I don't flinch,*
 *Fill the bowl up again,*
*Then give us a pinch*
 *Of your sneezing, a* Yean.
*Good Lord, what a sight,*
 *After all their good cheer,*
*For people to fight*

*In the midst of their beer:*
*They rise from their feast,*
  *And hot are their brains,*
*A cubit at least*
  *The length of their skenes.\**
*What stabs and what cuts,*
  *What clattering of sticks,*
*What strokes on the guts,*
  *What bastings and kicks!*
*With cudgels of oak,*
  *Well hardened in flame,*
*An hundred heads broke,*
  *An hundred struck lame.*
*You churl, I'll maintain*
  *My father built Lusk,*
*The castle of Slane,*
  *And Carrickdrumrusk:*
*The Earl of Kildare,*
  *And Moynalta, his brother,*
*As great as they are,*
  *I was nursed by their mother.*
*Ask that of old Madam,*
  *She'll tell you who's who,*
*As far up as Adam,*
  *She knows it is true,*
*Come down with that beam,*
  *If cudgels are scarce,*
*A blow on the wame,\*\**
  *Or a kick on the arse.*

\*Daggers
\*\*Belly

◻◇◻

## For the Literary Traveler

Swift served as the dean of ST. PATRICK'S CATHEDRAL in one of Dublin's least elegant neighborhoods from 1713 to 1745 and his greatest writings are the fruit of these years. At Essex Quay in Temple Bar, turn left up the hill toward Fishamble Street. This is the area called the "shambles," where the fishmongers of the Dublin ballad "Molly Malone" lived and hawked their cockles and mussels. It's also the site of the first performance of Handel's *Messiah* in 1742. To the right is Wood Quay, the bland new municipal offices of the Dublin Corporation, built over the bulldozed ninth- and tenth-century Viking city and Swift's medieval Dublin, despite massive protest marches in the 1980s. Continuing into Patrick's Street, you're at the Cathedral in about fifteen minutes unless you stop along the way for "Dublinia," Christchurch Cathedral's audiovisual introduction to the multilayered history of "Black Pool"—*Duibhlinn* in Irish, *Dyfflin* in Norse.

Swift was a friend of Turlough O' Carolan, the blind Irish poet, composer, and harpist, and Dublin lore has it that he entertained him at the cathedral's DEANERY. O' Carolan set this poem about the Irish Feast (it's also called "O'Rourke's Feast") to music; Swift translated it from its original Irish into English, enjoying not only the intemperance of the tale but also, as a master of scatology, its excrementitious aftermath. "Man is never more contemplative than when he is at stool," he once said. (There's a monument commemorating O' Carolan, also an earthy sort, in the north aisle of the cathedral.) The present deanery of 1781, diagonally across from the cathedral's entrance, was rebuilt after Swift's burned down, but the gardens he nurtured—his "Naboth's Vineyard"—remain. "I am as busy in my little spot of town garden, as ever I was in the *grand monde*," he wrote to a friend.

Just down from the deanery in St. Patrick's Close is MARSH'S LIBRARY (1701), named for its sober founder Archbishop Narcissus Marsh, the Provost at Trinity College during Swift's student days, who said the dean had been "remarkable for nothing else but making a good fire." His fine brick building at the curve in the road is Dublin's first public

library, its reading cages originally open to "All Graduates and Gentlemen," including Swift. Joyce read there in October 1902. The wired
cages (alcoves) in which readers were locked with their rare books
under the eye of a librarian (many of the books were once chained to
the shelves) turn up in *Ulysses* as the "stagnant bay in Marsh's Library".
(Mon., Weds., Thurs., Fri. 10–12:45, 2–5; Sat. 10:30–12:45; closed Tues.
and Sun.)

## FROM "THE DRAPIER'S FOURTH LETTER"

### TO THE WHOLE PEOPLE OF IRELAND.

*M*Y *Dear Countrymen,*
　　Having already written *Three Letters* upon so disagreeable
a Subject as Mr. *Wood* and his *Half-pence*; I conceived my Task was
at an End. . . .

I thought I had sufficiently shewn to all who could want Instruc-
tion, by what Methods they might safely proceed, whenever this
*Coyn* should be offered to them: And I believe there hath not been
for many Ages an Example of any Kingdom so firmly united in a
Point of great Importance, as this of Ours is at present, against that
detestable Fraud. . . .

But the *Love and Torrent* of Power prevailed. Indeed the Arguments on both sides were invincible; For in *Reason*, all *Government*
without the Consent of the *Governed* is the *very Definition of Slavery*: But in *Fact, Eleven Men well Armed will certainly subdue one
Single Man in his Shirt*. But I have done. . . .

The Remedy is wholly in your own Hands, and therefore I have
digressed a little in order to refresh and continue that *Spirit* so sea-
sonably raised amongst you, and to let you see that by the Laws of
GOD, of NATURE, of NATIONS, and of your own Country,
you ARE and OUGHT to be as FREE a People as your Brethren in
*England.*

## For the Literary Traveler

As dean of St. Patrick's, in the capital city of a desperately poor colony
of the British Empire, Swift made his pulpit an organ of conscience.
His greatest writings, *The Drapier's Letters* (1724–25), *Gulliver's Travels*
(1726), and *A Modest Proposal* (1729) show that, for him, religion, politics, and morality cannot be separated. In sermons, pamphlets, and the
brilliant satires he insisted on their common purpose: the promotion
of justice and liberty for all. Many of his parishioners were Huguenot
refugees, the Dublin weavers, tailors, and craftsmen of the COOMBE, a
nearby neighborhood at the southern end of the area called THE LIBER-
TIES. Walk west from the cathedral, along DEAN STREET, into a maze of
working-class streets crowded with markets, small shops, new luxury
apartments, and trendy bars and music halls. Walk north—back
toward Christchurch—turning left into Back Lane, forking off High
Street, to see another site known to Swift and his parishioners,
Dublin's only surviving guild hall, the TAILORS' GUILD HALL (1706). It's
been nicely restored and bears a plaque with the names of the masters of the tailors' guild from 1419 to 1841. THE BRAZEN HEAD, the city's
oldest pub (which Joyce liked), is back across High Street, past the medieval ST. AUDOEN'S ARCH, and down to the left off lower Bridge Street.
In Swift's day, the workers of the Coombe were victims of British mer-
cantilist policies that banned the export of Irish textiles to England or
abroad. In their defense came Swift's pamphlet "A Proposal for the
Universal Use of Irish Manufacture," in which he advocated a boycott
of everything British, including her coal.

When England was on the verge of flooding the Irish market with a
cheap new currency—the coins were to be made of copper—Swift,
adopting the persona of a shopkeeper named M. B. Drapier, wrote
seven subversive pamphlets. They were known as *The Drapier's Letters*
and protested the implementation of this new monetary policy that
threatened economic disaster for Ireland. His protest worked. England
abandoned the copper currency, and Swift was hailed by his parishioners and all Dublin workers as the "Hibernian Patriot." Whenever he

returned to the city after an absence, bells were rung and bonfires lit. It was the psychological effect of his protest that was the most danger-ous for the Empire: for a time *The Drapier's Letters* united native Catholic and Anglo-Irish Ireland by defining their common interests and their enemy. England's American colonies also heard the Drapier's challenge: "by the laws of God, of nature, of nations, and of your own country, you are and ought to be as free a people as your own bretheren in England." Thirty years after his death, Swift's declaration that "in rea-son all government without the consent of the governed is the very definition of slavery" resonated in America's Declaration of Indepen-dence in 1776.

Throughout his life Swift was afflicted by dizziness, nausea, and ring-ing in his middle ear. In his last three years, these symptoms (defined as Menière's disease only in 1861) combined with a loss of memory and the effects of a stroke to produce the label of madness mistakenly ap-plied to him by critics. In fact, he acted as a compassionate and gener-ous pastor until his death, willing his modest income to found a residence for destitute elderly women and the still-in-operation ST. PATRICK'S HOSPITAL (or Swift's Hospital) for the mentally ill. As he him-self explained:

> He gave the little wealth he had
> To build a House for Fools and Mad;
> And show'd by one satiric touch,
> No Nation wanted it so much.

Located near the junction of Bow Lane and James's Street—near the Guinness brewery—along bus routes 21A, 78, 79, and 90, the hospi-tal's handsome main building (1749) contains a small museum of Swift's possessions.

ST. PATRICK'S CATHEDRAL, however (modeled on Salisbury Cathedral), is his best-known memorial. Along its aisles are informative exhibits about the many themes of the prophetic dean's sermons. The dignity of the main altar and the sanctuary, graceful beneath three lancet stained-glass windows, evokes the power of the great dean's prose and conviction: "We have just enough religion to make us hate, but not enough to make us love one another." His body is buried at the rear of the church next to the mysterious woman he called Stella. She was his most intimate friend, the recipient of his poems and letters under the title *Journal to Stella*, and possibly his wife. His Latin epitaph, on a tablet above a bust of his likeness, reads in English:

> Here lies the body of Jonathan Swift, Doctor of Divinity,
> Dean of this Cathedral Church,
> Where savage indignation can no longer rend the heart
> Go, traveller, and imitate, if you can,
> This dedicated champion of human liberty.

# Sean O'Casey

## 1880–1964

*George Bernard Shaw called him "Titan," and Harold Macmillan said he was the kindest man he'd ever met. For others, he's the Irish writer closest in spirit to the "savage indignation" of Jonathan Swift. O'Casey grew up on Dublin's seedy north side (like Joyce), the thirteenth child (only five survived) of a widowed mother whose indomitable spirit became the heroic ground of his great dramatic trilogy,* The Shadow of the Gunman *(1923),* Juno and the Paycock *(1925), and* The Plough and the Stars *(1926). At the age of fourteen, O'Casey went to work as a manual laborer—docker and pick-and-shovel navvy—later joining the Gaelic League (he became fluent in Irish) and serving as secretary of the Irish Transport and General Workers Union under union organizer Jim Larkin and the socialist rebel leader James Connolly. A socialist in politics (he became a communist after he moved to England), in his plays he repudiates the violence of the fanatical Irish nationalists and the British army. His compassionate eye always on the tenement poor—the victims of the gunslinging, high-theory patriotism he hated—he made their voices the heart of his tragicomedies.*

FROM *THE SHADOW OF THE GUNMAN*, ACT II

*Davoren, an ineffectual dreamer, and Seumas, a disillusioned former gun-toting patriot, argue about the self-deceptions of Ireland's warriors/saviors.*

SEUMAS. Everything is very quiet now; I wonder what time is it?

DAVOREN. The village cock hath thrice done salutation to the morn.

SEUMAS. Shakespeare, Richard the III, Act Five, Scene III. It was Ratcliffe said that to Richard just before the battle of Bosworth. . . . How peaceful the heavens look now with the moon in the middle; you'd never think there were men prowlin' about tryin' to shoot each other. I don't know how a man who has shot any one can sleep in peace at night.

DAVOREN. There's plenty of men can't sleep in peace at night now unless they know that they have shot somebody.

SEUMAS. I wish to God it was all over. The country is gone mad. Instead of counting their beads now they're countin' bullets; their Hail Marys and paternosters are burstin' bombs—burstin' bombs an' the rattle of machine-guns; petrol is their holy water; their Mass is a burnin' buildin'; their De Profundis is 'The Soldiers' Song,'* an' their creed is, I believe in the gun almighty, maker of heaven an' earth—an' it's all for 'the glory o' God an' the honour o' Ireland.'

DAVOREN. I remember the time when you yourself believed in nothing but the gun.

SEUMAS. Ay, when there wasn't a gun in the country; I've a different opinion now when there's nothin' but guns in the country. . . . An' you daren't open your mouth, for Kathleen ni Houlihan is very different now to the woman who used to play the harp an' sing 'Weep on, weep on, your hour is past', for she's a ragin' divil now, an' if you only look crooked at her you're sure of a punch

---

*Now the national anthem of the Republic of Ireland; written by Peadar Kearney

in th' eye. But this is the way I look at it—I look at it this way: You're not goin'—you're not goin' to beat the British Empire— the British Empire, by shootin' an occasional Tommy at the corner of an occasional street. Besides, when the Tommies have the wind up—when the Tommies have the wind up they let bang at everything they see—they don't give a God's curse who they plug.

DAVOREN. Maybe they ought to get down off the lorry and run to the Records Office to find out a man's pedigree before they plug him.

SEUMAS. It's the civilians that suffer; when there's an ambush they don't know where to run. Shot in the back to save the British Empire, an' shot in the breast to save the soul of Ireland. I'm a Nationalist meself, right enough—a Nationalist right enough, but all the same—I'm a Nationalist right enough; I believe in the freedom of Ireland, an' that England has no right to be here, but I draw the line when I hear the gunmen blowin' about dyin' for the people, when it's the people that are dyin' for the gunmen! With all due respect to the gunmen, I don't want them to die for me.

## For the Literary Traveler

In O'CASEY'S DUBLIN, the "iffy" neighborhood (as one cabdriver put it) north of the Liffey, the talk flows on.

Close by his birthplace (now a bank) at 85 UPPER DORSET STREET, you turn south along North Frederick Street, home of Walton's Music Store, the womb of rock-happy Dublin since the 1960s. (Peter Sheridan describes Dublin's rock-and-roll love affair—as well as his debt to O'Casey—in his 1999 memoir 44: Dublin Made Me. He and his filmmaker brother, Jim Sheridan, who made In the Name of the Father and My Left Foot, grew up on Sheriff Street, in O'Casey's dockside territory near the Liffey.) At the Parnell Monument, you turn right and then left into the MOORE STREET MARKETS. This is the best place to hear the

accent of O'Casey's characters, which tourists often miss. In late afternoon, when the likelihood of unsold produce increases, the women
behind the stalls—the heroines of Brendan O'Carroll's comic novel
*The Mammy* and its movie version, Anjelica Huston's *Agnes Browne*—
raise the volume. "Meushereu-ums! Berreussel sperreou-uts!" Behind
the women, butchers shout the prices of their "lovely lamb chops."
Long before Joyce began imitating the Moore Street chants at parties
and O'Casey gave their accents to the Bessie Burgesses and the Junos
of his plays, Swift had loved these hawkers and written for them
"Verses made for Women who cry Apples, &c.": "Ripe 'sparagrass / Fit
for a lad or lass, / To make their water pass." At night the people of the
surrounding multiethnic streets—Henrietta Street, Dominick Street,
Bolton Street, Mary Street, and Jervis Street, the streets of O'Casey's
boyhood—queue up at the nine-screen Virgin Cinema (01-872-8400)
and the Ambassador cinema (01-872-7000) on Parnell Street. Almost
no one on the lines for tickets, popcorn, or the toilet keeps their
mouth shut for long.

Tacky by day and boisterous at night, O'CONNELL STREET (Sackville
Street before independence)—the widest thoroughfare in Europe, ac-
cording to the Irish—cuts south from Parnell Square to O'Connell
Bridge at the Liffey. The statue of PARNELL at its head and of JIM LARKIN
on the paved stretch in the middle—near the GPO, or GENERAL POST
OFFICE—are O'Casey icons. Eleven when Parnell was betrayed, young
Johnnie, as Sean was called then, revered Ireland's "Uncrowned King."
Jim Larkin, however, the Irish labor leader and the organizer of Dublin
workers, was the hero of O'Casey's adulthood. Poverty and high mor-
tality rates from typhoid and tuberculosis were extreme in turn-of-
the-century Dublin tenements, which were the settings of all of
O'Casey's plays. In these abandoned Georgian mansions owned by English absentee landlords, a single room was often inhabited by one
large family, and rats the size of large kittens had the run of large base-
ments polluted with human excrement. One-third of the population
of 305,000 suffered such conditions, always afraid of being evicted for
not being able to make the rent.

Preaching "the divine mission of discontent," in 1909 Jim Larkin organized Dublin's unskilled workers into the Irish Transport and General Workers' Union, sending a militant message of hope into the

slums. Imprinted on his fine statue are the words of Larkin himself:
"The great appear great because we are on our knees. Let us rise." A
huge man and a charismatic orator, he called the General Strike of
1913 as a last resort, after the employers and owners, supported by
the Irish clergy who opposed the trade union movement, refused to
negotiate. Like his second in command, James Connolly, and his assistant, O'Casey, he was less interested in the issue of Irish nationalism
than in organizing political resistance for the cause of just wages and
fair housing for workers. After the strike failed, he left to raise money
in America but became trapped by World War I: England and Ireland
conspired to refuse the dangerous agitator reentry, and in Red-scared
America his radical politics landed him in Sing Sing. It was only the pardon of Governor Al Smith that finally brought him back to Dublin in
1923. By then the nationalists—the ex-gunmen—were in control
of the new Free State; the rights of workers were not their issue.
O'Casey's disillusion with the new state—one of the reasons for his
self-exile to England—drives the antiheroic animus of his great trilogy.
(James Plunkett's novel *Strumpet City* tells Jim Larkin's story.)

    In O'Casey's plays, the politics behind the Easter Rising of April 24,
1916, when the GPO was taken over by the rebels and bombarded by
the British (though restored, the façade still shows bullet holes from
the siege, which is re-created in Neil Jordan's movie *Michael Collins*)
turn into matters of life and death for fools, frauds, and holy innocents.
A good place to contemplate O'Casey's point of view on violent nationalism is out at KILMAINHAM GAOL (take bus 21A, 78, 78B, 79, or 90),
where sixteen of the Easter Rising leaders were executed in the
prison yard. It was only after the executions, as the tour guide explains,
that the Irish people came to support the rebel cause. Roddy Doyle's
first historical novel, *A Star Called Henry* (1999), builds on O'Casey's
iconoclastic point of view toward the ideologues and martyrs.

    Leaving O'Connell Street at the GPO, O'Casey Country turns east
down Lower Abbey Street to Marlborough Street, where he tri-
umphed as an artist in the ABBEY THEATRE (this is not the original building or location), the cultural monument established by Yeats and Lady
Gregory to prove that Ireland was not "the home of buffoonery and
of easy sentiment" but of "an ancient idealism." It was Lady Gregory
who encouraged the forty-three-year-old cement mixer to keep on

revising his first play, *The Shadow of a Gunman,* until it became a successful Abbey production. O'Casey's critical take on romantic Ireland's
Easter Monday bloodbath in *The Plough and the Stars* (1926) had chau-
vinist audiences throwing veggies and fists at the Abbey's stage. As a
student at Trinity, Beckett saw his plays, liking *Juno and the Paycock* the
best, and later praised O'Casey as "a master of knockabout in this very
serious and honourable sense—that he discerns the principle of disin-
tegration in even the most complacent solidities, and activates it to
their explosion. This is the energy of his theatre, the triumph of the
principle of knockabout." These days it's easy to get tickets to the Abbey's
productions (tel. 01-878-7222); there's experimental theater downstairs in the Peacock Theatre. Other theaters offering a variety of Irish
classics, musicals, and progressive performance art include Andrew's
Lane Theatre, Focus Theatre, the Gaiety, the Gate, and the Project Arts
Center in Temple Bar, where contemporary playwrights Marina Carr
and Tom MacIntyre are produced in the Project's black-box theater.
For schedules, see *The Irish Times.*

While O'Casey was writing *The Shadow of a Gunman,* he was living
in a tenement at 35 MOUNTJOY SQUARE—renamed Hilljoy Square in
the play—that was raided one night by the Black and Tans. What happened next is all in the play. Once the home of the most elegant mansions on Dublin's earliest Georgian square, Mountjoy is a short walk
from the Abbey (across and north of Parnell Street). Designed for
Luke Gardiner, Lord Mountjoy, banker, landlord, and English military
leader, the square's once-crumbling tenements (also part of Joyce's
Dublin) are now being restored. Facing a park and playground in which
people of all ages enjoy themselves, Mountjoy Square raises the hopes
of all city lovers, a good ending for O'Casey Country. "The kingdom
of heaven in the nature of everyman" was the playwright's lifelong
belief.

# James Joyce

## 1882–1941

*Joyce told a friend, "There was an English Queen who said that when she died the word 'Calais' would be written on her heart. 'Dublin' will be found on mine." And he used to boast that if Dublin somehow disappeared, it could be rebuilt from his books. He abandoned his hometown with Nora Barnacle in 1904, when he was twenty-two, and except for three short visits, he never saw it again. But on the evidence of* Dubliners *(1914),* A Portrait of the Artist as a Young Man *(1916),* Ulysses *(1922), and* Finnegans Wake *(1939), he never left the city where he grew up and came of age as an artist. Though exile from Ireland was a necessary condition of his vocation (as it was for Shaw, Wilde, O'Casey, Beckett, and Edna O'Brien), it is "dear dirty Dublin," the literal, sensual, and mythological city of his youth, that is the pulsing heart of each masterpiece. As a young man, he told his brother: "I am trying . . . to give people some kind of intellectual pleasure or spiritual enjoyment by converting the bread of everyday life into something that has a permanent artistic life of its own. . . . It is my idea of the significance of trivial things that I want to give the two or three unfortunate wretches who may eventually read me." More than a century after his birth, droves of "wretches," his passionate readers, roam Dublin in search of him. The current of literary pilgrims coursing through streets and pubs, over strands and quays and Liffey bridges, amounts to a rite of celebration of Joyce the Dubliner as the twentieth century's first genius of fiction and* Ulysses *as its greatest novel.*

FROM *A PORTRAIT OF THE ARTIST AS A*
*YOUNG MAN*

*Joyce's autobiographical novel re-creates the passage of his alter ego Stephen Dedalus from infancy to adolescent independence. At the end he claims "silence, exile, and cunning" as his means of escape from the labyrinth of family, church, and country. The emotional high point occurs at the end of Book IV, which follows here. Stephen sees a girl wading in Dublin Bay on a day of "dappled seaborne clouds," a vision of idealized beauty he interprets as an epiphany— a revelation of his artistic destiny.*

He turned seaward from the road at Dollymount and as he passed on to the thin wooden bridge he felt the planks shaking with the tramp of heavily shod feet. A squad of christian brothers was on its way back from the Bull and had begun to pass, two by two, across the bridge. Soon the whole bridge was trembling and resounding. The uncouth faces passed him two by two, stained yellow or red or livid by the sea, and as he strove to look at them with ease and indifference, a faint stain of personal shame and commiseration rose to his own face. . . .

He passed from the trembling bridge on to firm land again. At that instant, as it seemed to him, the air was chilled and looking askance towards the water he saw a flying squall darkening and crisping suddenly the tide. A faint click at his heart, a faint throb in his throat told him once more of how his flesh dreaded the cold infrahuman odour of the sea: yet he did not strike across the downs on his left but held straight on along the spine of rocks that pointed against the river's mouth.

A veiled sunlight lit up faintly the grey sheet of water where the river was embayed. In the distance along the course of the slowflowing Liffey slender masts flecked the sky and, more distant still, the dim fabric of the city lay prone in haze. Like a scene on some vague arras, old as man's weariness, the image of the seventh city of christendom was visible to him across the timeless air, no older nor more weary nor less patient of subjection than in the days of the thingmote. . . .

He looked northward towards Howth. The sea had fallen below the line of seawrack on the shallow side of the breakwater and already the tide was running out fast along the foreshore. Already one long oval bank of sand lay warm and dry amid the wavelets. Here and there warm isles of sand gleamed above the shallow tide, and about the isles and around the long bank and amid the shallow currents of the beach were lightclad gayclad figures, wading and delving.

In a few moments he was barefoot, his stockings folded in his pockets and his canvas shoes dangling by their knotted laces over his shoulders: and, picking a pointed salteaten stick out of the jetsam among the rocks, he clambered down the slope of the breakwater.

There was a long rivulet in the strand: and, as he waded slowly up its course, he wondered at the endless drift of seaweed. Emerald and black and russet and olive, it moved beneath the current, swaying and turning. The water of the rivulet was dark with endless drift and mirrored the highdrifting clouds. The clouds were drifting above him silently and silently the seatangle was drifting below him; and the grey warm air was still: and a new wild life was singing in his veins.

Where was his boyhood now? Where was the soul that had hung back from her destiny, to brood alone upon the shame of her wounds and in her house of squalor and subterfuge to queen it in faded cerements and in wreaths that withered at the touch? Or where was he?

He was alone. He was unheeded, happy and near to the wild heart of life. He was alone and young and wilful and wildhearted, alone amid a waste of wild air and brackish waters and the seaharvest of shells and tangle and veiled grey sunlight and gayclad lightclad figures, of children and girls and voices childish and girlish in the air.

A girl stood before him in midstream, alone and still, gazing out to sea. She seemed like one whom magic had changed into the likeness of a strange and beautiful seabird. Her long slender bare legs were delicate as a crane's and pure save where an emerald trail of seaweed had fashioned itself as a sign upon the flesh. Her thighs, fuller and softhued as ivory, were bared almost to the hips where the white fringes of her drawers were like featherings of soft white down. Her slateblue skirts were kilted boldly about her waist and dovetailed behind her. Her bosom was as a bird's soft and slight, slight and soft as the breast of some darkplumaged dove. But her long fair hair was girlish: and girlish, and touched with the wonder of mortal beauty, her face.

She was alone and still, gazing out to sea; and when she felt his presence and the worship of his eyes her eyes turned to him in quiet sufferance of his gaze, without shame or wantonness. Long, long she suffered his gaze and then quietly withdrew her eyes from his and bent them towards the stream, gently stirring the water with her foot hither and thither. The first faint noise of gently moving water broke the silence, low and faint and whispering, faint as the bells of sleep; hither and thither, hither and thither: and a faint flame trembled on her cheek.

—Heavenly God! cried Stephen's soul, in an outburst of profane joy.

He turned away from her suddenly and set off across the strand. His cheeks were aflame; his body was aglow; his limbs were trembling. On and on and on and on he strode, far out over the sands, singing wildly to the sea, crying to greet the advent of the life that had cried to him.

Her image had passed into his soul for ever and no word had broken the holy silence of his ecstasy. Her eyes had called him and his soul had leaped at the call. To live, to err, to fall, to triumph, to recreate life out of life! A wild angel had appeared to him, the angel of mortal youth and beauty, an envoy from the fair courts of life, to throw open before him in an instant of ecstasy the gates of all the ways of error and glory. On and on and on and on!

He halted suddenly and heard his heart in the silence. How far had he walked? What hour was it?

There was no human figure near him nor any sound borne to him over the air. But the tide was near the turn and already the day was on the wane. He turned landward and ran towards the shore and, running up the sloping beach, reckless of the sharp shingle, found a sandy nook amid a ring of tufted sandknolls and lay down there that the peace and silence of the evening might still the riot of his blood.

He felt above him the vast indifferent dome and the calm processes of the heavenly bodies; and the earth beneath him, the earth that had borne him, had taken him to her breast.

He closed his eyes in the languor of sleep. His eyelids trembled as if they felt the vast cyclic movement of the earth and her watches, trembled as if they felt the strange light of some new world. His soul was swooning into some new world, fantastic, dim, uncertain as under sea, traversed by cloudy shapes and beings. A world, a glimmer, or a flower? Glimmering and trembling, trembling and unfolding, a breaking light, an opening flower, it spread in endless succession to itself, breaking in full crimson and unfolding and fading to palest rose, leaf by leaf and wave of light by wave of light, flooding all the heavens with its soft flushes, every flush deeper than other.

Evening had fallen when he woke and the sand and arid grasses of his bed glowed no longer. He rose slowly and, recalling the rapture of his sleep, sighed at its joy.

He climbed to the crest of the sandhill and gazed about him. Evening had fallen. A rim of the young moon cleft the pale waste of sky like the rim of a silver hoop embedded in grey sand; and the tide was flowing in fast to the land with a low whisper of her waves, islanding a few last figures in distant pools.

⊏◇⊐

## For the Literary Traveler

In Book II of *Portrait*, Stephen Dedalus explores his neighborhood north of the Liffey, discovering as he walks the "paralysis" of Dublin in the 1890s (the theme of the short stories of *Dubliners*). Joyce knew every inch of the seedy northside. In the years of his youth, his feckless father, John Joyce, had rented fourteen different houses here for his large family. Stephen's main route, between MOUNTJOY SQUARE and the

CUSTOM HOUSE, had been Joyce's own. The square, once the most fashionable address in Dublin, with a downhill view of the Custom House, had become derelict after 1800, a symbol of Ireland's economic and political impotence. After the Irish Parliament (which Swift excoriates in "The Legion Club") was dissolved by the Act of Union in 1800, the disestablished lords turned from politics to real estate, selling their northside mansions for quick cash or converting them to multiple dwellings and then retiring to London as absentee slum lords. The brothels of the notorious "Monto" district down around the docks and the noble eighteenth-century Custom House ("Nighttown" in *Ulysses*) did a brisk business. Stephen, Catholic schoolboy and Prefect of the Sodality of the Blessed Virgin Mary, is a guilt-ridden customer. Closer to home (and just west of Mountjoy Square) was BELVEDERE COLLEGE at 6 Great Denmark Street, the Jesuit high school where he hears the hellfire Retreat sermons (in Book III) and rejects (in Book IV) a Jesuit's seductive invitation to become a priest. Built in 1775, this Georgian mansion with its fine interiors is still a school and open to visitors when it's convenient.

The ecstatic climax of *Portrait*—at the end of Book IV—comes miles beyond this grim northside on BULL ISLAND (or the NORTH BULL) at DOLLYMOUNT STRAND and the shores of DUBLIN BAY. Joyce, who walked everywhere in Dublin, often walked out here, where the city's delightful maritime prospect is enjoyed by Dubliners but often missed by tourists. (Bus 30, in Marlborough Street, will take you here, along the Clontarf Road.) Stephen walks onto the island, a bird sanctuary and now a UNESCO Biosphere Reserve, over the wooden bridge (now open to car traffic) passing a squad of Christian Brothers, whom his father calls the "Paddy Stinks and Mickey Muds" of Irish education. Beyond the bridge is the Bull Wall, the northern breakwater of Dublin harbor, extending a mile and a half into Dublin Bay. From here you can see ships still following "the course of the slowflowing Liffey" past the two lighthouses and north to HOWTH; to the south you see the chimneys of the Pigeon House (the electricity supply station) and behind it the Dublin mountains and the Great Sugarloaf in Wicklow. DOLLYMOUNT STRAND is a long beach with high sand dunes, a peaceful waterscape under a wide sky, within the city limits. Another causeway, just up the Clontarf Road, also leads to the beach and an Interpretive Center with exhibits about Bull Island's flora and fauna. As prolific as the flocks of seabirds and tall grasses you find along the strand are the interpretations of the Bull Island climax of *Portrait* that continue to issue from the academic "Joyce Industry." In Stephen's reverie, critics find everything from youthful narcissism to art conceived of as a transcendental vocation.

To follow Dedalus through the conclusion of *Portrait* (Book V)— more of an epilogue after the apocalyptic finale of Book IV—is to take his "morning walk across the city." This will take you down the North Strand Road, across O'Connell Bridge, past "the grey block of Trinity ... set heavily in the city's ignorance like a great dull stone set in a cumbrous ring," and up Grafton Street to "my Green," where "the trees in Stephen's Green were fragrant of rain and the rainsodden earth gave forth its mortal odour." A public common since the twelfth century and until the eighteenth century the scene of public executions, STEPHEN'S GREEN today is the city center's most popular park, with fountains, flower gardens, and sculptures of Ireland's writers and heroes: Joyce's bronze head by Marjorie Fitzgibbon faces the southern promenade, across the road from his alma mater, UNIVERSITY COLLEGE, the "sombre" destination of his daily walk in the years 1898–1902. The university's newly restored eighteenth-century townhouses, collectively named Newman House after John Henry Newman (1801–1890), the founder of the university in 1853 and author of *The Idea of a University*, whose "silverveined prose" Stephen savors as he walks across the city to class, are open to visitors in the summer, when it hosts the James Joyce Summer School in July (June–Sept., Tues.–Fri. 10–4; Sat. 12–4:30). The reliefs and ceilings of the Italian *stuccodores* Paul and Phillip Lafranchini are exquisite. A lecture hall has been restored in the manner of Joyce's student days. In the lovely University Chapel next door, Cardinal Newman preached to his Dublin students, and during his tenure as rector (1852–1859) he wrote to the Jesuit poet Gerard Manley Hopkins, also on the faculty of University College Dublin (UCD), "If I were Irish I would be—in my heart—a rebel."

Stephen's final walks around Dublin end at the NATIONAL LIBRARY in Kildare Street among other students "sheltering under the arcade," across the quad from its twin building, the NATIONAL MUSEUM. (Both flank Leinster House, now the seat of the Irish Parliament.) Joyce was a regular visitor to the library's READING ROOM from 1894 to 1904, sitting up front on the right-hand side near the entrance, writing poetry on call slips, applying unsuccessfully for a job as librarian. Thomas Lyster, the librarian who insisted on readers' complete silence, turns up as the urbane purring Quaker librarian in the "Scylla and Charybdis" episode of *Ulysses*. By showing a passport, visitors may also spend time in this room of warm mahogany woodwork at the top of a marble staircase.

Stephen comes down to earth in *Ulysses*. Here he meets the protagonist of Joyce's maturity, the Jewish Dubliner Leopold Bloom, another north-sider who wanders around town but not with his head in the "dappled seaborne clouds": he pays attention to the city's motley, its faces and bodies and voices. He's much more fun to walk around Dublin with than the abstracted Stephen, who pays attention mostly to himself.

FROM *ULYSSES*

*Modeled upon the structure of Homer's* Odyssey, *the action of the novel is concentrated into the events of eighteen hours in Dublin on June 16, 1904, the date when Joyce first went out with Nora Barnacle, the woman with whom he would live the rest of his life and have two children. The eighteen episodes center on Leopold Bloom, an advertising salesman, and his unfaithful wife, Molly—both of 7 Eccles Street on the city's north side—and on Stephen Dedalus (of* Portrait*), now an idling university graduate—three unheroic and modern versions of Ulysses, Penelope, and Telemachus.*

FROM CYCLOPS, 5:00 P.M.

*Different narrators are heard here among the voices of the men drinking in Barney Kiernan's Pub—Joe, John Wyse, Lenehan, Martin Cunningham, Jack Power—but the main action is Bloom's confrontation with "the Citizen," a rabid*

*Irish nationalist and anti-Semite. Bloom's humanity, kind,*
*tolerant, and comic, emerges as the heart of both this section*
*and of the entire novel.*

—Will you try another, citizen? says Joe.

—Yes, sir, says he, I will.

—You? Says Joe.

—Beholden to you, Joe, says I. May your shadow never grow less.

—Repeat that dose, says Joe.

Bloom was talking and talking with John Wyse and he quite excited with his dunducketymudcoloured mug on him and his old
plumeyes rolling about.

—Persecution, says he, all the history of the world is full of it.
Perpetuating national hatred among nations.

—But do you know what a nation means? says John Wyse.

—Yes, says Bloom.

—What is it? says John Wyse.

—A nation? says Bloom. A nation is the same people living in
the same place.

—By God, then, says Ned, laughing, if that's so I'm a nation for
I'm living in the same place for the past five years.

So of course everyone had a laugh at Bloom and says he, trying
to muck out of it:

—Or also living in different places.

—That covers my case, says Joe.

—What is your nation if I may ask, says the citizen.

—Ireland, says Bloom. I was born here. Ireland.

The citizen said nothing only cleared the spit out of his gullet
and, gob, he spat a Red bank oyster out of him right in the corner.

—After you with the push, Joe, says he, taking out his handkerchief to swab himself dry.

—Here you are, citizen, says Joe. Take that in your right hand
and repeat after me the following words.

The muchtreasured and intricately embroidered ancient Irish
facecloth attributed to Solomon of Droma and Manus Tomaltach
og Mac Donogh, authors of the Book of Ballymote, was then carefully
produced and called forth prolonged admiration. No need to dwell

on the legendary beauty of the cornerpieces, the acme of art, wherein one can distinctly discern each of the four evangelists in turn presenting to each of the four masters his evangelical symbol a bogoak sceptre, a North American puma (a far nobler king of beasts than the British article, be it said in passing), a Kerry calf and a golden eagle from Carrantuohill. * . . .

—Show us over the drink? says I. Which is which?

—That's mine, says Joe, as the devil said to the dead policeman.

—And I belong to a race too, says Bloom, that is hated and persecuted. Also now. This very moment. This very instant.

Gob, he near burnt his fingers with the butt of his old cigar.

—Robbed, says he. Plundered. Insulted. Persecuted. Taking what belongs to us by right. At this very moment, says he, putting up his fist, sold by auction off in Morocco like slaves or cattle.

—Are you talking about the new Jerusalem? says the citizen.

—I'm talking about injustice, says Bloom.

—Right, says John Wyse. Stand up to it then with force like men.

That's an almanac picture for you. Mark for a softnosed bullet. Old lardyface standing up to the business end of a gun. Gob, he'd adorn a sweepingbrush, so he would, if he only had a nurse's apron on him. And then he collapses all of a sudden, twisting around all the opposite, as limp as a wet rag.

—But it's no use, says he. Force, hatred, history, all that. That's not life for men and women, insult and hatred. And everybody knows that it's the very opposite of that that is really life.

—What? says Alf.

—Love, says Bloom. I mean the opposite of hatred. I must go now, says he to John Wyse. Just round to the court a moment to see if Martin is there. If he comes just say I'll be back in a second. Just a moment.

Who's hindering you? And off he pops like greased lightning.

—A new apostle to the gentiles, says the citizen. Universal love.

*The highest mountain in Ireland, in Kerry

—Well, says John Wyse. Isn't that what we're told. Love your neighbours.

—That chap? says the citizen. Beggar my neighbour is his motto. Love, Moya! He's a nice pattern of a Romeo and Juliet.

Love loves to love love. Nurse loves the new chemist. Constable 14 A loves Mary Kelly. Gerty Mac Dowell loves the boy that has the bicycle. M. B. loves a fair gentleman. Li Chi Han lovey up kissy Cha Pu Chow. Jumbo, the elephant, loves Alice, the elephant. Old Mr Verschoyle with the ear trumpet loves old Mrs Verschoyle with the turnedin eye. The man in the brown macintosh loves a lady who is dead. His Majesty the King loves Her Majesty the Queen. Mrs Norman W. Tupper loves officer Taylor. You love a certain person. And this person loves that other person because everybody loves somebody but God loves everybody. . . .

—I know where he's gone, says Lenehan, cracking his fingers.

—Who? says I.

—Bloom, says he, the courthouse is a blind. He had a few bob on *Throwaway* and he's gone to gather in the shekels.

—Is it that whiteeyed kaffir? says the citizen, that never backed a horse in anger in his life.

—That's where he's gone, says Lenehan. I met Bantam Lyons going to back that horse only I put him off it and he told me Bloom gave him the tip. Bet you what you like he has a hundred shillings to five on. He's the only man in Dublin has it. A dark horse.

—He's a bloody dark horse himself, says Joe.

—Mind, Joe, says I. Show us the entrance out.

—There you are, says Terry.

Goodbye Ireland I'm going to Gort. So I just went round to the back of the yard to pumpship and begob (hundred shillings to five) while I was letting off my (*Throwaway* twenty to) letting off my load gob says I to myself I knew he was uneasy in his (two pints off of Joe and one in Slattery's off) in his mind to get off the mark to (hundred shillings is five quid) and when they were in the (dark horse) Pisser Burke was telling me card party and letting on the child was sick (gob, must have done about a gallon) flabbyarse of a wife speaking down the tube *she's better* or *she's* (ow!) all a plan so he could vamoose with the pool if he won or (Jesus, full up I was) trading without a licence (ow!) Ireland my nation says he (hoik! phthook!) never be up to those bloody (there's the last of it) Jerusalem (ah!) cuckoos.

So anyhow when I got back they were at it dingdong, John Wyse saying it was Bloom gave the idea for Sinn Fein to Griffith to put in his paper all kinds of jerrymandering, packed juries and swindling the taxes off of the Government and appointing consuls all over the world to walk about selling Irish industries. Robbing Peter to pay Paul. Gob, that puts the bloody kybosh on it if old sloppy eyes is mucking up the show. Give us a bloody chance. God save Ireland from the likes of that bloody mouseabout. Mr Bloom with his argol bargol. . . .

So in comes Martin asking where was Bloom.

—Where is he? says Lenehan. Defrauding widows and orphans.

—Isn't that a fact, says John Wyse, what I was telling the citizen about Bloom and the Sinn Fein?

—That's so, says Martin. Or so they allege.

—Who made those allegations? says Alf.

—I, says Joe. I'm the alligator.

—And after all, says John Wyse, why can't a jew love his country like the next fellow?

—Why not? says J. J., when he's quite sure which country it is.

—Is he a jew or a gentile or a holy Roman or a swaddler or what the hell is he? says Ned. Or who is he? No offence, Crofton.

—We don't want him, says Crofter the Orangeman or presbyterian.

—Who is Junius? says J. J.

—He's a perverted jew, says Martin, from a place in Hungary and it was he drew up all the plans according to the Hungarian system. We know that in the castle.

—Isn't he a cousin of Bloom the dentist? says Jack Power.

—Not at all, says Martin. Only namesakes. His name was Virag.

The father's name that poisoned himself. He changed it by deed-poll, the father did.

—That's the new Messiah for Ireland! says the citizen. Island of saints and sages!

—Well, they're still waiting for their redeemer, says Martin. For that matter so are we. . . .

—Have you time for a brief libation, Martin? says Ned.

—Only one, says Martin. We must be quick. J. J. and S.

—You, Jack? Crofton? Three half ones, Terry.

—Saint Patrick would want to land again at Ballykinlar and convert us, says the citizen, after allowing things like that to contaminate our shores.

—Well, says Martin, rapping for his glass. God bless all here is my prayer.

—Amen, says the citizen.

—And I'm sure he will, says Joe. . . .

I was just looking round to see who the happy thought would strike when be damned but in he comes again letting on to be in a hell of a hurry.

—I was just round at the courthouse, says he, looking for you. I hope I'm not . . .

—No, says Martin, we're ready.

Courthouse my eye and your pockets hanging down with gold and silver. Mean bloody scut. Stand us a drink itself. Devil a sweet fear! There's a jew for you! All for number one. Cute as a shithouse rat. Hundred to five.

—Don't tell anyone, says the citizen.

—Beg your pardon, says he.

—Come on boys, says Martin, seeing it was looking blue. Come along now.

—Don't tell anyone, says the citizen, letting a bawl out of him. It's a secret. And the bloody dog woke up and let a growl.

—Bye bye all, says Martin.

And he got them out as quick as he could, Jack Power and

Crofton or whatever you call him and him in the middle of them letting on to be all at sea and up with them on the bloody jaunting car.

—Off with you, says Martin to the jarvey. . . .

But begob I was just lowering the heel of the pint when I saw the citizen getting up to waddle to the door, puffing and blowing with the dropsy, and he cursing the curse of Cromwell on him, bell, book and candle in Irish, spitting and spatting out of him and Joe and little Alf round him like a leprechaun trying to peacify him.

—Let me alone, says he.

And begob he got as far as the door and they holding him and be bawls out of him:

—Three cheers for Israel!

Arrah, sit down on the parliamentary side of your arse for Christ' sake and don't be making a public exhibition of yourself. Jesus, there's always some bloody clown or other kicking up a bloody murder about bloody nothing. Gob, it'd turn the porter sour in your guts, so it would.

And all the ragamuffins and sluts of the nation round the door and Martin telling the jarvey to drive ahead and the citizen bawling and Alf and Joe at him to whisht and he on his high horse about the jews and the loafers calling for a speech and Jack Power trying to get him to sit down on the car and hold his bloody jaw and a loafer with a patch over his eye starts singing *If the man in the moon was a jew, jew, jew* and a slut shouts out of her:

—Eh, mister! Your fly is open, mister!

And says he:

—Mendelssohn was a jew and Karl Marx and Mercadante and Spinoza. And the Saviour was a jew and his father was a jew. Your God.

—He had no father, says Martin. That'll do now. Drive ahead.

—Whose God! says the citizen.

—Well, his uncle was a jew, says he. Your God was a jew. Christ was a jew like me.

Gob, the citizen made a plunge back into the shop.

—By Jesus, says he, I'll brain that bloody jewman for using the holy name. By Jesus, I'll crucify him so I will. Give us that biscuit-box here.

—Stop! stop! says Joe. . . .

Gob, the devil wouldn't stop him till he got hold of the bloody tin anyhow and out with him and little Alf hanging on to his elbow and he shouting like a stuck pig, as good as any bloody play, in the Queen's royal theatre.

—Where is he till I murder him?

And Ned and J. G. paralysed with the laughing.

—Bloody wars, says I, I'll be in for the last gospel.

But as luck would have it the jarvey got the nag's head round the other way and off with him.

—Hold on, citizen, says Joe. Stop!

Begob he drew his hand and made a swipe and let fly. Mercy of God the sun was in his eyes or he'd have left him for dead. Gob, he near sent it into the county Longford. The bloody nag took fright and the old mongrel after the car like bloody hell and all the populace shouting and laughing and the old tinbox clattering along the street. . . .

You never saw the like of it in all your born puff. Gob, if he got that lottery ticket on the side of his poll he'd remember the gold cup, he would so, but begob the citizen would have been lagged for assault and battery and Joe for aiding and abetting. The jarvey saved his life by furious driving as sure as God made Moses. What? O, Jesus, he did. And he let a volley of oaths after him.

—Did I kill him, says he, or what?

And he shouting to the bloody dog:

—After him, Garry! After him, boy!

And the last we saw was the bloody car rounding the corner and old sheepsface on it gesticulating and the bloody mongrel after it with his lugs back for all he was bloody well worth to tear him limb from limb. Hundred to five! Jesus, he took the value of it out of him, I promise you.

When, lo, there came about them all a great brightness and they beheld the chariot wherein He stood ascend to heaven. And they beheld Him in the chariot, clothed upon in the glory of the brightness, having raiment as of the sun, fair as the moon and terrible that for awe they durst not look upon Him. And there came a voice out of heaven, calling: *Elijah! Elijah!* And He answered with a main cry: *Abba! Adonai!* And they beheld Him even Him, ben Bloom Elijah, amid clouds of angels ascend to the glory of the brightness at an angle of fortyfive degrees over Donohoe's in Little Green Street like a shot off a shovel.

### *For the Literary Traveler*

Barney Kiernan's pub at 8–10 Little Britain Street, where assorted Dubliners drink and talk while the Citizen targets Bloom the Jew, is long gone. But the neighborhood's political landmarks still stand, backgrounds of the history that has poisoned the Citizen—"Cyclops," the one-eyed monster who, with his dog (the patriotically named Garry Owen), attacks Bloom viciously.

LITTLE BRITAIN STREET is close to the markets and ringed by several institutions established to dispense justice, the cardinal virtue of Bloom's politics: the FOUR COURTS; DUBLIN CASTLE, the seat of British power until independence (just across the Liffey, on the southside); and the GREEN STREET COURTHOUSE, between 26 Green Street and Halston Street. It's injustice, however, that dominates the scene in the pub, as it has centuries of Irish history.

From the Ormond Hotel on the quays (the setting of "Sirens," episode 11), Bloom walks north on CAPEL STREET. Off to the left, through the side streets, you can see the FOUR COURTS on Upper Ormond Quay, seat of the High Court of Justice of Ireland, the second masterpiece of James Gandon, the architect of the Custom House. After antitreaty forces occupied the Four Courts in 1922, it was bombarded by Michael Collins, and the priceless archives of Ireland were destroyed. Though Joyce referred in *Dubliners* to "the dull inelegance of Capel Street," a description that fits today, it became a different memory for him when he was living in Paris. "Dublin," he told a friend, "is the nearest city to the Continent. Places here in Paris on a Saturday night are like Capel St. and Thomas St. There are the same joy and excitement, as though bargaining for Sunday's dinner was a holiday." As a boy, he was—like O'Casey—a regular at the Capel Street public library. Slattery's pub (at 129 Capel), mentioned in the episode, is still there, holding weekly traditional music and jazz sessions. At the top of the street, bear left (into North King Street) and left again into GREEN STREET. Now you are approaching Little Britain Street from the direction taken by the narrator and his anonymous friend. You'll pass the back of the GREEN STREET COURTHOUSE (where Bloom has a date to meet Martin Cunningham at 5:00 P.M.); its front entrance is on the other side of the park on Halston Street. The Green Street Central Criminal Court, built between 1792 and 1799, was the place of trial of the patriots Robert Emmet, the brothers Sheare, William Smith O'Brien, and the Fenian leaders of 1867; now it's the Special Criminal Court, which, according to the garda (policeman) staked out front, handles "subversives"—"the IRA, missus." Green Street Park (at the corner of Little Britain Street) is the site of the old Newgate Prison, where the United Irishman Lord Edward Fitzgerald died in 1798 and the Young Irelanders of 1848 were imprisoned. A neighborhood so highly marked by reminders of the unjust courts of British imperialism and the violent resistance of Irish nationalism fits well with this episode in which the mythology of Sinn Fein bares its teeth and the voice of truth—"Your God was a jew. Christ was a jew like me"—must run for his life.

Many landmarks from Joyce's Dublin have been destroyed by the wars for independence and, since the 1950s, a rapacious real-estate industry. Yet it's possible to find many reminders of the "Bloomtime" city. (Every year on Bloomsday, June 16, literary pilgrims do just that, with gusto. For information about the festivities—walking tours, lectures, readings, Bloomsday breakfasts of Guinness and kidneys—contact the James Joyce Centre at joycecen@iol.ie. The Internet has many sites that open up Joyce's world to everyone: www.globalirish.com; www.2street.com/joyce; "DYOUBLONG," an online celebration of Bloomsday, is at www.irish-times.com/bloomsday).

Tracking Bloom and Stephen Dedalus around Dublin—as you go back and forth across the Liffey with map in hand—you can easily find, in no particular order: north of the Liffey, the ORMOND QUAY HOTEL at 7–11 UPPER ORMOND QUAY, which attempts to bring back the musical atmosphere of "Sirens" (especially on Bloomsday), in the Siren's Lounge, the Joyce Room, and the Ulysses Room. South of the Liffey, DAVY BYRNE'S "moral pub" at 21 Duke Street—off Grafton Street—has a painting of Joyce and reminders of Bloom's lunchtime visit in the eighth episode, "Lestrygonians." South of the city center, the MARTELLO TOWER at SANDYCOVE, where Stephen lives with Buck Mulligan and Haines in episode 1, "Telemachus," is now a Joyce museum (Apr.–Oct., Mon.–Sat. 10–5; Sun. 2–6; take the number 8 Dalkey bus from Eden Quay). Five miles north of the tower is SANDYMOUNT STRAND, where in the morning Stephen walks in episode 3, "Proteus": "Signatures of all things I am here to read, seaspawn and seawrack, the nearing tide"; and in the evening, his eye on Gerty MacDowell's thighs, Bloom worships wetly in "Nausikaa," the episode that horrified the New York Society for the Suppression of Vice. Acting *in loco Dei*, it banned *Ulysses* from the United States until 1934. Bloom's first appearance in the novel is all self-control and domestic responsibility in episode 4, "Calypso," in his kitchen in 7 ECCLES STREET, north of the Liffey. Though the house is gone (there is a plaque), the neighborhood of UPPER DORSET STREET has maintained the working-class flavor of 1904. SAINT GEORGE'S CHURCH is now the Temple Theatre. Along Bloom's route in episode 5, "Lotus Eaters," SWENY'S CHEMIST'S SHOP, south of the Liffey in Lincoln Place, still sells lemon soap, and there's a daily morning Mass at SAINT ANDREW'S (ALL HALLOWS) in Westland Row (the rear entrance is on Cumberland Street). (Across the road, at 21 Westland Row, Oscar Wilde was born in 1854.)

    In its haphazard displays, the DUBLIN WRITERS MUSEUM at 18–19 Parnell Square North matches the randomness of Bloom's impressions as he walks through Dublin. He'd like its café, and the bookstore is excellent. A few blocks northeast is BELVEDERE COLLEGE; facing it is NORTH GREAT GEORGE'S STREET and THE JAMES JOYCE CENTRE at 35 Great Denmark Street, an elegantly restored Georgian mansion. This was Mr. Denis J. Maginni's dancing school in *Ulysses* and it is filled with enough memorabilia to satisfy the most voracious pilgrim: portraits of Joyce's ancestors and of Nora Barnacle; the door of 7 Eccles Street; editions of *Ulysses* in many languages and a tape of Joyce's voice reading from the "Wandering Rocks" episode; a video of Dublin in 1904. The book-shop sells "The *Ulysses* Map of Dublin," a useful checklist for the places you might have missed. On Bloomsday, Joyceans dressed up in period costumes gather at this house for an all-day celebration featuring (in 1999) readings by Edna O'Brien and actor Stephen Rea, street theater, jugglers, and pints of Guinness. Contemporary writers toast the legacy of Dublin's first genius. As novelist John Banville offered, "No other modernist has Joyce's humaneness, humor, and love of the ordinary stuff of life. *Ulysses* is an enduring work of art."

◊    ◊

The soliloquy of Molly Bloom, the most famous female literary charac-ter since Chaucer's Wife of Bath, is the final act of *Ulysses* and is named "Penelope" after Odysseus's faithful wife in Homer's *Odyssey*. Joyce once said that a film on astronomy, in particular some sequences dealing with the moon, gave him the idea for its rhythm. It is a half-asleep reverie with memories of different men and many places—Gilbraltar, Lombard Street, Bloom, and the rhododendron gardens on HOWTH HEAD, where Joyce took Nora Barnacle in the summer of 1904 before they left Ireland for good in October. In her biography of Joyce, Edna O'Brien defends the erotic Molly from the charges of Marilyn French and Kate Millett, for whom Joyce's portrait shows his contempt for women and his own naivete in creating this sexual primitive. "There's nothing naive in Joyce," replies O'Brien, "and if he depicted women as sexually primitive he was more prescient than anyone be-fore or since. In fact he was far more indulgent of women than of men." According to O'Brien, Molly's credo was "Let's have a bit of fun first." Her creator despised all literary arguments, telling Beckett he'd rather talk about turnips.

(Howth bus 31 from Lower Abbey Street takes half an hour and is crowded on weekends; you can also get there on the northbound Howth Dublin Area Rapid Transit.) There are houses now in the inte-rior of the Howth Head peninsula, but a footpath runs around the coast and to the summit—it's called the Top View—or you can take the 31B bus to get up to the cliffs. Up here you can look down over Lambay and Ireland's Eye, small rocky islands to the north, a crowded Howth harbor, Dublin Bay, the Dublin and Wicklow mountains, Dublin city, and the flower gardens of Howth demesne. Howth, which in early human history was an island, is said to have the largest flowers of any place in Ireland. It's easy to find a private spot to enjoy the flowing language of Molly Bloom—Bloom's resting place and Joyce's most life-affirming voice.

*FROM* PENELOPE

### EPISODE 18

I love flowers Id love to have the whole place swimming in roses God of heaven theres nothing like nature the wild mountains then the sea and the waves rushing then the beautiful country with fields of oats and wheat and all kinds of things and all the fine cattle going about that would do your heart good to see rivers and lakes and flowers all sorts of shapes and smells and colours springing up even out of the ditches primroses and violets nature it is as for them saying theres no God I wouldnt give a snap of my two fingers for all their learning why dont they go and create something I often asked him atheists or whatever they call themselves go and wash the cobbles off themselves first then they go howling for the priest and they dying and why why because theyre afraid of hell on account of their bad conscience ah yes I know them well who was the first person in the universe before there was anybody that made it all who ah that they dont know neither do I so there you are they might as well try to stop the sun from rising tomorrow the sun shines for you he said the day we were lying among the rhododendrons on Howth head in the grey tweed suit and his straw hat the day I got him to propose to me yes first I gave him the bit of seedcake out of my mouth and it was leapyear like now yes 16 years ago my God after that long kiss I near lost my breath yes he said I was a flower of the mountain yes so we are flowers all a womans body yes that was one true thing he said in his life and the sun shines for you today yes that was why I liked him because I saw he understood or felt what a woman is and I knew I could always get round him and I gave him all the pleasure I could leading him on till he asked me to say yes and I wouldnt answer first only looked out over the sea and the

sky I was thinking of so many things he didnt know of Mulvey and
Mr Stanhope and Hester and father and old captain Groves and
the sailors playing all birds fly and I say stoop and washing up
dishes they called it on the pier and the sentry in front of the gover-
nors house with the thing round his white helmet poor devil half
roasted and the Spanish girls laughing in their shawls and their tall
combs and the auctions in the morning the Greeks and the jews
and the Arabs and the devil knows who else from all the ends of
Europe and Duke street and the fowl market all clucking outside
Larby Sharons and the poor donkeys slipping half asleep and the
vague fellows in the cloaks asleep in the shade on the steps and
the big wheels of the carts of the bulls and the old castle thousands
of years old yes and those handsome Moors all in white and tur-
bans like kings asking you to sit down in their little bit of a shop
and Ronda with the old windows of the posadas glancing eyes a lat-
tice hid for her lover to kiss the iron and the wineshops half open at
night and the castanets and the night we missed the boat at Algeci-
ras the watchman going about serene with his lamp and O that awful deepdown torrent O and the sea the sea crimson sometimes like
fire and the glorious sunsets and the figtrees in the Alameda gardens yes and all the queer little streets and pink and blue and yellow houses and the rosegardens and the jessamine and geraniums
and cactuses and Gibraltar as a girl where I was a Flower of the
mountain yes when I put the rose in my hair like the Andalusian
girls used or shall I wear a red yes and how he kissed me under the
Moorish wall and I thought well as well him as another and then I
asked him with my eyes to ask again yes and then he asked me
would I yes to say yes my mountain flower and first I put my arms
around him yes and drew him down to me so he could feel my
breasts all perfume yes and his heart was going like mad and yes I
said yes I will Yes.

# Samuel Beckett

## 1906–1989

*Of his early years in Foxrock, a south Dublin suburb, Beckett said, "You might say I had a happy childhood. . . . My parents did everything they could to make a child happy . . . although I had little talent for happiness." According to biographer James Knowlson, son and mother "rarely saw eye to eye on anything concerning himself." With his father the young Beckett took long walks and bicycle rides in the Dublin hills and learned to swim and dive from the rocks at the Forty-Foot in Sandycove. He was a brilliant student of French and Italian literature at Trinity College, winning an exchange lectureship in Paris, where he first met James Joyce in 1928 and became his assistant. In later years, acknowledging the influence of Joyce's dedication to his work, Beckett said, "Joyce taught me what it meant to be a real artist." After Joyce's death, Beckett called him "a very lovable human being." Returning to Dublin to lecture at Trinity, he found he hated academic life and resigned after a year. During this period, he worked on the stories that became* More Pricks than Kicks *(1934). Eventually, after years of nomadic poverty, he settled in Paris. During World War II, he joined the French Resistance, for which he received the Croix de Guerre. Though he had published poetry and fiction—*More Pricks than Kicks *(1934),* Murphy *(1938),* Molloy *(1951),* Malone Dies *(1951), and* The Unnamable *(1953)—his first success came with the production of his play* Waiting for Godot *(1953) in Paris. Despising the fame that assaulted him after* Endgame *(1956),* Krapp's Last Tape *(1958), and* Happy Days *(1961), he refused to attend the ceremony when he was awarded the Nobel Prize for Litera-*

*ture in 1969. He gave a good portion of his prize money to the library of Trinity College.*

### DING DONG

More Pricks than Kicks, *from which this story is taken, was written in Dublin and has the atmosphere of the city in the late twenties when Beckett was a student at Trinity. The title comes from Jesus' words to Saul in the* Acts of the Apostles: *"I am Jesus whom thou persecutist; it is hard for thee to kick against the pricks" (9:5).*

*Beckett took the name of Belacqua, the picaresque anti-hero, from a penitent in Dante's* Purgatorio *notorious for his sloth. Belacqua, a comic and impotent Don Juan who is a student of languages at Trinity, is pursued through Dublin by a variety of women, and he finally dies. Of the ten stories in the collection, only the first ("Dante and the Lobster") and third ("Ding Dong") are detachable. The rest read like a novel.*

My sometime friend Belacqua enlivened the last phase of his solipsism, before he toed the line and began to relish the world, with the belief that the best thing he had to do was to move constantly from place to place. He did not know how this conclusion had been gained, but that it was not thanks to his preferring one place to another he felt sure. He was pleased to think that he could give what he called the Furies the slip by merely setting himself in motion. But as for sites, one was as good as another, because they all disappeared as soon as he came to rest in them. The mere act of rising and going, irrespective of whence and whither, did him good. That was so. He was sorry that he did not enjoy the means to indulge this humour as he would have wished, on a large scale, on land and sea. Hither and thither on land and sea! He could not afford that, for he was poor. But in a small way he did what he could. From the ingle to the window, from the nursery to the bedroom, even from one quarter of the town to another, and back, these little acts of motion he was in a fair way of making, and they certainly did do him some good as a rule. It was the old story of the salad days, torment in the terms and in the intervals a measure of ease.

Being by nature however sinfully indolent, bogged in indolence, asking nothing better than to stay put at the good pleasure of what he called the Furies, he was at times tempted to wonder whether the remedy were not rather more disagreeable than the complaint. But he could only suppose that it was not, seeing that he continued to have recourse to it, in a small way it is true, but nevertheless for years he continued to have recourse to it, and to return thanks for the little good it did him.

The simplest form of this exercise was boomerang, out and back; nay, it was the only one that he could afford for many years. Thus it is clear that his contrivance did not proceed from any discrimination between different points in space, since he returned directly, if we except an occasional pause for refreshment, to his point of departure, and truly no less recruited in spirit than if the interval had been whiled away abroad in the most highly reputed cities.

I know all this because he told me. We were Pylades and Orestes for a period, flattened down to something very genteel; but the relation abode and was highly confidential while it lasted. I have witnessed every stage of the exercise. I have been there when he set out, springing up and hastening away without as much as by your leave, impelled by some force that he did not care to gainsay. I have had glimpses of him enjoying his little trajectory. I have been there again when he returned, transfigured and transformed. It was very nearly the reverse of the author of the Imitation's "glad going out and sad coming in."

He was at pains to make it clear to me, and to all those to whom he exposed his manoeuvre, that it was in no way cognate with the popular act of brute labour, digging and such like, exploited to disperse the dumps, an antidote depending for its efficaciousness on mere physical exhaustion, and for which he expressed the greatest contempt. He did not fatigue himself, he said; on the contrary. He lived a Beethoven pause, he said, whatever he meant by that. In his anxiety to explain himself he was liable to come to grief. Nay, this anxiety in itself, or so at least it seemed to me, constituted a breakdown in the self-sufficiency which he never wearied of arrogating to himself, a sorry collapse of my little internus homo, and alone sufficient to give him away as inept ape of his own shadow. But he wriggled out of everything by pleading that he had been drunk at the time, or that he was an incoherent person and content to remain so, and so on. He was an impossible person in the end. I gave him up in the end because he was not *serious*.

One day, in a positive geyser of confidence, he gave me an account of one of these "moving pauses." He had a strong weakness for oxymoron. In the same way he over-indulged in gin and tonic-water.

Not the least charm of this pure blank movement, this "gress" or "gression," was its aptness to receive, with or without the approval of the subject, in all their integrity the faint inscriptions of the outer world. Exempt from destination, it had not to shun the unforeseen nor turn aside from the agreeable odds and ends of vaudeville that are liable to crop up. This sensitiveness was not the least charm of this roaming that began by being blank, not the least charm of this pure act the alacrity with which it welcomed defilement. But very nearly the least.

Emerging, on the particular evening in question, from the underground convenience in the maw of College Street, with a vague impression that he had come from following the sunset up the Liffey till all the colour had been harried from the sky, all the tulips and aerugo expunged, he squatted, not that he had too much drink taken but simply that for the moment there were no grounds for his favouring one direction rather than another, against Tommy Moore's plinth. Yet he durst not dally. Was it not from brooding shill I, shall I, dilly, dally, that he had come out? Now the summons to move on was a subpoena. Yet he found he could not, any more than Buridan's ass, move to right or left, backward or forward. Why this was he could not make out at all. Nor was it the moment for self-examination. He had experienced little or no trouble coming back from the Park Gate along the north quay, he had taken the Bridge and Westmoreland Street in his stride, and now he suddenly found himself good for nothing but to loll against the plinth of this bull-necked bard, and wait for a sign.

There were signs on all hands. There was the big Bovril sign to begin with, flaring beyond the Green. But it was useless. Faith, Hope and—what was it?—Love, Eden missed, every ebb derided, all the tides ebbing from the shingle of Ego Maximus, little me. Itself it went nowhere, only round and round, like the spheres, but mutely. It could not dislodge him now, it could only put ideas into his head. Was it not from sitting still among his ideas, other people's ideas, that he had come away? What would he not give now to get on the move again! Away from ideas!

Turning aside from this and other no less futile emblems, his attention was arrested by a wheel-chair being pushed rapidly under the arcade of the Bank, in the direction of Dame Street. It moved in and out of sight behind the bars of the columns. This was the blind paralytic who sat all day near to the corner of Fleet Street, and in bad weather under the shelter of the arcade, the same being wheeled home to his home in the Coombe. It was past his time and there was a bitter look on his face. He would give his chairman a piece of his mind when he got him to himself. This chairman, hireling or poor relation, came every evening a little before the dark, unfastened from the beggar's neck and breast the placard announcing his distress, tucked him up snugly in his coverings and wheeled him home to his supper. He was well advised to be assiduous, for this beggar was a power in the Coombe. In the morning it was his duty to shave his man and wheel him, according to the weather, to one or other of his pitches. So it went, day after day.

This was a star the horizon adorning if you like, and Belacqua made off at all speed in the opposite direction. Down Pearse Street, that is to say, long straight Pearse Street, its vast Barrack of Glencullen granite, its home of tragedy restored and enlarged, its coal merchants and Florentine Fire Brigade Station, its two Cervi saloons, ice-cream and fried fish, its dairies, garages and monumental sculptors, and implicit behind the whole length of its southern frontage the College. Perpetuis futuris temporibus duraturum.* It was to be hoped so, indeed.

*"For all future time it ought to be preserved."

It was a most pleasant street, despite its name, to be abroad in, full as it always was with shabby substance and honest-to-God coming and going. All day the roadway was a tumult of buses, red and blue and silver. By one of these a little girl was run down, just as Belacqua drew near to the railway viaduct. She had been to the Hibernian Dairies for milk and bread and then she had plunged out into the roadway, she was in such a childish fever to get back in record time with her treasure to the tenement in Mark Street where she lived. The good milk was all over the road and the loaf, which had sustained no injury, was sitting up against the kerb, for all the world as though a pair of hands had taken it up and set it down there. The queue standing for the Palace Cinema was torn between conflicting desires: to keep their places and to see the excitement. They craned their necks and called out to know the worst, but they stood firm. Only one girl, debauched in appearance and swathed in a black blanket, fell out near the sting of the queue and secured the loaf. With the loaf under her blanket she sidled unchallenged down Mark Street and turned into Mark Lane. When she got back to the queue her place had been taken of course. But her sally had not cost her more than a couple of yards.

Belacqua turned left into Lombard Street, the street of the sanitary engineers, and entered a public house. Here he was known, in the sense that his grotesque exterior had long ceased to alienate the curates and make them giggle, and to the extent that he was served with his drink without having to call for it. This did not always seem a privilege. He was tolerated, what was more, and let alone by the rough but kindly habitués of the house, recruited for the most part from among dockers, railwaymen and vague joxers on the dole. Here also art and love, scrabbling in dispute or staggering home, were barred, or, perhaps better, unknown. The aesthetes and the impotent were far away.

These circumstances combined to make of this place a very grateful refuge for Belacqua, who never omitted, when he found himself in its neighbourhood with the price of a drink about him, to pay it a visit.

When I enquired how he squared such visits with his anxiety to keep on the move and his distress at finding himself brought to a standstill, as when he had come out of the underground in the mouth of College Street, he replied that he did not. "Surely" he said "my resolution has the right to break down." I supposed so indeed. "Or" he said "if you prefer, I make the raid in two hops instead of non-stop. From what" he cried "does that disqualify me, I should very much like to know." I hastened to assure him that he had a perfect right to suit himself in what, after all, was a manoeuvre of his own contriving, and that the raid, to adopt his own term, lost nothing by being made in easy stages. "Easy!" he exclaimed, "how easy?"

But notice the double response, like two holes to a burrow.

Sitting in this crapulent den, drinking his drink, he gradually ceased to see its furnishings with pleasure, the bottles, representing centuries of loving research, the stools, the counter, the powerful screws, the shining phalanx of the pulls of the beer-engines, all cunningly devised and elaborated to further the relations between purveyor and consumer in this domain. The bottles drawn and emptied in a twinkling, the casks responding to the slightest pressure on their joysticks, the weary proletarians at rest on arse and elbow, the cash register that never complains, the graceful curates flying from customer to customer, all this made up a spectacle in which Belacqua was used to take delight and chose to see a pleasant instance of machinery decently subservient to appetite. A great major symphony of supply and demand, effect and cause, fulcrate on the middle C of the counter and waxing, as it proceeded, in the charming harmonics of blasphemy and broken glass and all the aliquots of fatigue and ebriety. So that he would say that the only place where he could come to anchor and be happy was a low public-house, and that all the wearisome tactics of gress and dud Beethoven would be done away with if only he could spend his life in such a place. But as they closed at ten, and as residence and good faith were viewed as incompatible, and as in any case he had not the means to consecrate his life to stasis, even in the meanest bar, he supposed he must be content to indulge this whim from time to time, and return thanks for such sporadic mercy.

All this and much more he laboured to make clear. He seemed to derive considerable satisfaction from his failure to do so.

But on this particular occasion the cat failed to jump, with the result that he became as despondent as though he were sitting at home in his own great armchair, as anxious to get on the move and quite as hard put to it to do so. Why this was he could not make out. Whether the trituration of the child in Pearse Street had upset him without his knowing it, or whether (and he put forward this alternative with a truly insufferable complacency) he had come to some parting of the ways, he did not know at all. All he could say was that the objects in which he was used to find such recreation and repose lost gradually their hold upon him, he became insensible to them little by little, the old itch and algos crept back into his mind. He had come briskly all the way from Tommy Moore, and now he suddenly found himself sitting paralysed and grieving in a pub of all places, good for nothing but to stare at his spoiling porter, and wait for a sign.

To this day he does not know what caused him to look up, but look up he did. Feeling the impulse to do this strong upon him, he forced his eyes away from the glass of dying porter and was rewarded by seeing a hatless woman advancing slowly towards him up the body of the bar. No sooner had she come in than he must have become aware of her. That was surely very curious in the first instance. She seemed to be hawking some ware or other, but what it was he could not see, except that it was not studs or laces or matches or lavender or any of the usual articles. Not that it was unusual to find a woman in that public-house, for they came and went freely, slaking their thirst and beguiling their sorrows with no less freedom than their men-folk. Indeed it was always a pleasure to see them, their advances were always most friendly and honourable, Belacqua had many a delightful recollection of their commerce.

Hence there was no earthly reason why he should see in the advancing figure of this mysterious pedlar anything untoward, or in the nature of the sign in default of which he was clamped to his stool till closing-time. Yet the impulse to do so was so strong that he yielded to it, and as she drew nearer, having met with more rebuffs than pence in her endeavours to dispose of her wares, whatever they were, it became clear to him that his instinct had not played him false, in so far at least as she was a woman of very remarkable presence indeed.

Her speech was that of a woman of the people, but of a gentle-woman of the people. Her gown had served its time, but yet contrived to be respectable. He noticed with a pang that she sported about her neck the insidious little mock fur so prevalent in tony slumland. The one deplorable feature of her get up, as apprehended by Belacqua in his hasty survey, was the footwear—the cruel strait outsizes of the suffragette or welfare worker. But he did not doubt for a moment that they had been a gift, or picked up in the pop for a song. She was of more than average height and well in flesh. She might be past middle-age. But her face, ah her face, was what Belacqua had rather refer to as her countenance, it was so full of light. This she lifted up upon him and no error. Brimful of light and serene, serenissime, it bore no trace of suffering, and in this alone it might be said to be a notable face. Yet like tormented faces that he had seen, like the face in the National Gallery in Merrion Square by the Master of Tired Eyes, it seemed to have come a long way and subtend an infinitely narrow angle of affliction, as eyes focus a star. The features were null, only luminous, impassive and secure, petrified in radiance, or words to that effect, for the reader is requested to take notice that this sweet style is Belacqua's. An act of expression, he said, a wreathing or wrinkling, could only have had the effect of a dimmer on a headlight. The implications of this triumphant figure, the just and the unjust, etc., are better forgone.

At long last she addressed herself to Belacqua.

"Seats in heaven" she said in a white voice "tuppence apiece, four fer a tanner."

"No" said Belacqua. It was the first syllable to come to his lips. It had not been his intention to deny her.

"The best of seats" she said "again I'm sold out. Tuppence apiece the best of seats, four fer a tanner."

This was unforeseen with a vengeance, if not exactly vaudeville. Belacqua was embarrassed in the last degree, but transported also. He felt the sweat coming in the small of his back, above his Montrouge belt.

"Have you got them on you?" he mumbled.

"Heaven goes round" she said, whirling her arm, "and round and round and round and round and round."

"Yes" said Belacqua "round and round."

"Rowan" she said, dropping the d's and getting more of a spin into the slogan, "rowan an' rowan an' rowan."

Belacqua scarcely knew where to look. Unable to blush he came out in this beastly sweat. Nothing of the kind had ever happened to him before. He was altogether disarmed, unsaddled and miserable. The eyes of them all, the dockers, the railwaymen and, most terrible of all, the joxers, were upon him. His tail drooped. This female dog of a pixy with her tiresome Ptolemy, he was at her mercy.

"No" he said "no thank you, no not this evening thank you."

"Again I'm sold out" she said "an' buked out, four fer a tanner."

"On whose authority . . ." began Belacqua, like a Scholar.

"For yer frien' " she said "yer da, yer ma an' yer motte, four fer a tanner." The voice ceased, but the face did not abate.

"How do I know" piped Belacqua "you're not sellin' me a pup?"

"Heaven goes rowan an' rowan . . ."

"Rot you" said Belacqua "I'll take two. How much is that?"

"Four dee" she said.

Belacqua gave her a sixpence.

"Gobbless yer honour" she said, in the same white voice from which she had not departed. She made to go.

"Here" cried Belacqua "you owe me twopence." He had not even the good grace to say tuppence.

"Arragowan" she said "make it four cantcher, yer frien', yer da, yer ma an' yer motte."

Belacqua could not bicker. He had not the strength of mind for that. He turned away.

"Jesus" she said distinctly "and his sweet mother preserve yer honour."

"Amen" said Belacqua, into his dead porter.

Now the woman went away and her countenance lighted her to her room in Townsend Street.

But Belacqua tarried a little to listen to the music. Then he also departed, but for Railway Street, beyond the river.

⊏◇⊐

## For the Literary Traveler

The voices in "Ding Dong" are Irish voices; Dublin, meandering and talky, takes on the prominence of a main character. When Belacqua, who likes his gin-and-tonics, agrees to describe for the narrator of this story his hedonistic ramblings, it's possible to follow him, thanks to Eoin O'Brien's marvelous *The Beckett Country: Samuel Beckett's Ireland* (1986).

First Belacqua arrives in COLLEGE STREET, an approach to that bastion of Protestant privilege, TRINITY COLLEGE. Beckett's feelings toward the academic life come through in a poem entitled "Gnome," published in the years he was writing *More Pricks than Kicks*.

> *Spend the years of learning squandering*
> *Courage for the years of wandering*
> *Through the world politely turning*
> *From the loutishness of learning*

In 1959, however, he agreed to show up to receive an honorary doctorate from Trinity, which had obviously forgiven him for walking out on his teaching job in 1931.

Belacqua now uses the underground urinal behind THOMAS MOORE'S STATUE, "the plinth of [the] bull-necked bard." The place (and lyrics) most associated with Moore is the Vale of Avoca—more an industrial area than a sylvan site today—where his tree stands at the "Meeting of the Waters," the Avonmore and Avonbeg Rivers in southeastern Wicklow. (In *Ulysses*, Joyce says of "Tommy Moore," "They did right to put him up over a urinal: meeting of the waters.")

Belacqua continues down PEARSE STREET, the northern perimeter of TRINITY COLLEGE, which has an entrance to THE SAMUEL BECKETT THEATRE, housed in a modern wooden pagoda on the Trinity campus. The adjoining box office sells tickets just before the productions of Trinity's award-winning Dublin Players, and there's an exhibit space with photographs of Beckett by John Minihan and a painting by Louis le Brocquey.

MARK STREET, home of the child who is run down near the railway viaduct (now gone), is off Pearse Street to the left, an area of plain public flats where tenements stood in Beckett's time. In response to the little girl's tragic death, Belacqua's tone is characteristically abstract and callous. Beckett, however, according to his biographer, was devastated by this event, which he witnessed. He repeats the accidental death of a child under a train in his radio play All that Fall (1956). It was over this issue, in particular—of a God who allows innocent people to suffer—that Beckett, who was raised in the Church of Ireland, abandoned his religious faith.

At the intersection of PEARSE STREET, LOMBARD STREET, and Westland Row, Belacqua turns left into Lombard Street and enters a pub popular among dockers, railway workers, and men on the dole. His taste in pubs reflects Beckett's: he patronized only those where he could read his newspaper and be left alone, avoiding pubs frequented by politicians, poets, and intellectuals—"aesthetes and the impotent," as Belacqua calls them.

(The Literary Pub Crawl, which delights large numbers of tourists, would horrify the likes of Belacqua and his creator. It starts nightly at 7:30 from Easter to Oct. 21; Nov.–Mar., Thu.–Sat. only; there's also one year round at noon on Sundays, at The Duke at 8–9 Duke Street. Two actors, reciting bits of Waiting for Godot and scenes from Behan, Wilde, and Plunkett, lead the group from pub to pub, stopping for drinks and gossip about which writer drank himself to death where. Other pubs where, like Beckett/Belacqua, you can keep to yourself and read if you wish, include the nearby Lincoln's Inn at 19 Lincoln Place—hard by where Joyce first met Nora Barnacle—the Pembroke, and Kehoe's, a traditional pub with cozy snugs just off Grafton Street, at 9 South Anne Street.)

As Belacqua drinks and meditates—in luminous prose—about the sometime happiness of pub life, a pedlar woman, La Serenissima, interrupts his reverie. At the end of the story, the woman heads home, and Belacqua continues on to RAILWAY STREET, formerly, but no longer, an address in the Kips, the red-light district.

Beckett first saw the face of Belacqua's pedlar, La Serenissima, in a painting—A Portrait of an Old Lady by the Master of the Tired Eyes—in the NATIONAL GALLERY. From Lombard Street, it's south along Westland

Row, left around Lincoln Place (you cross Clare Street, where above his father's offices of Beckett and Medcalf at number 6, Beckett lived while he wrote *More Kicks* and started *Murphy*), and straight on into Merrion Square West (Mon.–Sat. 10–6; Thu. until 9; Sun. 2–5). *More Pricks than Kicks* is filled with references to the paintings on view in one of Dublin's most delightful interiors. (The bookshop, café, and free concerts are also good.)

Deeply interested in painting, Beckett spent a good deal of time here during his years at Trinity and afterward. He was a friend of the painter Jack Yeats (1871–1957), W. B. Yeats's younger brother, whose work he ranked with that of Kandinsky, Klee, Rouault, and Braque, because, like them, "he illuminated existence." Yeats's work, he said, was a tremendous influence on him. It's located on the first floor in rear gallery 6, "The Irish School": *The Liffey Swim* (which Joyce bought, commenting, "There are great silences in that picture.... Jack Yeats and I have the same method"), *Islandbridge Regatta,* and *Morning in a City* are all Dublin scenes. Of his friend's art, Beckett said, "Simply bow down, in wonderment."

He also loved the Italian paintings of Titian, Tintoretto, and Bellini (he spent hours looking at the Perugino *Pietà*, admiring the "spunky" Christ, making Belacqua's girlfriend in the story "Love and Lethe" resemble its Magdalene). The silence and mysticism of Rembrandt's *The Rest on the Flight into Egypt* (in the museum's wing of European art) and other small Dutch masters for which the National Gallery is known—these Beckett cherished for his entire life, sixty years later remembering their precise details. His passion for the visual arts contributed to the symbiosis of literature and painting that many critics have seen in the stark stage directions of his plays; the dislocations of modern art, especially in the work of Cézanne, influenced every aspect of his dramaturgy.

The National Gallery, with paintings of Lady Gregory, O'Casey, Joyce, and Seamus Heaney, has near the entrance a statue of George Bernard Shaw, who left one-third of his estate to the gallery that in *Sixteen Self Sketches* he praises for having nourished his imagination in the years of his poor, "frightful and loveless" Dublin childhood.

Beckett left Ireland in the 1930s. Some say it was the banning of *More Pricks than Kicks* in 1934 that was a crucial moment of alienation for him. But he made many return visits to his family in Foxrock and to Jack Yeats, who had his studio in nearby Fitz-william Square. "We used to go for walks.... We didn't talk very much," Beckett remembered much later. Jack Yeats's house and the gracious square where it is located—along Belacqua's routes—are at the heart of some of Dublin's finest Georgian neighborhoods and streetscapes.

At Number One Merrion Square North—"Wilde's Corner"—dramatist and poet Oscar Wilde (1854–1900) lived until he left for Oxford. A secluded and lovely memorial sculpture garden in the square's northwest corner looks across at his house. From the National Gallery, the walk along Merrion Square South, past William Butler Yeats's house at number 82, affords a fine classical vista of Upper Mount Street with St. Stephen's church closing it in the distance.

At the end of Mount Street, rounding the crescent behind the church, you come to the pretty Italianate HUBAND BRIDGE on the GRAND CANAL (extending 340 miles west to the River Shannon), Dublin's "Bridge of Sighs."

Besides marking Belacqua Shuah's late-night path of debauchery, the towpaths along the canal and the streets on either side of the canal bridges are literary landmarks: Elizabeth Bowen's birthplace and childhood home at 15 Herbert Place, the subject of her memoir *Seven Winters: Memories of a Dublin Childhood* (1942). Beside the Baggot Street Bridge, inside the reedy paths on Wilton Terrace, a statue of the poet from rural Monaghan, Patrick Kavanagh (who lived just south of the bridge at 62 Pembroke Road and drank at the still-commodious Waterloo House at 36 Upper Baggot Street) sits on a bench, the exact memorial he requested from his friends in his poem "Lines Written on a Seat on the Grand Canal":

> *O COMMEMORATE me where there is water*
> *Canal water preferably, so stilly*
> *Greeny at the heart of summer. Brother*
> *Commemorate me thus beautifully.*
> *Where by a rock Niagariously roars*

> *The falls for those who sit in the tremendous silence*
> *Of mid-July.*

It was on the canal's north bank that Beckett's mother lay dying in the Merrion Nursing Home at 21 Herbert Street in the summer of 1950. Beckett sat with her through her last agony, taking breaks to walk alone along the canal, waiting for her suffering to be over. In 1958 he dramatized this time and place as *Krapp's Last Tape*. The narrator, no longer the pedantic young Dubliner of *More Pricks*, remembers "the house on the canal where mother lay a-dying, in the late autumn, after her long viduity."

When the blind was lowered in the window of the nursing home, he knew it was "All over and done with, at last." Every year since he'd settled in Paris, Beckett had come home to Dublin to visit his mother for a month. He was heartbroken by the Parkinson's disease that for several years made her suffer terribly: "I gaze into the eyes of my mother, never so blue, so stupefied, so heart-rending ... these are the first eyes I think I truly see. I do not need to see others; there is enough there to make one love and weep." In the play, Krapp also remembers his walks with his father in the Wicklow mountains. Beckett, in these years, wrote to a friend, "At night when I can't sleep, I do the old walks again and stand beside him again one Christmas morning in the fields near Glencullen."

To see the landscapes of Beckett's childhood—in his words, a lifelong "obsessional" memory—you can return to Pearse Street and the train station (formerly Westland Row Station) and take the southbound DART, an efficient electric train system, in the direction of Bray and the Wicklow mountains. (Nonstop, the ride takes about half an hour. If you buy an all-day excursion ticket, you can get off and on the train all along this route and explore this magnificent coast on the Irish Sea.) The train passes along the sweep of Dublin Bay, with panoramic vistas of places that appear repeatedly in Beckett's (and Shaw's and Yeats's and Joyce's) writing: the lighthouses and pier at Dun Laoghaire, the harbors and small islands in the sea, Dalkey, the shimmering blue-green bay and white crescent beach beneath Killiney Hill.

Disembarking at DALKEY and climbing Dalkey Hill on Torca Road, midway up you come to Torca Cottage or Shaw's Cottage, marked with a plaque and closed to the public. Shaw attributed the growth of his artistic imagination to his removal "at the age of ten from the [Dublin] street in which I was born [33 Synge Street] to the heights of Dalkey Hill," where he loved the sunsets. Along Dalkey Avenue you'll find "lions couchant on the pillars" of the gate to the former Clifton School, the setting of "Nestor," episode 2 in *Ulysses*, where Stephen Dedalus (like Joyce) taught at a boys' school.

Further south along the coast, KILLINEY BAY and strand cut a wide arc beneath the hill, overgrown in spring and summer with wildflowers. The best approach to this stretch of coast is on the DART (though you can also climb up Dalkey Hill to the park and obelisk on top of KILLINEY HILL, overlooking the bay). As the train emerges from the Dalkey tunnel, the view of Killiney Bay is perhaps as beautiful as any seascape you'll see in Ireland—the comparison of Killiney to the Bay of Naples is not an exaggeration. The light, if not the temperature, is Mediterranean. As an adult visiting his brother's home on Killiney Hill, Beckett often fell asleep at night listening to the sea.

In 1959, when Beckett's companion (and later wife), Suzanne Deschevaux-Dumesil, visited Ireland for the first time, he drove her south into these Dublin and Wicklow mountains, a granite chain extending seventy miles between Dalkey and Wexford, the longest mass of granite in Britain and Ireland. They belong to the earliest and deepest emotional ground of Beckett Country, to which his father, an indefatigable walker, had first introduced him: Glencullen (now a suburb), the Devil's Elbow, pretty Enniskerry (as a Dubliner, walking out from Rathfarnham on a Sunday, he stopped here for his favorite Beamish stout at the Powerscourt Arms Hotel, still a pleasant place to drink and read the paper), Glencree, Sallygap, the Military Road, Prince William's Seat, Luggala, Annamoe. These are also the tramping grounds of Synge (see p. 117), whose plays Beckett knew well and admired. It was for these lonesome high places—especially as they looked east to the sea—that Ireland always remained deep in Beckett's affections. In *Worstward Ho*, he remembers:

> Where then but there see now another. Bit by bit an old man and child. In the dim void bit by bit an old man and child ... Hand in hand with equal plod they go. In the free hands—no. Free

empty hands … The child hand raised to reach the holding hand. Hold the old holding hand. Hold and be held. Plod on and never recede … Backs turned. Both bowed. Joined by held holding hands. Plod on as one.

Two wanderers on the open road, isolated and together, going on, no matter what: this is *Waiting for Godot* Country. Its dialectic—the play of opposites—enacts his ambiguous feelings about Ireland and towards life and death. Like Joyce, Beckett exiled himself from his country. Also like Joyce, he took the place with him—voices, faces, jokes, and the map of Dublin, city and hills.

# Eavan Boland

## 1944 –

*Currently Ireland's preeminent female poet, Boland has published eight volumes of poetry, has received numerous literary awards, and is director of the creative writing program at Stanford University. In her commencement address at Stanford in May 1999, she referred to Ireland as a country that is famous for the way in which "it values and loves the written and spoken word … for the way it promotes language as a means of life." But within that literary tradition, as she argues in the essay "A Kind of Scar" (1989), the experience and writing of women have been largely ignored. Boland, who helped found the feminist Arlen House Press, has tried to reverse the traditional pattern. Rejecting as false the nationalistic images of women in Irish poetry—the Cathleen Ní Houlihans and Dark Rosaleens who are the passive and silent objects of stereotypical emotions—she makes explicit in many of her poems the psychological and sexual themes of women's experience. She has also observed, however, that over the last twenty years, many Irish women have moved from being the subjects of Irish poems to being the authors of them.*

## ANNA LIFFEY

*As a young married woman, Boland moved from Dublin to Dundrum, seven miles to the south, where she gave birth to and raised her children and wrote poetry. From her front door she could see the mountains of Wicklow, where the Liffey begins as a stream in a peat bog. Here she contemplates the flow of the river, a journey of eighty miles, through Wicklow and the plain of Kildare, bending east into Dublin (where she and her country were born), and finally out into the Irish Sea— a metaphor for the passage of her life. The poem's verses, like the river's currents, move through her past youth and into her present middle age.*

> Life, *the story goes,*
> *Was the daughter of Cannan,*
> *And came to the plain of Kildare.*
> *She loved the flat-lands and the ditches*
> *And the unreachable horizon.*
> *She asked that it be named for her.*
> *The river took its name from the land.*
> *The land took its name from a woman.*
>
> *A woman in the doorway of a house.*
> *A river in the city of her birth.*
>
> *There, in the hills above my house,*
> *The river Liffey rises, is a source.*
> *It rises in rush and ling heather and*
> *Black peat and bracken and strengthens*
> *To claim the city it narrated.*
> *Swans. Steep falls. Small towns.*
> *The smudged air and bridges of Dublin.*
>
> *Dusk is coming.*
> *Rain is moving east from the hills.*
> *If I could see myself*
> *I would see*
> *A woman in a doorway*

*Wearing the colours that go with red hair.*
*Although my hair is no longer red.*

*I praise*
*The gifts of the river.*
*Its shiftless and glittering*
*Re-telling of a city,*
*Its clarity as it flows,*
*In the company of runt flowers and herons,*
*Around a bend at Islandbridge*
*And under thirteen bridges to the sea.*
*Its patience at twilight—*
*Swans nesting by it,*
*Neon wincing into it.*

*Maker of*
*Places, remembrances,*
*Narrate such fragments for me:*

*One body. One spirit.*
*One place. One name.*
*The city where I was born.*
*The river that runs through it.*
*The nation which eludes me.*
*Fractions of a life*
*It has taken me a lifetime*
*To claim.*

*I came here in a cold winter.*

*I had no children. No country.*
*I did not know the name for my own life.*

*My country took hold of me.*
*My children were born.*

*I walked out in a summer dusk*
*To call them in.*

*One name. Then the other one.*
*The beautiful vowels sounding out home.*

*Make of a nation what you will*
*Make of the past*
*What you can—*

*There is now*
*A woman in a doorway.*

*It has taken me*
*All my strength to do this.*

*Becoming a figure in a poem.*

*Usurping a name and a theme.*

*A river is not a woman.*
   *Although the names it finds*
      *The history it makes*
*And suffers—*
   *The Viking blades beside it,*
      *The muskets of the Redcoats,*
         *the flames of the Four Courts*
*Blazing into it*
   *Are a sign.*
      *Anymore than*
*A woman is a river,*
   *Although the course it takes,*
      *Through swans courting and distraught willows,*
*Its patience*
   *Which is also its powerlessness,*
      *From Callary to Islandbridge.*
         *And from source to mouth,*
*Is another one.*
*And in my late forties*
*Past believing*
   *Love will heal*
      *What language fails to know*
*And needs to say—*
   *What the body means—*
      *I take this sign*

And I make this mark:
    A woman in the doorway of her house.
        A river in the city of her birth.
The truth of a suffered life.
        The mouth of it.

The seabirds come in from the coast.
The city wisdom is they bring rain.
I watch them from my doorway.
I see them as arguments of origin—
Leaving a harsh force on the horizon
Only to find it
Slanting and falling elsewhere.

Which water—
The one they leave or the one they pronounce—
Remembers the other?

I am sure
The body of an ageing woman
Is a memory
And to find a language for it
Is as hard
As weeping and requiring
These birds to cry out as if they could
Recognize their element
Remembered and diminished in
A single tear.

An aging woman
Finds no shelter in language.
She finds instead
Single words she once loved
Such as "summer" and "yellow"
And "sexual" and "ready"
Have suddenly become dwellings
For someone else—
Rooms and a roof under which someone else
Is welcome, not her. Tell me,

*Anna Liffey,*
*Spirit of water,*
*Spirit of place,*
*How is it on this*
*Rainy Autumn night*
*As the Irish Sea takes*
*The names you made, the names*
*You bestowed, and gives you back*
*Only wordlessness?*

*Autumn rain is*
*Scattering and dripping*
*From carports*
*And clipped hedges.*
*The gutters are full.*

*When I came here*
*I had neither*
*children nor country.*
*The trees were arms.*
*The hills were dreams.*

*I was free*
*to imagine a spirit*
*in the blues and greens,*
*the hills and fogs*
*of a small city.*

*My children were born.*
*My country took hold of me.*
*A vision in a brick house.*
*Is it only love*
*that makes a place?*

*I feel it change.*
*My children are*
*growing up, getting older.*
*My country holds on*
*to its own pain.*

*I turn off*
*the harsh yellow*
*porch light and*
*stand in the hall.*
*Where is home now?*

*Follow the rain*
*out to the Dublin hills.*
*Let it become the river.*
*Let the spirit of place be*
*a lost soul again.*

*In the end*
*It will not matter*
*That I was a woman. I am sure of it.*
*The body is a source. Nothing more.*
*There is a time for it. There is a certainty*
*About the way it seeks its own dissolution.*
*Consider rivers.*
*They are always en route to*
*their own nothingness. From the first moment*
*They are going home. And so*
*when language cannot do it for us,*
*cannot make us know love will not diminish us,*
*there are these phrases*
*of the ocean*
*to console us.*
*Particular and unafraid of their completion*
*In the end*
*everything that burdened and distinguished me*
*will be lost in this:*
*I was a voice.*

◘

## For the Literary Traveler

The River Liffey was known as "Anna Liffey" or "Anna Livia" long before Joyce celebrated her as Anna Livia Plurabelle in *Finnegans Wake*.
For those who, like Boland, love the LIFFEY, there are many prospects to
be had on her in Dublin, where she reigns as the fair city's watery ma-
trix of beauty, commerce, and history. For better and worse, her banks
received Dublin's first Christian foundations and provided access to
Ireland's interior, first to the marauding Vikings in 841, then the Normans, and for centuries the British, who in 1916 climaxed their occupation by sailing a gunboat on her (it was actually an armed fishing
vessel) and bombarding the city.

Walking past the CUSTOM HOUSE on the north quays, you can see
Anna Livia represented in stone in the archway over the riverfront entrance to this eighteenth-century architectural masterpiece by James
Gandon. (The Custom House Visitors Center is worth a stop.) Celtic
religion revered rivers as female deities, but this English construct features Anna Livia, wreathed in garlands of thick braided hair, as the only
female on the building, Ireland's single river goddess among thirteen
sculpted river gods (who include—as an Irish river—the Atlantic
Ocean).

You can walk the river's thirteen bridges. QUEEN'S BRIDGE at Usher's
Quay (15 Usher's Island, the home of Joyce's aunts, was the setting of
"The Dead") is said to be the most beautiful. From here (and from
other bridges) you can see the spires and domes that grace the quays,
the huge dome of the FOUR COURTS on the north side, and the
CHURCH OF ADAM AND EVE (named for a tavern in Cook Street) in Merchant's Quay on the south side, which Joyce immortalizes in the opening lines of *Finnegans Wake*: "riverrun, past Eve and Adam's, from
swerve of shore to bend of bay, brings us by a commodius vicus of re-
circulation back to Howth Castle and Environs."

On a rainy day, or anytime at all, a striking overview of the polluted
river as it flows beneath HA'PENNY BRIDGE (so called because once you
had to pay a halfpenny toll to cross it) is from the top floor of the

WINDING STAIR CAFÉ AND BOOKSHOP on the river's north side at 40 Lower Ormond Quay. Housed in an ancient warehouse, the Winding Stair has a first-rate used-book store on the first and second floors and serves real coffee at the top, where you can sit beneath tall windows as long as you like. It's a great place to listen to Dubliners, watch the river run below, or read more Eavan Boland: "Dublin is a city of foghorns and gritty rain in the winter. And a city of beautiful distances and ocean colors in the summer. It is a city that is passionately loved by its own people," as she told her Stanford audience. (Colum McCann's "Along the Riverwall," from the prize-winning *Fishing the Sloe-Backed River* (1994), is a superb Liffey-centered story.)

Boland is well known in Dublin. "I was a voice," she declares with absolute precision in "Anna Liffey." (An easy way to find out if other women writers' voices are carrying in Ireland is by asking for them by name—the wonderful Dublin poet Paula Meehan or novelists Clare Boylan and Anne Enright—at Dublin's many bookstores. Around the corner from the Winding Stair is Eason's in O'Connell Street, next to the GPO, a good place to start. South of the Liffey are Greene's Bookshop in Clare Street, Fred Hanna's in Nassau Street, Books Upstairs in College Green, and Hodges Figges and Waterstone's in Dawson Street. Fitzgerald's bookstall at the Merchants' Arch on the southern end of the Ha'penny Bridge, where Bloom rents *Sweets of Sin* for Molly, has changed hands.) In a city dominated by writers of savage indignation, Boland's voice, her river sense of the beauty of being in time, carries you a far distance.

# Nuala O'Faolain

1 9 4 ? –

*Nuala O'Faolain grew up in north County Dublin, out along the Clon-*
*liffe Road in the areas of Baldoyle, Portmarnock, and Malahide when*
*they were still open country. Her life as the second of nine children of*
*an alcoholic mother and absent father drives the story behind* Are You
Somebody? The Accidental Memoir of a Dublin Woman, *a best-*
*seller in Ireland and the United States. A columnist for* The Irish
Times, *O'Faolain was asked to write an introduction to a collection of*
*her journalism; the introduction turned into this book. National Book*
*Award novelist Alice McDermott called it "a beautiful exploration of*
*human loneliness and happiness, of contentment and longing." Frank*
*McCourt said, "You don't want the book to end: it glows with compas-*
*sion." Her most recent book is a first novel,* I Dream of You (2001), *a*
*passionate story of Ireland's sexual politics, past and present.*

## FROM *ARE YOU SOMEBODY?*

Where we lived was beautiful, then. Not the big flat fields
around the bungalow—though even there, on a winter afternoon, I saw my first heron rise into the sky from a pond, grey on
grey—but the beaches and the cornfields and the old woods. And
the winding country roads, so little used then—at Malahide and
Rob's Walls and the front at Portmarnock—that sand drifted
across them and collected on them. In winter great wild waves
crashed up the sand at Portmarnock and broke over the road, and

across from the dunes there was a little wooden pub and some holiday shacks and then fields. The road around the estuary to Baldoyle flooded quickly and silently in winter, and we ran along the
grassy bank to school between silver sheets of floodwater. There
were no new houses. The parkland and fine houses of the landlords
stretched back almost to the edge of the city. Near us, there was a
deserted big house, shuttered and silent in the middle of woods.
The peacocks had been left behind there and gone wild, and they
called to each other all the night. We walked a mile to where the
bus from Dublin turned around. It was a country bus, going
through countryside on its way into town, stopping at the pubs that
marked each little hamlet. Everything was clean and bright.

At the shabby end of the main street of Malahide, where the air
was scented by a little candy factory, you turned down past a de-
crepit, elegant terrace, and at the bottom, at the water's edge, a
man with a rowboat would take you across to the sand and marram
grass of Malahide Island, where seabirds' eggs lay lavishly on the
ground, as at the Creation. You rang a big bell on a pole at the end
of the day, and the boatman came back across the water, shining
and still in the evening, to collect you. Or you stayed on Malahide
beach with your jam sandwiches and bottle of milk, and the people
in the houses would boil your kettle for the tea for a penny. . . .

◊        ◊

The outer boundaries of my experience when I was a student were,
in one direction, literature and the people who were opening my
mind to it, and, in the other direction, the business of love. Those
were what mattered. I had confidence about the learning. . . .

Yet I had no confidence at all at the other boundary—at the
business of love. Over the next few years, the few times I more or
less went "all the way," it wasn't because I wanted to but because I
was too shy about intimate things to talk about it. I didn't have the
self-confidence to indicate "no." Or when it came up, wordlessly,
the first time, I didn't have the words to say I didn't want to. Then,
by doing it, I gained the confidence to say we should stop. This was
the worst possible way of being with young men who were at least
as confused as I was.

The boys and girls at University College Dublin, as far as I know, were prudish, and they often lived at home or in hostels run by priests and nuns, and they were prone—I was, anyway—to ambush by Catholic scruples. Honest randiness was not admitted, even by the students across Dublin at Trinity College, except by some wistful rugby types from Northern Ireland I somehow knew, who persisted in believing that Catholic girls were "easy." But even the older men at Trinity—men from Britain who had done National Service, or former servicemen from America—had to bow to the customs of quiet contraceptive-free Dublin. Drinking and talking and incessant going to the pictures were, among other things, sublimation. . . .

Having friends was new. Learning from the enthusiasms of other people my own age was new. Knowing boys and men as companions was new. Not many people got to college thirty-odd years ago, and my fellow students, though often poor, were usually carefully raised. Most people left school at eleven, or fourteen, or after the Inter. They didn't get much of a chance to make friends of the opposite sex. They were meant to sense each other out at dances. That I did know about: the intensities in the laneways behind dance halls and coming out of the cinema with sore lips and swollen breasts. I did not know in any stable way how to behave. There was a cheap "invalid" wine then, called Vintara. I used to drink a lot of it. Onlookers, particularly if they had led sheltered lives, were appalled by how uninhibited it allowed a person to be.

It seemed to me that I was finished when I dropped out of UCD. Months of despair in London followed. I didn't even have the money to go to London, but that I took a job as a domestic in a hospital there. An agency in O'Connell Street paid your boat fare to that kind of job, the lowest of the low; then they took the money back out of your wages, so it was nearly impossible to save the fare home. I lived in a hostel near the hospital. I worked by myself in a basement room. There was a big tin machine that took dirty dishes in at one end and produced them at the other, a bit less dirty. I was in charge of that. I had been having a wonderful time at college. I'd had friends. Now I was so lonely in the evenings, lying on the bed, looking up at the window high in the wall, that my skin hurt. I tried not to think about Dublin, because all that was over, and as far as I knew for the rest of my life, I'd be some kind of an Irish worker in England. This experience of complete hopelessness went very deep. There were hardly any black people in England then, and no Asians. The Irish and—more recently—Cypriots were the servant class. Down at my level you just lived to work to earn enough to live another week of work. I didn't see any way out.

An accident got me the fare back to Ireland. Lives were ruined at that time, thousands and thousands of them, quite casually, by the rules the patriarchy made for young women. They were hotly pursued, and half longed to yield, but they were not able to defend themselves against pregnancy, and they were destroyed if they got pregnant. I got the fare back to Ireland through one of those tragic pregnancies.

An Irishwoman I knew—a successful, well-dressed executive assistant who normally wouldn't have mixed with me—thought she might be pregnant. She came to me and we went to a doctor. She took off her jumper and bra and he just peered at her and said yes, she was pregnant. He said it coldly. She paid him. Outside, it was a winter night. She held on to the wall, dry-eyed, trying to grasp the ruin that faced her. Almost the worst thing was: How would she tell her parents? In the end, I was given the fare to go back to Ireland to tell them, while she waited in London to hear how they took it.

That was how I got back to Dublin.

This young woman had barely begun her life when pregnancy struck her. But that is her story, for her to tell. All I know is that she hid out in Belfast and that I was there with her for the last few days before the baby was born. We walked around all the time, aimlessly, because we had no money to go in anywhere. I saw her a few hours after the birth, weeping in her bed, her milk seeping through the bandages she was tightly bound with. Her father came up from Dublin, and he and I were the only people in a side chapel when a priest baptised the baby. Then I took the baby to the train for Dublin. In Dublin I got a bus to a suburb. I handed the baby in to the nun in a home there, to be kept until it was adopted. All that way, the baby never cried. I didn't know until many years later that the mother used to go out to that home and look through the hedge at the children's playtime, in the hope of seeing a child who looked like herself.

◊ ◊

I did, after a year of near desperation, get back into college. The writer Mary Lavin—whose fondness for me was one of my strokes of luck—gave me an allowance for six weeks, to study to redo the exams. I had exactly enough for a room in Pembroke Street and a chip supper—which I thought about all day—in Cafolla's of Baggot Street Bridge. . . .

◊ ◊

Writing in itself was not revered in literary Dublin. A lot of people wrote, and no bones were made about it. It was not thought of as a raid on the inarticulate, or anything like that, so much as a craft that you might keep yourself by practising. It was something anyone might be engaged in. When I was around Dublin in the early 1960s I might call in to the National Library to see Mary Lavin. She wrote there, and in the foyer of Buswell's, and on a breadboard sitting up in her bed in Bective in the early morning, before she got her daughters up for school. Round in McDaid's, the novelist John Broderick might be getting ready to go home to Athlone, where his business was writing. Down in the Stag's Head, the playwright Tom McIntyre might be talking about writing with playwright Tom Kilroy, who was writing. Myles na Gopaleen* might be in Neary's, not talking to anyone. (I spent an evening there once with poet Louis MacNeice and the two men didn't address each other.) The novelist Ben Kiely might be in the White Horse on Burgh Quay, hypnotizing some young woman with his talk. My friend Sean Mac Réamoinn might be in the Tower Bar with a visiting writer, like Anthony Burgess. Liam O'Flaherty might be walking home along the canal. . . .

*Also known as Flann O'Brien (pseud. of Brian O'Nolan), author of *At Swim-Two-Birds*

Biographers of Irish writers will be scraping the barrel very deep if they ever come to me. But I'm representative of a certain milieu. For every real writer around, there were ten merely literary-minded people like me. Perhaps "literary Dublin" needed both kinds. It was a real place, even in the 1960s. Without question, writing mattered more than money or possessions or status in any other field. But the culture was terribly dependent on drink. There was too much public anecdotal life and not enough personal lyric life. There was too much drinking. Drinking means bad breath and crusted shirtfronts and shaking hands and bottles of milk wolfed down as a meal and waking in the morning on a pile of coats with no clean knickers and being thin, being cold, being sick. And drinking is, after all, about getting drunk. Fine people all but prostituted themselves to get the money to get stupidly drunk every single night. I saw Myles na Gopaleen urinate against the counter in Neary's one night. That's what being a drunk means: waking to the evidence of repeated lonely humiliations, that drive you further and further away from anything but drink. And whatever that kind of drinking did to men, it ruined women. I can think of only a few of the women (and I'm not one of them) who hung around McDaid's who were not, sometimes, squalid. You would think that way of life had been designed to test people to their limits. Certainly it could not be survived, only abandoned.

## For the Literary Traveler

Though the bucolic MALAHIDE, where O'Faolain grew up, is now car-choked on Saturday afternoons, it's still a lovely, peaceful place down on MALAHIDE BEACH on any sunny day. You're a literal stone's throw across from Donabate Peninsula and MALAHIDE ISLAND. As you head south toward Dublin, the coast road winds around the scenic points of Portmarnock, Lambay Island, and Howth, past Dollymount Strand and Bull Island, and down the CLONTARF ROAD into town. In the beginning of her memoir, O'Faolain describes walking this coast road into the city:

I could not get enough of looking at Dublin, which was Joyce's Dublin still, then, brown and dusty and dense with street life.... I would walk along Summerhill, which was a canyon of Georgian tenements then, with women sitting on the worn and beautiful front steps all the day long.... I would ... stop to look at anything.... No one sees a child watching.... Perhaps that habit of observation helped me to get my job with *The Irish Times*.

THE IRISH TIMES (its building is in D'Olier Street, between O'Connell Bridge and the junction of College and Pearse Streets) is a good source of the widely ranging opinion on the cultural revolution that Ireland has experienced since the repressiveness of O'Faolain's student years at UNIVERSITY COLLEGE DUBLIN (UCD). The turning point came in 1972, when the Irish people voted to join the EEC (the European Economic Community, now the EU), effectively removing the special position of the Roman Catholic Church from the Irish constitution. Subsequent referenda legalized contraception in 1986 and divorce (by a fraction of a percentage point) in 1997. Abortion was rejected in 1992. O'Faolain's portrait of extramarital sex and pregnancy as a punitive business in a pre-EEC Dublin is confirmed by novelist Roddy Doyle's comment: "Writing about herself, Nuala O'Faolain has also written about Ireland. It is a cruel and wounded place—and this book has become an important part of the cure."

O'Faolain's university career was saved by the writer Mary Lavin of Bective in Meath (see p. 98) and of 11 LAD LANE, a Dublin mews just off Baggot Street and FITZWILLIAM SQUARE EAST. Lavin's home and literary salon, where she gave so generously to young writers such as Nuala O'Faolain, is now occupied by a nurses' association that welcomes visitors. The view along Fitzwilliam Street East is glorious in both directions (except for the gauge left by a moronic Electricity Supply Board). Looking southwest, you see the Dublin mountains as the street's closing vista. To the northeast, down past the east side of Merrion Square, you see the HOLLES STREET HOSPITAL (the NATIONAL MATERNITY HOSPITAL), the setting of the "Oxen of the Sun" episode in *Ulysses* (where Bloom inquired after his friend Mrs. Purefoy, who'd been in labor for three days), as well as the setting of some of O'Faolain's fine *Irish Times* columns. In her student days, Dublin hospitals were not hospitable havens for women "in trouble." (In these not-so-long-ago "good old days"—a phrase still used in letters to *The Irish Times*—unmarried mothers, after having to give up their "illegitimate" babies for adoption or to an orphanage, were forced to live in a cloister and work in its laundry for the rest of their lives; *Eclipsed,* a 1999 play by Patricia Burke Brogan, dramatizes the lives of four young women confined to the infamous "Magdalene Laundries" in the 1960s.)

O'Faolain's point of view on literary Dublin's pub culture diverges from the Irish Tourist Board's promotion of the institution of the pub—and tourist pub crawls—as the cradle of the Irish writer's genius. She's a woman who's been there. Mapping the culture of booze, her book finds waste of talent, early burnout, and the abuse of women and children. From the hub of GRAFTON STREET, now a pedestrian shopping strip, you can find your way to a few legendary writers' hangouts on which O'Faolain casts her sharp, sober eye: NEARY'S in Chatham Street, favored by novelist Flann O'Brien (a.k.a. columnist Myles na Gopaleen), the author of *At Swim-Two-Birds* (1939), who died of alcoholism at the age of fifty-five. McDAID'S in Harry Street was the second home of poet Patrick Kavanagh* and dramatist Brendan Behan (1923–1964), author of *The Quare Fellow* (1956) and *The Hostage* (1958), who performed here alongside Gainor Crist, the model for the hero of J. P. Donleavy's novel, *The Ginger Man* (1955). Further down Grafton Street, past Trinity, and left into Fleet Street, THE PALACE, all old wood and glass, was in O'Faolain's student days a favorite haunt of *Irish Times* journalists and writers published and unpublished.

Dublin writers did—and do—take coffee breaks: in BEWLEY'S (in both Grafton Street and Westmoreland Street), where Joyce, Leopold Bloom, Beckett, and Belacqua Shuah were customers and which the *Blue Guide* ranks alongside other famous survivals of European cafes, such as the Café Greco in Rome, and Paris's Café Flore. Of the three, Bewley's is the friendliest. You can enjoy the company of friends or a book—and Harry Clarke's stained-glass windows—for as long as you

*Kavanagh, according to his friend Anthony Cronin, died after two decades of compulsive, "suicidal" drinking.

care to sit. Roddy Doyle prefers KYLEMORE'S BAKERY across from the GPO in Earl Street North.

O'Faolain's view of her native city's pub life—these days less self-conscious and much more fun—hits like a jolt of caffeine. It's consistent with the way she doesn't cover up her dysfunctional and alcoholic family, keeping you alert to the bracing truth telling and smart comedy of her story. O'Faolain and her transatlantic publishing success represents the Irish woman writer coming through despite a culture of drunken "geniuses" that once kept her silent. Today women are holding their own in literary Dublin that not so long ago was a fiercely besotted boys-only establishment.

# Roddy Doyle

## 1958–

*Born in working-class north Dublin, Doyle attended University College Dublin (UCD) before he became an secondary-school teacher in Kilbarrack (1979–93), the Barrytown of his fiction. He wrote (and self-published)* The Commitments *(1989), the first novel in the Barrytown Trilogy, over school holidays, then sent it out to publishers in England, who mailed it back to him unopened. It was Alan Parker's film of this novel about the rise and fall of a rock band who brought soul to Dublin that rocketed Doyle to fame. Six novels later—*The Snapper *(1990),* The Van *(1991),* Paddy Clarke Ha Ha Ha *(1993), which won the Booker, Britain's highest literary award,* The Woman Who Walked into Doors *(1996), and the historical masterpiece* A Star Called Henry *(1999)—he is arguably contemporary Ireland's most original and popular writer. His compassionate and fiercely comic insight into a Dublin culture of poverty, alcohol, and family has deepened with each book. The feisty, rude characters of* The Commitments—*manager Jimmy Rabbitte, Outspan, Derek, singer*

*Deco, James on keyboard, trumpeter Joey the Lips, drummer Billy Mooney, Dean Fay on sax, and singers Imelda, Bernie, and Natalie— embody Doyle's respect for the resourceful people of the so-called anonymous wasteland of Kilbarrack. His ear for "Dubliny" dialogue is pitch perfect. It's a special sound, and in the later novels the emotional complexity it captures is astounding.*

FROM CHAPTER 1, *THE COMMITMENTS*

We'll ask Jimmy, said Outspan. —Jimmy'll know.
Jimmy Rabbitte knew his music. He knew his stuff alright. You'd never see Jimmy coming home from town without a new album or a 12-inch or at least a 7-inch single. Jimmy ate Melody Maker and the NME every week and Hot Press every two weeks. He listened to Dave Fanning and John Peel. He even read his sisters' Jackie when there was no one looking. So Jimmy knew his stuff.

The last time Outspan had flicked through Jimmy's records he'd seen names like Microdisney, Eddie and the Hot Rods, Otis Redding, The Screaming Blue Messiahs, Scraping Foetus off the Wheel (—Foetus, said Outspan. —That's the little young fella inside the woman, isn't it?

—Yeah, said Jimmy.

—Aah, that's fuckin' horrible, tha' is.); groups Outspan had never heard of, never mind heard. Jimmy even had albums by Frank Sinatra and The Monkees.

So when Outspan and Derek decided, while Ray was out in the jacks, that their group needed a new direction they both thought of Jimmy. Jimmy knew what was what. Jimmy knew what was new, what was new but wouldn't be for long and what was going to be new. Jimmy had Relax before anyone had heard of Frankie Goes to Hollywood and he'd started slagging them months before anyone realized that they were no good. Jimmy knew his music.

Outspan, Derek and Ray's group, And And And, was three days old; Ray on the Casio and his little sister's glockenspiel, Outspan on his brother's acoustic guitar, Derek on nothing yet but the bass guitar as soon as he'd the money saved.

—Will we tell Ray? Derek asked.

—Abou' Jimmy? Outspan asked back.

—Yeah.

————Better not. Yet annyway.

Outspan was trying to work his thumb in under a sticker, This Guitar Kills Fascists, his brother, an awful hippy, had put on it.

—There's the flush, he said. —He's comin' back. We'll see Jimmy later.

They were in Derek's bedroom.

Ray came back in.

—I was thinkin' there, he said. —I think maybe we should have an exclamation mark, yeh know, after the second And in the name.

—Wha'?

—It'd be And And exclamation mark, righ', And. It'd look deadly on the posters.

Outspan said nothing while he imagined it.

—What's an explanation mark? said Derek.

—Yeh know, said Ray.

He drew a big one in the air.

—Oh yeah, said Derek. —An' where d'yeh want to put it again?

—And And,

He drew another one.

—And.

—Is it not supposed to go at the end?

—It should go up his arse, said Outspan, picking away at the sticker.

Jimmy was already there when Outspan and Derek got to the Pub.

—How's it goin', said Jimmy.

—Howyeh, Jim, said Outspan.

—Howayeh, said Derek.

They got stools and formed a little semicircle at the bar.

—Been ridin' annythin' since I seen yis last? Jimmy asked them.

—No way, said Outspan. —We've been much too busy for tha' sort o' thing. Isn't tha' righ'?

—Yeah, that's righ', said Derek.

—Puttin' the finishin' touches to your album? said Jimmy.

—Puttin' the finishin' touches to our name, said Outspan.

—Wha' are yis now?

—And And exclamation mark, righ'? ——And, said Derek.
Jimmy grinned a sneer.

—Fuck, fuck, exclamation mark, me. I bet I know who thought
o' tha'.

—There'll be a little face on the dot, righ', Outspan explained.

—An' yeh know the line on the top of it? That's the dot's fringe.

—Black an' whi'e or colour?

—Don't know.

—It's been done before, Jimmy was happy to tell them. —Ska.
Madness, The Specials. Little black an' whi'e men. ———I told
yis, he hasn't a clue.

———Yeah, said Outspan.

—He owns the synth though, said Derek.

—Does he call tha' fuckin' yoke a synth? said Jimmy.

—Annyway, no one uses them annymore. It's back to basics.

—Just as well, said Outspan. —Cos we've fuck all else.

—Wha' tracks are yis doin'? Jimmy asked.

—Tha' one, Masters and Servants.

—Depeche Mode?

—Yeah.

Outspan was embarrassed. He didn't know why. He didn't
mind the song. But Jimmy had a face on him.

—It's good, tha', said Derek. —The words are good, yeh know
———good.

—It's just fuckin' art school stuff, said Jimmy.

That was the killer argument, Outspan knew, although he didn't
know what it meant.

Derek did.

—Hang on, Jimmy, he said. —That's not fair now. The Beatles
went to art school.

—That's different.

—Me hole it is, said Derek. —An' Roxy Music went to art
school an' you have all their albums, so yeh can fuck off with
yourself.

Jimmy was fighting back a redner.

—I didn't mean it like tha', he said. —It's not the fact tha' they went to fuckin' art school that's wrong with them. It's—(Jimmy was struggling.) —more to do with—(Now he had something.)— —the way their stuff, their songs like, are aimed at gits like them-selves. Wankers with funny haircuts. An' rich das. ——An' fuck all else to do all day 'cept prickin' around with synths.

—Tha' sounds like me arse, said Outspan. —But I'm sure you're righ'.

—Wha' else d'yis do?

—Nothin' yet really, said Derek. —Ray wants to do tha' one, Louise. It's easy.

—Human League?

—Yeah.

Jimmy pushed his eyebrows up and whistled.

They agreed with him.

Jimmy spoke. —Why exactly ——d'yis want to be in a group?

—Wha' d'yeh mean? Outspan asked.

He approved of Jimmy's question though. It was getting to what was bothering him, and probably Derek too.

—Why are yis doin' it, buyin' the gear, rehearsin'? Why did yis form the group?

—Well——

—Money?

—No, said Outspan. —I mean, it'd be nice. But I'm not in it for the money.

—I amn't either, said Derek.

—The chicks?

—Jaysis, Jimmy!

—The brassers, yeh know wha' I mean. The gee. Is tha' why?

———No, said Derek.

—The odd ride now an' again would be alrigh' though wouldn't it? said Outspan.

—Ah yeah, said Derek. —But wha' Jimmy's askin' is is tha' the reason we got the group together. To get our hole.

—No way, said Outspan.

—Why then? said Jimmy.

He'd an answer ready for them.

—It's hard to say, said Outspan.

That's what Jimmy had wanted to hear. He jumped in.

—Yis want to be different, isn't tha' it? Yis want to do somethin' with yourselves, isn't tha' it?

—Sort of, said Outspan.

—Yis don't want to end up like (he nodded his head back) —these tossers here. Amn't I righ'?

Jimmy was getting passionate now. The lads enjoyed watching him.

—Yis want to get up there an' shout I'm Outspan fuckin' Foster.

He looked at Derek.

—An' I'm Derek fuckin' Scully, an' I'm not a tosser. Isn't tha' righ'? That's why yis're doin' it. Amn't I righ'?

—I s'pose yeh are, said Outspan.

—Fuckin' sure I am.

—With the odd ride thrown in, said Derek.

They laughed.

Then Jimmy was back on his track again.

—So if yis want to be different what're yis doin' doin' bad versions of other people's poxy songs?

That was it. He was right, bang on the nail. They were very impressed. So was Jimmy.

—Wha' should we be doin' then? Outspan asked.

—It's not the other people's songs so much, said Jimmy. —It's which ones yis do.

—What's tha' mean?

—Yeh don't choose the songs cos they're easy. Because fuckin' Ray can play them with two fingers.

—Wha' then? Derek asked.

Jimmy ignored him.

—All tha' mushy shite abou' love an' fields an' meetin' mots in supermarkets an' McDonald's is gone, ou' the fuckin' window. It's dishonest, said Jimmy. —It's bourgeois.

—Fuckin' hell!

—Tha' shite's ou'. Thank Jaysis.

—What's in then? Outspan asked him.

—I'll tell yeh, said Jimmy. —Sex an' politics.

—WHA'?

—Real sex. Not mushy I'll hold your hand till the end o' time stuff. ——Ridin'. Fuckin'. D'yeh know wha' I mean?

—I think so.

—Yeh couldn't say Fuckin' in a song, said Derek.

—Where does the fuckin' politics come into it? Outspan asked.

—Yeh'd never get away with it.

—Real politics, said Jimmy.

—Not in Ireland annyway, said Derek. —Maybe England. But they'd never let us on Top o' the Pops.

—Who the fuck wants to be on Top o' the Pops? said Jimmy.

Jimmy always got genuinely angry whenever Top of the Pops was mentioned although he never missed it.

—I never heard anyone say it on The Tube either, said Derek.

—I did, said Outspan. —Your man from what's their name said it tha' time the mike hit him on the head.

Derek seemed happier.

Jimmy continued. He went back to sex.

—Believe me, he said. —Holdin' hands is ou'. Lookin' at the moon, tha' sort o' shite. It's the real thing now.

He looked at Derek.

—Even in Ireland. ——Look, Frankie Goes To me arse were shite, righ'?

They nodded.

—But Jaysis, at least they called a blow job a blow job an' look at all the units they shifted?

—The wha'?

—Records.

They drank.

Then Jimmy spoke. —Rock an' roll is all abou' ridin'. That's wha' rock an' roll means. Did yis know tha'? (They didn't.) —Yeah, that's wha' the blackies in America used to call it. So the time has come to put the ridin' back into rock an' roll. Tongues, gooters, boxes, the works. The market's huge.

—Wha' abou' this politics?

—Yeah, politics. ——Not songs abou' Fianna fuckin' Fail or annythin' like tha'. Real politics. (They weren't with him.) —Where are yis from? (He answered the question himself.) —Dublin. (He asked another one.) —Wha' part o' Dublin? Barrytown. Wha' class are yis? Workin' class. Are yis proud of it? Yeah, yis are. (Then a practical question.) —Who buys the most records? The workin' class. Are yis with me? (Not really.) —Your music should be abou' where you're from an' the sort o' people yeh come from. ——— Say it once, say it loud, I'm black an' I'm proud.

They looked at him.

—James Brown. Did yis know————never mind. He sang tha'. ———An' he made a fuckin' bomb.

They were stunned by what came next.

—The Irish are the niggers of Europe, lads.

They nearly gasped: it was so true.

—An' Dubliners are the niggers of Ireland. The culchies have fuckin' everythin'. An' the northside Dubliners are the niggers o' Dublin. ———Say it loud, I'm black an' I'm proud.

He grinned. He'd impressed himself again.

He'd won them. They couldn't say anything.

—Yis don't want to be called And And exclamation mark And, do yis? Jimmy asked.

—No way, said Outspan.

—Will yeh manage us, Jimmy? said Derek.

—Yeah, said Jimmy. —I will.

They all smiled.

—Am I in charge? Jimmy asked them.

—Yeah.

—Righ' then, said Jimmy. —Ray isn't in the group annymore.

This was a shock.

—Why not?

—Well, first we don't need a synth. An' second, I don't like the cunt.

They laughed.

—I never have liked him. I fuckin' hate him to be honest with yis.

————I don't like him much meself, said Outspan.

—He's gone so?

He was gone.

—Wha' sort o'stuff will we be doin'? Derek asked.

—Wha' sort o'music has sex an' politics? Jimmy asked.

—Reggae, said Derek.

—No, not tha'.

—It does.

—Yeah, but we won't be doin' it. We'll leave the reggae to the skinheads an' the spacers.

—Wha' then?

—Soul.

—Soul?

—Soul?

—Soul. Dublin soul.

Outspan laughed. Dublin soul sounded great.

—Another thing, said Jimmy. —Yis aren't And And And annymore.

This was a relief.

—What are we Jimmy?

—The Commitments.

Outspan laughed again.

—That's a rapid name, said Derek.

—Good, old fashioned THE, said Jimmy.

—Dublin soul, said Outspan.

He laughed again.

—Fuckin' deadly.

The day after the formation of The Commitments Jimmy sent an ad into the Hot Press classifieds:

—Have you got Soul? If yes, The World's Hardest Working Band is looking for you. Contact J. Rabbitte, 118, Chestnut Ave., Dublin 21. Rednecks and southsiders need not apply.

◻◇◻

## For the Literary Traveler

KILBARRACK, the actual setting of Doyle's Barrytown trilogy (*The Commitments, The Snapper,* and *The Van*), lies in a no-frills north Dublin neighborhood of housing estates off the Clontarf/Howth Road, about a mile beyond Stephen Dedalus's Bull Island. You can get here in about half an hour on the Howth-bound city bus (31) or the northbound DART, or you can take a taxi. Don't listen to either the cabbies who warn you Kilbarrack's no place for a "daycent" person like yourself or the literary critics who advise that, in the words of one, "Kilbarrack contains not a single place to which a tourist to Ireland might choose to go." Along streets of small houses, a few parks, churches, and the GREENDALE COMMUNITY SCHOOL (where Doyle taught geography and English while writing the trilogy), kids kick soccer balls, ride bikes, play hookey. In the early 1990s, drugs were part of the turf. Doyle, whose understanding of the working-class poor has been compared to Sean O'Casey's, has listened to his neighbors, his students, and their families, picking up on their quick-wittedness, their love of fun, their refusals of despair. Wandering through these streets—Saint Margaret's Avenue, Greendale Road, Briarfield Road—you pass the homes of many families like Jimmy Rabbitte's of *The Commitments* (and of his father, Jimmy Rabbitte Sr., in *The Snapper* and *The Van*). You can also listen to their Dublinese ("English as she is spoke in Dublin") in nearby pubs on Malahide, Raheny, and Kilbarrack Roads or further south on DOLLYMOUNT STRAND, where members of the band joke about getting a ride in the dunes, and where in *The Van* Bimbo and the great Jimmy Rabbitte Sr. drive into the sea. (The ILAC LIBRARY in the ILAC Shopping Centre on Parnell Street, around the corner from the markets of Moore Street—in the "city centre," as Kilbarrack people refer to Dublin—is where Jimmy Senior hangs out in the early days of his unemployment, before the van takes over his life. Like most public libraries, this one, rich in faces and vivid details, is worth a visit.)

Though the word *possibility* does not come to mind as you walk around Kilbarrack, that is exactly what Doyle has uncovered and brought to life in his novels about its people. Like writers everywhere who have paid attention in such plain places as Bathgate Avenue in the Bronx, Mango Street in Chicago, or Testaccio in Rome, Doyle has seen that beneath the monotonous surfaces failure is not inevitable. Defiantly, local life springs eternal.

⊏◇⊐

# James Joyce
## 1882–1941

*At the age of six, Joyce was enrolled in Clongowes Wood College, a Jesuit boarding school for wealthy boys in County Kildare and the setting for a good part of Book I of* A Portrait of the Artist as a Young Man. *In 1891, Joyce's father, no longer able to pay the tuition fees, withdrew his oldest son from Clongowes. A few years later, the Jesuit Father Conmee, remembering Joyce's academic gifts, accepted him into Belvedere College on a full-tuition scholarship. Though Joyce later left the Catholic Church, he always valued his fourteen years as a student among the Jesuits. "You allude to me as a Catholic . . . now you ought to allude to me, for the sake of precision and to get the correct contour on me, . . . as a Jesuit. From them I have learnt to arrange things in such a way that they become easy to survey and to judge."*

FROM *A PORTRAIT OF THE ARTIST
        AS A YOUNG MAN*

BOOK I

O nce upon a time and a very good time it was there was a moocow coming down along the road and this moocow that was coming down along the road met a nicens little boy named baby tuckoo. . . .

His father told him that story: his father looked at him through a glass: he had a hairy face.

He was a baby tuckoo. The moocow came down the road where Betty Byrne lived: she sold lemon platt.

> O, the wild rose blossoms
> On the little green place.

He sang that song. That was his song.

> O, the green wothe botheth.

When you wet the bed first it is warm then it gets cold. His mother put on the oilsheet. That had the queer smell.

His mother had a nicer smell than his father. She played on the piano the sailor's hornpipe for him to dance. He danced:

> Tralala lala
> Tralala tralaladdy
> Tralala lala
> Tralala lala.

Uncle Charles and Dante clapped. They were older than his father and mother but uncle Charles was older than Dante. . . .

Sitting in the studyhall he opened the lid of his desk and changed the number pasted up inside from seventy-seven to seventy-six. But the Christmas vacation was very far away: but one time it would come because the earth moved round always.

There was a picture of the earth on the first page of his geography: a big ball in the middle of clouds. Fleming had a box of crayons and one night during free study he had coloured the earth green and the clouds maroon. That was like the two brushes in Dante's press, the brush with the green velvet back for Parnell and the brush with the maroon velvet back for Michael Davitt. But he had not told Fleming to colour them those colours. Fleming had done it himself.

He opened the geography to study the lesson; but he could not learn the names of places in America. Still they were all different places that had those different names. They were all in different countries and the countries were in continents and the continents were in the world and the world was in the universe.

He turned to the flyleaf of the geography and read what he had written there: himself, his name and where he was.

*Stephen Dedalus*
*Class of Elements*
*Clongowes Wood College*
*Sallins*
*County Kildare*
*Ireland*
*Europe*
*The World*
*The Universe*

That was in his writing: and Fleming one night for a cod had written on the opposite page:

*Stephen Dedalus is my name,*
*Ireland is my nation.*
*Clongowes is my dwellingplace*
*And heaven my expectation.*

He read the verses backwards but then they were not poetry. Then he read the flyleaf from the bottom to the top till he came to his own name. That was he: and he read down the page again. What was after the universe? Nothing. But was there anything round the universe to show where it stopped before the nothing place began? It could not be a wall but there could be a thin thin line there all round everything. It was very big to think about every-thing and everywhere. Only God could do that. He tried to think what a big thought that must be but he could think only of God. God was God's name just as his name was Stephen. *Dieu* was the French for God and that was God's name too; and when anyone prayed to God and said *Dieu* then God knew at once that it was a

French person that was praying. But though there were different names for God in all the different languages in the world and God understood what all the people who prayed said in their different languages still God remained always the same God and God's real name was God.

The bell rang for night prayers and he filed out of the studyhall after the others and down the staircase and along the corridors to the chapel. The corridors were darkly lit and the chapel was darkly lit. Soon all would be dark and sleeping. There was cold night air in the chapel and the marbles were the colour the sea was at night. The sea was cold day and night: but it was colder at night. It was cold and dark under the seawall beside his father's house. But the kettle would be on the hob to make punch.

The prefect of the chapel prayed above his head and his memory knew the responses:

> *O Lord, open our lips*
> *And our mouth shall announce Thy praise.*
> *Incline unto our aid, O God!*
> *O Lord, make haste to help us!*

There was a cold night smell in the chapel. But it was a holy smell. It was not like the smell of the old peasants who knelt at the back of the chapel at Sunday mass. That was a smell of air and rain and turf and corduroy. But they were very holy peasants. They breathed behind him on his neck and sighed as they prayed. They lived in Clane, a fellow said.

⊏◇⊐

## For the Literary Traveler

*A Portrait* opens with a memory of Joyce's birthplace at 41 Brighton Square West in RATHGAR, a suburb south of Dublin. (Take the number 15 bus from O'Connell Bridge to Brighton Road. The house is marked with a plaque.) The home that Stephen daydreams about at school still stands beside the sea at BRAY, a Wicklow town thirteen miles south of Dublin. The Christmas dinner scene, with its furious argument over Parnell and religion, took place here, at 1 Martello Terrace (visible from the Bray DART station), the house where the Joyces moved when Joyce was five years old.

The sensuality of particular places is the language Stephen loves to the point of ecstasy in *A Portrait of the Artist*. In all its dark and open spaces, CLONGOWES WOOD COLLEGE, still a boarding school for boys, makes a strong imprint on the map of his unfolding imagination. (If you call in advance—(045) 868202—or show up when a Jesuit is free to escort you, you can visit the buildings and grounds.) The forty-five-minute drive from Dublin goes west to the N7 and Naas; exit at Sallins/Clane, go north through Sallins to Clane, and turn left onto the L25. A mile and a half out of Clane, on the right, Clongowes's high, un-marked gates open upon a long avenue of limetrees leading to CASTLE BROWN, the school's main building. The dormitories, refectory, and classrooms have been rebuilt since Joyce's time, but the old chapel where in the novel Stephen attends night prayers is still open to stu-dents and people from Sallins and Clane. The indoor swimming pool and the infirmary where Stephen fantasizes about death are also in use and unaltered. Upstairs a reception room overlooks the playing fields and the moat or "ha ha" where in 1794 the patriot Hamilton Rowan threw his hat from the window as a decoy to the British sol-diers who were shooting at him through the front doors, a story of cunning in the face of brute force that made a deep impression on Joyce. The most dramatic change at Clongowes is the addition of Joyce's picture—next to Father Conmee's—in the SERPENTINE GALLERY, "the low dark narrow corridor that led to the castle," its walls hung with framed faces from the Jesuit past, where Stephen walked on his way to the rector's office to complain about injustice. It wasn't so long ago that the Irish Jesuits kept a tight-lipped silence about their famous alumnus. Now, about Joyce (whose books are in the school library), they've loosened up. "It's a much happier place now," my Jesuit guide, who'd taught at Clongowes for fifty years, told me. "There was too much fear then."

# Cormac Mac Airt

### d. 267?

*Ancient lore, according to historian Peter Harbison, sees the mythical Cormac Mac Airt as the most famous king who reigned on the Hill of Tara, the seat of the High Kings of pagan Celtic Ireland, "in the early centuries after Christ." The grandson of Conn of the Hundred Battles, Cormac appears in* The Cycle of the Kings *as a lost boy raised by she-wolves, "the delight of many for his beauty and grace and dignity and strength and judgment." He grew up to become the legendary hero of the golden age of the pre-Christian Celtic warrior aristocracy. Also according to legend, after his conversion to Christianity he was cursed by a druid and later choked to death on a salmon bone. He was buried not among his pagan ancestors in* Bruig na Boinne *(the nearby Knowth, Dowth, and Newgrange, one of the largest and best-preserved clusters of passage graves in western Europe), but in* Rath na Riogh *(Rosnaree) with his body facing due east, toward the rising sun.*

## CORMAC MAC AIRT PRESIDING AT TARA

Beautiful was the appearance of Cormac in that assembly, flowing and slightly curling was his golden hair. A red buckler with stars and animals of gold and fastenings of silver upon him. A crimson cloak in wide descending folds around him, fastened at his neck with precious stones. A torque of gold around his neck. A white shirt with a full collar, and intertwined with red gold thread upon him. A girdle of gold, inlaid with precious stones, was around him. Two wonderful shoes of gold, with golden loops upon his feet.

Two spears with golden sockets in his hands, with many rivets of red bronze. And he was himself, besides, symmetrical and beautiful of form, without blemish or reproach.

*Version: Douglas Hyde*

## *For the Literary Traveler*

The HILL OF TARA, "the glory of the Gael" in royal Meath, is halfway between Dublin and Navan (off the N3). An interpretive center in the nineteenth-century church on the hill (May through mid-June, 9:30–5; mid-June through mid-Sept., 9:30–6:30; mid-Sept. through Oct., 10–5) introduces Tara as an important site in every stage of Ireland's history: prehistoric religious and domestic settlement; the royal acropolis of the High Kings of Celtic Ireland; as a site of Christian assembly and pilgrimage; and as the location of one of Daniel O'Connell's political "monster rallies" of one million people for the cause of Catholic emancipation.

A guided tour identifies the important earthworks spread over these low, unspectacular hills: THE BANQUET HALL, where everyone sat in places according to status; GRAINNE'S FORT, whence Grainne, Cormac's daughter, ran off with young Diarmuid, instead of marrying her father's long-in-the-tooth general Finn MacCool (the event on which the tragic tale of the *Pursuit of Diarmuid and Grainne* is based); the RATH OF THE SYNODS, a ring fort where Patrick supposedly held church assemblies; the MOUND OF THE HOSTAGES, where good King Cormac imprisoned his captives from Connacht who then died within the chamber, and the LIA FAIL (Stone of Destiny), the stone used in the inauguration of the High Kings and popularly known as BOD FHEARGHUIS ("Fergus's Penis"), said to cry out in confirmation when a true king stood on it. To the south is the RATH OF HIGH KING LAOGHAIRE, who forced a confrontation with Patrick when he saw his Easter fire glowing from the nearby Hill of Slane (see p. 97). About a half a mile south is RATH MEDB (Maeve's hill fort), in some legends linked to Maeve (her name is a cognate in many languages for intoxication, "the one who makes drunk"), the ruling queen/earth goddess of the royal hill, as she was also of the Hill of Rathcroghan in Roscommon. The man who would be king was required to bed her after he had drunk wine or ale in acknowledgment of her sovereignty. The mounds of Tara are rich with stories of passion and pride, but it is from the solitary heights that you can best imagine back into the past: see the Celts when, sometime around 350 B.C., they first discovered this great hill fort of their Stone Age ancestors and "as soon as they set eyes on it," in the words of William Trevor, knew it as "a holy place."

⊏◇⊐

# Thomas Cahill

## 1940 –

*Thomas Cahill grew up in the Bronx listening to his mother's stories about the Kerry and Galway that his grandparents knew. When he first saw Ireland with his own eyes, it was the remains of the pre-Christian and early Christian past strewn all over the landscape that struck his imagination. After many Irish journeys and a book (*A Literary Guide to Ireland, *co-written with this author), he wrote* How the Irish Saved Civilization: The Untold Story of Ireland's Heroic Role from the Fall of Rome to the Rise of Medieval Europe *(1995), of which Thomas Keneally, Irish-Australian author of* Schindler's List *and* The Great Shame, *said, "It reads like a love story, it sings to the imagination. It connects Celtic legend to Irish history, Celtic lore to Irish politics, and proves the persistence of wild Celtic love and mysticism. For its portrait of St. Patrick alone, it will resonate in the memory."*

FROM *HOW THE IRISH SAVED CIVILIZATION*

### CHAPTER IV, "GOOD NEWS FROM FAR OFF: THE FIRST MISSIONARY"

Of the many legends surrounding Patrick, few can be authenticated. He did not chase the snakes out of Ireland. There is no way of knowing whether he used the shamrock to explain the Trinity. He probably did have a confrontation with a king, possibly the high king at Tara, and it may have been over his right to commemorate Christ's resurrection by lighting a bonfire—the same fire that has become a permanent feature of all Easter liturgies. Even Patrick's great prayer in Irish—sometimes called "Saint Patrick's Breastplate" because it was thought to protect him from hostile powers, sometimes called "The Deer's Cry" because it was thought to make him resemble a deer to the eyes of those seeking to do him harm—cannot be definitely ascribed to him. Characteristics of its language would assign it to the seventh, or even to the eighth, century. On the other hand, it is Patrician to its core, the first ringing assertion that the universe itself is the Great Sacrament, magically designed by its loving Creator to bless and succor human beings. The earliest expression of European vernacular poetry, it is, in attitude, the work of a Christian druid, a man of both faith and magic. Its feeling is entirely un-Augustinian; but it is this feeling that will go on to animate the best poetry of the Middle Ages. If Patrick did not write it (at least in its current form), it surely takes its inspiration from him. For in this cosmic incantation, the inarticulate outcast who wept for slaves, aided common men in difficulty, and loved sunrise and sea at last finds his voice. Appropriately, it is an Irish voice:

*I arise today*
*Through a mighty strength, the invocation of the Trinity,*
*Through belief in the threeness,*
*Through confession of the oneness*
*Of the Creator of Creation.*

*I arise today*
*Through the strength of Christ's birth with his baptism,*
*Through the strength of his crucifixion with his burial,*
*Through the strength of his resurrection with his ascension,*
*Through the strength of his descent for the judgment of Doom.*

*I arise today*
*Through the strength of the love of Cherubim,*
*In obedience of angels,*

*In the service of archangels,*
*In hope of resurrection to meet with reward,*
*In prayers of patriarchs,*
*In predictions of prophets,*
*In preaching of apostles,*
*In faith of confessors,*
*In innocence of holy virgins,*
*In deeds of righteous men.*

*I arise today*
*Through the strength of heaven:*
*Light of sun,*
*Radiance of moon,*
*Splendor of fire,*
*Speed of lightning,*
*Swiftness of wind,*
*Depth of sea,*
*Stability of earth,*
*Firmness of rock.*

*I arise today*
*Through God's strength to pilot me:*
*God's might to uphold me,*
*God's wisdom to guide me,*
*God's eye to look before me,*
*God's ear to hear me,*
*God's word to speak for me,*
*God's hand to guard me,*
*God's way to lie before me,*
*God's shield to protect me,*
*God's host to save me*
*From snares of devils,*
*From temptations of vices,*
*From everyone who shall wish me ill,*
*Afar and anear,*
*Alone and in multitude.*

*I summon today all these powers between*
  *me and those evils,*

*Against every cruel merciless power that may oppose my*
    *body and soul*
*Against incantations of false prophets,*
*Against black laws of pagandom,*
*Against false laws of heretics,*
*Against craft of idolatry,*
*Against spells of witches and smiths and wizards,*
*Against every knowledge that corrupts man's body and soul.*

*Christ to shield me today*
*Against poison, against burning,*
*Against drowning, against wounding,*
*So that there may come to me abundance of reward.*
*Christ with me, Christ before me, Christ behind me,*
*Christ in me, Christ beneath me, Christ above me,*
*Christ on my right, Christ on my left,*
*Christ when I lie down, Christ when I sit down, Christ*
    *when I arise,*
*Christ in the heart of every man who thinks of me,*
*Christ in the mouth of everyone who speaks of me,*
*Christ in every eye that sees me,*
*Christ in every ear that hears me.*

*I arise today*
*Through a mighty strength, the invocation of the Trinity,*
*Through belief in the threeness,*
*Through confession of the oneness,*
*Of the Creator of Creation.*

The key to Patrick's confidence—and it is the sort of ringing, rock-solid confidence on which a civilization may be built, an un-muffled confidence not heard since the Golden Ages of Greece and Rome—is in his reliance on "the Creator of Creation," the phrase with which the "Breastplate" opens and closes. Our Father in heaven, having created all things, even things that have since be-come bent or gone bad, will deliver us, his children, from all evil. . . . [And] from the celebratory spirit of the "Breastplate" will spring the characteristic art and poetry of the western world—the immense symbolic power of the medieval liturgy, the smiling angels of Gothic art, the laughable demons, the sweetness of poets like Francis of Assisi (whose "Canticle of the Sun" could almost be mistaken for a Celtic poem), Dante (who spoke of "the love that moves the sun and the other stars"), and Chaucer (whose "Crea-*tour* of every crea*ture*" is almost a line from the "Breastplate"). Nor did this spirit die at the close of the Middle Ages. For it remains a continuing tradition in British and Irish poetry that takes us down to the present—from the gentle visions of George Herbert and Thomas Traherne to the excited ecstasies of Gerard Manley Hopkins, from the mysticism of Joseph Plunkett—who wrote "I See His Blood upon the Rose" not in the fifth century but in the twentieth—to the Christian druidism of Seamus Heaney, who to this day is carving out poems that might stop even Derdriu in her tracks.

In this tradition, there is a trust in the objects of sensory perception, which are seen as signposts from God. But there is also a sensuous reveling in the splendors of the created world, which would have made Roman Christians exceedingly uncomfortable. I think it likely that, had Augustine ever read the "Breastplate," he would have sniffed heresy. Even in Patrick's *Confession* and *Letter*, which no one disputes came from his pen, there are emphases and omissions that Augustine would have found unnerving. Where, in Patrick's own story, is there any negative treatment of the temptations of the flesh? . . . Patrick is as silent about sex as are the Gospels.

## For the Literary Traveler

Kidnapped as a teenager from his home near the west coast of Roman Britain by Irish pirates and slave traders, Patrick spent six years as a slave tending pigs on Slemish Mountain in Antrim (see p. 434) before escaping. Years later, by his own request, he returned to Ireland, where he spent the rest of his life doing dangerous and difficult missionary work. Though he was aware of his lack of education (and the con-tempt in which the educated British clergy held him), he traveled everywhere, overcoming the old warrior religion with the message of the Gospel. He became, in Cahill's words, "the first human being in the history of the world to speak out unequivocally against slavery." The origin of "St. Patrick's Breastplate" is, like much of what we've heard about him, a mix of fact and fiction. Supposedly composed in 433 in the reign of the pagan King Laoghaire of Tara who ordered Patrick to Tara after his defiant lighting of the Easter fire on the nearby Hill of Slane—the druidic fire on Tara was always to be lit first—the lines were Patrick's song, a shield against danger, as he walked straight into enemy territory.

THE HILL OF SLANE is one of the loveliest destinations in the BOYNE VALLEY. Less than a mile north of the village of Slane (eight miles north-west of Navan), it overlooks the whole of the Boyne Valley, from Trim to Drogheda. The site of Patrick's first countercultural Easter liturgy, Slane has become the symbolic setting of the kindling of the Christian message throughout Ireland. Patrick's friend, St. Erc, whose hermitage is not yet open to the public, founded a monastery here; there was also a medieval abbey. The present friary on the hill dates from a small Franciscan foundation of 1512. From the church's tower, you can look down over the Meath countryside, a sweep of lush and rolling pas-tureland. It calls to mind Patrick's mystical Christianity, a "sense of the world as holy, as the Book of God—as a healing mystery." The Hill of Slane is also the contemporary setting of an annual rite of summer—rock concerts by U2, the Rolling Stones, and many others, drawing au-diences of up to a hundred thousand.

# Mary Lavin

## 1912–1996

*"I cannot think of any Irish writer who has gone so profoundly with-
out fear into the Irish heart. This fearlessness makes her remarkable." The praise of V. S. Pritchett, a master of the short story himself,
underscores Mary Lavin's prominence on modern Ireland's literary
landscape. She started out in Massachusetts, then moved to Ireland
with her Irish parents at the age of ten. As an adult, she lived in a
house across the fields from Bective Abbey in County Meath beside
the River Boyne. At University College Dublin, she was writing her
doctoral dissertation on Virginia Woolf when her first short story
came to her. That was the end of her as an academic. Never again did
she write "a single paragraph that has not had its source in the imagination." She married, bore three daughters, and, left a widow in
1954, supported her family by farming as well as writing—a few novels and twelve volumes of short stories. Of these, Alice Munro has
said: "Mary Lavin's stories have always given me a feeling of wonder
and security—security because of the way the view keeps opening up,
with such ease and authority, and wonder because she is, after all, so
intrepid, so original and astonishing."*

## IN THE MIDDLE OF THE FIELDS

Like a rock in the sea, she was islanded by fields, the heavy grass
washing about the house, and the cattle wading in it as in water.
Even their gentle stirrings were a loss when they moved away at
evening to the shelter of the woods. A rainy day might strike a wet
flash from a hay barn on the far side of the river—not even a habi-

tation! And yet she was less lonely for him here in Meath than else-where. Anxieties by day, and cares, and at night vague, nameless fears—these were the stones across the mouth of the tomb. But who understood that? People thought she hugged tight every memory she had of him. What did they know about memory? What was it but another name for dry love and barren longing? They even tried to unload upon her their own small purposeless memories. "I imagine I see him every time I look out there," they would say as they glanced nervously over the darkening fields when they were leaving. "I think I ought to see him coming through the trees." Oh, for God's sake! she'd think. I'd forgotten him for a minute!

It wasn't him *she* saw when she looked out at the fields. It was the ugly tufts of tow and scutch that whitened the tops of the grass and gave it the look of a sea in storm, spattered with broken foam. That grass would have to be topped. And how much would it cost?

At least Ned, the old herd, knew the man to do it for her. "Bart-ley Crossen is your man, ma'am. Your husband knew him well."

She couldn't place him at first. Then she remembered. "Oh, yes—that's his hay barn we see, isn't it? Why, of course! I know him well—by sight, I mean." And so she did—splashing past on the road in a big muddy car, the wheels always caked with clay, and the wife in the front seat beside him.

"I'll get him to call around and have a word with you, ma'am," said the herd.

"Before dark!" she cautioned.

But there was no need to tell him. The old man knew how she always tried to be upstairs before it got dark, locking herself into her room, which opened off the room where the children slept, praying devoutly that she wouldn't have to come down again for anything—above all, not to answer the door. That was what in par-ticular she dreaded: a knock after dark.

"Ah, sure, who'd come near you, ma'am, knowing you're a woman alone with small children that might be wakened and set crying? And, for that matter, where could you be safer than in the middle of the fields, with the innocent beasts asleep around you?"

If he himself had to come to the house late at night for any reason—to get hot water to stoup the foot of a beast, or to call the
vet—he took care to shout out long before he got to the gable. "It's
me, ma'am!" he'd shout. "Coming! Coming!" she'd cry, gratefully,
as quick on his words as their echo. Unlocking her door, she'd run
down and throw open the hall door. No matter what the hour! No
matter how black the night! "Go back to your bed now, you,
ma'am," he'd say from the darkness, where she could see the
swinging yard lamp coming nearer and nearer like the light of a little boat drawing near to a jetty. "I'll put out the lights and let myself out." Relaxed by the thought that there was someone in the
house, she would indeed scuttle back into bed, and, what was
more, she'd be nearly asleep before she'd hear the door slam. It
used to sound like the slam of a door a million miles away.

There was no need to worry. He'd see that Crossen came early.

◊    ◊

It was well before dark when Crossen did drive up to the door. The
wife was with him, as usual, sitting up in the front seat the way people sat up in the well of little tub traps long ago, their knees pressed
together, allowing no slump. The herd had come with them, but
only he and Crossen got out.

"Won't your wife come inside and wait, Mr. Crossen?" she
asked.

"Oh, not at all, ma'am. She likes sitting in the car. Now, where's
this grass that's to be cut? Are there any stones lying about that
would blunt the blade?" Going around the gable of the house, he
looked out over the land.

"There's not a stone or a stump in it," Ned said. "You'd run
your blade over the whole of it while you'd be whetting it twenty
times in another place!"

"I can see that," said Bartley Crossen, but absently, she thought.

He had walked across the lawn to the rickety wooden gate that
led into the pasture, and leaned on it. He didn't seem to be looking
at the fields at all, though, but at the small string of stunted thorns
that grew along the riverbank, their branches leaning so heavily

out over the water that their roots were almost dragged clear of the clay.

Suddenly he turned around and gave a sigh. "Ah, sure, I didn't need to look! I know it well!" As she showed surprise, he gave a little laugh, like a young man. "I courted a girl down there when I was a lad," he said. "That's a queer length of time ago now, I can tell you!" He turned to the old man. "You might remember it." Then he looked back at her. "I don't suppose you were thought of at all in those days, ma'am," he said, and there was something kindly in his look and in his words. "You'd like the mowing done soon, I suppose? How about first thing in the morning?"

Her face lit up. But there was the price to settle. "It won't be as dear as cutting meadow, will it?"

"Ah, I won't be too hard on you, ma'am," he said. "I can promise you that!"

"That's very kind of you," she said, but a little doubtfully.

Behind Crossen's back, Ned nodded his head in approval. "Let it go at that, ma'am," he whispered as they walked back toward the car. "He's a man you can trust."

And when Crossen and the wife had driven away, he reassured her again. "A decent man," he said. Then he gave a laugh—it, too, was a young kind of laugh for a man of his age; it was like a nudge. "Did you hear what he said, though—about the girl he courted down there? Do you know who that was? It was his first wife! You know he was twice married? Ah, well, it's so long ago I wouldn't wonder if you never heard it. Look at the way he spoke about her himself, as if she was some girl he'd all but forgotten! The thorn trees brought her to his mind! That's where they used to meet, being only youngsters, when they first took up with each other.

"Poor Bridie Logan—she was as wild as a hare. And she was mad with love, young as she was! They were company-keeping while they were still going to school. Only nobody took it seriously—him least of all, maybe—till the winter he went away to the agricultural college in Athenry. She started writing to him then. I used to see her running up to the postbox at the crossroads every other evening. And sure, the whole village knew where the letter was going. His people were fit to be tied when he came home in the summer and said he wasn't going back, but was going to marry Bridie. All the same, his father set them up in a cottage on his own land. It's the cottage that's used now for stall-feds—it's back of the new house. Oh, but you can't judge it now for what it was then! Giddy and all as she was—as lightheaded as a thistle—you should have seen the way she kept that cottage. She'd have had it scrubbed away if she didn't start having a baby. He wouldn't let her take the scrubbing brush into her hands after that!"

"But she wasn't delicate, was she?"

"Bridie? She was as strong as a kid goat, that one! But I told you she was mad about him, didn't I? Well, after she was married to him she was no better—worse, you'd say. She couldn't do enough for him! It was like as if she was driven on by some kind of a fever. You'd only to look in her eyes to see it. Do you know! From that day to this, I don't believe I ever saw a woman so full of going as that one! Did you ever happen to see little birds flying about in the air like they were flying for the divilment of it and nothing else? And did you ever see the way they give a sort of a little leap in the air, like they were forcing themselves to go a bit higher still—higher than they ought? Well, it struck me that was the way Bridie was acting, as she rushed about that cottage doing this and doing that to make him prouder and prouder of her. As if he could be any prouder than he was already and the child getting noticeable!"

"She didn't die in childbed?"

"No. Not in a manner of speaking, anyway. She had the child, nice and easy, and in their own cottage, too, only costing him a few shillings for one of the women that went in for that kind of job long ago. And all went well. It was no time till she was let up on her feet again. I was there the first morning she had the place to herself! She was up and dressed when I got there, just as he was going out to milk.

" 'Oh, it's great to be able to go out again,' she said, taking a great breath of the morning air as she stood at the door looking after him. 'Wait! Why don't I come with you to milk!' she called suddenly. Then she threw a glance back at the baby asleep in its crib by the window.

" 'Oh, it's too far for you, Bridie!' " he cried. The cows were down in the little field by the river—you know the field, alongside the road at the foot of the hill on this side of the village. And knowing she'd start coaxing him, he made out of the gate with the cans.

" 'Good man!' I said to myself. But the next thing I knew, she'd darted across the yard.

" 'I can go on the bike if it's too far to walk!' she said. And up she got on her old bike, and out she pedaled through the gate.

" 'Bridie, are you out of your mind?' he shouted as she whizzed past him.

" 'Arrah, what harm can it do me?' she shouted back.

"I went stiff with fright looking after her. And I thought it was the same with him, when he threw down the cans and started down the hill after her. But looking back on it, I think it was the same fever as always was raging in her that started raging in him, too. Mad with love, that's what they were, both of them—she only wanting to draw him on, and he only too willing!

" 'Wait for me!' he shouted, but before she'd even got to the bottom she started to brake the bike, putting down her foot like you'd see a youngster do, and raising up such a cloud of dust we could hardly see her."

"She braked too hard!"

"Not her! In the twinkle of an eye she'd stopped the bike, jumped off, turned it round, and was pedaling madly up the hill again, her head down on the handlebars like a racing cyclist. But that was the finish of her!"

"Oh, no! What happened?"

"She stopped pedaling all of a sudden, and the bike half stopped, and then it started to go back down the hill a bit, as if it skidded on the loose gravel at the side of the road. That's what I thought happened, and him, too, I suppose, because we both began to run down the hill. She didn't get time to fall before we got to her. But what use was that? It was some kind of internal bleeding that took her. We got her into the bed, and the neighbors came running, but she was gone before the night."

"Oh, such a thing to happen! And the baby?"

"Well, it was a strong child! And it grew into a fine lump of a lad. That's the fellow that drives the tractor for him now—the oldest son, Bartley."

"Well, I suppose his second marriage had more to it, when all was said and done."

"That's it. And she's a good woman—the second one. The way she brought up that child of Bridie's! And filled the cradle, year after year, with sons of her own. Ah sure, things always work out for the best in the end, no matter what!" he said, and he started to walk away.

"Wait a minute, Ned," she said urgently. "Do you really think he forgot about her—for years, I mean?"

"I'd swear it," said the old man. And then he looked hard at her. "It will be the same with you, too," he added kindly. "Take my word for it. Everything passes in time and is forgotten."

As she shook her head doubtfully, he nodded emphatically. "When the tree falls, how can the shadow stand?" he said. And he walked away.

I wonder! she thought as she walked back to the house, and she envied the practical country way that made good the defaults of nature as readily as the broken sod knits back into the sward.

◊      ◊

Again that night, when she went up to her room, she looked down toward the river and she thought of Crossen. Had he really forgotten? It was hard for her to believe, and with a sigh she picked up her hairbrush and pulled it through her hair. Like everything else about her lately, her hair was sluggish and hung heavily down, but after a few minutes under the quickening strokes of the brush, it lightened and lifted, and soon it flew about her face like the spray above a weir. It had always been the same, even when she was a child. She had only to suffer the first painful drag of the bristles when her mother would cry out, "Look! Look! That's electricity!" and a blue spark would shine for an instant like a star in the gray depths of the mirror.

That was all they knew of electricity in those dim-lit days when valleys of shadow lay deep between one piece of furniture and another. Was it because rooms were so badly lit then that they saw it

so often, that little blue star? Suddenly she was overcome by longing to see it again, and, standing up impetuously, she switched off
the light.

It was just then that, down below, the iron fist of the knocker
was lifted and, with a loud, confident stroke, brought down on the
door.

It wasn't a furtive knock. She admitted that even as she sat stark
with fright in the darkness. And then a voice that was vaguely familiar called out—and confidently—from below.

"It's me, ma'am! I hope I'm not disturbing you!"

"Oh, Mr. Crossen!" she cried out with relief, and, unlocking her
door, she ran across the landing and threw up a window on that
side of the house. "I'll be right down!" she called.

"Don't come down, ma'am!" he shouted. "I only want one
word with you."

"But of course I'll come down!" She went back to get her dressing gown and pin up her hair, but as she did she heard him stomp-
ing his feet on the gravel. It had been a mild day, but with night a
chill had come in the air, and, for all that it was late spring, there
was a cutting east wind coming across the river. "I'll run down and
let you in from the cold," she called, and, twisting up her hair, she
held it against her head with her hand without waiting to pin it,
and she ran down the stairs in her bare feet to unbolt the door.

"You were going to bed, ma'am!" he said accusingly the minute
she opened the door. And where he had been so impatient a
minute beforehand, he stood stock-still in the open doorway. "I
saw the lights were out downstairs when I was coming up the
drive," he said contritely. "But I didn't think you'd gone up for the
night!"

"Neither had I!" she said lyingly, to put him at his ease. "I was
just upstairs brushing my hair. You must excuse me!" she added,
because a breeze from the door was blowing her dressing gown
from her knees, and to pull it across she had to take her hand from
her hair, so that the hair fell down about her shoulders. "Would
you mind closing the door for me?" she said, with some embarrassment, and she began to back up the stairs. "Please go inside to the
sitting room, won't you?" she said, nodding toward the door of the

small room off the hall. "Put on the light. I'll be down in a minute."

But although he had obediently stepped inside the door and closed it, he stood stoutly in the middle of the hall. "I shouldn't have come in at all," he said. "I know you were going to bed! Look at you!" he cried again in the same accusing voice, as if he dared her this time to deny it. He was looking at her hair. "Excuse my saying so, ma'am, but I never saw such a fine head of hair. God bless it!" he said quickly, as if afraid he had been rude. "Doesn't a small thing make a big differ," he said impulsively. "You look like a young girl!"

In spite of herself, she smiled with pleasure. She wanted no more of it, all the same. "Well, I don't feel like one!" she said sharply.

What was meant for a quite opposite effect, however, seemed to delight him and put him wonderfully at ease. "Ah sure, you're a sensible woman! I can see that," he said, and, coming to the foot of the stairs, he leaned comfortably across the newel post. "Let you stay the way you are, ma'am," he said. "I've only a word to say to you, and it's not worth your while going up them stairs. Let me have my say here and now and be off about by business! The wife will be waiting up for me, and I don't want that!"

She hesitated. Was the reference to his wife meant to put her at *her* ease? "I think I ought to get my slippers," she said cautiously. Her feet were cold.

"Oh, yes, put something on your feet!" he cried, only then seeing that she was in her bare feet. "But as to the rest, I'm long gone beyond taking any account of what a woman has on her. I'm gone beyond taking notice of women at all."

But she had seen something to put on her feet. Under the table in the hall was a pair of old boots belonging to Richard, with fleece lining in them. She hadn't been able to make up her mind to give them away with the rest of his clothes, and although they were big and clumsy on her, she often stuck her feet into them when she came in from the fields with mud on her shoes. "Well, come in where it's warm, so," she said. She came back down the few steps and stuck her feet into the boots, and then she opened the door of the sitting room.

She was glad she'd come down. He'd never have been able to put on the light. "There's something wrong with the center light," she said as she groped along the wainscot to find the socket for the reading lamp. It was in an awkward place, behind the desk. She had to go down on her knees.

"What's wrong with it?" he asked, as, with a countryman's interest in practicalities, he clicked the switch up and down to no effect.

"Oh, nothing much, I'm sure," she said absently. "There!" She had found the socket. The room was lit up with a bright white glow.

"Why don't you leave the plug in the socket, anyway?" he asked critically.

"I don't know," she said. "I think someone told me it's safer, with reading lamps, to pull them out at night. There might be a short circuit, or mice might nibble at the cord, or something— I forget what I was told. I got into the habit of doing it, and now I keep on." She felt a bit silly.

But he was concerned about it. "I don't think any harm could be done," he said gravely. Then he turned away from the problem. "About tomorrow, ma'am," he said, somewhat offhandedly, she thought. "I was determined I'd see you tonight, because I'm not a man to break my word—above all, to a woman."

What was he getting at?

"Let me put it this way," he said quickly. "You'll understand, ma'am, that as far as I am concerned, topping land is the same as cutting hay. The same time. The same labor cost. And the same wear and tear on the blade. You understand that?"

On her guard, she nodded.

"Well now, ma'am, I'd be the first to admit that it's not quite the same for you. For you, topping doesn't give the immediate return you'd get from hay—"

"There's no return from it!" she exclaimed crossly.

"Oh, come now, ma'am, come! Good grassland pays as well as anything—you know you won't get nice sweet pickings for your beasts from neglected land, but only dirty old tow grass knotting under their feet. It's just that it's not a quick return, and so—as you know—I made a special price for you."

"I do know!" she said impatiently. "But I thought that part of it was settled and done."

"Oh, I'm not going back on it, if that's what you think," he said affably. "I'm glad to do what I can for you, ma'am, the more so seeing you have no man to attend to these things for you but only yourself alone."

"Oh, I'm well able to look after myself," she said, raising her voice.

Once again her words had an opposite effect to what she intended. He laughed good-humoredly. "That's what all women like to think!" he said. "Well, now," he said in a different tone of voice, and it annoyed her to see he seemed to think something had been settled between them, "it would suit me—and I'm sure it's all the same with you—if we could leave your little job till later in the week, say till nearer to the time of the haymaking generally. Because by then I'd have the cutting bar in good order, sharpened and ready for use. Whereas now, while there's still a bit of ploughing to be done here and there, I'll have to be chopping and changing, between the plough and the mower, putting one on one minute and the other the next!"

"As if anyone is still ploughing this time of the year!" Her eyes hardened.

"Harrowing then," he conceded.

"Who are you putting before me?" she demanded.

"Now, take it easy, ma'am. No one. Leastways, not without getting leave first from you."

"Without telling me you're not coming, you mean!"

"Oh, now, ma'am, don't get cross. I'm only trying to make matters easy for everyone."

But she was very angry now. "It's always the same story. I thought you'd treat me differently! I'm to wait till after this one, and after that one, and in the end my fields will go wild!"

He looked a bit shamefaced. "Ah now, ma'am, that's not going to be the case at all. Although, mind you, some people don't hold with topping, you know."

"I hold with it."

"Oh, I suppose there's something in it," he said reluctantly. "But the way I look at it, cutting the weeds in July is a kind of a topping."

"Grass cut before it goes to seed gets so thick at the roots no weeds can come up!" she cried, so angry she didn't realize how authoritative she sounded.

"Faith, I never knew you were so well up, ma'am," he said, looking at her admiringly, but she saw he wasn't going to be put down by her. "All the same now, ma'am, you can't say a few days here or there could make any difference?"

"A few days could make all the difference! This farm has a gravely bottom to it, for all it's so lush. A few days of drought could burn it to the butt. And how could I mow it then? What cover would there be for the 'nice sweet pickings' you were talking about a minute ago?" Angrily, she mimicked his own accent without thinking.

He threw up his hands. "Ah well, I suppose a man may as well admit when he's bested," he said. "Even by a woman. And you can't say I broke my promise."

"I can't say but you tried hard enough," she said grudgingly, although she was mollified that she was getting her way. "Can I offer you anything?" she said then, anxious to convey an air of finality to their discussion.

"Oh, not at all, ma'am! Nothing, thank you! I'll have to be getting home." He stood up.

She stood up, too.

"I hope you won't think I was trying to take advantage of you," he said as they went toward the door. "It's just that we must all make out as best we can for ourselves—isn't that so? Not but you're well able to look after yourself, I must say. No one ever thought you'd stay on here after your husband died. I suppose it's for the children you did it?" He looked up the well of the stairs. "Are they asleep?"

"Oh, long ago," she said indifferently. She opened the hall door.

The night air swept in immediately, as it had earlier. But this time, from far away, it bore along on it the faint scent of new-mown hay. "There's hay cut somewhere already!" she exclaimed in surprise. And she lifted her face to the sweetness of it.

For a minute, Crossen looked past her out into the darkness, then he looked back. "Aren't you ever lonely here at night?" he asked suddenly.

"You mean frightened?" she corrected quickly and coldly.

"Yes! Yes, that's what I meant," he said, taken aback. "Ah, but why would you be frightened! What safer place could you be under the sky than right here with your own fields all about you!"

What he said was so true, and he himself as he stood there, with his hat in his hand, so normal and natural it was indeed absurd to think that he would no sooner have gone out the door than she would be scurrying up the stairs like a child. "You may not believe it," she said, "but I am scared to death sometimes! I nearly died when I heard your knock on the door tonight. It's because I was scared that I was upstairs," she said, in a further burst of confidence. "I always go up the minute it gets dark. I don't feel so frightened up in my room."

"Isn't that strange now?" he said, and she could see he found it an incomprehensibly womanly thing to do. He was sympathetic all the same. "You shouldn't be alone! That's the truth of the matter," he said. "It's a shame!"

"Oh, it can't be helped," she said. There was something she wanted to shrug off in his sympathy, while at the same time there was something in it she wanted to take. "Would you like to do something for me?" she asked impulsively. "Would you wait and put out the lights down here and let me get back upstairs before you go?"

After she had spoken, for a minute she felt foolish, but she saw at once that, if anything, he thought it only too little to do for her. He was genuinely troubled about her. And it wasn't only the present moment that concerned him; he seemed to be considering the whole problem of her isolation and loneliness. "Is there nobody could stay here with you—at night even? It would have to be another woman, of course," he added quickly, and her heart was warmed by the way—without a word from her  he rejected that solution out of hand. "You don't want a woman about the place," he said flatly.

"Oh, I'm all right, really. I'll get used to it," she said.

"It's a shame, all the same," he said. He said it helplessly, though, and he motioned her toward the stairs. "You'll be all right for tonight, anyway," he said. "Go on up the stairs now, and I'll put out the lights." He had already turned around to go back into the sitting room.

Yet it wasn't quite as she intended for some reason, and it was somewhat reluctantly that she started up the stairs.

"Wait a minute! How do I put out this one?" he called from the sitting room door before she was halfway up the stairs.

"Oh, I'd better put out that one myself," she said, thinking of the awkward position of the socket. She ran down again, and, going past him into the little room, she knelt and pulled at the cord. Instantly the room was deluged in darkness. And instantly she felt that she had done something stupid. It was not like turning out a light by a switch at the door and being able to step back at once into the lighted hall. She got to her feet as quickly as she could, but as she did, she saw that Crossen was still in the doorway. His bulk was blocked out against the light beyond. "I'll leave the rest to you," she said, in order to break the peculiar silence that had come down on the house.

But he didn't move. He stood there, the full of the doorway.

"The other switches are over there by the hall door," she said, unwilling to brush past him. Why didn't he move? "Over there," she repeated, stretching out her arm and pointing, but instead of moving he caught at her outstretched arm, and, putting out his other hand, he pressed his palm against the door jamb, barring the way.

"Tell me," he whispered, his words falling over each other, "are you never lonely—at all?"

"What did you say?" she said in a clear voice, because the thickness of his voice sickened her. She had hardly heard what he said. Her one thought was to get past him.

He leaned forward. "What about a little kiss?" he whispered, and to get a better hold on her he let go the hand he had pressed against the wall, but before he caught at her with both hands she had wrenched her arm free of him, and, ignominiously ducking under his armpit, she was out next minute in the lighted hall.

Out there—because light was all the protection she needed from him, the old fool—she began to laugh. She had only to wait for him to come sheepishly out.

But there was something she hadn't counted on; she hadn't counted on there being anything pathetic in his sheepishness. There was something pitiful in the way he shambled into the light, not raising his eyes. And she was so surprisingly touched by him that before he had time to utter a word she put out her hand. "Don't feel too bad," she said. "I didn't mind."

Even then, he didn't look at her. He just took her hand and pressed it gratefully, his face still turned away. And to her dismay she saw that his nose was running water. Like a small boy, he wiped it with the back of his fist, streaking his face. "I don't know what came over me," he said slowly. "I'm getting on to be an old man now. I thought I was beyond all that." He wiped his face again. "Beyond letting myself go, anyway," he amended miserably.

"Oh, it was nothing," she said.

He shook his head. "It wasn't as if I had cause for what I did."

"But you did nothing," she protested.

"It wasn't nothing to me," he said dejectedly.

For a minute, they stood there silent. The hall door was still ajar, but she didn't dare to close it. What am I going to do with him now, she thought. I'll have him here all night if I'm not careful. What time was it, anyway? All scale and proportion seemed to have gone from the night. "Well, I'll see you in the morning, Mr. Crossen," she said, as matter-of-factly as possible.

He nodded, but made no move. "You know I meant no disrespect to you, ma'am, don't you?" he said then, looking imploringly at her. "I always had a great regard for you. And for your husband, too. I was thinking of him this very night when I was coming up to the house. And I thought of him again when you came to the door looking like a young girl. I thought what a pity it was him to be taken from you, and you both so young! Oh, what came over me at all? And what would Mona say if she knew?"

"But you wouldn't tell her, I hope!" she cried. What sort of a figure would she cut if he told about her coming down in her bare feet with her hair down her back? "Take care would you tell her!" she warned.

"I don't suppose I ought," he said, but he said it uncertainly and morosely, and he leaned back against the wall. "She's been a good woman, Mona. I wouldn't want anyone to think different. Even the boys could tell you. She's been a good mother to them all these years. She never made a bit of difference between them. Some say she was better to Bartley than to any of them! She reared him from a week old. She was living next door to us, you see, at the time"—he hesitated—"At the time I was left with him," he finished in a flat voice. "She came in that first night and took him home to her own bed—and, mind you, that wasn't a small thing for a woman who knew nothing about children, not being what you'd call a young girl at the time, in spite of the big family she gave me afterwards. She took him home that night, and she looked after him. It isn't every woman would care to be responsible for a newborn baby. That's a thing a man doesn't forget easy! There's many I know would say that if she hadn't taken him someone else would have, but no one only her would have done it the way she did.

"She used to have him all day in her own cottage, feeding him and the rest of it. But at night, when I'd be back from the fields, she'd bring him home and leave him down in his little crib by the fire alongside of me. She used to let on she had things to do in her own place, and she'd slip away and leave us alone, but that wasn't her real reason for leaving him. She knew the way I'd be sitting looking into the fire, wondering how I'd face the long years ahead, and she left the child there with me to break my thoughts. And she was right. I never got long to brood. The child would give a cry, or a whinge, and I'd have to run out and fetch her to him. Or else she'd hear him herself maybe, and run in without me having to call her at all. I used often think she must have kept every window and door in her place open, for fear she'd lose a sound from either of us. And so, bit by bit, I was knit back into a living man. I often wondered what would have become of me if it wasn't for her. There are men and when the bright way closes to them there's no knowing but they'll take a dark way. And I was that class of man.

"I told you she used to take the little fellow away in the day and bring him back at night? Well, of course, she used to take him away again coming on to the real dark of night. She'd take him away to her own bed. But as the months went on and he got bigger, I could see she hated taking him away from me at all. He was beginning to smile and play with his fists and be real company. 'I wonder ought I leave him with you tonight?' she'd say then, night after night. And sometimes she'd run in and dump him down in the middle of the big double bed in the room off the kitchen, but the next minute she'd snatch him up again. 'I'd be afraid you'd overlie him! You might only smother him, God between us and all harm!' 'You'd better take him,' I'd say. I used to hate to see him go myself by this time. All the same, I was afraid he'd start crying in the night, and what would I do then? If I had to go out for her in the middle of the night, it could cause a lot of talk. There was talk enough as things were, I can tell you, although there was no grounds for it. I had no more notion of her than if she wasn't a woman at all— would you believe that? But one night when she took him up and put him down, and put him down and took him up, and went on and went on about leaving him or taking him, I had to laugh. 'It's a pity you can't stay along with him, and that would settle all,' I said. I was only joking her, but she got as red as fire, and next thing she burst out crying! But not before she'd caught up the child and wrapped her coat around him. Then, after giving me a terrible look, she ran out of the door with him.

"Well, that was the beginning of it. I'd no idea she had any feelings for me. I thought it was only for the child. But men are fools, as women well know, and she knew before me what was right and proper for us both. And for the child, too. Some women have great insight into these things! And God opened my own eyes then to the woman I had in her, and I saw it was better I took her than wasted away after the one that was gone. And wasn't I right?"

"Of course you were right," she said quickly.

But he slumped back against the wall, and the abject look came back into his eyes.

I'll never get rid of him, she thought desperately. "Ah, what ails you!" she cried impatiently. "Forget it, can't you?"

"I can't," he said simply. "And it's not only me—it's the wife I'm thinking about. I've shamed her!"

"Ah, for heaven's sake. It's nothing got to do with her at all."

Surprised, he looked up at her. "You're not blaming yourself, surely?" he asked.

She'd have laughed at that if she hadn't seen she was making headway. Another stroke and she'd be rid of him. "Arrah, what are you blaming any of us for!" she cried. "It's got nothing to do with any of us—with you, or me, or the woman at home waiting for you. It was the other one! That girl—your first wife—Bridie! It was her! Blame her! She's the one did it!" The words had broken from her. For a moment, she thought she was hysterical and that she could not stop. "You thought you could forget her," she said, "but see what she did to you when she got the chance!" She stopped and looked at him.

He was standing at the open door. He didn't look back. "God rest her soul," he said, and he stepped into the night.

## *For the Literary Traveler*

Lavin introduces us to BECTIVE, a small village about six miles southwest of Tara (or left off the Navan/Trim road [R162] going south), in "A Likely Story" in *Tales from Bective Bridge*:

> Do you know Bective? Like a bird in the nest, it presses close to the soft green mound of the river bank, its handful of houses no more significant by day than the sheep that dot the far fields. But at night, when all its little lamps are lit, house by house, it is marked out on the hillside as clearly as the Great Bear is marked

out in the sky. And on a still night it throws its shape in glitter on the water.

Just beside the triple-arched BECTIVE BRIDGE over the RIVER BOYNE there's a spiked gate, and beyond it the gray ruins of BECTIVE ABBEY. From the road you can see the stone cottage with the tin roof, which local people point out as the place where Mary Lavin wrote her stories; you can't see ABBEY FARM, the house where she raised her family, now occupied by a new owner. Bective Abbey, in the middle of fields where cattle graze, is the second of forty Cistercian abbeys in Ireland, a daughter (founded 1146) of the mother house, Mellifont Abbey in County Louth (just north of Slane). This landscape feels eternal, like the voice of the story: "Like a rock in the sea, she was islanded by fields, the heavy grass washing about the house, and the cattle wading in it as in water." The quiet presence of Lavin Country, well suited to the art she called "looking closer than normal into the human heart," continues along the back roads around Bective. You pass a few gone-to-seed houses and heaps of junk. The conversation among the customers in the combination pub and grocery at the Bective/Tara crossroad comes across as uneventful, like this rural backwater looks. At first glance you think nothing much is going on in Bective. But as in Lavin's fiction, beneath the still surfaces everything that matters might be going on.

Maps of the Boyne River Valley Scenic Walk are available in the local Tourist Information Offices of County Meath and in the Meath Heritage Centre in nearby Trim. In the lounge bar of the Wellington Court Hotel (on the Summerhill Road, leaving Trim), there's a local clientele that puts a face to some of Mary Lavin's volatile characters. There's also a receptionist, who in 1999—three years after Lavin's death—dished out a sample of an Irish Fact (definable, in the words of Hugh Kenner, "as anything they will tell you in Ireland, where you get told a great deal and had best assume a demeanor of wary appreciation"). In response to the receptionist's asking what brought me to Trim, I mentioned my interest in the local writer Mary Lavin. "Is it Mary Lavin you're after, is it?" said she. "Ah, she comes in here for her tea. A lovely woman! You've only just missed her!"

# JOHN MILLINGTON SYNGE

### 1871–1909

*The man whose plays launched the Abbey Theatre spent many summers walking through Wicklow, where his Anglo-Irish family owned property. What the city is to Joyce's fiction, the open road is to Synge's drama: a random world he transformed into art in many poems and in the plays* In the Shadow of the Glen, The Well of the Saints, The Tinker's Wedding, *and* The Playboy of the Western World. *For himself and for his characters, the journeys through the heathery mountains and valleys of Wicklow were adventures of escape and liberation. Synge, who also explored the Aran Islands (see p. 339), Kerry (see p. 229), and Mayo (see p. 361), had no use for late-Victorian drawing rooms or their cultural conventions. An outsider in a family that never stopped disapproving of him (they attended none of his plays), he preferred the company of itinerant beggars and local folk who inspired his dramatic characters' rich individuality. The dialogue he wrote for them brought audiences to riot in Dublin, New York, and Philadelphia. Synge's independent mind and the support of Yeats, who was director of the Abbey Theatre at the time, sustained him as the major playwright of the Celtic Revival (or Irish Literary Renaissance) despite the loud resistance of nationalists and the bourgeoisie to the realism of his plays.*

*He died of Hodgkin's disease at the age of thirty-seven in the Elpis Nursing Home on Lower Mount Street in Dublin, near Merrion Square. (Beckett, who admired Synge's plays and shared his love of walking the Dublin and Wicklow hills, chose this setting for the death of his "hero" Belacqua in* More Pricks than Kicks.*) George Moore recalls the scene in his autobiography* Hail and Farewell:

An hour before he died he asked the nurse to wheel his bed into a room whence he could see the Wicklow mountains . . . and he was wheeled into the room, but the mountains could not be seen from the windows; to see them it was necessary to stand up, and Synge couldn't stand or sit up in his bed, so his last wish remained ungratified and he died with tears in his eyes.

## IN GLENCULLEN

*Thrush, linnet, stare and wren,*
*Brown lark beside the sun,*
*Take thought of kestril, sparrow-hawk,*
*Birdlime and roving gun.*

*You great-great-grand-children*
*Of birds I've listened to,*
*I think I robbed your ancestors*
*When I was young as you.*

## TO THE OAKS OF GLENCREE

*My arms are round you, and I lean*
*Against you, while the lark*
*Sings over us, and golden lights, and green*
*Shadows are on your bark.*

*There'll come a season when you'll stretch*
*Black boards to cover me:*
*Then in Mount Jerome\* I will lie, poor wretch,*
*With worms eternally.*

*The Protestant cemetery in Dublin

## PRELUDE

*Still south I went and west and south again,*
*Through Wicklow from the morning till the night,*
*And far from cities, and the sights of men,*
*Lived with the sunshine and the moon's delight.*

*I knew the stars, the flowers, and the birds,*
*The grey and wintry sides of many glens,*
*And did but half remember human words,*
*In converse with the mountains, moors, and fens.*

## IS IT A MONTH

*Is it a month since I and you*
*In the starlight of Glen Dubh*
*Stretched beneath a hazel bough*
*Kissed from ear and throat to brow,*
*Since your fingers, neck, and chin*
*Made the bars that fenced me in,*
*Till Paradise seemed but a wreck*
*Near your bosom, brow, and neck*
*And stars grew wilder, growing wise,*
*In the splendour of your eyes!*
*Since the weasel wandered near*
*Whilst we kissed from ear to ear*
*And the wet and withered leaves*
*Blew about your cap and sleeves,*
*Till the moon sank tired through the ledge*
*Of the wet and windy hedge?*
*And we took the starry lane*
*Back to Dublin town again.*

⊏◇⊐

## *For the Literary Traveler*

Less than an hour from Dublin, SYNGE COUNTRY is accessible by bus, but driving or walking the seventy-mile WICKLOW WAY, the first long-distance walking route in the Republic, is the best way of seeing the places you find in his poetry and plays. Synge's Wicklow is at once beautiful and lonely: crossing its desolate mountains, tracking a writer for whom these glens were a timeless paradise, you may stop to won-der if you're still in the modern world. RATHFARNHAM, his suburban birthplace, is the gateway to the DUBLIN MOUNTAINS, through the Feath-erbed Pass, leading to GLENCREE. Also en route to the pretty village of Enniskerry is GLENCULLEN, though it's no longer the solitary sanctuary of birds that Synge recalls in "In Glencullen." A mile beyond Enniskerry are the gardens and waterfall—at four hundred feet, the highest in Ire-land and England—of the beautifully landscaped Powerscourt, aptly named given its Anglo-Irish prominence at the heart of the English Pale. Also at Rathfarnham begins the MILITARY HIGHWAY or Wilderness Highway (R115), a forty-five-mile more-or-less scenic straightaway over the Wicklow Mountains south to Aghavannagh, built by the Brit-ish to open up access to the hideouts of the rebels of the 1798 Rising. At that time Wicklow was described as "a wilderness as impenetrable as the jungles of the Amazon." From GLENCREE you can see Lower and Upper Lough Bray and further east the majestic cones of the Great Sugar Loaf and Little Sugar Loaf Mountains. The "Oaks of Glencree," once a forest of oak preserved by the British sovereign as a royal park, is now a dismal plantation of conifer trees (to the east along the Enniskerry/Glencree road), one of many such groves created in the name of reforestation that you see all over Ireland.

"Still south I went and west and south again": moving in the direc-tion of Synge's "Prelude," you come to SALLYGAP, Ireland's highest crossroads between Kippure and Djouce Mountains. From Sallygap, detour west (toward Blessington) to see perhaps the most literary point of origin on Ireland's natural landscape: the River Liffey, which be-gins in Wicklow as a tiny stream ten miles from Dublin. The road west of Sallygap cuts across miles of peat bog, past grazing sheep who also waddle along the open road. Then, all at once, you're next to Anna Liffey in her first beauty: she's there on the right, just over the small Liffey Bridge, a clear sparkling natural pool (with a NO SWIMMING signpost) backdropped by fields and soft gray granite hills. To find her on foot, Joss Lyman's *Best Irish Walks* gives the route from the Kippure Mountain carpark. From her quiet brookside seclusion, Anna Livia flows north through County Kildare, entering Dublin considerably wider and browner at Leixlip.

Returning to Sallygap, this time travel east from the crossroads, stopping, as Synge often did, above LOUGH TAY, (also called Luggala), a mirage-like radiance far beneath you on the glen floor, buttressed by the black walls of Fancy Mountain. LOUGH DAN, a long tongue of water, is also visible from this spectacular road (R579), which continues to wind down toward Sraghmore. (There's a wonderful walk on the Wicklow Way between Lough Tay and Lough Dan.)

Within the triangle of the villages of ROUNDWOOD (on its green, Synge photographed the markets, writing the local talk into his notebook), ANNAMOE, and ASHFORD are a few places Synge knew well. A road ascends the valley about a mile northwest of Ashford on the Vartry River into the strange DEVIL'S GLEN, its waterfall, wild scenery, and the remains of Glanmore, a castle built for Francis Synge, his great-grandfather, a frequent destination:

> Towards the top of the hill I passed through a narrow gap with high rocks on one side of it and fir trees above them, and a handful of jagged sky filled with extraordinarily brilliant stars. In a few moments I passed out on the brow of the hill that runs behind the Devil's Glen and smelt the fragrance of the bogs. I mounted again. There was not light enough to show the mountains round me, and the earth seemed to have dwindled away into a mere platform where an astrologer might watch. Among these emotions of the night one cannot wonder that the madhouse is so often named in Wicklow.

(Mental instability is often on Synge's mind in his journals where he ponders the consequences of geographic isolation and the strategies people devise to create alternatives to the bleakness of their lives.) Outside Annamoe is CASTLE KEVIN, a Georgian house behind high stone gates where Synge spent his summers from 1892 to 1907, and TOMRI-LANDS FARM, the second-to-last house on the left before TOMRILANDS CROSSROADS, where he wrote *In the Shadow of the Glen*:

> When I was writing *In the Shadow of the Glen* some years ago, I got more aid than any learning could have given me from a chink in the floor of the old Wicklow house where I was staying, that let me hear what was being said by the servant girls in the kitchen.

GLENMALURE, the setting of this play, spreads through a long, bleak valley to the southwest of Annamoe and Laragh. Whereas only thirty years ago this glen was as empty as the young wife Nora suffers it day in and day out, today there are houses and more houses scattered helter-skelter along the floor of the Avonbeg River. But some of what Synge saw hasn't changed: in his words, "after a stormy night's rain the whole valley is filled with a riot of waterfalls." Nora is alive to nature's tempests. Leaving her loveless marriage to the money-obsessed Dan Burke, she runs off with her sweet-talking Tramp, up the glen and over TABLE MOUNTAIN to Brittas. (For its theme of women's liberation, the play was castigated by Dublin critics as "a slur on Irish womanhood." During his last illness, Synge liked to talk about feminism—never a popular subject in Ireland—with his nurses.) You can follow Nora's escape route over the WICKLOW GAP—skirting the potholes is an adventure in itself—with its ample views of LUGNAQUILLA (at 3,039 feet the highest peak in Ireland outside Kerry), the Glen of Imaal, and the open, wild country of West Wicklow, a fine place, as Synge knew, for "lying down under the Heavens."

## FROM *IN THE SHADOW OF THE GLEN*

TRAMP *(going over to Nora)*. We'll be going now, lady of the house—the rain is falling, but the air is kind and maybe it'll be a grand morning by the grace of God.

NORA. What good is a grand morning when I'm destroyed surely, and I going out to get my death walking the roads?

TRAMP. You'll not be getting your death with myself, lady of the house, and I knowing all the ways a man can put food in his mouth.... We'll be going now, I'm telling you, and the time you'll be feeling the cold, and the frost, and the great rain, and the sun again, and the south wind blowing in the glens, you'll not be sitting up on a wet ditch, the way you're after sitting in the place, making yourself old with looking on each day, and it passing you by. You'll be saying one time, "It's a grand evening, by the grace of God," and another time, "It's a wild night, God help us, but it'll pass surely." You'll be saying—

DAN *(goes over to them crying out impatiently)*. Go out of that door, I'm telling you, and do your blathering below in the glen.

*[Nora gathers a few things into her shawl.]*

TRAMP *(at the door)*. Come along with me now, lady of the house, and it's not my blather you'll be hearing only, but you'll be hearing the herons crying out over the black lakes, and you'll be hearing the grouse and the owls with them, and the larks and the big thrushes when the days are warm, and it's not from the like of them you'll be hearing a talk of getting old like Peggy Cavanagh, and losing the hair off you, and the light of your eyes, but it's fine songs you'll be hearing when the sun goes up, and there'll be no old fellow wheezing, the like of a sick sheep, close to your ear.

NORA. I'm thinking it's myself will be wheezing that time with lying down under the Heavens when the night is cold; but you've a fine bit of talk, stranger, and it's with yourself I'll go.

There was nothing haphazard about this defiant play's setting, chosen by a writer who called himself a radical, "someone who wanted to change things root and branch": Wicklow was known throughout Ireland as "a favorite retreat of fugitives from authority."

The only route that delivers the full impact of the power of GLEN-MACNASS and GLENMACNASS WATERFALL is the steep road north out of LARAGH. This is the unforgettable highlight of the Wicklow landscape. Synge's poem voices the pleasure of this beauty taken in the company of his beloved, Molly Allgood, the Abbey Theatre actress to whom he was engaged to be married at the time of his death.

### QUEENS

Seven dog-days we let pass
Naming queens in Glenmacnass,
All the rare and royal names
Wormy sheepskin yet retains,
Etain, Helen, Maeve, and Fand,
Golden Deirdre's tender hand,
Bert, the big-foot, sung by Villon,
Cassandra, Ronsard found in Lyon.
Queens of Sheba, Meath and Connaught,
Coifed with crown, or gaudy bonnet,
Queens whose finger once did stir men,
Queens were eaten of fleas and vermin,
Queens men drew like Monna Lisa,
Or slew with drugs in Rome and Pisa,
We named Lucrezia Crivelli,
And Titian's lady with amber belly,
Queens acquainted in learned sin,
Jane of Jewry's slender shin:
Queens who cut the bogs of Glanna,
Judith of Scripture, and Gloriana,
Queens who wasted the East by proxy,
Or drove the ass-cart, a tinker's doxy,
Yet these are rotten—I ask their pardon—
And we've the sun on rock and garden,
These are rotten, so you're the queen
Of all are living, or have been.

Though Synge died in his prime, the Wicklow mountains and glens he loved—six times as old as the Himalayas and the Alps—remain. Wicklow County Tourism (fax 04-04 66057) offers two annual Walking Festivals:

the May Walk, centered around the Wicklow Gap and West Wicklow, and the Autumn Walk, around Glenmalure. The Wicklow County Tourism Map and the Wicklow Way Map Guide are available at local bed-and-breakfasts and from Wicklow Tourism on Kilmantin Hill, Wicklow Town.

Coach tours of Wicklow move quickly through AVONDALE HOUSE in RATHDRUM, the Wicklow home of Charles Stewart Parnell (1846–1891), the monumental nineteenth-century champion of Home Rule who was born and raised here and loved this countryside. But it's a lovely place to take your time. Synge visited this house in which the tastefully restored rooms look out on the Vale of Avoca; the book corner and video center introduce the Parnell family and its famous son, the casualty of a priest-ridden Ireland mourned in the Christmas dinner scene of Joyce's *Portrait of the Artist*: " 'Poor Parnell!' [Mr. Casey] cried loudly. 'My dead king!' " (A summary of F. S. L. Lyons's biography of Parnell is for sale, and there are cartoons on the walls outside the dining room of the models for the characters in Joyce's "Ivy Day in the Committee Room," the *Dubliners* story about the craven politicians who obeyed the priests and deserted Parnell when his adulterous affair with Katharine O'Shea was discovered.) The exotic tree walk through AVONDALE takes you through ancient groves of hazelwood and beech. Though Anglo-Irish Wicklow was reputedly a county where Protestantism and loyalty to England ran deep, its hills were the hideouts of Republican rebels. As in the years of Jonathan Swift's *Drapier's Letters* (see p. 12) and the Rising of 1798, when both the Protestant and Catholic Irish came together for a short time, so in the 1870s and 1880s both sides supported the Anglo-Irish Parnell when he stood up for Ireland in the British House of Commons. Lyons connects the strength of Parnell's determined Irish patriotism with his native place, where his "basic Wicklow granite had stubbornly resisted all those diverse and futile attempts to put an English polish on it."

(For information about the annual week-long Synge Summer School (July) and the Parnell Summer School (August), both held in Rathdrum, contact Mrs. Irene Parsons, (tel. 04-04 46131), or Wicklow Tourism at www.wicklow.ie and www.countywicklow.com).

◻◇◻

# Seamus Heaney

## 1939–

*After Bloody Sunday,\* Heaney moved his young family out of Northern Ireland, settling in Wicklow, near Ashford. In his Nobel lecture, "Crediting Poetry," he told a story about the founder of the monastery at Glendalough:*

This is a story about another monk holding himself up valiantly in the posture of endurance. It is said that once upon a time St. Kevin was kneeling with his arms stretched out in the form of a cross in Glendalough, a monastic site not too far from where we lived in County Wicklow, a place which to this day is one of the most wooded and watery retreats in the whole of the country. Anyhow, as Kevin knelt and prayed, a blackbird mistook his outstretched hand for some kind of roost and swooped down upon it, laid a clutch of eggs in it and proceeded to nest in it as if it were the branch of a tree. Then, overcome with pity and constrained by his faith to love the life in all creatures great and small, Kevin stayed immobile for hours and days and nights and weeks, holding out his hand until the eggs hatched and the fledglings grew wings, true to life if subversive of common sense, at the intersection of natural process and the glimpsed ideal.

---

\* The day in 1972 when the British army shot dead thirteen civil rights demonstrators and wounded twenty-eight others, which led to years of violence and political upheaval in the North.

*This story, for Heaney, illuminates the contours of his own vocation as a poet: he's no longer the earnest youth "bowed to the desk like some monk over his prie-dieu . . . in an attempt to bear his portion of the weight of the world." Like Kevin, he's now seasoned enough "to make space . . . for the marvellous as well as the murderous."*

## ST. KEVIN AND THE BLACKBIRD

*And then there was St Kevin and the blackbird.*
*The saint is kneeling, arms stretched out, inside*
*His cell, but the cell is narrow, so*

*One turned-up palm is out the window, stiff*
*As a crossbeam, when a blackbird lands*
*And lays in it and settles down to nest.*

*Kevin feels the warm eggs, the small breast, the tucked*
*Neat head and claws and, finding himself linked*
*Into the network of eternal life,*

*Is moved to pity: now he must hold his hand*
*Like a branch out in the sun and rain for weeks*
*Until the young are hatched and fledged and flown.*

*And since the whole thing's imagined anyhow,*
*Imagine being Kevin. Which is he?*
*Self-forgetful or in agony all the time*

*From the neck on out down through his hurting forearms?*
*Are his fingers sleeping? Does he still feel his knees?*
*Or has the shut-eyed blank of underearth*

*Crept up through him? Is there distance in his head?*
*Alone and mirrored clear in love's deep river,*
*'To labour and not to seek reward,' he prays,*

*A prayer his body makes entirely*
*For he has forgotten self, forgotten bird*
*And on the riverbank forgotten the river's name.*

## For the Literary Traveler

By Synge's time the Irish Church had hitched its interests to the British Crown and preached a culture of conformity. But Seamus Heaney's poem recalls the idealism of early Christianity and of GLENDALOUGH—the Glen of the Two Lakes—when it was young. St. Kevin started his community of monks in the sixth century out of a desire to love a God who was alive in all the creatures of his creation and to become himself a more free human being.

Fifteen centuries later, the valley at times still has the peace of the monks' mystical desire. On the shores of the UPPER LAKE, ringed by mountains, the beauty of nature seems an incontrovertible fact of life. A contemplative mood is hard to sustain, though, since Glendalough is a favorite destination of tourist buses. Even so, in late afternoon, when the crowds have gone, the Upper Lake radiates the silence of twilight.

Near the LOWER LAKE, inside the medieval gateway, are the fine ruins. The monastery in its heyday would have included, besides ecclesiastical buildings, workshops, sites for manuscript writing and copying, guest houses, an infirmary, farm buildings, and dwellings for both the monks and the large numbers of pilgrims. None of these survived the destruction of the city by English forces in 1398.

Follow the GREEN ROAD to the Upper Lake: it's a forest walk past ancient oak trees and thick holly trees, home to lapwings, wagtails, singing blackbirds, and, in spring, purple violets, myrtle, gorse, geraniums, butterwort, St. John's wort, and the Poulanass waterfall flooding the paths and misting the bright lush air. West of REEFERT CHURCH, you can make the slippery climb up to the ruins of ST. KEVIN'S CELL, the setting of Heaney's poem. If you climb the Spink, the steep wooded bank behind the beehive-shaped cell, and follow the forest road to the northern brow of Derrybawn Mountain—the finest ridge in Wicklow, according to Joss Lynam's *Best Irish Walks*—the Upper Lake stretches out below in all the wonder it must once have had for Glendalough's first pilgrims. (The seven-and-a-half-mile walking trail returns you to the Poulanass waterfall in about four and a half hours.)

St. Kevin's retreat grew eventually into the University of Glendalough, drawing thousands of students from all over Europe, people in search of a counterculture. The Venerable Bede weaves a tableau of the place in full swing:

> Many of the nobles of the English nation and lesser men also had set out thither, forsaking their native island either for the grace of sacred learning or a more austere life. And some of them indeed soon dedicated themselves faithfully to the monastic life, others rejoiced rather to give themselves to learning, going about from one master's cell to another. All these the Irish willingly received, and saw to it to supply them with food day by day without cost, and books for their studies, and teaching, free of charge.

Some of the monks were poets in their free time, making monasteries like Glendalough important literary as well as religious landmarks. The old monastic poem "The Scholar and His Cat" (written by a ninth-century Irish monk at Saint Gallen in Switzerland and translated from the Irish by Robin Flower) belongs to the imaginative ground of such a watery place, where rats undoubtedly tried the patience of saints and manic cats entertained everyone.

### PANGUR BAN

*I and Pangur Ban my cat,*
*'Tis a like task we are at:*
*Hunting mice is his delight,*
*Hunting words I sit all night.*

*'Tis a merry thing to see*
*At our tasks how glad are we,*
*When at home we sit and find*
*Entertainment to our mind.*

*'Gainst the wall he sets his eye,*
*Full and fierce and sharp and sly;*

'Gainst the wall of knowledge I
All my little wisdom try.

So in peace our task we ply,
Pangur Ban, my cat and I;
In our arts we find our bliss,
I have mine and he has his.

# THE
# PROVINCE OF
# MUNSTER

---

TIPPERARY
WATERFORD
CORK
KERRY
LIMERICK
CLARE

---

Jan Morris · William Trevor

Dervla Murphy · Sean O'Faolain

Frank O'Connor · Lorrie Moore

Elizabeth Bowen · Eileen O'Connell

Anonymous · Liam Dall O'hlfearnáin

John Millington Synge

Nuala Ní Dhomhnaill

Mary Carbery · Kate O'Brien

Frank McCourt · Sean O'Faolain

Brian Merriman · Edna O'Brien

# Jan Morris

## 1926 –

*The Anglo-Welsh travel writer Jan Morris lives in Wales when she's not on the road researching her internationally renowned books on such places as Venice, Spain, Manhattan, and the Middle East. Now she's written* Ireland: Your Only Place, *about the country she calls "the most pungently individualistic part of Europe." The "hazed allure" of Ireland has always tantalized—it's so close to her home in Wales "that on clear days we can see it on our western horizon." Her book—an essay, really—focuses on specific sites which are revelatory of Ireland's "secrets and surprises." In the following selection about the view from the Rock of Cashel she works her twin passions for history and exotic places to yield another richly textured cultural portrait.*

FROM *IRELAND: YOUR ONLY PLACE*

I stood one evening on ... the Rock of Cashel in Tipperary, capped with its tall thicket of ruins—where Brian Boru held court as High King of Ireland, where archbishops dispensed theology and the renegade Earl of Inchiquin, 'The Burner O'Brien', came slaughtering and profaning through the sacred precincts. I stood on this commanding place one summer evening and, looking down to the fields below, observed a black mare with her foal. There were cattle about too, munching and lolloping, and through them those two equines, mother and son, picked their way with fastidious grace. They seemed to me more than animals; the poor cows would eventually be slaughtered, but the mare and her foal looked timeless, as though they would be sauntering always there through the lush grass, in the soft of the evening, beneath the towers of Cashel.

. . . These creatures did exemplify for me some spirit of the island itself. It was a legitimate fancy. In the worst days of English oppression the very name of Ireland was transmuted into a series of exquisite eponyms, presenting the country as a flower, an animal or most often as a lovely girl—Dark Rosaleen, Cathleen ni Houlihan, My Little Dark Rose. The convention survived, and in modern times too artists have habitually portrayed Ireland in metaphor. 'Did you see an old woman going down the road?' asked one character of another in a play by Yeats, resuscitating one of the oldest of these fantasies. 'I did not; but I saw a young girl, and she had the walk of a queen,' says the other—and everyone knew that he was speaking of Ireland.

So I could be forgiven for seeing Ireland in those lovely horses. Recognizable always in this country, it seems to me, are elemental essences—suggestions of fire, love, ethereal beauty, superstition, battle and death. 'I loved the young men whose horses galloped over many an open plain, beating lightning from the ground,' says an old woman in a Gaelic poem, and she too was allegorizing the country, which has always boasted of its hell-for-leather young bloods, and always loved its horses. When they erected a memorial to the dead of the Easter Rising, within the Dublin General Post Office which was the focus of the rebellion, they chose a figure of the mythical hero Cuchulain, who had himself lashed to a rock rather than submit to his enemies—and whose bronze legs in the Post Office are now shining from the touch of so many respectful customers.

◊     ◊

The Irish language was always the messenger of these emotions, and it remains today a kind of *memento vitae*—a reminder of Ireland's Celtic origins, and of its immemorial sovereignty. Irish—by then, as the poet Thomas Kettle put it, 'the secret scripture of the poor'—was the symbolical language of the patriots who finally achieved independence from England, and it remains the first language of the Irish State. The Republic of Ireland is officially Poblacht na hÉireann, the President of Ireland is Uachtarán na hÉireann, the Prime Minister is the Taoiseach, the Parliament the Oireachtas. Street signs and official announcements are generally in Irish and in English, in theory Government servants are bilingual, and every Irish schoolchild learns at least a smattering of Irish.

It is a proud but wishful formality—hardly more. The Irish language, passionately revived in the first years of independence, never did become popular, and today it is spoken as a first language only in the areas officially designated as Gaeltacht or Gaelic areas. A visit to one of these enclaves is a haunting experience, especially perhaps for a Welsh wanderer. Disregard the effluvia of tourism, never mind the sometimes silly manifestations of Celticness that other Irishmen like to mock—to stand on a rocky shore in Kerry, say, on the ultimate edge of western Europe, and to hear hanging on the air the cadences of that infinitely ancient and lyrical tongue, echoing from a farm door perhaps, or shouted over the beat of rock music from a café, is to sense the deepest power and poignancy of Ireland. Who can doubt that it was Irish that my mare spoke to her colt, as she led him through the meadows of Cashel? . . .

The echo of the Irish language, if not the language itself, has helped to preserve Ireland's links with the pre-industrial world, and almost anywhere in the island I seem to feel myself closer to the pastoral society that has been destroyed almost everywhere else in Europe. Its images are ubiquitous still in the countryside— donkeys, horses, haystacks, black curraghs on the Connemara shore, a couple of goats shackled together in a field, horses, tinker caravans in shambled laager, fusty corner shops, pubs with signs saying 'Musicians Welcome', an old woman leading a cow, grinning imp-like children—and a flavour of esoteric whimsy often reaches us still out of the peasant past. . . .

◊     ◊

'Musicians Welcome.' The harp of the wandering minstrel is the official emblem of the Irish Republic, appearing on all its coins, besides being the universally known trade-mark of Guinness, the brewers. Nothing is truer to the old spirit than Irish traditional music, which has lately enjoyed a dramatic revival, establishing a cult following all over the world, and which expresses itself most characteristically in pubs. All over Ireland there are taverns known to musicians (and some, like the ones at Doolin in County Clare, have become so famous as to be insufferable, at least during the tourist season). To walk into one sufficiently late on a summer evening can be a startling experience—like coming face to face with a medieval minstrelsy. Solemn in a corner of the bar four or five musicians will be playing some immemorial jiggety air, on tin whistle, guitar, fiddle and drum. The music is flighty, rhythmic, insistent and intoxicating, like the music of fiddlers in fairy tales; the musicians, thumping their feet to its rhythm, are bent over their instruments altogether seriously, almost reverently in fact. Jammed suffocatingly all around them, beer in hand, the young crowd watches and listens as though bewitched, and standing on top of the bar, so as to be seen across their heads, the bar-tender too looks as though he has been magicked there. When the tune ends the players, breaking into satisfied smiles, and exchanging brisk words of badinage with their audience, drink deep of Guinnesses; and very often one sees young foreigners, Germans perhaps, or Scandinavians, staring at them as though they are seeing ghosts.

ᴄ◇ᴅ

### For the Literary Traveler

Approach the clifftop ROCK OF CASHEL from the north (M8) or the west, if possible. A massive ancient stone, it climbs the air above you like a gothic dream, ominous, proud, thrilling. Once you've climbed up to the entrance and made your way inside, the views from the Rock— if the day is clear—take you down again in all directions: in the foreground (looking from all sides of the cathedral shell) is the GOLDEN VALE, the wide green pastureland of grazing cattle and horses that strikes Jan Morris. Further in the distance, to the south, are the GALTEES, the COMERAGHS, and the KNOCKMEALDOWN Mountains. To the east is the isolated dome of SLIEVENAMAN ("Mountain of the Women," at 2,564 feet), a conspicuous landmark from many parts of Tipperary and Waterford. (It's so named, according to legend, for a rite of betrothal: old Finn MacCool, unable to choose a wife, sat on the summit observing all the available young women race up the hill toward him; the winner would land herself a husband. When Grainne, the daughter of King Cormac of Tara—see p. 90—reached Finn first, she turned around and ran off with young Diarmuid.)

The force of the wind up on the Rock—it's also called ST. PATRICK'S ROCK—is as powerful as its impression of utter domination you feel down below. If not *the* most impressive (as some guidebooks claim), Cashel is surely among the most impressive sites in Ireland. It's Cashel's physical situation as well as its resonances of the old Gaelic world of the Irish language and music that pull Morris in. The history of the site also has connections with her own Celtic origins.

By the year 400, Eoganacht chiefs (known subsequently by the surname MacCarthy), who had probably come over from Morris's Wales, conquered this Munster countryside (and Clare to the north), setting up a defensive fortress on the Rock. They became the kings of Cashel, which was synonymous with being the kings of Munster. According to legend, on the spot where the HIGH CROSS now stands, St. Patrick baptized King Aengus, the Rock's first Christian occupant, and in the course of the ceremony accidentally stuck his crozier through Aengus's foot. The proud warrior didn't flinch, thinking this ordeal part of the ceremony. When the Eoganacht kings (the MacCarthys) eventually abandoned the Cashel district, to carve out a new kingdom in Cork (Desmond), their cultural finale was King Cormac MacCarthy's building of CORMAC'S CHAPEL in 1127–1134, the earliest and most beautiful Romanesque church in Ireland.

The exterior is a warm red sandstone. With its fantastic stone decorations of beasts devouring beasts and of human heads above the chancel arch, the interior reflects the turbulent history of Cashel, the centuries of tribal warfare—bloody victories, bloody defeats—and the fusion of church and state in the person of one all-powerful and polymorphous man, pagan, Christian, druid, bishop, king. There are more inscrutable faces in stone relief on the altar tombs and tomb

chests in the transepts of the larger thirteenth-century unroofed
CATHEDRAL.

Over the centuries, religious fanaticism claimed this hill for a variety
of holy causes. In 1647, when the renegade "Burner O'Brien" mentioned by Jan Morris attacked Cashel with a Cromwellian army, the
townspeople hid on the Rock; O'Brien burned them out and slaughtered them. About his Irish campaigns, Cromwell wrote home that he
could feel the presence of the Holy Spirit as the flames laid waste and
the blood flowed.

Cashel is open mid-June to mid-Sept., daily 9–7:30; mid-Mar. to
mid-June, daily 9:30–5:30; mid-Sept. to mid-Mar., Mon.–Sat. 9:30–4:30,
Sun. 2–5. Tourist traffic is heavy in summer. Traditional-music sessions—
for Jan Morris and many others, the continuing expression of the ancient Gaelic culture—are held June 15–Sept. 15, Tues.–Sat. at 9 P.M., at
the BRU BORU (Brian Boru) HERITAGE CENTRE at the base of the Rock.

# William Trevor

### 1928–

*"Probably the greatest living writer of short stories in the English
language," according to* The New Yorker, *William Trevor spent a
peripatetic Protestant childhood in Ireland as his bank-manager father was moved around from town to town, from Trevor's birthplace
in Mitchelstown, Cork, to Skibbereen to Youghal. The southeast
counties of Tipperary and Waterford were close neighbors he came to
know well. After graduating from Trinity College in History, he
started out as a sculptor and wood carver, then moved to London and
a job as an advertising copywriter, publishing his first novel in 1958.
Since then his novels (including* Death in Summer *and* Felicia's
Journey) *and collections of short stories (*The Ballroom of Romance,
Angels at the Ritz, Beyond the Pale) *have appeared regularly, win-*

*ning many literary prizes and hats-off reviews. His recent fiction has
been more and more concerned with Irish subjects and settings, (such
as the tragic consequences of the civil war in* The Silence in the Garden). *Compared to Chekhov ("Trevor never raises his voice," wrote
one critic, "reminding us of the line from Yeats: 'Rhetoric is heard.
Poetry is overheard' "), he has often been mentioned as a writer deserving of the Nobel Prize. In addition to the characters he brings to
life with poignant sympathy, he is deeply attached to places, a passion
obvious in his study of the Irish landscape in literature,* A Writer's
Ireland *(1984), and in his memoir,* Excursions in the Real World
*(1993). Trevor's memoir ends with a portrait of Clonmel in County
Tipperary—you come to feel the town is Trevor's friend—and a walk
through the Nire Valley in County Waterford.*

## FROM *EXCURSIONS IN THE REAL WORLD: MEMOIRS*

### THE NIRE

County Tipperary is divided into two: the North Riding and the
South Riding. The town of Clonmel—Cluain Meala, the
honey meadow—is the administrative centre of the South Riding,
and the capital of the county. It's interesting in all sorts of ways: a
town of the ancient territory of the Decies, Anglo-Norman, mas-
sively fortified in the fourteenth century—a protection that stood it
in good stead when Cromwell, riding by, decided to besiege it.

The River Suir gives Clonmel much of its character, and the
mountains that surround it add something to that, but the town has
its own provincial idiosyncrasy. Spacious O'Connell Street, Gladstone Street and Irishtown may be a far cry from a honey meadow,
but the centuries that have passed since this was a designation have
left an insistent mark. There is a faded grandeur about Clonmel: a
prosperous past is evoked by the Georgian symmetry of Anne
Street, by the mill buildings of the Quakers, the mementoes of
Carlo Bianconi, the Main Guard. The West Gate, with a plaque to
a native—Laurence Sterne—was rebuilt in the 1830s. Greater antiquity is mostly buried, or remains in bits and pieces. Somewhere
beneath Old St Mary's church are the foundations of the Church

of Our Ladye of Clonmel, built when the de Burgo family was the one that locally mattered most. The Abbey of St Francis has a fourteenth-century tower.

You begin in Clonmel when you walk out of the realities of the twentieth century into the timeless stretches of the Nire Valley. Personally, I begin at Hickey's bakery with a cup of coffee in Nuala's tiny coffee shop, then drive south into County Waterford. Bungalows with handkerchief trees and fancy façades decorate the roadside, each one vying with the next. At Ballymacarbry there's Doocey's filling station and grocery. At Melody's lounge bar you turn off and head for the hills.

Between the Monavullagh Mountains and the Comeraghs, the River Nire—or Nier—descends from Coumalocha and is repeatedly joined by tributaries of its own en route to becoming a tributary of the Suir, west of Newcastle. The ascent to Coumalocha begins ordinarily enough, and so do you if you choose the lane through Lyre, leaving behind you when you begin your walk a couple of old vans that serve as sheep shelters, the ruins of a house usefully adapted as a docking pen, and two scarecrows that are the hillside's protection for its lambs. The going is easy until the bogs begin, the incline gentle. You walk in a balm of silence, hardly disturbed by the larks that dart out of the bracken or become agitated above your head if their nests seem endangered by the tramp of your feet. After heavy rain the areas of bog pose a problem; you do your best to skirt them.

The scarecrows have lost their outlines when you look back. The vans are coloured dots. The farmhouse, the red barn roof, the clump of firs, are nothing much either. The ground is drier after an hour or so, the ascent steeper. Seefin, Coumfea, Milk Hill, Knockaunapeebra, Crotty's Rock: slowly you move into their territory, welcomed only by sheep. But there are foxes here too, their holes among the rocks. And buzzards hang stealthily.

When you reach the first of the corrie lakes, tucked in below Coumfea, the silence seems almost palpable. The dark water is as still as ice, and as cold. The lake has a lonely look up there on its own, as if aware that it has been forgotten. Steeply encasing it, the mountain of which it's a part rises on three sides; looking up, you can guess where the first of the higher lakes is—similarly cradled, similarly fed by an orderly torrent that disappears when it goes underground.

I met an old man once in the Nire Valley. He was poking his way along the lane at Lyre. He said he had walked to Waterford in his youth, thirty miles away. He said he had walked to Cork, which is more than sixty. He didn't like roads, he never had. I asked him why he'd walked to Waterford and Cork, and he explained that he had wanted to see them. The time he was talking about was 1910 or so, he couldn't be certain exactly. But whenever it was, he insisted, in those days people walked more in Ireland. There was a man he knew who walked from Waterford to Dublin.

The encounter was unusual because you don't meet many people when you leave the beaten track in the Nire Valley. Usually you meet no one at all. But occasionally a dog is barking, miles away, scurrying after the sheep. On distant roads, cars creep along the Nire Drive; busy on a slope, a tractor goes about its task as leisurely as a snail.

There are other places as peaceful, but outside Ireland there are few in Europe as accessible. For the imaginative walker, the temptation is to find the Nire's bleak splendour a symbol for the island that contains it, as in the past other elements have been symbols of the Irish whole. James Clarence Mangan's 'seas of corn' were that. Kilcash was that, and the Tipperary Woodlands, and St Columba's little oak grove. Patrick Kavanagh saw it in the black hills of Shancoduff, Yeats in his lake isle.

But, somehow, in the Nire poetry is limited, there being no human connection, nor a past to mourn. No Mass was ever said here, no earls arrayed themselves in splendour, no different landscape can be regretted. Yet looking down from these modest heights at lush fields and managed forests, you feel that here, not there, the elusive spirit of Ireland might just possibly be—not packaged as Dark Rosaleen or Cathleen ní Houlihan or the Old Woman of Beare, but in the chilly air and sheep scratching for nourishment. Nature is defiant on Europe's western rock, and you would swear that this Ireland all around you has never been different. It is the only wisp of romance you are offered as you tramp on, up to the next small lake.

It's a personal attachment, of course: your own place. For others, there is Kerry or Connemara, the Wicklow Hills, Donegal, Mayo; and it is rarely easy to assess why fondness for particular landscape comes about. All you know is that affectionately you remember where the patches of cropped grass are, the ferns, the gulches, the best approach when the going's mushy, the way around the shale. It is affection, you are equally aware, that causes you to want to know what you never will: every single yard of this vast place intimately, in all weathers, at every time of day. The secret of beauty may be here, and probably is, but it isn't yours to discover either. All there is, as you descend, is a litany of sounds that echoes perfectly what you see: Knockanaffrin, Knockeen, Spilloge Loughs, Shanballyanne, Fauscoum, Glenahiry, Toorala.

In Hickey's bakery, where yesterday's bread is still being sold at reduced prices, the spell cast by that landscape doesn't evaporate. It seems irrelevant that a man has reached a hundred and two in Thomastown, as the *Nationalist* reports, or that there's been malicious damage at the Rock of Cashel. In Nuala's coffee shop housewives consume barm brack and tea, an elderly couple decide on salad sandwiches, young mothers quieten their children with cake. The talk is of the Strawberry Fair, and the Clonmel Festival Majorettes on parade. The town has had its first new heart, and next week will have a new mayor. The *Nationalist* reports that a Clonmel man has been warned that wives are not footballs to be kicked around; three publicans have been fined for after-hours offences; Tipp's last hope of a title is the minor hurlers on Sunday. In Hickey's bakery the real world presses its claims again, ephemeral, mortal.

◻◇◻

## For the Literary Traveler

From Cashel, you'll find CLONMEL—"the Honey Meadow"—fifteen miles southeast through the gentle SUIR VALLEY. (Take N8 to New Inn, turn left onto R687.) After Clonmel, Trevor's route continues south into the NIRE VALLEY and the Comeragh Mountains, visible from the acropolis-like heights of Cashel.

But first the Anglo-Norman town of Clonmel that Trevor likes so much. Its outskirts are built up and trafficked at rush hour, but once inside the old walls, the rhythm changes. You can't miss the "faded grandeur" that often brings him back here. It's palpable along the RIVER WALK on the RIVER SUIR (pronounced "sure") that passes the old mill buildings and warehouses (now under restoration) and Suir Island. The river and riverwalk parallel the main street—O'CONNELL STREET—whose western end begins as you pass through the WEST GATE, a nineteenth-century version of a fourteenth-century original. It bears a plaque commemorating Laurence Sterne (born here, in his mother's native town, in 1713), the comic genius and "British Rabelais" who wrote the anti-novel *Tristram Shandy* and whose favorite reading was Rabelais and an Irish songbook. Opposite West Gate, at the eastern end of the street, is the MAIN GUARD (c. 1675), the oldest public classical building in Ireland. (Walking west to east along O'Connell Street, at number 13 is Sean Tierney's Bar, for eight years running either Tipperary or Munster "Pub of the Year," which deserves another prize for friendliness and the many black-and-white prints of Clonmel on the walls. For travelers who like a read or a chat with their drinks, there are cushioned snugs and bookshelves full of Dickens and the Brontës, but no William Trevor.)

Turn right at the eastern end of O'Connell Street into Sarsfield Street, where on the right the Clonmel Arms Hotel holds music sessions on weekends; on the left the Irish Tourist Board has a helpful staff, a good Clonmel Heritage Trail map, and maps of the walking trails to the south that Trevor knows so well. Straight ahead the RIVER SUIR sparkles at dusk beneath a wall of mountain.

Maybe the plainest place to eat, read, or enjoy the company of the townspeople is Trevor's favorite, HICKEY'S BAKERY, and the adjoining NUALA'S COFFEE SHOP, just outside West Gate on the right. Facing the flank of a mountain, the interior is a place to feel the current of small-town life: there are local people reading newspapers, whispery couples, women of all ages with children edgy over the soccer balls the women say they may not kick in Nuala's place (though easygoing Nuala might not mind). Leaving the bakery—in Irishtown, the section to which the non-Anglo-Norman (or native Irish) population was once confined—continue west and turn right into Wolfe Tone Street. Passing the one-story bungalows and the Quaker graveyard on the left, with its memorial to the Quakers for their contributions to the famine relief work of 1845–53 (nineteenth-century Clonmel was known as "the Quaker City of the South"), you come to what Trevor calls "the Georgian symmetry" of ANNE STREET. At its other end, in Mary Street, is Old St. Mary's Church, built over the foundations of the thirteenth-century church of Our Ladye of Clonmell. It's so low-key and pretty back here. You could easily miss Anne Street, the perfect introduction to Trevor Country.

"The timeless stretches of the NIRE VALLEY," in his words, begin south of Clonmel. Take the Dungarvin/Youghal road south to BALLYMACARBRY ("Ballymac") and cross the border into County Waterford. A few miles south, on the right, at MELODY'S NIRE VIEW BAR (Trevor calls it "Melody's lounge bar"), if you're lucky enough to meet up with the knowledge-able Carmel Melody or her husband (who runs pony treks through the valley and whose family has lived here for generations), you'll receive a comprehensive and colorful introduction to the history, folklore, and topography of the region. The pub, built on the site of a courthouse, is a friendly haven during June hailstorms, whether you're walking or driving; traditional music sessions are held here Wednesday nights. Adjoining the bar is a small Tourist Board office dispensing, during the summer months, a series of pamphlets covering six Nire Valley walks, with small maps of the various routes, their places of interest, and the length, difficulty, and walking time of each one. (The East Munster Way is another walking trail in this area, stretching from Carrick-on-Suir to Clogheen, part of it in close proximity to the Nire Valley, flanking the Comeragh and Knockmealdown Mountains. For information, contact the Tipperary County Council, County Hall, Clonmel, (052-25399.)

"At Melody's lounge bar you turn off and head for the hills," reports Trevor, who from this point on is on foot. If you plan to follow him through this river valley running with tributaries, bring waterproof footwear and maps. The left turn from Melody's into the signposted scenic Nire Valley leads straight to Hanora's Cottage, a comfortable and idyllic base (whose chef was trained at the acclaimed Ballymaloe House in Cork) from which to hike for longer than one afternoon (Seamus and Mary Wall, proprietors; tel. (052) 36134, fax (052) 36540).

If you're driving, you can turn either left or right at Hanora's Cottage for beautiful tours. The left turn takes you along the Nire Valley Scenic Drive, over the Nire Bridge—painted black and white—uphill. If you then take the second right turn to Rathgormack, the ride follows the top of a ridge with views of all the mountain ranges of this area. Instead of taking this right turn, you can continue along the Scenic Drive.

If you turn right at Hanora's Cottage, you pass the Nire Church (1856) on your left (inside, St. Helena, mother of the emperor Constantine, wears ruby red in the stained glass over the altar). Continue along a narrow road for a few kilometers, passing a stone farmhouse, until you come to the grassy KNOCKANAFFRIN LAY-BY. Knockanaffrin—Cnoc an Aiffrin in Irish—means "Hill of the Mass," recalling the years of the Penal Laws, when the Catholic Mass was outlawed but still celebrated in hidden places in the open air. Looking south, across hills of cultivated green fields, you are ringed by the COMERAGHS here. The only sound is of mountain streams rushing down from the hills at your back. In May and June, the wind blows petals from blossoming apple trees. The road ends here. If you want to reach the GAP, a great wide sweep between the ending of KNOCKANAFFRIN RIDGE, on the left, and the rocky outcrop of CARRIGSHANEAN ("Old Birds Rock"), on the right, continue along the white-posted mountain track for about two miles. On a clear day, the walk takes about an hour.

Trevor loves the names of the Nire Valley: the KNOCKEEN, TOORALA, CROTTY'S ROCK, MILK HILL, "the CORRIE LAKES tucked in below COUMFEA." You can find them on the Ordnance Survey maps and in the Nire Valley walkers' pamphlets. (Lonely Planet's Walking in Ireland has a few good pages on walking Knockanaffrin Ridge and the Monavullagh Mountains.) Trevor's affection for this valley and his feeling that "the elusive spirit of Ireland" might just possibly be here on these "modest heights" are completely persuasive along these empty roads. Like him, you want to come back. As he puts it, "The secret of beauty may be here." In the title story of his latest collection, *The Hill Bachelors* (2000), this mountain country of small farmers casts a spell on its main character almost as binding as love.

In *Excursions in the Real World*, Trevor also remembers YOUGHAL, to the south, and going to school in SKIBBEREEN, in southwest County Cork. These coastal towns are delightful, though Youghal is busier than the southwest. Skibbereen, capital of the CARBERIES, and CASTLETOWNSHEND are also the home ground of the Anglo-Irish writers Somerville and Ross (Edith Oenone Somerville, 1858–1949; Violet Martin, 1862–1915), authors of the novel *The Real Charlotte* (about the collapse of Big House culture) and the comic stories *Some Experiences of an Irish R. M.* (criticized for its stage-Irish characters), of whom Trevor writes with admiration in *A Writer's Ireland*. Some critics compare them to Jane Austen, finding in Somerville and Ross a similar sympathy with women dependent on the money that social codes prohibit them from earning for themselves. In Castletownshend, you can still see the Somerville home, DRISHANE HOUSE, and the Townshend castle, facing the harbor behind the huge tree at the dead-end bottom of the steep main street. Somerville's and Ross's graves are side by side in the hilltop graveyard, overlooking the bay, behind ST. BARRAHANE'S CHURCH, where Edith Somerville played the organ for seventy years, observing from the loft the vanity of her fellow churchgoers, who then showed up in her books. The nearby harbor towns and musical pubs of Glandore, Union Hall, and Leap are wonderful. (Jonathan Swift loved this part of Ireland, staying in these towns and in Castletownshend in 1723, writing in Latin the poem "Carberiae Rupes.") If you hang around in Skibbereen (the excellent WEST CORK ARTS CENTER is on the left at the head of its narrow main street), listening to the lilt of the talk and watching the faces lit with a mad merriment, you might develop a taste for Somerville and Ross country without opening a book. You'll see why, after all these years the place is still alive in Trevor's memory.

# Dervla Murphy

1931–

*One of the world's most intrepid bicyclists, Dervla Murphy longed to see strange places even before she could read. As the only child of the county librarian in Lismore, a small town in the Blackwater Valley of County Waterford, she pored over her parents' nineteenth-century picture books, plotting imaginary travels through the engraved images of mountains. For her tenth birthday, she was given a bicycle and an atlas; the decision to bike to India dates from these gifts. But, as her autobiography* Wheels Within Wheels *tells so movingly, she didn't hit the road for another twenty years. At fourteen, she had to leave school to keep house for her parents and nurse her mother, who was all but paralyzed with rheumatoid arthritis. It was on the mountain roads through the Blackwater Valley—to which her autobiography is pure invitation—that she prepared for her future, cycling up to 120 miles in a day. After her parents' death, the faithful daughter was off, biking overland from Dunkirk to Delhi on a bicycle called Rozinante. When her own daughter was five, Murphy took her along. She writes her renowned books about her journeys (*Full Tilt, Tibetan Foothold, In Ethiopia with a Mule, On a Shoestring to Coorg, Transylvania and Beyond, South from the Limpopo, A Place Apart*) out of her home on the South Mall of Lismore's main street. Lismoreians, who know her from way back, call her "Nerveless Dervla."*

FROM *WHEELS WITHIN WHEELS*

A T 7:45 on the morning of November 28, 1931, a young woman in the first stage of labour was handed by her husband into Lismore's only hackney-car. The couple were slowly driven east to Cappoquin along a narrow road, in those days potholed and muddy. It was a mild, still, moist morning. During the journey a pale dawn spread over the Blackwater valley, a place as lovely in winter as in summer—a good place to be born.

The woman had waist-length chestnut hair, wavy, glossy and thick. Her features were classically regular, her wide-set eyes dark blue, her complexion had never known—or needed—cosmetics. She had an athletic build, with shoulders too broad for feminine grace. On the previous day, impatient because the baby was a week late, she had walked fifteen miles. . . .

Two days later I was christened in Cappoquin's parish church. At first the priest refused to baptise me, insisting peevishly that 'Dervla' was a pagan name and must be changed to something respectably Catholic like Mary or Brigid. My father, however, would not give in. He recalled that a sixth-century St Dervla was reputed to have lived in Co Wexford and that from Ireland the name had spead throughout Europe. Then he carefully explained, to an increasingly impatient curate, that Dearbhail meant True Desire in Gaelic and that the English, French and Latin versions were Dervla, Derval and Dervilla. Finally they compromised; my birth certificate names me as Dervilla Maria.

Although my mother's recovery was rapid we were not allowed home until December 12. Then my first journey took me through countryside that had scarcely changed since Thackeray described it in 1842: 'Beyond Cappoquin, the beautiful Blackwater river suddenly opened before us, and driving along it for three miles through some of the most beautiful rich country ever seen, we came to Lismore. Nothing certainly can be more magnificent than this drive. Parks and rocks covered with the grandest foliage; rich handsome seats of gentlemen in the midst of fair lawns and beautiful bright plantations and shrubberies; and at the end, the graceful spire of Lismore church, the prettiest I have seen in or, I think, out of Ireland. Nor in any country that I have visited have I seen a view more noble—it is too rich and peaceful to be what is called romantic, but lofty, large and *generous*, if the term may be used; the river and banks as fine as the Rhine; the castle not as large but as noble and picturesque as Warwick. As you pass the bridge, the banks stretch away on either side in amazing verdure, and the castle walks remind one somewhat of the dear old terrace of St Germains, with its groves, and long, grave avenues of trees.'

From that bridge it was about a quarter of a mile to my first home on the eastern edge of Lismore. There my parents had rented half a decaying mini-mansion. The other half was occupied by the owner, an obese, elderly, gossipy widow who always smelt of camphorated oil. Her habit of glancing through opened letters, and asking our maid what the Murphys were having for dinner, did not endear her to my mother. . . .

◊     ◊

Two miles south of Lismore a wooded ridge—Ballinaspic—forms the watershed between the Bride and the Blackwater valleys. Standing on a certain gatepost on Ballinaspic's crest one can survey the whole sweep of West Waterford, and always I feel an intoxication of joy as my eye travels from the coast near Dungarvan to the Cork border near Macollop. There are profound differences between one's responses to familiar and unfamiliar landscapes. The incomparable grandeur of the Himalayas fills me with a mixture of exaltation and humility. But the beauty of the Blackwater valley is so much a part of me that it inspires an absurd pride—almost as though I had helped to make it, instead of the other way round.

Looking across that fertile valley from Ballinaspic one sees three mountain ranges. The Comeraghs, above the sea to the north-east, seem like the long, casual strokes of some dreamy painter's brush. The Knockmealdowns, directly overlooking Lismore, are gently curved and oddly symmetrical and display as many shades of blue-brown-purple as there are days in the year. And the Galtees—more distant, to the north-west—rise angular and stern above the lonely moors of Araglen. Opposite Ballinaspic, another long, heavily wooded ridge separates the lower slopes of the Knockmealdowns from the lushness at river-level and is marked by several deep glens, each contributing a noisy stream to the quiet width of the Black-water. And south-east of Ballinaspic, amidst a calm glory of ancient woods and irregular little fields, one can glimpse the marriage of the Bride and the Blackwater—after the latter has abruptly turned south at Cappoquin.

Due north of Lismore a mountain pass forms the letter V against the sky and is known, with un-Irish prosaicness, as the Vee. Less than three hundred years ago wolves were hunted hereabouts and not much more than one hundred years ago evicted peasants were forced to settle on the barren uplands of Ballysaggart. More fortu-nate settlers arrived in 1832, a group of Cistercian monks who were presented with a mountain-side by Sir Richard Keane of Cappo-quin. Ten years later Thackeray observed that 'the brethren have cultivated their barren mountain most successfully', and now the grey Abbey of Mount Mellery stands solitary and conspicuous against its background of blue hills—an echo of those ancient monasteries which once made known, throughout civilised Eu-rope, the name of Lismore.

In the seventh century St Carthage founded a cathedral and col-lege in Lismore and by the eighth century the place had become a university city where in time both King Alfred the Great and King John (while still Earl of Morton) were to study. In 1173 the 'famous and holy city' was ransacked by Raymond le Gros; and when King John replaced the razed college with a castle it, too, was destroyed. Soon, however, the local bishops had built another castle, which Sir Walter Raleigh eventually acquired. But Sir Walter was not a very competent landowner and in 1602 he gladly sold his castle, surrounded by a little property of 42,000 acres, to Richard Boyle, First Earl of Cork. Some two hundred years later an heiress of the Earl of Cork married a Cavendish and Lismore Castle is still owned by the Devonshire family. Thackeray observed: 'You hear praises of the Duke of Devonshire as a landlord wherever you go among his vast estates: it is a pity that, with such a noble residence as this, and with such a wonderful country round about it, his Grace should not inhabit it more.'

Between the sixteenth and twentieth centuries West Waterford had to endure less than its share of Ireland's woes. The Villiers-Stuarts of Dromana and the Keanes of Cappoquin always lived on their estates and generally were compassionate landlords—while the Devonshires, though absentees, were not more than usually un-scrupulous. Moreover, a local historian, Canon Power, noted that the region 'seems to have been largely cleared of its original Celtic stock on the conclusion of the Desmond wars and . . . the first earl of Cork was able to boast that he had "no Irishe tenant on his land" '.

◊　◊

Fanciful though this may sound, the Blackwater River was among the chief and best-loved companions of my youth. To me, it has al-ways seemed Lismore's most tangible link with the saints and sin-ners and scholars of the past. Many centuries ago it was most appropriately known as *Nem*, an Irish word meaning 'Heaven'. Much later, Spenser mentioned it in *The Faery Queen*—'Swifte Aw-naduff which of the English man is Cal'de Blackewater'. Later still, some enthusiastic Victorian tourist (Thackeray, I think) decided to rename it the Irish Rhine and this inanity—as absurd as calling Swat the Switzerland of the East—has earned him the undying gratitude of the Irish Tourist Board.

The Blackwater—one of Europe's great salmon rivers—rises near Killarney and flows for seventy miles through the counties of Kerry, Cork and Waterford. In the twelfth century both Dromana House and Lismore Castle were granted charters entitling their owners to extensive fishing rights and even now these charters of King John of England remain good in law, much to the annoyance of certain local rod fishers.

A river shows different aspects to the fisherman, the naturalist, the trader, the artist, the soldier, the boatman and the swimmer. I formed my relationship with the Blackwater as a swimmer. Before I can remember, my father regularly immersed me in the cool, dark silkiness of its depths and I swam almost as soon as I could walk. It is a good thing to have had a river among one's mentors; its strength develops the body, its beauty develops the soul, its ageless-ness develops the imagination. Also, its moods teach respect for the mindless power of nature. The Blackwater is very moody: it has deep holes, sudden floods, hidden rocks, tricky currents and sly weeds. It claims at least three lives a year and I was not allowed to bathe alone until I was twelve. Although I could easily have broken this rule without being detected, it never occurred to me to do so.

Our shared devotion to the Blackwater had always been important to my father and myself. It was not simply that we were both keen swimmers; our bathing was as much a rite as a pastime and during the summer, whether the weather was summery or not, we met outside the Library at five-thirty every afternoon and went together to the river. . . .

## For the Literary Traveler

The BLACKWATER RIVER starts out in Kerry, flowing east through Cork and Waterford into the fertile BLACKWATER VALLEY, one of the longest stretches of lushness—flowering glens, woodlands, dark green hillsides— in Ireland. At LISMORE, the Blackwater curves a bit on its way toward CAPPOQUIN, where it turns south toward Youghal and the sea. The steep roads of this valley, north and south of Lismore, the more out of the way the better, are Murphy Country: growing up here, Dervla Murphy walked and biked them all, imagining herself some faraway day on the mountain ranges of other continents. *Wheels Within Wheels* can be read as a guide to the local places she loved as a girl, places that saved her body and soul during the hard years of dutiful daughterhood.

Among the most scenic routes through this beautiful West Waterford river valley are the ones she mentions:

"Due north of Lismore a mountain pass forms the letter V against the sky." This pass is known as THE VEE. You can begin the (signposted) drive into it four miles east of Lismore at Cappoquin (where Molly Bloom's Captain Mulvey came from).

A slight (signposted) detour off the main route into the Vee leads to MOUNT MELLERAY, the Cistercian (Trappist) monastery on the flanks of the KNOCKMEALDOWNS, where in Joyce's "The Dead" the alcoholic Freddy Malins is going to take the cure and it is said the monks sleep in their coffins (they don't).

The main route winds along the floor beneath mountains, their sides moving with the shadows of scudding clouds and bursts of sunlight. Up here in the high blue air in early June, there's not a car or person in sight. (Mount Melleray, now a school, is bustling by comparison.)

You can also approach the Vee from Lismore, taking the road north to Clogheen and Cahir, in about three miles picking up the Munster Way, which leads to the V-shaped sides of the gap itself. As you climb (or hit the gas), you realize where Murphy got the legs to bike herself and her child through Nepal.

Another of her favorite treks is on the other side of the Blackwater: "Two miles south of Lismore a wooded ridge—BALLINASPIC—forms the watershed between the BRIDE and the BLACKWATER valleys." Few Lismoreians can direct you to tiny Ballinaspic, only a few miles from town (and where, before she became an invalid, Murphy's mother used to wheel baby Dervla in the carriage), but it's worth taking the time to find it. The morning I asked for directions, a crowd gathered, each person confessing, "I haven't a clue," and suggesting I call in on Dervla, who lives just down there. Finally one man, summoned with shouts, came in off the street to point me in the right direction: Chapel Street, the road to the south, begins at the town monument, heading away from the castle; you pass the small bungalows of Irishtown, St. Carthage's Catholic cathedral, and the cemetery for Famine victims (a gift from the Duke of Devonshire, whose family still occupies Lismore's Castle), and in less than a mile, you come to a dump or "amenity site." Just past this landmark, turn right into a hilly boreen or narrow road (deserted except for one idyllic cottage and a few farms) and proceed uphill. At the road's crest, you come to the view of the Blackwater Valley of West Waterford and Lismore's spire and castle in the distance, exactly as Murphy describes it. (Inching past the postman's van on this narrow back road, I asked him if I was now in Ballinaspic. I mentioned my quest for the places of Dervla Murphy. "Indeed you are," he said. "And I know the lady. I deliver her post. She gave me this watch." He held his left arm toward me out the window of his cab

so I could see the fine watch. He assured me I was looking at the COM-
ERAGHS, the KNOCKMEALDOWNS, and the GALTEES. Their shapes and loca-
tions will be familiar by now, since you first saw them from the Rock of
Cashel (see p. 133).

To find the River BRIDE, the postman told me to bear left at the end
of the ridge road we were stopped on and head straight on down the
mountain—"You can't go wrong." To the southeast then, downhill all
the way, past gardens and wooded river banks, you do in a few minutes come upon children fishing in the River Bride, fishermen stopping
at the Brideview Bar at Tallowbridge (just outside Tallow), which overlooks the river as it flows east to meet its larger relation, the Blackwater, flowing south since Cappoquin.

In addition to the scenery around Lismore, the town itself is treasure. The handsome red brick and terra-cotta CARNEGIE LIBRARY (closed
on weekends), where Murphy's father worked his entire life, is up the
main street, past the monument, across the road from the Bank of Ireland. The places Thackeray so admired when he was on the road in
1842 writing his *Irish Sketch Book*, published under the pseudonym Michael Angelo Titmarsh, are as they were then. As you enter Lismore
from the direction of Cappoquin (though this road has changed since
he described it) or coming down from the Vee, you look up from the
bridge over the Blackwater and there is LISMORE CASTLE, poised magnificently above the river in its cliff-top woodlands, fine gardens, and
eight-hundred-year-old yew walk. (It's now open to the public daily in
summer 1:45–4:45 except Sat.)

At the end of a long stairway leading from the road that passes
beneath the castle (Castle Avenue) is ST. CARTHAGE'S CATHEDRAL, its
setting—in an old tumbling churchyard of yews and lime trees—as appealing as its interior. Stained glass by the pre-Raphaelite artist Edward
Burne-Jones is the highlight of St. Columba's Chapel, which is dedicated to peace and affixed with a notice that early Celtic Christianity
was marked by "a respect for plants, birds, and animals and the awareness that God is present in all creation." The ceiling of the choir, with
large rosettes in its vaulting, adds to the impression of good cheer in
this church.

Thackeray, who had good taste in lodgings, stayed at the Lismore
Hotel, in the center of Main Street, still a fine building that served as an

annex to house the overflow of guests from the castle. (Thus its original name, the Devonshire Arms.) Today the hotel's Green Room lounge is decorated with Jack Yeats prints from the Cuala Press and photographs of Irish writers. There's music on weekends, the Blackwater salmon is excellent, and the people are good company. Diagonally across the street from the Lismore Hotel is the old courthouse, which houses the Lismore interpretive center. Its audiovisual history of the town (though it could do without the fake fey "Brother Declan" narrator) is informative: Lismore began as a monastic settlement founded by St. Carthage in 635, eventually becoming one of the most prestigious of the monastic university "cities," despite centuries of invasion and attack by Vikings and Normans who sailed up the Blackwater from Youghal.

The shop of the interpretive centre stocks former Lismoreian/ Georgetown University professor George O'Brien's memoir *The Village of Longing* (1987), winner of awards and plaudits from Seamus Heaney, Dervla Murphy, and the poet Derek Mahon. "Nothing is phony, nothing made up," says Mahon. "His picture of Irish life is a delight, an imaginative feast." As a boy growing up in the economically stagnant Lismore of the fifties ("compared to [Lismore], the paralysis of Joyce's Dublin was a veritable St. Vitus's dance"), O'Brien watched the busloads of tourists—"the new invaders"—stopping on the bridge below the castle, where they still park:

> The tourists were real Yanks, just riding through. They fascinated us. We'd seen their movies, heard their songs, knew their twangy accents. Now we were getting to see them, live—inhabitants of the future we desired for ourselves (money, cars, blondes), war-winners, bulwarks against the red menace and the yellow peril. And a lot of them were good Catholics.
>
> And they looked so healthy, these Yanks, tall, tan, plump: the only blemish we could see was that they all seemed to wear spectacles. Their clothes were great: devastating checks, shirts like postcards of a tropical paradise, big-butted matrons in cerise dungarees. You could tell by their appearance that they didn't give a damn what anyone thought of them. That was the kind of

freedom we craved—to be able to tell the world to bugger off, to turn ourselves into sartorial Caesar's salads precisely as and when it pleased us, to stare vacantly into the middle distance with cigars the size of small trees clamped between jaws smooth as steel. They're children at heart, we thought, wishing that we could think of ourselves as half so gay and simple.

These days, local people, commenting quietly amongst themselves, still observe the tourist buses disgorging their hordes to check out the Castle and little else.

Fred Astaire was among the Yankee visitors to Lismore. He came to see his sister Adele, who married the son of a Devonshire duke. He was a regular patron of the historic MADDEN'S BAR, just down from the Lismore Hotel on Main Street, on the left, near the North Mall. Its All-Ireland award-winning chef, Owen Madden, has made it into a good eatery.

⊏◇⊐

# Sean O'Faolain

1900–1991

*Born John Whelan in Cork City, O'Faolain changed his name into the Irish language after Independence, when it became politically popular to do so. All his life he waged a struggle against the "old" Ireland, by which he meant the repressive and the "deadly dull provincialism" of De Valera's Irish Free State. (On the occasion of his centenary, his daughter, the writer Julia O'Faolain, commented, "Now that it* has *changed, the old Ireland seems so remote that, I am told, few young Irish people know it existed at all.") Throughout his long resistance, he wrote novels (*A Nest of Simple Folk*), criticism, essays, biographies, autobiography (*Vive Moi!*), travel books (*An* Irish Journey—see p. 274*), and the short stories for which he is best*

*known. Reviewing his three-volume* Collected Stories *(1980–82),
V. S. Pritchett called O'Faolain "the most authoritative and diverse,"
among many first-rate Irish storytellers. In America (if not in Ireland) he was acknowledged for many years as the "first Irish man of
letters." About his native Cork, to which as an adult he did not return, he said, "I cannot be objective about Cork. . . . It is one of those
towns you love and hate."*

<h3 style="text-align:center">THE TALKING TREES</h3>

There were four of them in the same class at the Red Abbey, all
under fifteen. They met every night in Mrs Coffey's sweetshop
at the top of Victoria Road to play the fruit machine, smoke fags
and talk about girls. Not that they really talked about them—they
just winked, leered, nudged one another, laughed, grunted and
groaned about them, or said things like 'See her legs?' 'Yaroosh!'
'Whamm!' 'Ouch!' 'Ooof!' or 'If only, if only!' But if anybody had
said, 'Only what?' they would not have known precisely what.
They knew nothing precisely about girls, they wanted to know
everything precisely about girls, there was nobody to tell them all
the things they wanted to know about girls and that they thought
they wanted to do with them. Aching and wanting, not knowing,
half guessing, they dreamed of clouds upon clouds of fat, pink,
soft, ardent girls billowing towards them across the horizon of their
future. They might just as well have been dreaming of pink porpoises moaning at their feet for love.

In the sweetshop the tall glass jars of coloured sweets shone in
the bright lights. The one-armed fruit machine went zing. Now
and again girls from St Monica's came in to buy sweets, giggle
roguishly and over-pointedly ignore them. Mrs Coffey was young,
buxom, fair-haired, blue-eyed and very good-looking. They admired her so much that one night when Georgie Watchman whispered to them that she had fine bubs Dick Franks told him curtly
not to be so coarse, and Jimmy Sullivan said in his most toploftical
voice, 'Georgie Watchman, you should be jolly well ashamed of
yourself, you are no gentleman,' and Tommy Gong Gong said

nothing but nodded his head as insistently as a ventriloquist's dummy.

Tommy's real name was Tommy Flynn, but he was younger than any of them so that neither he nor they were ever quite sure that he ought to belong to the gang at all. To show it they called him all sorts of nicknames, like Inch because he was so small; Fatty because he was so puppy-fat; Pigeon because he had a chest like a woman; Gong Gong because after long bouts of silence he had a way of suddenly spraying them with wild bursts of talk like a fire alarm attached to a garden sprinkler.

That night all Georgie Watchman did was to make a rude blubber-lip noise at Dick Franks. But he never again said anything about Mrs Coffey. They looked up to Dick. He was the oldest of them. He had long eyelashes like a girl, perfect manners, the sweetest smile and the softest voice. He had been to two English boarding schools, Ampleforth and Downside, and in Ireland to three, Clongowes, Castleknock and Rockwell, and had been expelled from all five of them. After that his mother had made his father retire from the Indian Civil, come back to the old family house in Cork and, as a last hope, send her darling Dicky to the Red Abbey day-school. He smoked a corncob pipe and dressed in droopy plus fours with chequered stockings and red flares, as if he was always just coming from or going to the golf course. He played cricket and tennis, games that no other boy at the Red Abbey could afford to play. They saw him as the typical school captain they read about in English boys' papers like *The Gem* and *The Magnet*, *The Boy's Own Paper*, *The Captain*, and *Chums*, which was where they got all those swanky words like Wham, Ouch, Yaroosh, Ooof and Jolly Well. He was their Tom Brown, their Bob Cherry, their Tom Merry, those heroes who were always leading Greyfriars School or Blackfriars School to victory on the cricket field amid the cap-tossing huzzas of the juniors and the admiring smiles of visiting parents. It never occurred to them that *The Magnet* or *The Gem* would have seen all four of them as perfect models for some such story as *The Cads of Greyfriars*, or *The Bounders of Blackfriars*, low types given to secret smoking in the spinneys, drinking in the Dead Woman's Inn, or cheating at examinations, or worst crime of all, betting on horses with red-faced bookies' touts down from London, while the rest of the school was practising at the nets—a quartet of rotters fated to be caned ceremoniously in the last chapter before the entire awe-struck school, and then whistled off at dead of night back to their heartbroken fathers and mothers.

It could not have occurred to them because these crimes did not exist at the Red Abbey. Smoking? At the Red Abbey any boy who wanted to was free to smoke himself into a galloping consumption so long as he did it off the premises, in the jakes or up the chimney. Betting? Brother Julius was always passing fellows sixpence or even a bob to put on an uncle's or a cousin's horse at Leopardstown or the Curragh. In the memory of man no boy had ever been caned ceremoniously for anything. Fellows were just leathered all day long for not doing their homework, or playing hooky from school, or giving lip, or fighting in class—and they were leathered hard. Two years ago Jimmy Sullivan had been given six swingers on each hand with the sharp edge of a metre-long ruler for pouring the contents of an inkwell over Georgie Watchman's head in the middle of a history lesson about the Trojan Wars, in spite of his wailing explanation that he had only done it because he thought Georgie Watchman was a scut and all Trojans were blacks. Drink? They did not drink only because they were too poor. While, as for what *The Magnet* and *The Gem* really meant by 'betting'—which, they dimly understood, was some sort of depravity that no decent English boy would like to see mentioned in print—hardly a week passed that some brother did not say that a hard problem in algebra, or a leaky pen, or a window that would not open or shut was 'a blooming bugger'.

There was the day when little Brother Angelo gathered half a dozen boys about him at playtime to help him with a crossword puzzle.

'Do any of ye,' he asked, 'know what Notorious Conduct could be in seven letters?'

'Buggery?' Georgie suggested mock-innocently.

'Please be serious!' Angelo said. 'This is about Conduct.'

When the solution turned out to be *Jezebel*, little Angelo threw up his hands, said it must be some queer kind of foreign woman

and declared that the whole thing was a blooming bugger. Or there
was that other day when old Brother Expeditus started to tell them
about the strict lives and simple food of Dominican priests and
Trappist monks. When Georgie said, 'No tarts, Brother?' Expeditus had laughed loud and long.

'No, Georgie!' he chuckled. 'No pastries of any kind.'

They might as well have been in school in Arcadia. And every
other school about them seemed to be just as hopeless. In fact they
might have gone on dreaming of pink porpoises for years if it was
not for a small thing that Gong Gong told them one October night
in the sweetshop. He sprayed them with the news that his sister
Jenny had been thrown out of class that morning in St Monica's for
turning up with a red ribbon in her hair, a mother-of-pearl brooch
at her neck and smelling of scent.

'Ould Sister Eustasia,' he fizzled, 'made her go out in the yard
and wash herself under the tap, she said they didn't want any girls
in their school who had notions.'

The three gazed at one another, and began at once to discuss all
the possible sexy meanings of notions. Georgie had a pocket dictionary. 'An ingenious contrivance'? 'An imperfect conception
(US)'? 'Small wares'? It did not make sense. Finally they turned to
Mrs Coffey. She laughed, nodded towards two giggling girls in the
shop who were eating that gummy kind of block toffee that can gag
you for half an hour, and said, 'Why don't you ask *them*?' Georgie
approached them most politely.

'Pardon me, ladies, but do you by any chance happen to have
notions?'

The two girls stared at one another with cow's eyes, blushed
scarlet and fled from the shop shrieking with laughter. Clearly a notion was very sexy.

'Georgie!' Dick pleaded. 'You're the only one who knows anything. What in heaven's name is it?'

When Georgie had to confess himself stumped they knew at last
that their situation was desperate. Up to now Georgie had always
been able to produce some sort of answer, right or wrong, to all
their questions. He was the one who, to their disgust, told them
what he called conraception meant. He was the one who had ex-

plained to them that all babies are delivered from the navel of the mother. He was the one who had warned them that if a fellow kissed a bad woman he would get covered by leprosy from head to foot. The son of a Head Constable, living in the police barracks, he had collected his facts simply by listening as quietly as a mouse to the other four policemen lolling in the dayroom of the barracks with their collars open, reading the sporting pages of *The Freeman's Journal*, slowly creasing their polls and talking about colts, fillies, cows, calves, bulls and bullocks and 'the mysteerious nachure of all faymale wimmen'. He had also gathered a lot of useful stuff by dutiful attendance since the age of eleven at the meetings and marchings of the Protestant Boys' Brigade, and from a devoted study of the Bible. And here he was, stumped by a nun!

Dick lifted his beautiful eyelashes at the three of them, jerked his head and led them out on the pavement.

'I have a plan,' he said quietly. 'I've been thinking of it for some time. Chaps! Why don't we see everything with our own eyes?' And he threw them into excited discussion by mentioning a name. 'Daisy Bolster?'

Always near every school, there is a Daisy Bolster—the fast girl whom everybody has heard about and nobody knows. They had all seen her at a distance. Tall, a bit skinny, long legs, dark eyes, lids heavy as the dimmers of a car lamp, prominent white teeth, and her lower lip always gleaming wet. She could be as old as seventeen. Maybe even eighteen. She wore her hair up. Dick told them that he had met her once at the tennis club with four or five other fellows around her and that she had laughed and winked very boldly all the time. Georgie said that he once heard a fellow in school say, 'She goes with boys.' Gong Gong bubbled that that was true because his sister Jenny told him that a girl named Daisy Bolster had been thrown out of school three years ago for talking to a boy outside the convent gate. At this Georgie flew into a terrible rage.

'You stupid slob!' he roared. 'Don't you know yet that when anybody says a boy and girl are talking to one another it means they're doing you-know-what?'

'I don't know you-know-what,' Gong Gong wailed. 'What what?'

'I heard a fellow say,' Jimmy Sullivan revealed solemnly, 'that she has no father and that her mother is no better than she should be.'

Dick said in approving tones that he had once met another fellow who had heard her telling some very daring stories.

'Do you think she would show us for a quid?'

Before they parted on the pavement that night they were talking not about a girl but about a fable. Once a girl like that gets her name up she always ends up as a myth, and for a generation afterwards, maybe more, it is the myth that persists. 'Do you remember,' some old chap will wheeze, 'that girl Daisy Bolster? She used to live up the Mardyke. We used to say she was fast.' The other old boy will nod knowingly, the two of them will look at one another inquisitively, neither will admit anything, remembering only the long, dark avenue, its dim gas lamps, the stars hooked in its trees.

Within a month Dick had fixed it. Their only trouble after that was to collect the money and to decide whether Gong Gong should be allowed to come with them.

Dick fixed that, too, at a final special meeting in the sweetshop. Taking his pipe from between his lips, he looked speculatively at Gong Gong, who looked up at him with eyes big as plums, trembling between the terror of being told he could not come with them and the greater terror of being told that he could.

'Tell me, Gong Gong,' Dick said politely, 'what exactly does your father do?'

'He's a tailor,' Tommy said, blushing a bit at having to confess it knowing that Jimmy's dad was a bank clerk, that Georgie's was a Head Constable, and that Dick's had been a Commissioner in the Punjab.

'Very fine profession,' Dick said kindly. 'Gentleman's Tailor and Outfitter. I see, Flynn and Company. Or is it Flynn and Sons? Have I seen his emporium?'

'Ah, no!' Tommy said, by now as red as a radish. 'He's not that sort of tailor at all, he doesn't build suits, ye know, that's a different trade altogether, he works with me mother at home in Tuckey Street, he tucks things in and lets things out, he's what they call a mender and turner, me brother Turlough had this suit I have on me now before I got it, you can see he's very good at his job, he's a real dab . . .'

Dick let him run on, nodding sympathetically—meaning to convey to the others that they really could not expect a fellow to know much about girls if his father spent his life mending and turning old clothes in some side alley called Tuckey Street.

'Do you fully realize, Gong Gong, that we are proposing to behold the ultimate in female beauty?'

'You mean,' Gong Gong smiled fearfully, 'that she'll only be wearing her nightie?'

Georgie Watchman turned from him in disgust to the fruit-machine. Dick smiled on.

'The thought had not occurred to me,' he said. 'I wonder, Gong Gong, where do you get all those absolutely filthy ideas. If we subscribe seventeen and sixpence, do you think you can contribute half a crown?'

'I could feck it, I suppose.'

Dick raised his eyelashes.

'Feck?'

Gong Gong looked shamedly at the tiles.

'I mean steal,' he whispered.

'Don't they give you any pocket money?'

'They give me threepence a week.'

'Well, we have only a week to go. If you can, what was your word, feck half a crown, you may come.'

The night chosen was a Saturday—her mother always went to town on Saturdays; the time of meeting, five o'clock exactly; the place, the entrance to the Mardyke Walk.

On any other occasion it would have been a gloomy spot for a rendezvous. For adventure, perfect. A long tree-lined avenue, with, on one side, a few scattered houses and high enclosing walls; on the other side the small canal whose deep dyke had given it its name. Secluded, no traffic allowed inside the gates, complete silence. A place where men came every night to stand with their girls behind the elm trees kissing and whispering for hours. Dick and Georgie were there on the dot of five. Then Jimmy Sullivan came swiftly loping. From where they stood, under a tree beyond the porter's lodge, trembling with anticipation, they could see clearly for only about a hundred yards up the long tunnel of elms lit by the first stars above the boughs, one tawny window streaming across a dank garden, and beyond that a feeble perspective of pendant lamps fading dimly away into the blue November dusk. Within another half-hour the avenue would be pitch black between those meagre pools of light.

Her instructions had been precise. In separate pairs, at exactly half past five, away up there beyond the last lamp, where they would be as invisible as cockroaches, they must gather outside her house.

'You won't be able even to see one another,' she had said gleefully to Dick, who had stared coldly at her, wondering how often she had stood behind a tree with some fellow who would not have been able even to see her face.

Every light in the house would be out except for the fanlight over the door.

'Ooo!' she had giggled. 'It will be terribly oohey. You won't hear a sound but the branches squeaking. You must come along to my door. You must leave the other fellows to watch from behind the trees. You must give two short rings. Once, twice. And then give a long ring, and wait.' She had started to whisper the rest, her hands by her sides clawing her dress in her excitement. 'The fanlight will go out if my mother isn't at home. The door will open slowly. You must step into the dark hall. A hand will take your hand. You won't know whose hand it is. It will be like something out of Sherlock Holmes. You will be simply terrified. You won't know what I'm wearing. For all you'll know I might be wearing nothing at all!'

He must leave the door ajar. The others must follow him one by one. After that . . .

It was eleven minutes past five and Gong Gong had not yet come. Already three women had passed up the Mardyke carrying parcels, hurrying home to their warm fires, forerunners of the home-for-tea crowd. When they had passed out of sight Georgie growled, 'When that slob comes I'm going to put my boot up his backside.' Dick, calmly puffing his corncob, gazing wearily up at the stars, laughed tolerantly and said, 'Now Georgie, don't be impatient. We shall see all! We shall at last know all!'

Georgie sighed and decided to be weary too.

'I hope,' he drawled, 'this poor frail isn't going to let us down!'

For three more minutes they waited in silence, and then Jimmy Sullivan let out a cry of relief. There was the small figure hastening towards them along the Dyke Parade from one lamppost to another.

'Puffing and panting as usual, I suppose,' Dick chuckled. 'And exactly fourteen minutes late.'

'I hope to God,' Jimmy said, 'he has our pound note. I don't know in hell why you made that slob our treasurer.'

'Because he is poor,' Dick said quietly. 'We would have spent it.'

He came panting up to them, planted a black violin case against the tree and began rummaging in his pockets for the money.

'I'm supposed to be at a music lesson, that's me alibi, me father always wanted to be a musician but he got married instead, he plays the cello, me brother Turlough plays the clarinet, me sister Jenny plays the viola, we have quartets, I sold a Haydn quartet for one and six, I had to borrow sixpence from Jenny, and I fecked the last sixpence from me mother's purse, that's what kept me so late . . .'

They were not listening, staring into the soiled and puckered handkerchief he was unravelling to point out one by one, a crumpled half-note, two half-crowns, two shillings and a sixpenny bit.

'That's all yeers, and here's mine. Six threepenny bits for the quartet. That's one and six. Here's Jenny's five pennies and two ha'pence. That makes two bob. And here's the tanner I just fecked from me mother's purse. That makes my two and sixpence.'

Eagerly he poured the mess into Dick's hands. At the sight of the jumble Dick roared at him.

'I told you, you bloody little fool, to bring a pound note!'

'You told me to bring a pound.'

'I said a pound note. I can't give this dog's breakfast to a girl like Daisy Bolster.'

'You said a pound.'

They all began to squabble. Jimmy Sullivan shoved Gong Gong.

Georgie punched him. Dick shoved Georgie. Jimmy defended
Georgie with 'We should never have let that slob come with us.'
Gong Gong shouted, 'Who's a slob?' and swiped at him. Jimmy
shoved him again so that he fell over his violin case, and a man
passing home to his tea shouted at them, 'Stop beating that little
boy at once!'

Tactfully they cowered. Dick helped Gong Gong to his feet.
Georgie dusted him lovingly. Jimmy retrieved his cap, put it back
crookedly on his head and patted him kindly. Dick explained in his
best Ampleforth accent that they had merely been having 'a trifling
discussion', and 'our young friend here tripped over his suitcase'.
The man surveyed them dubiously, growled something and went
on his way. When he was gone Georgie pulled out his pocketbook,
handed a brand-new pound note to Dick, and grabbed the dirty
jumble of cash. Dick at once said, 'Quick march! Two by two!' and
strode off ahead of the others, side by side with Tommy in his
crooked cap, lugging his dusty violin case, into the deepening dark.

They passed nobody. They heard nothing. They saw only the
few lights in the sparse houses along the left of the Mardyke. On
the other side was the silent, railed-in stream. When they came in
silence to the wide expanse of the cricket field the sky dropped a
blazing veil of stars behind the outfield nets. When they passed the
gates of the railed-in public park, locked for the night, darkness returned between the walls to their left and the overgrown laurels
glistening behind the tall railings on their right. Here Tommy
stopped dead, hooped fearfully towards the laurels.

'What's up with you?' Dick snapped at him.

'I hear a noise, me father told me once how a man murdered a
woman in there for her gold watch, he said men do terrible things
like that because of bad women, he said that that man was hanged
by the neck in Cork Jail, he said that was the last time the black flag
flew on top of the jail. Dick! I don't want to go on!'

Dick peered at the phosphorescent dial of his watch, and strode
ahead, staring at the next feeble lamp hanging crookedly from its
black iron arch. Tommy had to trot to catch up with him.

'We know,' Dick said, 'that she has long legs. Her breasts will be
white and small.'

'I won't look!' Tommy moaned.

'Then don't look!'

Panting, otherwise silently, they hurried past the old corrugated-iron building that had once been a roller-skating rink and was now empty and abandoned. After the last lamp the night became impenetrable, then her house rose slowly to their left against the starlight. It was square, tall, solid, brick fronted, three storeyed, and jet black against the stars except for its half-moon fanlight. They walked a few yards past it and halted, panting, behind a tree. The only sound was the squeaking of a branch over their heads. Looking backwards, they saw Georgie and Jimmy approaching under the last lamp. Looking forwards, they saw a brightly lit tram, on its way outward from the city, pass the far end of the tunnel, briefly light its maw and black it out again. Beyond that lay wide fields and the silent river. Dick said, 'Tell them to follow me if the fanlight goes out,' and disappeared.

Alone under the tree, backed still by the park, Tommy looked across to the far heights of Sunday's Well dotted with the lights of a thousand suburban houses. He clasped his fiddle case before him like a shield. He had to force himself not to run away towards where another bright tram would rattle him back to the city. Suddenly he saw the fanlight go out. Strings in the air throbbed and faded. Was somebody playing a cello? His father bowed over his cello, jacket off, shirt sleeves rolled up, entered the Haydn; beside him Jenny waited, chin sidewards over the viola, bosom lifted, bow poised, the tendons of her frail wrist hollowed by the lamplight, Turlough facing them lipped a thinner reed. His mother sat shawled by the fire, tapping the beat with her toe. Georgie and Jimmy joined him.

'Where's Dick?' Georgie whispered urgently.

'Did I hear music?' he gasped.

Georgie vanished, and again the strings came and faded. Jimmy whispered, 'Has she a gramophone?' Then they could hear nothing but the faint rattle of the vanished tram. When Jimmy slid away from him, he raced madly up into the darkness, and then stopped dead half-way to the tunnel's end. He did not have the penny to pay for the tram. He turned and raced as madly back the way he

had come, down past her house, down to where the gleam of the
laurels hid the murdered woman, and stopped again. He heard a
rustling noise. A rat? He looked back, thought of her long legs and
her small white breasts, and found himself walking heavily back to
her garden gate, his heart pounding. He entered the path, fumbled
for the dark door, pressed against it, felt it slew open under his
hand, stepped cautiously into the dark hallway, closed the door,
saw nothing, heard nothing, stepped onward, and fell clattering on
the tiles over his violin case.

A door opened. He saw firelight on shining shinbones and bare
knees. Fearfully, his eyes moved upwards. She was wearing nothing
but gym knickers. He saw two small birds, white, soft, rosy-tipped.
Transfixed by joy he stared and stared at them. Her black hair hung
over her narrow shoulders. She laughed down at him with white
teeth and wordlessly gestured him to get up and come in. He faltered after her white back and stood inside the door. The only light
was from the fire.

Nobody heeded him. Dick stood by the corner of the mantelpiece, one palm flat on it, his other hand holding his trembling
corncob. He was peering coldly at her. His eyelashes almost met.
Georgie lay sprawled in a chintzy armchair on the other side of the
fire wearily flicking the ash from a black cigarette into the fender.
Opposite him Jimmy Sullivan sat on the edge of a chair, his elbows
on his knees, his eyeballs sticking out as if he just swallowed something hot, hard and raw. Nobody said a word.

She stood in the centre of the carpet, looking guardedly from
one to the other of them out of her hooded eyes, her thumbs inside
the elastic of her gym knickers. Slowly she began to press her
knickers down over her hips. When Georgie suddenly whispered
'The Seventh veil!' he at once wanted to batter him over the head
with his fiddle case, to shout at her to stop, to shout at them that
they had seen everything, to shout that they must look no more. Instead, he lowered his head so that he saw nothing but her bare toes.
Her last covering slid to the carpet. He heard three long gasps, became aware that Dick's pipe had fallen to the floor, that Georgie
had started straight up, one fist lifted as if he was going to strike
her, and that Jimmy had covered his face with his two hands.

A coal tinkled from the fire to the fender. With averted eyes he went to it, knelt before it, wet his fingers with his spittle as he had often seen his mother do, deftly laid the coal back on the fire and remained so for a moment watching it light up again. Then he sidled back to his violin case, walked out into the hall, flung open the door on the sky of stars, and straightway started to race the whole length of the Mardyke from pool to pool of light in three gasping spurts.

After the first spurt he stood gasping until his heart had stopped hammering. He heard a girl laughing softly behind a tree. Just before his second halt he saw ahead of him a man and a woman approaching him arm in arm, but when he came up to where they should have been they too had become invisible. Halted, breathing, listening, he heard their murmuring somewhere in the dark. At his third panting rest he heard an invisible girl say, 'Oh, no, oh no!' and a man's urgent voice say, 'But yes, but yes!' He felt that behind every tree there were kising lovers, and without stopping he ran the gauntlet between them until he emerged from the Mardyke among the bright lights of the city. Then, at last, the sweat cooling on his forehead, he was standing outside the shuttered plumber's shop above which they lived. Slowly he climbed the bare stairs to their floor and their door. He paused for a moment to look up through the window at the stars, opened the door and went in.

Four heads around the supper table turned to look up enquiringly at him. At one end of the table his mother sat wearing her blue apron. At the other end his father sat, in his rolled-up shirt sleeves as if he had only just laid down the pressing iron. Turlough gulped his food. Jenny was smiling mockingly at him. She had the red ribbon in her hair and the mother-of-pearl brooch at her neck.

'You're bloody late,' his father said crossly. 'What the hell kept you? I hope you came straight home from your lesson. What way did you come? Did you meet anybody or talk to anybody? You know I don't want any loitering at night, I hope you weren't cadeying with any blackguards? Sit down, sir, and eat your supper. Or did your lordship expect us to wait for you? What did you play tonight? What did Professor Hartmann give you to practise for your next lesson?'

He sat in his place. His mother filled his plate and they all ate in silence.

Always the questions! Always talking at him! They never let him alone for a minute. His hands sank. She was so lovely. So white. So soft. So pink. His mother said gently, 'You're not eating, Tommy. Are you all right?'

He said, 'Yes, yes, I'm fine, Mother.'

Like birds. Like stars. Like music.

His mother said, 'You are very silent tonight, Tommy. You usually have a lot of talk after you've been to Professor Hartmann. What were you thinking of?'

'They were so beautiful!' he blurted.

'What was so bloody beautiful?' his father rasped. 'What are you blathering about?'

'The stars,' he said hastily.

Jenny laughed. His father frowned. Silence returned.

He knew that he would never again go back to the sweetshop. They would only want to talk and talk about her. They would want to bring everything out into the light, boasting and smirking about her, taunting him for having run away. He would be happy for ever if only he could walk every night of his life up the dark Mardyke, hearing nothing but a girl's laugh from behind a tree, a branch squeaking, and the far-off rattle of a lost tram; walk on and on, deeper and deeper into the darkness until he could see nothing but one tall house whose fanlight she would never put out again. The doorbell might ring, but she would not hear it. The door might be answered, but not by her. She would be gone. He had known it ever since he heard her laughing softly by his side as they ran away together, for ever and ever, between those talking trees.

◁◇▷

## For the Literary Traveler

"There is a long walk in Cork known as the Mardyke," O'Faolain writes in *An Irish Journey*, "a mile of trees with lamps at intervals, lost in the leaves spanning the gravel. It starts with old weather-slated houses and ends on the green verge of the city.... the Cork smut-hounds actually tarred those trees man-high to prevent lovers from sheltering behind them at night!" Before the tar brush, a Cork joke had it that "the trees of the Mardyke are more sinned against than sinning."

The MARDYKE, a footpath along the south side of the River Lee, and its environs—Fitzgerald Park, the view across the RIVER LEE of the houses and terraces of SUNDAY'S WELL, the University of Cork Sports Grounds, and the DYKE FIELDS—are the setting of "The Talking Trees," O'Faolain's story of the sexual initiation of Tommy Gong Gong (né Flynn) at the breasts of Daisy Bolster.

One approach to the Mardyke from the city center that makes for a pleasant walk—and walking is the only way to see Cork, whose streets were once a maze of waterways—is from the NORTH MALL, a terrace of early-eighteenth-century houses on the River Lee, which is to Cork as the Liffey is to Dublin: its winding and watery heart. At the Irish Distilleries, turn left, crossing the footbridge over the Lee into Grenville Place (the North Channel banked by willow trees will be on your right), bearing right onto Dyke Parade, past the Granary, University College Cork's Theatre, and continuing straight on. The Mardyke has been spruced up in recent years, and FITZGERALD PARK, on your right, Cork's largest public green, is an oasis in a busy city, especially on weekends, when Corkonians are out with their children (May–Aug., daily 8 A.M.–10 P.M.; Sept.–Apr., daily 8–5). The sculptures you see around the park have an aesthetic energy, strong emblems for a story about embodied, naked beauty. The figure beside the huge copper beach tree, the "Shawlie" (in O'Faolain's time the garb of Cork's poor old women), is without attribution, but the other pieces are by Ireland's best sculptors: *Adam and Eve* by Edward Delaney, *Dreamline* by Seamus Murphy, and *Girl Dancing* by Oisin Kelly.

To return to the north side of the Lee, leave Fitzgerald Park through its gates at the western end and cross the narrow white suspension bridge that Cork people call Daly Bridge or the Shaky Bridge into SUNDAY'S WELL. Joyce's father, John Joyce, whose memory for stories, ballads, and gab is immortalized in *Ulysses*, grew up here; in *A Portrait of the Artist as a Young Man*, Simon and Stephen Dedalus visit Cork together, Stephen observing the word *foetus* cut into a desk at the university and "the leaves of the trees along the Mardyke ... astir and whispering in the sunlight." Sunday's Well Road leads east back toward the city (a bit further on there are steps down from these heights into the North Mall where you started out) past pretty houses with flowering terraces overlooking the city and the Lee, with a good view from the parking lot of St. Vincent de Paul's Catholic church. (The high view is prettier than the close-up look you get down on the quays, where too many ugly stores have gone up in the last twenty years.) The church's interior, with its stained glass above the choir loft of saints and dancing angels playing musical instruments, gives an exuberance to the church, a quality O'Faolain missed in the Irish churches he was raised in. In "A Portrait of the Artist as an Old Man," he wrote, "I was in fact forty-six years old before I finally abandoned the faith of my fathers, and, under the life-loving example of Italy, became converted to Roman Catholicism."

In the furtive background of "The Talking Trees" is Irish puritanism, his writings the object of O'Faolain's contempt. Its manifestation in the Censorship of Publications Act, passed by the Irish government in 1929, had deadening effects on Ireland's literary life. The works of most Irish authors who were any good, especially those with a reputation in Europe and America (Beckett, O'Faolain, O'Connor, Kate O'Brien, and later Edna O'Brien), were banned. The censorship, according to poet Robert Graves, was "the fiercest ... this side of the iron curtain—and I do not except Spain." In 1949, Orwell's *1984* was banned. In the early sixties, novelist Brigid Brophy saw a sign in a Dublin bookstore: THERE ARE OVER 8,000 BOOKS BANNED IN IRELAND. IF BY CHANCE WE HAVE ONE ON DISPLAY, PLEASE INFORM US, AND IT WILL BE DESTROYED.

O'Faolain's neighborhood for his first twenty-six years was below in the city, on the south side of the Lee, in Half-Moon Street, a block south of the new, soulless opera house in Emmet Place (home of the popular Guinness Jazz Festival the last weekend in October) and across from the handsome CRAWFORD MUNICIPAL ART GALLERY (Mon.–Sat. 10–4:45), with Rodin bronzes and a good café run by chefs from that culinary paradise, Ballymaloe House, twenty miles to the southeast, in Shanagarry, Cork (www.ballymaloe.com).

A useful supplement to a walking tour of O'Faolain's "The Talking

Trees" is the Tourist Trail Walking Guide or the Cork City Area Guide, available at the Tourist Office on GRAND PARADE. Cork Harbor Cruises (44 Grand Parade) clarify Cork's geography as an ancient port town (originally a marsh, or *corcach*), spread over thirteen small islands in the River Lee, with many bridges and quays. Some visitors find the layout of Cork so strange they miss it altogether. Others come to love this town, the way it comes at you out of hidden alleys—the colorful English Market where Frank Hederman of Cobh sells his superb smoked wild salmon (between Grand Parade and Princes Street), the bookstore in Carey's Lane, the musicians in Rory Gallagher Square off Paul Street, and the singsong accents of Cork people, who, despite the mixed reviews they get from the native literati, are about as un-processed as you'll find. For a brilliant overview on the subject of Cork's literary tradition, there's Terry Eagleton's "Cork and the Carniva-lesque," in his essay collection on Irish culture, *Crazy John and the Bishop* (1998).

# Frank O'Connor

## 1903–1966

*Frank O'Connor, the pseudonym of Michael O'Donovan, grew up dirt poor in Cork, the only child of a violent, alcoholic father and a mother whom he worshiped.*

*One of the modern masters of the short story—Yeats said he did for Ireland what Chekhov did for Russia—at fourteen O'Connor left the Christian Brothers school where they considered him, in his words, "a complete fool." Thereafter he educated himself in the Carnegie Public Library on Grand Parade. Like O'Faolain, he joined the Republican army during the civil war. Cork City, the base of the nineteenth-century Fenian movement, with a long history of resistance to the English, was known as "Rebel Cork." Taken prisoner,*

*O'Connor landed in a Free State jail, where he worked on his Gaelic and changed his politics. (His famous story "Guests of the Nation" reflects his gradual disillusionment with revolutionaries.) After the war, he became a translator of early Irish lyrics (his collection* Kings, Lords, and Commons *is a masterpiece), director of the Abbey Theatre, and writer of novels, travel books, criticism, the autobiographies* An Only Child *and* My Father's Son, *and the great short stories such as "My Oedipus Complex," "First Confession," "The Long Road to Ummera," and "The Mad Lomasneys," many of them first published in* The New Yorker. *In 1951, with much of his work banned in Ireland, he moved to the United States, attracting as a teacher and writer a devoted following among American college students. He came back home at least once a year, he said, so he wouldn't forget what a terrible place it was.*

## THE DRUNKARD

It was a terrible blow to Father when Mr. Dooley on the terrace died. Mr. Dooley was a commercial traveller with two sons in the Dominicans and a car of his own, so socially he was miles ahead of us, but he had no false pride. Mr. Dooley was an intellectual, and, like all intellectuals the thing he loved best was conversation, and in his own limited way Father was a well-read man and could appreciate an intelligent talker. Mr. Dooley was remarkably intelligent. Between business acquaintances and clerical contacts, there was very little he didn't know about what went on in town, and evening after evening he crossed the road to our gate to explain to Father the news behind the news. He had a low, palavering voice and a knowing smile, and Father would listen in astonishment, giving him a conversational lead now and again, and then stump triumphantly in to Mother with his face aglow and ask: "Do you know what Mr. Dooley is after telling me?" Ever since, when somebody has given me some bit of information off the record I have found myself on the point of asking: "Was it Mr. Dooley told you that?"

Till I actually saw him laid out in his brown shroud with the rosary beads entwined between his waxy fingers I did not take the report of his death seriously. Even then I felt there must be a catch and that some summer evening Mr. Dooley must reappear at our gate to give us the lowdown on the next world. But Father was very upset, partly because Mr. Dooley was about one age with himself, a thing that always gives a distinctly personal turn to another man's demise; partly because now he would have no one to tell him what dirty work was behind the latest scene at the Corporation. You could count on your fingers the number of men in Blarney Lane who read the papers as Mr. Dooley did, and none of these would have overlooked the fact that Father was only a laboring man. Even Sullivan, the carpenter, a mere nobody, thought he was a cut above Father. It was certainly a solemn event.

"Half past two to the Curragh," Father said meditatively, putting down the paper.

"But you're not thinking of going to the funeral?" Mother asked in alarm.

" 'Twould be expected," Father said, scenting opposition. "I wouldn't give it to say to them."

"I think," said Mother with suppressed emotion, "it will be as much as anyone will expect if you go to the chapel with him."

("Going to the chapel," of course, was one thing, because the body was removed after work, but going to a funeral meant the loss of a half-day's pay.)

"The people hardly know us," she added.

"God between us and all harm," Father replied with dignity, "we'd be glad if it was our own turn."

To give Father his due, he was always ready to lose a half day for the sake of an old neighbor. It wasn't so much that he liked funerals as that he was a conscientious man who did as he would be done by; and nothing could have consoled him so much for the prospect of his own death as the assurance of a worthy funeral. And, to give Mother her due, it wasn't the half-day's pay she begrudged, badly as we could afford it.

Drink, you see, was Father's great weakness. He could keep steady for months, even for years, at a stretch, and while he did he was as good as gold. He was first up in the morning and brought the mother a cup of tea in bed, stayed at home in the evenings and read the paper; saved money and bought himself a new blue serge suit and bowler hat. He laughed at the folly of men who, week in week out, left their hard-earned money with the publicans; and sometimes, to pass an idle hour, he took pencil and paper and calculated precisely how much he saved each week through being a teetotaller. Being a natural optimist he sometimes continued this calculation through the whole span of his prospective existence and the total was breathtaking. He would die worth hundreds.

If I had only known it, this was a bad sign; a sign he was becoming stuffed up with spiritual pride and imagining himself better than his neighbors. Sooner or later, the spiritual pride grew till it called for some form of celebration. Then he took a drink—not whiskey, of course; nothing like that—just a glass of some harmless drink like lager beer. That was the end of Father. By the time he had taken the first he already realized that he had made a fool of himself, took a second to forget it and a third to forget that he couldn't forget, and at last came home reeling drunk. From this on it was "The Drunkard's Progress," as in the moral prints. Next day he stayed in from work with a sick head while Mother went off to make his excuses at the works, and inside a fortnight he was poor and savage and despondent again. Once he began he drank steadily through everything down to the kitchen clock. Mother and I knew all the phases and dreaded all the dangers. Funerals were one.

"I have to go to Dunphy's to do a half-day's work," said Mother in distress. "Who's to look after Larry?"

"I'll look after Larry," Father said graciously. "The little walk will do him good."

There was no more to be said, though we all knew I didn't need anyone to look after me, and that I could quite well have stayed at home and looked after Sonny, but I was being attached to the party to act as a brake on Father. As a brake I had never achieved anything, but Mother still had great faith in me.

Next day, when I got home from school, Father was there before me and made a cup of tea for both of us. He was very good at tea, but too heavy in the hand for anything else; the way he cut bread was shocking. Afterwards, we went down the hill to the church, Father wearing his best blue serge and a bowler cocked to one side of his head with the least suggestion of the masher. To his great joy he discovered Peter Crowley among the mourners. Peter was another danger signal, as I knew well from certain experiences after Mass on Sunday morning; a mean man, as Mother said, who only went to funerals for the free drinks he could get at them. It turned out that he hadn't even known Mr. Dooley! But Father had a sort of contemptuous regard for him as one of the foolish people who wasted their good money in public-houses when they could be saving it. Very little of his own money Peter Crowley wasted!

It was an excellent funeral from Father's point of view. He had it all well studied before we set off after the hearse in the afternoon sunlight.

"Five carriages!" he exclaimed. "Five carriages and sixteen covered cars! There's one alderman, two councillors and 'tis unknown how many priests. I didn't see a funeral like this from the road since Willie Mack, the publican, died."

"Ah, he was well liked," said Crowley in his husky voice.

"My goodness, don't I know that?" snapped Father. "Wasn't the man my best friend? Two nights before he died—only two nights—he was over telling me the goings-on about the housing contract. Them fellows in the Corporation are night and day robbers. But even I never imagined he was as well connected as that."

Father was stepping out like a boy, pleased with everything: the other mourners, and the fine houses along Sunday's Well. I knew the danger signals were there in full force: a sunny day, a fine funeral, and a distinguished company of clerics and public men were bringing out all the natural vanity and flightiness of Father's character. It was with something like genuine pleasure that he saw his old friend lowered into the grave; with the sense of having performed a duty and the pleasant awareness that however much he would miss poor Mr. Dooley in the long summer evenings, it was he and not poor Mr. Dooley who would do the missing.

"We'll be making tracks before they break up," he whispered to Crowley as the gravediggers tossed in the first shovelfuls of clay, and away he went, hopping like a goat from grassy hump to hump. The drivers, who were probably in the same state as himself, though without months of abstinence to put an edge on it, looked up hopefully.

"Are they nearly finished, Mick?" bawled one.

"All over now bar the last prayers," trumpeted Father in the tone of one who brings news of great rejoicing.

The carriages passed us in a lather of dust several hundred yards from the public-house, and Father, whose feet gave him trouble in hot weather, quickened his pace, looking nervously over his shoulder for any sign of the main body of mourners crossing the hill. In a crowd like that a man might be kept waiting.

When we did reach the pub the carriages were drawn up outside, and solemn men in black ties were cautiously bringing out consolation to mysterious females whose hands reached out modestly from behind the drawn blinds of the coaches. Inside the pub there were only the drivers and a couple of shawly women. I felt if I was to act as a brake at all, this was the time, so I pulled Father by the coattails.

"Dadda, can't we go home now?" I asked.

"Two minutes now," he said, beaming affectionately. "Just a bottle of lemonade and we'll go home."

This was a bribe, and I knew it, but I was always a child of weak character. Father ordered lemonade and two pints. I was thirsty and swallowed my drink at once. But that wasn't Father's way. He had long months of abstinence behind him and an eternity of pleasure before. He took out his pipe, blew through it, filled it, and then lit it with loud pops, his eyes bulging above it. After that he deliberately turned his back on the pint, leaned one elbow on the counter in the attitude of a man who did not know there was a pint behind him, and deliberately brushed the tobacco from his palms. He had settled down for the evening. He was steadily working through all the important funerals he had ever attended. The carriages departed and the minor mourners drifted in till the pub was half full.

"Dadda," I said, pulling his coat again, "can't we go home now?"

"Ah, your mother won't be in for a long time yet," he said benevolently enough. "Run out in the road and play, can't you?"

It struck me as very cool, the way grown-ups assumed that you could play all by yourself on a strange road. I began to get bored as I had so often been bored before. I knew Father was quite capable of lingering there till nightfall. I knew I might have to bring him home, blind drunk, down Blarney Lane, with all the old women at their doors, saying: "Mick Delaney is on it again." I knew that my mother would be half crazy with anxiety; that next day Father wouldn't go out to work; and before the end of the week she would be running down to the pawn with the clock under her shawl. I could never get over the lonesomeness of the kitchen without a clock.

I was still thirsty. I found if I stood on tiptoe I could just reach Father's glass, and the idea occurred to me that it would be interesting to know what the contents were like. He had his back to it and wouldn't notice. I took down the glass and sipped cautiously. It was a terrible disappointment. I was astonished that he could even drink such stuff. It looked as if he had never tried lemonade.

I should have advised him about lemonade but he was holding forth himself in great style. I heard him say that bands were a great addition to a funeral. He put his arms in the position of someone holding a rifle in reverse and hummed a few bars of Chopin's Funeral March. Crowley nodded reverently. I took a longer drink and began to see that porter might have its advantages. I felt pleasantly elevated and philosophic. Father hummed a few bars of the Dead March in *Saul*. It was a nice pub and a very fine funeral, and I felt sure that poor Mr. Dooley in Heaven must be highly gratified. At the same time I thought they might have given him a band. As Father said, bands were a great addition.

But the wonderful thing about porter was the way it made you stand aside, or rather float aloft like a cherub rolling on a cloud, and watch yourself with your legs crossed, leaning against a bar counter, not worrying about trifles but thinking deep, serious, grown-up thoughts about life and death. Looking at yourself like that, you couldn't help thinking after a while how funny you looked, and suddenly you got embarrassed and wanted to giggle. But by the time I had finished the pint, that phase too had passed; I found it hard to put back the glass, the counter seemed to have grown so high. Melancholia was supervening again.

"Well," Father said reverently, reaching behind him for his drink, "God rest the poor man's soul, wherever he is!" He stopped, looked first at the glass, and then at the people round him. "Hello," he said in a fairly good-humored tone, as if he were prepared to consider it a joke, even if it was in bad taste, "who was at this?"

There was silence for a moment while the publican and the old women looked first at Father and then at his glass.

"There was no one at it, my good man," one of the women said with an offended air. "Is it robbers you think we are?"

"Ah, there's no one here would do a thing like that, Mick," said the publican in a shocked tone.

"Well, someone did it," said Father, his smile beginning to wear off.

"If they did, they were them that were nearer it," said the woman darkly, giving me a dirty look; and at the same moment the truth began to dawn on Father. I suppose I must have looked a bit starry-eyed. He bent and shook me.

"Are you all right, Larry?" he asked in alarm.

Peter Crowley looked down at me and grinned.

"Could you beat that?" he exclaimed in a husky voice.

I could, and without difficulty. I started to get sick. Father jumped back in holy terror that I might spoil his good suit, and hastily opened the back door.

"Run! run! run!" he shouted.

I saw the sunlit wall outside with the ivy overhanging it, and ran. The intention was good but the performance was exaggerated, because I lurched right into the wall, hurting it badly, as it seemed to me. Being always very polite, I said "Pardon" before the second bout came on me. Father, still concerned for his suit, came up behind and cautiously held me while I got sick.

"That's a good boy!" he said encouragingly. "You'll be grand when you get that up."

Begor, I was not grand! Grand was the last thing I was. I gave one unmerciful wail out of me as he steered me back to the

pub and put me sitting on the bench near the shawlies. They
drew themselves up with an offended air, still sore at the suggestion
that they had drunk his pint.

"God help us!" moaned one, looking pityingly at me, "isn't it
the likes of them would be fathers?"

"Mick," said the publican in alarm, spraying sawdust on my
tracks, "that child isn't supposed to be in here at all. You'd better
take him home quick in case a bobby would see him."

"Merciful God!" whimpered Father, raising his eyes to Heaven
and clapping his hands silently as he only did when distraught,
"what misfortune was on me? Or what will his mother say? . . . If
women might stop at home and look after their children themselves!" he added in a snarl for the benefit of the shawlies. "Are
them carriages all gone, Bill?"

"The carriages are finished long ago, Mick," replied the
publican.

"I'll take him home," Father said despairingly. . . . "I'll never
bring you out again," he threatened me. "Here," he added, giving
me a clean handkerchief from his breast pocket, "put that over
your eye."

The blood on the handkerchief was the first indication I got that
I was cut, and instantly my temple began to throb and I set up another howl.

"Whisht, whisht, whisht!" Father said testily, steering me out
the door. "One'd think you were killed. That's nothing. We'll wash
it when we get home."

"Steady now, old scout!" Crowley said, taking the other side of
me. "You'll be all right in a minute."

I never met two men who knew less about the effects of drink.
The first breath of fresh air and the warmth of the sun made me
groggier than ever and I pitched and rolled between wind and tide
till Father started to whimper again.

"God Almighty, and the whole road out! What misfortune was
on me didn't stop at my work! Can't you walk straight?"

I couldn't. I saw plain enough that, coaxed by the sunlight,
every woman old and young in Blarney Lane was leaning over her
half-door or sitting on her doorstep. They all stopped gabbling to

gape at the strange spectacle of two sober, middle-aged men bringing home a drunken small boy with a cut over his eye. Father, torn
between the shamefast desire to get me home as quick as he could,
and the neighborly need to explain that it wasn't his fault, finally
halted outside Mrs. Roche's. There was a gang of old women outside a door at the opposite side of the road. I didn't like the look of
them from the first. They seemed altogether too interested in me. I
leaned against the wall of Mrs. Roche's cottage with my hands in
my trouser pockets, thinking mournfully of poor Mr. Dooley in his
cold grave on the Curragh, who would never walk down the road
again, and, with great feeling, I began to sing a favorite song of
Father's.

> "Though lost to Mononia and cold in the grave
> He returns to Kincora no more."

"Wisha, the poor child!" Mrs. Roche said. "Haven't he a lovely
voice, God bless him!"

That was what I thought myself, so I was the more surprised
when Father said "Whisht!" and raised a threatening finger at me.
He didn't seem to realize the appropriateness of the song, so I sang
louder than ever.

"Whisht, I tell you!" he snapped, and then tried to work up a
smile for Mrs. Roche's benefit. "We're nearly home now. I'll carry
you the rest of the way."

But, drunk and all as I was, I knew better than to be carried
home ignominiously like that.

"Now," I said severely, "can't you leave me alone? I can walk all
right. 'Tis only my head. All I want is a rest."

"But you can rest at home in bed," he said viciously, trying to
pick me up, and I knew by the flush on his face that he was very
vexed.

"Ah, Jasus," I said crossly, "what do I want to go home for?
Why the hell can't you leave me alone?"

For some reason the gang of old women at the other side of the
road thought this very funny. They nearly split their sides over it. A
gassy fury began to expand in me at the thought that a fellow

couldn't have a drop taken without the whole neighborhood coming out to make game of him.

"Who are ye laughing at?" I shouted, clenching my fists at them. "I'll make ye laugh at the other side of yeer faces if ye don't let me pass."

They seemed to think this funnier still; I had never seen such ill-mannered people.

"Go away, ye bloody bitches!" I said.

"Whisht, whisht, whisht, I tell you!" snarled Father, abandoning all pretense of amusement and dragging me along behind him by the hand. I was maddened by the women's shrieks of laughter. I was maddened by Father's bullying. I tried to dig in my heels but he was too powerful for me, and I could only see the women by looking back over my shoulder.

"Take care or I'll come back and show ye!" I shouted. "I'll teach ye to let decent people pass. Fitter for ye to stop at home and wash yeer dirty faces."

" 'Twill be all over the road," whimpered Father. "Never again, never again, not if I lived to be a thousand!"

To this day I don't know whether he was forswearing me or the drink. By way of a song suitable to my heroic mood I bawled "The Boys of Wexford," as he dragged me in home. Crowley, knowing he was not safe, made off and Father undressed me and put me to bed. I couldn't sleep because of the whirling in my head. It was very unpleasant, and I got sick again. Father came in with a wet cloth and mopped up after me. I lay in a fever, listening to him chopping sticks to start a fire. After that I heard him lay the table.

Suddenly the front door banged open and Mother stormed in with Sonny in her arms, not her usual gentle, timid self, but a wild, raging woman. It was clear that she had heard it all from the neighbors.

"Mick Delaney," she cried hysterically, "what did you do to my son?"

"Whisht, woman, whisht, whisht!" he hissed, dancing from one foot to the other. "Do you want the whole road to hear?"

"Ah," she said with a horrifying laugh, "the road knows all about it by this time. The road knows the way you filled your unfortunate innocent child with drink to make sport for you and that other rotten, filthy brute."

"But I gave him no drink," he shouted, aghast at the horrifying interpretation the neighbors had chosen to give his misfortune. "He took it while my back was turned. What the hell do you think I am?"

"Ah," she replied bitterly, "everyone knows what you are now. God forgive you, wasting our hard-earned few ha'pence on drink, and bringing up your child to be a drunken corner-boy like yourself."

Then she swept into the bedroom and threw herself on her knees by the bed. She moaned when she saw the gash over my eye. In the kitchen Sonny set up a loud bawl on his own, and a moment later Father appeared in the bedroom door with his cap over his eyes, wearing an expression of the most intense self-pity.

"That's a nice way to talk to me after all I went through," he whined. "That's a nice accusation, that I was drinking. Not one drop of drink crossed my lips the whole day. How could it when he drank it all? I'm the one that ought to be pitied, with my day ruined on me, and I after being made a show for the whole road."

But next morning, when he got up and went out quietly to work with his dinner-basket, Mother threw herself on me in the bed and kissed me. It seemed it was all my doing, and I was being given a holiday till my eye got better.

"My brave little man!" she said with her eyes shining. "It was God did it you were there. You were his guardian angel."

**⊏◇⊐**

## For the Literary Traveler

O'Connor's Cork is not for tourists. Only aficionados of the great *Collected Stories* will make the trek up the hills north of the LEE. And we will be happy. There's still a street life of kids, corner boys, and mammies with prams; there's shouting and games, plain old women stopping to chat or give a stranger directions and tell you about their people in the States, and not a designer label on hide or head. Though as a young man, O'Connor called his native city a place of "barbarous mediocrity," in later years he spoke with affection of Cork's "warm dim odorous feckless evasive southern quality." He described his writing as "crab apple jelly," a sweet and tart mixture, arousing both laughter and sorrow. That's the mix you feel climbing the hill streets he knew as a child and put into the short story "The Drunkard" and the autobiography *An Only Child*. With a street map of Cork in hand, you enter O'Connor Country—with some irony—at the statue of Father Theobold Matthew, the "Apostle of Temperance," who stands at the top of PATRICK'S STREET (on the south side of the Lee). Crossing PATRICK'S BRIDGE, you climb one block north on vertiginous PATRICK'S HILL, at McCurtain Street turning right (past the Women's Poetry Center and the Metropole Hotel, where the lounges on the weekends of All-Ireland soccer matches are great places to get a firsthand look at—and earful of—the Irish love of sport). Heading northeast, you walk up SUMMERHILL, past ST. LUKE'S CROSS and GARDINER'S HILL under the high rock wall of the QUARRY (where *An Only Child* begins), until you come in about fifteen minutes to HARRINGTON SQUARE. There's a shrine to the Virgin Mary at the head of it and a plaque on the house at number 8: "Frank O'Connor, Writer, 1903–1966, lived here"—as did his mother, who, an orphan herself, refused to leave her drunken husband because she'd have had to put young Michael in an orphanage while she went out to work. (Snotty MONTENOTTE, the butt of many Cork jokes about the middle class and a neighborhood that figures in O'Connor's stories, is a short walk further east.)

Returning to the other side of Patrick's Hill (the downhill walk from Luke's Cross along Wellington Road is charming), head west along COBURG STREET until you hit Shandon Street, off which is BLARNEY LANE, now called Blarney Street (a busy pub neighborhood in many of the stories), where O'Connor spent his first five years. It's the down-and-dirty sidewalks and lanes and the tough, gossipy people (ask for directions and you win yourself half an hour of chat) that make this an O'Connor-hood. "Few writers from humble circumstances have begun quite so humbly as Frank O'Connor did," wrote Richard Ellmann, who might have been struck by this thought while hiking up Blarney Street. On the left you pass STRAWBERRY LANE, dropping down (past the Good Shepherd orphanage, where his mother grew up) into SUNDAY'S WELL,

the setting of "The Mad Lomasneys," who (like the garrulous John
Joyce) lived in a house "with a long sloping garden and a fine view of
the river and the city."

Returning to Shandon Street, you climb toward the steeple of
ST. ANNE'S SHANDON, the most prominent feature of Cork's north side.
Shandon steeple may be climbed and its bells played (June–Aug.,
Mon.–Sat. 9:30–5; winter, Mon.–Sat. 10–4). From its balcony there's a
view of the city—"strewn like a bouquet along the valley," said one native, who clearly was turning a blind eye to the blight down along the
quays. In the cemetery behind the church, Francis Sylvester Mahony
(a.k.a. Father Prout) is buried. He is the author of "The Bells of Shandon," a poem beloved in Cork, which, according to legend, he wrote
on the wall of his room in Rome when he was a seminarian lonesome
for home.

> With deep affection and recollection,
>   I often think of those Shandon bells,
> Whose sounds so wild would, in days of childhood,
>   Fling round my cradle their magic spells.
> On this I ponder, where'er I wander,
>   And thus grow fonder, sweet Cork, of thee;
>     With thy bells of Shandon,
>       That sound so grand on
> The pleasant waters of the river Lee.

A writer who worked to keep the ancient Irish literary tradition
alive, resisting at every turn the cultural stagnation of De Valera's Free
State, O'Connor would be pleased to find in the flat of the city—the
"flaat o' deh city"—the MUNSTER LITERATURE CENTER at 26 Sullivan's
Quay (across the Nano Nagle footbridge on Grand Parade), which
celebrates such Munster writers as O'Faolain, O'Connor, William
Trevor, Elizabeth Bowen, Kate O'Brien, Dervla Murphy, and Somerville
and Ross. The TRISKEL ARTS CENTER at the far end of the city park, just off
South Main Street, is Cork's contemporary film, music, and theater
house. These places and his own books, still in print and well stocked in
WATERSTONE'S on Grand Parade, represent the vital Ireland of the arts
that Frank O'Connor, Corkman, helped keep alive.

# Lorrie Moore

1957–

*Lorrie Moore was born Maria Lorena Moore in Glens Falls, New York, and grew up in a part-Irish Protestant family. Considered by many critics the most gifted fiction writer of her generation, her books include the once-read-never-forgotten novel* Who Will Run the Frog Hospital *(1994) and three acclaimed collections of short stories,* Self-Help *(1985),* Like Life *(1990), and* Birds of America *(1998), the last of these a National Book Award nominee and winner of the 1999* Irish Times *Literature Prize in International Fiction.*

*In the story "Which Is More than I Can Say About Some People" (from* Birds of America*), a mother and daughter take a car trip around Ireland. The purpose of the daughter's journey is to kiss the Blarney Stone and be healed: she is possessed by a terror of public speaking. Her part-Irish mother has come along for the ride. As a road story, it's not picture-postcard-friendly. Rather, it shows Moore's affinity with dark Irish humor, that mixture of hope and defeat that defines the shape of many Irish writers' art. The seriocomic way she depicts the devastation underlying human relationships recalls Beckett, in particular, in whom despair is a constant presence though never an absolute. In* Self-Help, *Moore quotes from his novel* Murphy: *"So all things limp together for the only possible." That line brings us back to the mother and daughter's Irish pilgrimage, as, at journey's end, they clink glasses in a Blarney pub.*

## WHICH IS MORE THAN I CAN SAY
## ABOUT SOME PEOPLE

It was a fear greater than death, according to the magazines. Death was number four. After mutilation, three, and divorce, two. Number one, the real fear, the one death could not even approach, was public speaking. Abby Mallon knew this too well. Which is why she had liked her job at American Scholastic Tests: she got to work with words in a private way. The speech she made was done in the back, alone, like little shoes cobbled by an elf: spider is to web as weaver is to *blank*. That one was hers. She was proud of that.

Also, *blank* is to heartache as forest is to bench.

◊    ◊

But then one day the supervisor and the AST district coordinator called her upstairs. She was good, they said, but perhaps she had become *too* good, too *creative*, they suggested, and gave her a promotion out of the composing room and into the high school auditoriums of America. She would have to travel and give speeches, tell high school faculty how to prepare students for the entrance exams, meet separately with the juniors and seniors and answer their questions unswervingly, with authority and grace. "You may have a vacation first," they said, and handed her a check.

"Thank you," she said doubtfully. In her life, she had been given the gift of solitude, a knack for it, but now it would be of no professional use. She would have to become a people person.

"A *peeper* person?" queried her mother on the phone from Pittsburgh.

"*People*," said Abby.

"Oh, those," said her mother, and she sighed the sigh of death, though she was strong as a brick.

◊    ◊

Of all Abby's fanciful ideas for self-improvement (the inspirational video, the breathing exercises, the hypnosis class), the Blarney Stone, with its whoring barter of eloquence for love—O GIFT OF

GAB, read the T-shirts—was perhaps the most extreme. Perhaps. There had been, after all, her marriage to Bob, her boyfriend of many years, after her dog, Randolph, had died of kidney failure and marriage to Bob seemed the only way to overcome her grief. Of course, she had always admired the idea of marriage, the citizenship and public speech of it, the innocence rebestowed, and Bob was big and comforting. But he didn't have a lot to say. He was not a verbal man. Rage gave him syntax—but it just wasn't enough! Soon Abby had begun to keep him as a kind of pet, while she quietly looked for distractions of depth and consequence. She looked for words. She looked for ways with words. She worked hard to befriend a lyricist from New York—a tepid, fair-haired, violet-eyed bachelor—she and most of the doctors' wives and arts administrators in town. He was newly arrived, owned no car, and wore the same tan blazer every day. "Water, water everywhere but not a drop to drink," said the bachelor lyricist once, listening wanly to the female chirp of his phone messages. In his apartment, there were no novels or bookcases. There was one chair, as well as a large television set, the phone machine, a rhyming dictionary continuously renewed from the library, and a coffee table. Women brought him meals, professional introductions, jingle commissions, and cash grants. In return, he brought them small piebald stones from the beach, or a pretty weed from the park. He would stand behind the coffee table and recite his own songs, then step back and wait fearfully to be seduced. To be lunged at and devoured by the female form was, he believed, something akin to applause. Sometimes he would produce a rented lute and say, "Here, I've just composed a melody to go with my Creation verse. Sing along with me."

And Abby would stare at him and say, "But I don't know the tune. I haven't heard it yet. You just made it up, you said."

Oh, the vexations endured by a man of poesy! He stood paralyzed behind the coffee table, and when Abby did at last step forward, just to touch him, to take his pulse, perhaps, *to capture one of his arms in an invisible blood-pressure cuff*! he crumpled and shrank. "Please don't think I'm some kind of emotional Epstein-Barr," he said, quoting from other arguments he'd had with

women. "I'm not indifferent or dispassionate. I'm calm. I'm romantic, but I'm calm. I have appetites, but I'm very calm about
them."

When she went back to her husband—"Honey, you're home!"
Bob exclaimed—she lasted only a week. Shouldn't it have lasted
longer—the mix of loneliness and lust and habit she always felt
with Bob, the mix that was surely love, for it so often felt like love,
how could it not be love, surely nature intended it to be, surely nature with its hurricanes and hail was counting on this to suffice?
Bob smiled at her and said nothing. And the next day, she booked
a flight to Ireland.

◊   ◊

How her mother became part of the trip, Abby still couldn't exactly recall. It had something to do with a stick shift: how Abby
had never learned to drive one. "In my day and age," said her
mother, "everyone learned. We all learned. Women had skills. They
knew how to cook and sew. Now women have no skills."

The stick shifts were half the rental price of the automatics.

"If you're looking for a driver," hinted her mother, "I can still
see the road."

"That's good," said Abby.

"And your sister Theda's spending the summer at your aunt's
camp again." Theda had Down's syndrome, and the family adored
her. Every time Abby visited, Theda would shout, "Look at you!"
and throw her arms around her in a terrific hug. "Theda's, of
course, sweet as ever," said her mother, "which is more than I can
say about some people."

"That's probably true."

"I'd like to see Ireland while I can. Your father, when he was
alive, never wanted to. I'm Irish, you know."

"I know. One-sixteenth."

"That's right. Of course, your father was Scottish, which is a totally different thing."

Abby sighed. "It seems to me that *Japanese* would be a totally
different thing."

*"Japanese?"* hooted her mother. "Japanese is close."

◊   ◊

And so in the middle of June, they landed at the Dublin airport together. "We're going to go all around this island, every last peninsula," said Mrs. Mallon in the airport parking lot, revving the
engine of their rented Ford Fiesta, "because that's just the kind of
crazy Yuppies we are."

Abby felt sick from the flight; and sitting on what should be the
driver's side but without a steering wheel suddenly seemed emblematic of something.

Her mother lurched out of the parking lot and headed for the
nearest roundabout, crossing into the other lane only twice. "I'll
get the hang of this," she said. She pushed her glasses farther up on
her nose and Abby could see for the first time that her mother's
eyes were milky with age. Her steering was jerky and her foot
jumped around on the floor, trying to find the clutch. Perhaps this
had been a mistake.

"Go straight, Mom," said Abby, looking at her map.

They zigged and zagged to the north, up and away from Dublin,
planning to return to it at the end, but now heading toward
Drogheda, Abby snatching up the guidebook and then the map
again and then the guidebook, and Mrs. Mallon shouting, "What?"
or "Left?" or "This can't be right; let me see that thing." The Irish
countryside opened up before them, its pastoral patchwork and
stone walls and its chimney aroma of turf fires like some other
century, its small stands of trees, abutting fields populated with
wildflowers and sheep dung and cut sod and cows with ear tags,
beautiful as women. Perhaps fairy folk lived in the trees! Abby
saw immediately that to live amid the magic feel of this place would
be necessarily to believe in magic. To live here would make you su-
perstitious, warm-hearted with secrets, unrealistic. If you were literal, or practical, you would have to move—or you would have to
drink.

They drove uncertainly past signs to places unmarked on the
map. They felt lost—but not in an uncharming way. The old narrow roads with their white side markers reminded Abby of the va-
cations the family had taken when she was little, the cow-country

car trips through New England or Virginia—in those days before there were interstates, or plastic cups, or a populace depressed by asphalt and french fries. Ireland was a trip into the past of America. It was years behind, unmarred, like a story or a dream or a clear creek. I'm a child again, Abby thought. I'm back. And just as when she was a child, she suddenly had to go to the bathroom.

"I have to go to the bathroom," she said. To their left was a sign that said ROAD WORKS AHEAD, and underneath it someone had scrawled, "No, it doesn't."

Mrs. Mallon veered the car over to the left and slammed on the brakes. There were some black-faced sheep haunch-marked in bright blue and munching grass near the road.

"Here?" asked Abby.

"I don't want to waste time stopping somewhere else and having to buy something. You can go behind that wall."

"Thanks," said Abby, groping in her pocketbook for Kleenex. She missed her own apartment. She missed her neighborhood. She missed the plentiful U-Pump-Itt's, where, she often said, at least they spelled *pump* right! She got out and hiked back down the road a little way. On one of the family road trips thirty years ago, when she and Theda had had to go to the bathroom, their father had stopped the car and told them to "go to the bathroom in the woods." They had wandered through the woods for twenty minutes, looking for the bathroom, before they came back out to tell him that they hadn't been able to find it. Her father had looked perplexed, then amused, and then angry—his usual pattern.

Now Abby struggled over a short stone wall and hid, squatting, eyeing the sheep warily. She was spacey with jet lag, and when she got back to the car, she realized she'd left the guidebook back on a stone and had to turn around and retrieve it.

"There," she said, getting back in the car.

Mrs. Mallon shifted into gear. "I always feel that if people would just be like animals and excrete here and there rather than in a single agreed-upon spot, we wouldn't have any pollution."

Abby nodded. "That's brilliant, Mom."

"Is it?"

They stopped briefly at an English manor house, to see the natural world cut up into moldings and rugs, wool and wood captive and squared, the earth stolen and embalmed and shellacked. Abby wanted to leave. "Let's leave," she whispered.

"What is it with you?" complained her mother. From there, they visited a neolithic passage grave, its floor plan like a birth in reverse, its narrow stone corridor spilling into a high, round room. They took off their sunglasses and studied the Celtic curlicues. "Older than the pyramids," announced the guide, though he failed to address its most important feature, Abby felt: its deadly maternal metaphor.

"Are you still too nervous to cross the border to Northern Ireland?" asked Mrs. Mallon.

"Uh-huh." Abby bit at her thumbnail, tearing the end of it off like a tiny twig.

"Oh, come on," said her mother. "Get a grip."

And so they crossed the border into the North, past the flak-jacketed soldiers patrolling the neighborhoods and barbed wire of Newry, young men holding automatic weapons and walking backward, block after block, their partners across the street, walking forward, on the watch. Helicopters flapped above. "This is a little scary," said Abby.

"It's all show," said Mrs. Mallon breezily.

"It's a scary show."

"If you get scared easily."

Which was quickly becoming the theme of their trip—Abby could see that already. That Abby had no courage and her mother did. And that it had forever been that way.

"You scare too easily," said her mother. "You always did. When you were a child, you wouldn't go into a house unless you were re-assured there were no balloons in it."

"I didn't like balloons."

"And you were scared on the plane coming over," said her mother.

Abby grew defensive. "Only when the flight attendant said there was no coffee because the percolator was broken. Didn't you find that alarming? And then after all that slamming, they still couldn't get one of the overhead bins shut." Abby remembered this like a distant, bitter memory, though it had only been yesterday. The plane had taken off with a terrible shudder, and when it proceeded with the rattle of an old subway car, particularly over Greenland, the flight attendant had gotten on the address system to announce there was nothing to worry about, especially when you think about "how heavy air really is."

Now her mother thought she was Tarzan. "I want to go on that rope bridge I saw in the guidebook," she said.

On page 98 in the guidebook was a photograph of a rope-and-board bridge slung high between two cliffs. It was supposed to be for fishermen, but tourists were allowed, though they were cautioned about strong winds.

"Why do you want to go on the rope bridge?" asked Abby.

"*Why?*" replied her mother, who then seemed stuck and fell silent.

◊    ◊

For the next two days, they drove east and to the north, skirting Belfast, along the coastline, past old windmills and sheep farms, and up out onto vertiginous cliffs that looked out toward Scotland, a pale sliver on the sea. They stayed at a tiny stucco bed-and-breakfast, one with a thatched roof like Cleopatra bangs. They slept lumpily, and in the morning in the breakfast room with its large front window, they ate their cereal and rashers and black and white pudding in an exhausted way, going through the motions of good guesthood—"Yes, the troubles," they agreed, for who could say for certain whom you were talking to? It wasn't like race-riven America, where you always knew. Abby nodded. Out the window, there was a breeze, but she couldn't hear the faintest rustle of it. She could only see it silently moving the dangling branches of the sun-sequined spruce, just slightly, like objects hanging from a rearview mirror in someone else's car.

She charged the bill to her Visa, tried to lift both bags, and then just lifted her own.

"Good-bye! Thank you!" she and her mother called to their host. Back in the car, briefly, Mrs. Mallon began to sing "Tooraloora-loora." " 'Over in Killarney, many years ago,' " she warbled. Her voice was husky, vibrating, slightly flat, coming in just under each note like a saucer under a cup.

And so they drove on. The night before, a whole day could have shape and design. But when it was upon you, it could vanish tragically to air.

They came to the sign for the rope bridge.

"I want to do this," said Mrs. Mallon, and swung the car sharply right. They crunched into a gravel parking lot and parked; the bridge was a quarter-mile walk from there. In the distance, dark clouds roiled like a hemorrhage, and the wind was picking up. Rain mizzled the windshield.

"I'm going to stay here," said Abby.

"You are?"

"Yeah."

"Whatever," said her mother in a disgusted way, and she got out, scowling, and trudged down the path to the bridge, disappearing beyond a curve.

Abby waited, now feeling the true loneliness of this trip. She realized she missed Bob and his warm, quiet confusion; how he sat on the rug in front of the fireplace, where her dog, Randolph, used to sit; sat there beneath the five Christmas cards they'd received and placed on the mantel—five, including the one from the paperboy—sat there picking at his feet, or naming all the fruits in his fruit salad, remarking life's great variety! or asking what was wrong (in his own silent way), while poking endlessly at a smoldering log. She thought, too, about poor Randolph, at the vet, with his patchy fur and begging, dying eyes. And she thought about the pale bachelor lyricist, how he had once come to see her, and how he hadn't even placed enough pressure on the doorbell to make it ring, and so had stood there waiting on the porch, holding a purple coneflower, until she just happened to walk by the front window and see him standing there. *O poetry!* When she invited him in, and he gave her the flower and sat down to decry the coded bloom and doom of all things, decry as well his own unearned deathlessness, how everything hurtles toward oblivion, except words, which assemble themselves in time like molecules in space, for God was an act—an act!—of language, it hadn't seemed silly to her, not really, at least not *that* silly.

The wind was gusting. She looked at her watch, worried now about her mother. She turned on the radio to find a weather report, though the stations all seemed to be playing strange, redone versions of American pop songs from 1970. Every so often, there was a two-minute quiz show—Who is the president of France? Is a tomato a vegetable or a fruit?—questions that the caller rarely if ever answered correctly, which made it quite embarrassing to listen to. Why did they do it? Puzzles, quizzes, game shows. Abby knew from AST that a surprising percentage of those taking the college entrance exams never actually applied to college. People just loved a test. Wasn't that true? People loved to put themselves to one.

Her mother was now knocking on the glass. She was muddy and wet. Abby unlocked the door and pushed it open. "Was it worth it?" Abby asked.

Her mother got in, big and dank and puffing. She started the car without looking at her daughter. "What a bridge," she said finally.

◊    ◊

The next day, they made their way along the Antrim coast, through towns bannered with Union Jacks and Scottish hymns, down to Derry with its barbed wire and IRA scrawlings on the city walls— "John Major is a Zionist Jew" ("Hello," said a British officer when they stopped to stare)—and then escaping across bandit country, and once more down across the border into the south, down the Donegal coast, its fishing villages like some old, never-was Cape Cod. Staring out through the windshield, off into the horizon, Abby began to think that all the beauty and ugliness and turbulence one found scattered through nature, one could also find in people themselves, all collected there, all together in a single place. No matter what terror or loveliness the earth could produce— winds, seas—a person could produce the same, lived with the same, lived with all that mixed-up nature swirling inside, every bit. There was nothing as complex in the world—no flower or stone— as a single hello from a human being.

◊   ◊

Once in a while, Abby and her mother broke their silences with
talk of Mrs. Mallon's job as office manager at a small flashlight
company—"I had to totally rearrange our insurance policies. The
dental and Major Medical were eating our lunch!"—or with questions about the route signs, or the black dots signifying the auto
deaths. But mostly, her mother wanted to talk about Abby's shaky
marriage and what she was going to do. "Look, another ruined
abbey," she took to saying every time they passed a heap of medieval stones.

"When you going back to Bob?"

"I went back," said Abby. "But then I left again. Oops."

Her mother sighed. "Women of your generation are always hoping for some other kind of romance than the one they have," said
Mrs. Mallon. "Aren't they?"

"Who knows?" said Abby. She was starting to feel a little tight-
lipped with her mother, crammed into this space together like as-
tronauts. She was starting to have a highly inflamed sense of event:
a single word rang and vibrated. The slightest movement could an-
noy, the breath, the odor. Unlike her sister, Theda, who had always
remained sunny and cheerfully intimate with everyone, Abby had
always been darker and left to her own devices; she and her mother
had never been very close. When Abby was a child, her mother had
always repelled her a bit—the oily smell of her hair, her belly but-
ton like a worm curled in a pit, the sanitary napkins in the bathroom wastebasket, horrid as a war, then later strewn along the curb
by raccoons who would tear them from the trash cans at night.
Once at a restaurant, when she was little, Abby had burst into an
unlatched ladies' room stall, only to find her mother sitting there in
a dazed and unseemly way, peering out at her from the toilet seat
like a cuckoo in a clock.

There were things one should never know about another
person.

Later, Abby decided that perhaps it hadn't been her mother
at all.

Yet now here she and her mother were, sharing the tiniest of cars, reunited in a wheeled and metal womb, sharing small double beds in bed-and-breakfasts, waking up with mouths stale and close upon each other, or backs turned and rocking in angry-seeming humps. *The land of ire!* Talk of Abby's marriage and its possible demise trotted before them on the road like a herd of sheep, insomnia's sheep, and it made Abby want to have a gun.

"I never bothered with conventional romantic fluff," said Mrs. Mallon. "I wasn't the type. I always worked, and I was practical, put myself forward, and got things done and over with. If I liked a man, I asked him out myself. That's how I met your father. I asked him out. I even proposed the marriage."

"I know."

"And then I stayed with him until the day he died. Actually, three days after. He was a good man." She paused. "Which is more than I can say about some people."

Abby didn't say anything.

"Bob's a good man," added Mrs. Mallon.

"I didn't say he wasn't."

There was silence again between them now as the countryside once more unfolded its quilt of greens, the old roads triggering memories as if it were a land she had traveled long ago, its mix of luck and unluck like her own past; it seemed stuck in time, like a daydream or a book. Up close the mountains were craggy, scabby with rock and green, like a buck's antlers trying to lose their fuzz. But distance filled the gaps with moss. Wasn't that the truth? Abby sat quietly, glugging Ballygowan water from a plastic bottle and popping Extra Strong Mints. Perhaps she should turn on the radio, listen to one of the call-in quizzes or to the news. But then her mother would take over, fiddle and retune. Her mother was always searching for country music, songs with the words *devil woman.* She loved those.

"Promise me one thing," said Mrs. Mallon.

"What?" said Abby.

"That you'll try with Bob."

At what price? Abby wanted to yell, but she and her mother were too old for that now.

Mrs. Mallon continued, thoughtfully, with the sort of pseudo-wisdom she donned now that she was sixty. "Once you're with a man, you have to sit still with him. As scary as it seems. You have to be brave and learn to reap the benefits of inertia," and here she gunned the motor to pass a tractor on a curve. LOOSE CHIPPINGS said the sign. HIDDEN DIP. But Abby's mother drove as if these were mere cocktail party chatter. A sign ahead showed six black dots.

"Yeah," said Abby, clutching the dashboard. "Dad was inert. Dad was inert, except that once every three years he jumped up and socked somebody in the mouth."

"That's not true."

"It's basically true."

In Killybegs, they followed the signs for Donegal City. "You women today," Mrs. Mallon said. "You expect too much."

◊   ◊

"If it's Tuesday, this must be Sligo," said Abby. She had taken to making up stupid jokes. "What do you call a bus with a soccer team on it?"

"What?" They passed a family of gypsies, camped next to a mountain of car batteries they hoped to sell.

"A football coach." Sometimes Abby laughed raucously, and sometimes not at all. Sometimes she just shrugged. She was waiting for the Blarney Stone. That was all she'd come here for, so everything else she could endure.

They stopped at a bookshop to get a better map and inquire, perhaps, as to a bathroom. Inside, there were four customers: two priests reading golf books, and a mother with her tiny son, who traipsed after her along the shelves, begging, "Please, Mummy, just a wee book, Mummy. Please just a wee book." There was no better map. There was no bathroom. "Sorry," the clerk said, and one of the priests glanced up quickly. Abby and her mother went next door to look at the Kinsale smocks and wool sweaters—tiny cardigans that young Irish children, on sweltering summer days of seventy-one degrees, wore on the beach, over their bathing suits. "So cute," said Abby, and the two of them wandered through the store, touching things. In the back by the wool caps, Abby's mother found a marionette hanging from a ceiling hook and began to play with it a little, waving its arms to the store music, which was a Beethoven concerto. Abby went to pay for a smock, ask about a bathroom or a good pub, and when she came back, her mother was still there, transfixed, conducting the concerto with the puppet. Her face was arranged in girlish joy, luminous, as Abby rarely saw it. When the concerto was over, Abby handed her a bag. "Here," she said, "I bought you a smock."

Mrs. Mallon let go of the marionette, and her face darkened. "I never had a real childhood," she said, taking the bag and looking off into the middle distance. "Being the oldest, I was always my mother's confidante. I always had to act grown-up and responsible. Which wasn't my natural nature." Abby steered her toward the door. "And then when I really was grown up, there was Theda, who needed all my time, and your father of course, with his demands. But then there was you. You I liked. You I could leave alone."

"I bought you a smock," Abby said again.

They used the bathroom at O'Hara's pub, bought a single mineral water and split it, then went on to the Drumcliff cemetery to see the dead Yeatses. Then they sped on toward Sligo City to find a room, and the next day were up and out to Knock to watch lame women, sick women, women who wanted to get pregnant ("Knocked up," said Abby) rub their rosaries on the original stones of the shrine. They drove down to Clifden, around Connemara, to Galway and Limerick—"There once were two gals from America, one named Abby and her mother named Erica. . . ." They sang, minstrel speed demons around the Ring of Kerry, its palm trees and blue and pink hydrangea like a set from an operetta. "Playgirls of the Western World!" exclaimed her mother. They came to rest, at dark, near Ballylickey, in a bed-and-breakfast, a former hunting lodge, in a glen just off the ring. They ate a late supper of toddies and a soda bread their hostess called "Curranty Dick."

"Don't I know it," said Mrs. Mallon. Which depressed Abby, like a tacky fixture in a room, and so she excused herself and went upstairs, to bed.

◊       ◊

It was the next day, through Ballylickey, Bantry, Skibbereen, and Cork, that they entered Blarney. At the castle, the line to kiss the stone was long, hot, and frightening. It jammed the tiny winding stairs of the castle's suffocating left tower, and people pressed themselves against the dark wall to make room for others who had lost their nerve and were coming back down.

"This is ridiculous," said Abby. But by the time they'd reached the top, her annoyance had turned to anxiety. To kiss the stone, she saw, people had to lie on their backs out over a parapet, stretching their necks out to place their lips on the underside of a supporting wall where the stone was laid. A strange-looking leprechaunish man was squatting at the side of the stone, supposedly to help people arch back, but he seemed to be holding them too loosely, a careless and sadistic glint in his eyes, and some people were changing their minds and going back downstairs, fearful and inarticulate as ever.

"I don't think I can do this," said Abby hesitantly, tying her dark raincoat more tightly around her.

"Of course you can," said her mother. "You've come all this way. This is why you came." Now that they were at the top of the castle, the line seemed to be moving quickly. Abby looked back, and around, and the view was green and rich, and breathtaking, like a photo soaked in dyes.

"Next!" she heard the leprechaun shouting.

Ahead of them, a German woman was struggling to get back up from where the leprechaun had left her. She wiped her mouth and made a face. "That vuz awfhul," she grumbled.

Panic seized Abby. "You know what? I don't want to do this," she said again to her mother. There were only two people ahead of them in line. One of them was now getting down on his back, clutching the iron supports and inching his hands down, arching at the neck and waist to reach the stone, exposing his white throat. His wife stood above him, taking his picture.

"But you came all this way! Don't be a ninny!" Her mother was bullying her again. It never gave her courage; in fact, it deprived her of courage. But it gave her bitterness and impulsiveness, which could look like the same thing.

"Next," said the leprechaun nastily. He hated these people; one could see that. One could see he half-hoped they would go crashing down off the ledge into a heap of raincoats, limbs, and traveler's checks.

"Go on," said Mrs. Mallon.

"I can't," Abby whined. Her mother was nudging and the leprechaun was frowning. "I can't. You go."

"No. Come on. Think of it as a test." Her mother gave her a scowl, unhinged by something lunatic in it. "You work with tests. And in school, you always did well on them."

"For tests, you have to study."

"You studied!"

"I didn't study the right thing."

"Oh, Abby."

"I can't," Abby whispered. "I just don't think I can." She breathed deeply and moved quickly. "Oh—okay." She threw her hat down and fell to the stone floor fast, to get it over with.

"Move back, move back," droned the leprechaun, like a train conductor.

She could feel now no more space behind her back; from her waist up, she was out over air and hanging on only by her clenched hands and the iron rails. She bent her head as far back as she could, but it wasn't far enough.

"Lower," said the leprechaun.

She slid her hands down farther, as if she were doing a trick on a jungle gym. Still, she couldn't see the stone itself, only the castle wall.

"Lower," said the leprechaun.

She slid her hands even lower, bent her head back, her chin skyward, could feel the vertebrae of her throat pressing out against the skin, and this time she could see the stone. It was about the size of a microwave oven and was covered with moisture and dirt and lipstick marks in the shape of lips—lavender, apricot, red. It seemed very unhygienic for a public event, filthy and wet, and so now instead of giving it a big smack, she blew a peck at it, then shouted, "Okay, help me up, please," and the leprechaun helped her back up.

Abby stood and brushed herself off. Her raincoat was covered with whitish mud. "Eeyuhh," she said. But she had done it! At least sort of. She put her hat back on. She tipped the leprechaun a pound. She didn't know how she felt. She felt nothing. Finally, these dares one made oneself commit didn't change a thing. They were all a construction of wish and string and distance.

"Now my turn," said her mother with a kind of reluctant determination, handing Abby her sunglasses, and as her mother got down stiffly, inching her way toward the stone, Abby suddenly saw something she'd never seen before: her mother was terrified. For all her bullying and bravado, her mother was proceeding, and proceeding badly, through a great storm of terror in her brain. As her mother tried to inch herself back toward the stone, Abby, now privy to her bare face, saw that this fierce bonfire of a woman had gone twitchy and melancholic—it was a ruse, all her formidable display. She was only trying to prove something, trying pointlessly to defy and overcome her fears—instead of just learning to live with them, since, hell, you were living with them anyway. "Mom, you okay?" Mrs. Mallon's face was in a grimace, her mouth open and bared. The former auburn of her hair had descended, Abby saw, to her teeth, which she'd let rust with years of coffee and tea.

Now the leprechaun was having to hold her more than he had the other people. "Lower, now lower."

"Oh, God, not any lower," cried Mrs. Mallon.

"You're almost there."

"I don't see it."

"There you got it?" He loosened his grip and let her slip farther.

"Yes," she said. She let out a puckering, spitting sound. But then when she struggled to come back up, she seemed to be stuck. Her legs thrashed out before her; her shoes loosened from her feet; her skirt rode up, revealing the brown tops of her panty hose. She was bent too strangely, from the hips, it seemed, and she was plump and didn't have the stomach muscles to lift herself back up. The leprechaun seemed to be having difficulty.

"Can someone here help me?"

"Oh my God," said Abby, and she and another man in line immediately squatted next to Mrs. Mallon to help her. She was heavy, stiff with fright, and when they had finally lifted her and gotten her sitting, then standing again, she seemed stricken and pale.

A guard near the staircase volunteered to escort her down.

"Would you like that, Mom?" and Mrs. Mallon simply nodded.

"You get in front of us," the guard said to Abby in the singsong accent of County Cork, "just in case she falls." And Abby got in front, her coat taking the updraft and spreading to either side as she circled slowly down into the dungeon-dark of the stairwell, into the black like a bat new to its wings.

◊     ◊

In a square in the center of town, an evangelist was waving a Bible and shouting about "the brevity of life," how it was a thing grabbed by one hand and then gone, escaped through the fingers. "God's word is quick!" he called out.

"Let's go over there," said Abby, and she took her mother to a place called Brady's Public House for a restorative Guinness. "Are you okay?" Abby kept asking. They still had no place to stay that night, and though it remained light quite late, and the inns stayed open until ten, she imagined the two of them temporarily homeless, sleeping under the stars, snacking on slugs. Stars the size of Chicago! Dew like a pixie bath beneath them! They would lick it from their arms.

"I'm fine," she said, waving Abby's questions away. "What a stone!"

"Mom," said Abby, frowning, for she was now wondering about a few things. "When you went across that rope bridge, did you do that okay?"

Mrs. Mallon sighed. "Well, I got the idea of it," she said huffily. "But there were some gusts of wind that caused it to buck a little, and though some people thought that was fun, I had to get down and crawl back. You'll recall there was a little rain."

"You crawled back on your hands and knees?"

"Well, yes," she admitted. "There was a nice Belgian man who helped me." She felt unmasked, no doubt, before her daughter and now gulped at her Guinness.

Abby tried to take a cheerful tone, switching the subject a little, and

it reminded her of Theda, Theda somehow living in her voice, her
larynx suddenly a summer camp for the cheerful and slow. "Well,
look at you!" said Abby. "Do you feel eloquent and confident, now
that you've kissed the stone?"

"Not really." Mrs. Mallon shrugged.

Now that they had kissed it, or sort of, would they become self-
conscious? What would they end up talking about?

Movies, probably. Just as they always had at home. Movies with
scenery, movies with songs.

"How about you?" asked Mrs. Mallon.

"Well," said Abby, "mostly I feel like we've probably caught
strep throat. And yet, and yet . . ." Here she sat up and leaned forward. No tests, or radio quizzes, or ungodly speeches, or songs
brain-dead with biography, or kooky prayers, or shouts, or prolix
conversations that with drink and too much time always revealed
how stupid and mean even the best people were, just simply this:
"A toast. I feel a toast coming on."

"You do?"

"Yes, I do." No one had toasted Abby and Bob at their little
wedding, and that's what had been wrong, she believed now. No
toast. There had been only thirty guests and they had simply eaten
the ham canapes and gone home. How could a marriage go right?
It wasn't that such ceremonies were important in and of themselves. They were nothing. They were zeros. But they were zeros as
placeholders; they held numbers and equations intact. And once
you underwent them, you could move on, know the empty power
of their blessing, and not spend time missing them.

From here on in, she would believe in toasts. One was collecting
itself now, in her head, in a kind of hesitant philately. She gazed
over at her mother and took a deep breath. Perhaps her mother
had never shown Abby affection, not really, but she had given her a
knack for solitude, with its terrible lurches outward, and its smooth
glide back to peace. Abby would toast her for that. It was really the
world that was one's brutal mother, the one that nursed and neglected you, and your own mother was only your sibling in that
world. Abby lifted her glass. "May the worst always be behind you.
May the sun daily warm your arms. . . ." She looked down at her

cocktail napkin for assistance, but there was only a cartoon of a big-chested colleen, two shamrocks over her breasts. Abby looked back up. *God's word is quick!* "May your car always start—" But perhaps God might also begin with tall, slow words; the belly bloat of a fib; the distended tale. "And may you always have a clean shirt," she continued, her voice growing gallant, public and loud, "and a holding roof, healthy children and good cabbages—and may you be with me in my heart, Mother, as you are now, in this place; always and forever—like a flaming light."

There was noise in the pub.

*Blank* is to childhood as journey is to lips.

"Right," said Mrs. Mallon, looking into her stout in a concentrated, bright-eyed way. She had never been courted before, not once in her entire life, and now she blushed, ears on fire, lifted her pint, and drank.

### For the Literary Traveler

Lorrie Moore's characters drive the perimeter of Ireland—the Antrim coast road, Donegal, Skibbereen—before arriving in BLARNEY, but if you're coming straight from Cork City, the easiest route is up Frank O'Connor's Blarney Street, the longest street in Cork, and then a pastoral five miles out of the city before landing in tourist hell. ("Blarney, along with Killarney, is probably the best known and most visited place in Ireland," reads the Tourist Board's guide to Cork.) Parking takes time, the line at the CASTLE is as Moore describes it, and the crowds ... well, by the time you've come down for air, Beckett's "Solitude is paradise" has come to feel like purest truth. Outside the castle, there are lots of shops and shoppers around the green in the center of the village. "Marilyn! Where yuh goin'? Don't go in there," a tourist shouted down a packed sidewalk at a woman who was heading into Blarney Woolens. "I already looked. There's nuthin' there." "Nuthin'?" screamed Marilyn, incredulous. "Whud I just say? *Nuthin'!*"

But as the site of the climax of this edgy mother-daughter pilgrim-

age, Blarney is inspired. After the rite of kissing THE STONE OF ELO-
QUENCE, the ultimate tourist nightmare (though the view from the
parapet is a pretty distraction), you don't expect a cure for Abby Mallon. So when it happens, it feels like a miracle. The castle that houses
the Stone, a massive keep with stepped battlements, was originally a
fortress of the MacCarthys, built around 1446; here they maintained
one of Ireland's longest-lived bardic schools. The term *blarney* is supposed to have been coined by Queen Elizabeth I, who, exasperated by
the unfulfilled promises of submission from Dermot MacCarthy, declared angrily, "This is all Blarney; what he says he never means." A few
years before her time, in 1540, the castle's poet, Donal MacCarthy invoked as true the nonverbal communication of lovers: "In language
beyond learning's touch/Passion can teach—/Speak in that speech beyond reproach/The body's speech."

The Irish, whether poets or peasants, are never at a loss for words,
or so the myth would have it. (William Trevor regards "the blarney and
the begorrah" as the curse of Irish writing, "born of whimsy and a desire to please the visitor or the family of the big house," signifying "an
innate inferiority complex in both life and art.") But it is the problem
of language, its insufficiency or incapacity to connect people on the
level of feeling, that nags at Moore's women on the road. The ending
shows that somewhere along her Irish-American or Irish itinerary
Moore picked up the words of a traditional Irish blessing, a pure piece
of prayer or blarney, depending on your temperament:

> *May the road rise to meet you,*
> *May the wind be always at your back,*
> *The sun shine warm upon your face,*
> *The rain fall soft upon your fields,*
> *And until we meet again, may God hold you in*
> *the hollow of his hand.*

# Elizabeth Bowen

## 1899–1973

*Though she lived mostly in England, novelist Elizabeth Bowen spent many summers and holidays at Bowen's Court, her family's Big House in North Cork ever since the first Bowen came to Ireland as a soldier in Cromwell's army. In two of her many novels,* The Last September *(1929) and* A World of Love *(1955), and in a number of short stories, Ireland is at the affectionate center—Bowen always called herself "an Irish novelist." In 1942 she published* Bowen's Court, *a history of the house, writing most of it while working as an air raid warden during the blitz in London. Poor finances forced her to sell the house in 1959 (the new owner demolished it the following year), but she revised* Bowen's Court *in 1963 at the request of her publishers.*

FROM *BOWEN'S COURT*

Up in the north-east corner of County Cork is a stretch of limestone country—open, airy, not quite flat; it is just perceptibly tilted from north to south, and the fields undulate in a smooth flowing way. Dark knolls and screens of trees, the network of hedges, abrupt stony ridges, slate glints from roofs give the landscape a featured look—but the prevailing impression is, emptiness. This is a part of Ireland with no lakes, but the sky's movement of clouds reflects itself everywhere as it might on water, rounding the trees with bloom and giving the grass a sheen. In the airy silence, any sound travels a long way. The streams and rivers, sunk in their valleys, are not seen until you come down to them.

Across the base of this tract of country the river Blackwater flows west to east, into the County Waterford. South of the Blackwater, from which they rise up steeply, Nagles Mountains cut off any further view. Behind Fermoy town these mountains end in a steep bluff: the main road from Cork to Dublin crosses the bridge at Fermoy, then runs due north over the Kilworth hills that close in this tract on the east. North of Kilworth lies Mitchelstown; above Mitchelstown the Galtees rise to powerful coloured peaks. Galtymore, the third highest mountain in Ireland, dominates this northeast corner of Cork. After their climax in Galtymore the Galtees drop into foothills, the Ballyhouras—this range of small shapely mountains borders the County Limerick and slides gently south, in promontories of bogland, into the County Cork fields. The Ballyhouras, forming its northern boundary, face down on Nagles Mountains across the open country of which I speak. The two blue lines, with space and a hidden river between them, run roughly parallel.

To the west extends a long flattish distance, beyond which, though only on very clear days, the Kerry Mountains are to be seen. The country in which Bowen's Court stands is, thus, squared in by hills or mountains on three sides, but melts off into the light and clouds of the west.

This limestone country is pitted with kilns and quarries; the hard white bye-roads run over rock. Our two rivers, the Funcheon and the Awbeg, have hollowed out for themselves, on their courses south to the Blackwater, rocky twisting valleys. Here and there down the valleys the limestone makes cliffs or amphitheatres. In places the rivers flow between steep woods; in places their valleys are open, shallow and lush—there are marshy reaches trodden by cattle, fluttered over by poplars from the embanked lanes. Herons cross these in their leisurely flopping flight; water peppermint grows among the rushes; the orchis and yellow wild iris flower here at the beginning of June. Lonely stone bridges are come on round turns of the stream, and old keeps or watch towers, called castles, command the valleys: some are so broken and weathered that they look like rocks, some have been almost blotted out by the ivy; some are intact shells whose stairs you can still climb.

There are mills on both rivers—one great mill is in ruins—and swans on the Funcheon and the Awbeg. Not far from the Awbeg, under Spenser's castle, there is a marsh where seagulls breed in spring. . . .

◊     ◊

Yes, there was the picture of peace—in the house, in the country round. Like all pictures, it did not quite correspond with any reality. Or, you might have called the country a magic mirror, reflecting something that could not really exist. That illusion—peace at its most ecstatic—I held to, to sustain me throughout war. I suppose that everyone, fighting or just enduring, carried within him one private image, one peaceful scene. Mine was Bowen's Court. War made me that image out of a house built of anxious history.

And so great and calming was the authority of the light and quiet round Bowen's Court that it survived war-time. And it did more than that, it survived the house. It remains with me now that the house has gone . . .

◊     ◊

Loss has not been entire. . . . There is a sort of perpetuity about livingness, and it is part of the character of Bowen's Court to be, in sometimes its silent way, very much alive.

### For the Literary Traveler

Crossing the highlands of the BLACKWATER VALLEY (on the N73 northeast of Mallow) between the BALLYHOURAS to the north and the NAGLES MOUNTAINS to the south—under a late afternoon sun you think you're seeing every shade of green the earth holds—you come to a sign on the left for FARAHY CHURCH AND CEMETERY and the site of BOWEN'S COURT. You can walk through the gates up the long drive across the fields where the house once stood and Bowen entertained her many literary friends, including Virginia Woolf. "We spent a night with the Bowens," she wrote to Vanessa. "Elizabeth's home was merely a great stone box, but full of Italian mantelpieces and decayed 18th Century furniture, and carpets all in holes—however they insisted on keeping up a ramshackle kind of state, dressing for dinner and so on." Another lane, left of the gates, leads to Farahy Church (1720), which Bowen, a lifelong churchgoer, attended. (In *Seven Winters: Memories of a Dublin Childhood*, she said of her Sunday mornings in Dublin's St. Stephen's, "The interior ... had authority—here one could feel a Presence, were it only the presence of an idea.") She's buried behind the church in Farahy's small graveyard, where, except for birdsong and the wind from the trees in Bowen's Court demesne, the silence is absolute. Every August, writers and scholars, including Bowen's biographer, Victoria Glendinning, assemble in this tiny church for lectures and hymn singing in Elizabeth Bowen's memory.

To walk the lovely BALLYHOURAS of Bowen Country—the route takes in the GLEN OF AHERLOW—contact the Ballyhoura Failte Society, (tel. 063-91300), Kilfinane, County Limerick, for the "Ballyhoura Way Map Guide." Or use Discovery Series Maps 65, 66, 73, and 74. From the summits, you can see the six counties of the province of Munster and the rolling fields of the Golden Vale.

Near Bowen's Court (three miles northwest of Doneraile on the road to Charleville) are the ruins of the poet Edmund Spenser's KILCOLMAN CASTLE and what's left of the three thousand acres of his estate, which, as secretary to the savage Lord Grey de Wilton, he came to possess in 1586 after the Earl of Desmond had been forced to forfeit them. Here Spenser (1552–1599) wrote the first three books of *The Faerie Queen* and his wedding poem, "Epithalamion." Though, like Bowen, he loved the Cork countryside, there was nothing tenderhearted about the civil servant Spenser's approach to the management of the native people who were his neighbors. In *A View of the Present State of Ireland* (1596), he advocated solving the problem of the dispossessed Irish with a strategic famine resulting in a genocide "which they themselves had wrought." "Surely ... there is no compassion to be had." When the Irish, who'd had their lands confiscated and turned over to settlers such as Spenser (and a century later the first Bowen) hid in the forests, the Elizabethans chopped down the trees, leaving the bare slopes and plains one sees everywhere today. Trees were sacred presences in pre-Christian Celtic religion. But the Protestant English, partial to a tamed and domesticated environment, associated marshy places and "wylde" forests with Irish Catholicism. Not all the forests fell at once, however. In 1598, the Irish hiding in the woods took revenge, burning Spenser out. Bowen tells the rest of the story in her memoir.

The American poet Marianne Moore (1887–1972), the daughter of an Irish father whom she never met, wrote poems about Shaw, George Moore, Yeats, and also about Spenser's Ireland:

> *Spenser's Ireland*
> *has not altered;*
> > *a place as kind as it is green,*
> *the greenest place I've never seen.*
> *Every name is a tune.*

People thought this poem was about loving Ireland, but as Elizabeth Bishop writes in her memoir of Moore, it was about *disapproving* of it. However, "she liked being of Irish descent: her great-great grandfather had run away from a house in Merrion Square," and to Ezra Pound she described herself as "pure Celt."

# Eibhlín Dhubh Ní Chonaill
## BLACK-HAIRED EILEEN O'CONNELL
### c. 1743–c. 1800

*The story behind what is considered the finest love poem in the Irish language is a tangle of facts and fictions. The poet, Eileen O'Connell, widowed after six months of marriage to an elderly man, took one look at handsome Art O'Leary beside the market house in Macroom, Cork (surely the most famous market house in Irish literary history),*

*and never looked back. Despite her family's disapproval (the aunt of
the "Liberator," Daniel O'Connell, Eileen was raised at Derrynane in
Kerry), Eileen left her father's house in 1767 and married O'Leary, a
hot-tempered and womanizing young Irishman with a captain's com-
mission in the Hungarian army. Their home was in West Cork, outside
of Macroom, and by 1774, the date of the poem's composition, they
were expecting their third child. Under the Penal Laws then in force in
Ireland, O'Leary, as a Catholic, was prohibited from owning a horse
worth more than five pounds. When a Protestant named Abraham
Morris offered O'Leary five pounds for his horse—by all accounts "a
splendid mare"—O'Leary, though required by law to accept the offer,
instead challenged Morris to a duel, for which Morris had him outlawed. O'Leary, with Eileen's help, went into hiding, but on May 4,
1774, he was ambushed and shot dead by British soldiers. The horse is
said to have returned home, whereupon Eileen rode out to Carriganimma, where his body was lying. She is supposed to have begun her
poem there and completed it during his wake. (The voices of Art's sister and father are also heard in the poem.) The poem is a traditional
lament or keen, with its incantatory verses about the dead person's dis-
tinctions interrupted by the loud wailing of men and women, and parts
of it are Eileen's responses to her mean-spirited sister-in-law, who had
criticized the newly widowed, pregnant mother of two small children
for not having been a full-time mourner at her husband's wake.*

## THE LAMENT FOR ART O'LEARY

*Translated by Frank O'Connor*

*My love and my delight,
The day I saw you first
Beside the market-house
I had eyes for nothing else
And love for none but you.
I left my father's house
And crossed the hills with you,
And it was no bad choice.
You gave me everything:*

*Parlours whitened for me,*
*Rooms painted for me,*
*Ovens reddened for me,*
*Loaves baked for me,*
*Roast spitted for me,*
*Beds made for me;*
*I took my ease on flock*
*Until the milking time*
*And later if I pleased.*

*My mind remembers*
*That bright spring day,*
*How a hat with a band of gold became you,*
*Your silver-hilted sword,*
*Your manly right hand,*
*Your horse on his mettle,*
*The foes around you*
*Cowed by your air*
*For when you rode by*
*On your white-nosed mare*
*The English bowed*
*To the ground before you,*
*Out of no love for you,*
*Out of their fear,*
*Though sweetheart of my soul,*
*The English killed you. . . .*

*My love and my secret*
*'Tis well you were suited*
*In a five-ribbed stocking*
*Your legs top-booted,*
*Your cornered Caroline*
*Your cracking whip.*
*Your sprightly gelding—*
*Oh, many's the girl*
*That would stop to behold you!*

*My love and my sweetheart,*
*When I come back*

*The little lad Conor*
*And Fiach the baby*
*Will ask me surely*
*Where I left their father;*
*I will say with anguish*
*'Twas in Kilnamartyr—*
*They will call the father*
*That will never answer.*

*My love and my darling*
*That I never thought dead*
*Till your horse came to me*
*With bridle trailing,*
*All blood from forehead*
*To polished saddle*
*Where you should be,*
*Sitting or standing;*
*I gave one leap to the threshold,*
*A second to the gate,*
*A third upon her back.*

*I clapped my hands*
*And off at a gallop,*
*I did not linger*
*Till I found you dead*
*By a little furze-bush,*
*Without pope or bishop*
*Or priest or cleric*
*One prayer to whisper,*
*But an old, old woman*
*And her cloak about you,*
*And your blood in torrents,*
*Art O'Leary,*
*I did not wipe it up,*
*I cupped it in my hands.*

*My love and my delight,*
*Rise up now beside me,*
*And let me lead you home!*

*Until I make a feast*
*And I shall roast your meat,*
*And send for company*
*And call the harpers in;*
*And I shall make your bed*
*Of soft and snowy sheets,*
*And blankets dark and rough*
*To warm the beloved limbs*
*An autumn blast has chilled.*

(His sister speaks)

*My love and my treasure!*
*What fine lovely lady*
*From Cork of the white sails*
*To the bridge of Tomey*
*With her dowry gathered*
*And cows at pasture*
*Would sleep alone*
*The night they waked you?*

(Eileen O'Connell replies)

*My darling, do not believe*
*One word she is saying!*
*It is a lie*
*That I slept while others*
*Sat up and waked you—*
*'Twas no sleep that took me*
*But the children crying:*
*They would not close their eyes*
*Without me beside them.*

*Oh, people, do not believe*
*Any lying story.*
*There is no woman in Ireland*
*That had slept beside him*
*And borne him three children*
*But would cry out*
*After Art O'Leary*

*That lies dead before me*
*Since yesterday morning.*

*Grief on you, Morris!*
*Heart's blood and bowel's blood!*
*May your eyes go blind*
*And your knees be broken!*
*You killed my darling*
*And no man in Ireland*
*Will fire the shot at you!*

*Grief and destruction!*
*Morris the traitor!*
*That took my man from me,*
*Father of three children;*
*There are two on the hearth*
*And one in the womb*
*I shall not bring forth.*

*My love and my sweetness,*
*Art, rise up to me,*
*And leap upon your mare,*
*And ride into Macroom*
*And Inchigeela beyond,*
*Clasping your flask of wine,*
*One going, one coming back,*
*As in your father's time.*

*My lasting misery*
*I was not by your side*
*The time they fired the shot*
*To catch it in my dress*
*Or in my heart, what harm,*
*If you but reached the hills,*
*Rider of the ready hands.*

*My love and my fortune,*
*'Tis an evil portion*
*To lay for a giant,*
*A shroud and a coffin;*

*For a big-hearted hero*
*That fished in the hill-streams;*
*And drank in bright halls*
*With white-breasted women.*

*My love and my delight,*
*As you went out the gate,*
*You turned and hurried back,*
*And kissed your handsome sons,*
*You came and kissed my hand.*
*And said 'Eileen, rise up*
*And set your business straight,*
*For I am leaving home,*
*I never may return.'*
*I laughed at what you said,*
*You had said as much before. . . .*

*But noble Art O'Leary,*
*Art of hair so golden,*
*Art of wit and courage,*
*Art the brown mare's master,*
*Swept last night to nothing*
*Here in Carriganimma—*
*Perish it, name and people! . . .*

*Ay, could calls but wake my kindred*
*In Derrynane across the mountains,*
*And Carhen of the yellow apples,*
*Many a proud and stately rider,*
*Many a girl with spotless kerchief*
*Would be here before tomorrow,*
*Shedding tears about your body,*
*Art O'Leary once so merry!*

*My love and my calf!*
*Noble Art O'Leary,*
*Son of Conor, son of Cady,*
*Son of Lewis O'Leary,*
*West of the valley,*

*And east of Greenan*
*(Where berries grow thickly*
*And nuts crowd on branches,*
*And apples in heaps fall*
*In their own season)*
*What wonder to any*
*If Iveleary lighted*
*And Ballingeary,*
*And Gugan of the saints\**
*For the smooth-palmed rider*
*The huntsman unwearied*
*That I would see spurring*
*From Grenagh without halting*
*When quick hounds had faltered?*
*Oh, rider of the bright eyes*
*What happened you yesterday?*
*I thought you in my heart*
*When I bought you your fine clothes*
*One the world could not slay. . . .*

*But cease your weeping now,*
*Women of the soft, wet eyes,*
*Till Art O'Leary drink,*
*Ere he go to the dark school,*
*Not to learn music or song*
*But to prop the earth and the stone.*

### For the Literary Traveler

The blood-soaked world of black-haired Eileen O'Connell and her murdered husband, Art O'Leary, gathers in the shadowed hills of WEST CORK, which rise higher and higher as you move through the western valley of the River Blackwater. This countryside is unpopulated, wrapped in a silence breathing secrets of old treachery and the furious

*Gougane Barra in West Cork

passion of Eileen O'Leary. Following the scenic Mallow/Killarney road west (N72) and turning south at the sign for MILLSTREET (R582), you see in front of you and off toward the right the naked humps of the DERRYNASAGGART MOUNTAINS. It was on the other side of this formidable border between Cork and Kerry that Eileen O'Connell lived when she fell in love with Art O'Leary. The handsome town of Millstreet is beautifully situated near the mouth of the pass between the Derrynasaggart and BOGGERAGH Mountains, where Art O'Leary rode his fine horse and later hid from the law. In the small village of CARRIGANIMMA (also spelled CARRIGANIMMY), on the left (going south) is Edmond Walsh's Pub, Spirits, and Grocery. Directly across the road from Walsh's, beside a hedge, is an opening to a narrow path, which passes a deserted stone house and leads to a footbridge. On the far side of the bridge, a wide, grassy path turning left and paralleling the river was the coach road in 1774. Along the bank are furze (or gorse) bushes, where Eileen found her husband's dead body, "your blood in torrents."

The dark hills are harshly beautiful south of Carriganimma, heading toward MACROOM, where Art O'Leary lived at Raleigh House (now gone) and where Eileen O'Connell, entering the town square beside the MARKET HOUSE, felt love—and the courage of love—at first sight. The present-day market house on a colorful square, with its pretty window and sculptured fountain of "The Family," is the early-nineteenth-century successor to the original. Across from this local gathering spot, the remains of Macroom Castle (admired by Jonathan Swift) overlook the banks of the River Sullane. Once a principal seat of the MacCarthys (the others being Blarney and Kilcrea), it was conquered by Cromwell, who gave it to Admiral Sir William Penn, father of William Penn, founder of Pennsylvania. Local people relax in Macroom's friendly Castle Hotel, some recommending a visit to another site of ambush (about twenty minutes southeast of where Art O'Leary died), the most famous ambush in modern Ireland's history: BEAL NA MBLATH ("the Mouth of Flowers") saw the "Big Fella," Michael Collins, the thirty-one-year-old commander of the Free State army in the civil war (and another renegade West Corkman), shot dead in August 1922 by one of his own, a former friend and comrade in arms. East of Macroom on the N22, turn south for Crookstown, following the signs for Beal na mBlath, now marked by a monument. West Cork people still like to argue and speculate about the question "Who killed Mick?"—the great Irish whodunit. (Tim Pat Coogan's biography (1992) answers the question.)

Also east of Macroom, south of the N22, is KILCREA ABBEY at OVENS, where in the southeast corner of the abbey's nave Art O'Leary's body was finally laid to rest. For years it was forbidden burial in any church-yard because in the view of England and her criminal justice system, he was an official outlaw. His epitaph, no doubt composed by Eileen, invokes in three adjectives the ideals of the aristocratic Gaelic order.

> LO ARTHUR LEARY
>
> GENROUS HANDSOME BRAVE
>
> SLAIN IN HIS BLOOM
>
> LIES IN THIS HUMBLE GRAVE

"The Lament for Art O'Leary," the dying Gaelic order's most pas-sionate testament, has also been called an early example of the litera-ture of resistance. All through the hills of West Cork, where for centuries the English were resisted by proud Gaels on foot and on horseback, Eileen maps her memories of the defiant Art O'Leary in the places of his native countryside. "Gugan of the saints" refers to GOUGANE BARRA, a deep black lake walled in on three sides by rocky precipices that turn into waterfalls after rain. Here, where the River Lee begins, St. Finbarr, according to legend, lived a hermit's life on an is-land in the lake; then he moved downriver to found the monastery that became Cork City. (Drive west toward Gougane Barra from Ovens, across TOON BRIDGE, through INCHIGEELAGH, around the north side of Lough Allua, heading south through the pass into the scooped-out hollow of Gougane Barra.) Beyond the island is Forest Park, a re-treat with waterfalls and walking trails through stands of oak, pine, beech, and ash trees. The stark natural landscape breathes with life, but only in the absence of the weekend busloads of religious pilgrims can Gougane Barra cast its almost mystical spell.

Facing the lake are Cronin's pleasant pub and a shop where you can buy the new edition of Eric Cross's *The Tailor and Ansty*: by reason of its pure authenticity, the book belongs to Eileen O' Connell's "Gougane of the saints."

When Eric Cross came to live here in Gougane Barra, he met the tailor, Timothy Buckley, and his sharp-tongued wife, Ansty or Anastasia. The area was still a Gaeltacht (an Irish-speaking district), and students, including Sean O'Faolain and Frank O'Connor, came here and to nearby Ballyvourney to study the Irish language. Cross (and O'Connor) spent many hours in the tailor's cottage (the third house, painted yellow, on the right going away from the lake) listening to his earthy stories. As Frank O'Connor wrote in his introduction to Cross's book, to Buckley and his wife, both of whom were bilingual, "sexual relations" were "the most entertaining subject for general conversation"; this was a feature of community life in Irish-speaking Ireland, where nary a puritan roamed. (The tailor's comment on the rise of fascism in the 1930s was, "There wouldn't be half this trouble if more people fell to breeding.") Every night the Buckleys' hearth was crowded with neighbors and visiting friends, for the tailor was a genuine and much-beloved shanachie (or *seanchaí*), an Irish storyteller who possessed a wide repertoire of folklore. But upon publication of Cross's book—it's a collection of the couple's irreverent stories—the Censorship Board lost its fragile mind. Banning the book as "in its general tendency indecent," it sent to Gougane Barra three priests who forced the old man, on his knees, to burn his copy of the book on his own hearth. The local people shunned their old friends. Before the book was unbanned, about ten years later, Timothy and Anastasia Buckley were dead. They're buried in the cemetery down the road opposite St. Finbarr's island.

The way out of Gougane Barra, north through the mountains, leaves behind Art O'Leary's Cork and returns to Eileen's native Kerry, a borderland marked with the prehistoric dominion of Ireland's earth goddess. En route (via Ballingeary and Glenflesk), you'll look up at THE PAPS—the Breasts of the goddess Dana—twin mountains massing on top of the world like the full breasts of a huge recumbent woman, each mound crowned by the nipple of a cairn. Nature and ancient history lend their stunning witness to black-haired Eileen's tragic love story.

# The Hag of Beara

*A female divinity or fertility goddess in early Irish literature and folk tradition, the hag associated with the landscape of the Beara Peninsula (which is part Cork and part Kerry) expresses herself here in two opposing voices: she's both the sensual pagan and the nun, the ascetic exemplar of the new Christian order. Poet and translator John Montague, observing that "early Irish poetry is the only literature in Europe, and perhaps in the world, where one finds a succession of women poets," names "The Hag of Beara" (ninth century) as the greatest of all the early poems by women: "[It] anticipates Villon by several centuries." More than a lament for the loss of one love (Eileen O'Connell's eighteenth-century "Lament for Art O'Leary" is the culmination of that form—see p. 213), this is a cry of anguish for the ravages of time in love's paradise—fertile young bodies, male and female.*

THE HAG OF BEARA

*Ebb tide has come for me:
My life drifts downwards
Like a retreating sea
With no tidal turn.*

*I am the Hag of Beare,
Fine petticoats I used to wear,*

223

*Today, gaunt with poverty,*
*I hunt for rags to cover me.*

*Girls nowadays*
*Dream only of money—*
*When we were young*
*We cared more for our men.*

*Riding over their lands*
*We remember how, like nobles,*
*They treated us well;*
*Courted, but didn't tell.*

*Today every upstart*
*Is a master of graft;*
*Skinflint, yet sure to boast*
*Of being a lavish host.*

*But I bless my King who gave—*
*Balanced briefly on time's wave—*
*Largesse of speedy chariots*
*And champion thoroughbreds.*

*These arms, now bony, thin*
*And useless to younger men,*
*Once caressed with skill*
*The limbs of princes!*

*Sadly my body seeks to join*
*Them soon in their dark home—*
*When God wishes to claim it,*
*He can have back his deposit.*

*No more gamy teasing*
*For me, no wedding feast:*
*Scant grey hair is best*
*Shadowed by a veil.*

*Why should I care?*
*Many's the bright scarf*
*Adorned my hair in the days*
*When I drank with the gentry.*

*So God be praised*
*That I mis-spent my days!*
*Whether the plunge be bold*
*Or timid, the blood runs cold.*

*After spring and autumn*
*Come age's frost and body's chill:*
*Even in bright sunlight*
*I carry my shawl.*

*Lovely the mantle of green*
*Our Lord spreads on the hillside!*
*Every spring the divine craftsman*
*Plumps its worn fleece.*

*But my cloak is mottled with age—*
*No, I'm beginning to dote—*
*It's only grey hair straggling*
*Over my skin like a lichened oak.*

*And my right eye has been taken away*
*As down-payment on heaven's estate;*
*Likewise the ray in the left*
*That I may grope to heaven's gate.*

*No storm has overthrown*
*The royal standing stone.*
*Every year the fertile plain*
*Bears its crop of yellow grain.*

*But I, who feasted royally*
*By candlelight, now pray*
*In this darkened oratory.*
*Instead of heady mead*

*And wine, high on the bench*
*With kings, I sup whey*
*In a nest of hags:*
God pity me!

*Yet may this cup of whey*
*O! Lord, serve as my ale-feast—*

*Fathoming its bitterness*
*I'll learn that you know best.*

*Alas, I cannot*
*Again sail youth's sea;*
*The days of my beauty*
*Are departed, and desire spent.*

*I hear the fierce cry of the wave*
*Whipped by the wintry wind.*
*No one will visit me today*
*Neither nobleman nor slave.*

*I hear their phantom oars*
*As ceaselessly they row*
*And row to the chill ford,*
*Or fall asleep by its side.*

*Flood tide*
*And the ebb dwindling on the sand!*
*What the flood rides ashore*
*The ebb snatches from your hand.*

*Flood tide*
*And the sucking ebb to follow!*
*Both I have come to know*
*Pouring down my body.*

*Flood tide*
*Has not yet rifled my pantry*
*But a chill hand has been laid*
*On many who in darkness visited me.*

*Well might the Son of Mary*
*Take their place under my roof-tree*
*For if I lack other hospitality*
*I never say 'No' to anybody—*

*Man being of all*
*Creatures the most miserable—*

*His flooding pride always seen*
*But never his tidal turn.*

*Happy the island in mid-ocean*
*Washed by the returning flood*
*But my ageing blood*
*Slows to final ebb.*

*I have hardly a dwelling*
*Today, upon this earth.*
*Where once was life's flood*
*All is ebb.*

## For the Literary Traveler

The best introduction to the BEARA (pronounced "BAR-ah") PENIN-
SULA'S dramatic contrasts of fertile green fields and desolate mountain
rockfaces is the ten-minute ferry ride from GLENGARRIFF across the
clear blue of BANTRY BAY to GARINISH ISLAND. (Tickets are sold along the
main street of Glengarriff.) As you cross the bay (past an island of
seals), the towering dark mountain wall of the peninsula's CAHA MOUN-
TAINS is at your back. On the island in front of you (where Shaw holed
up to work on *Saint Joan*), you find an orgy of flora in a Mediterranean
climate: lilacs the size of footballs; wisteria; blossoming chestnut trees;
rhododendron flowers in salmon, apricot, and palest pink with leaves
so deeply green the fertile soil seems the temple of some goddess of
vegetation; foxgloves; azaleas; gardenias; forget-me-nots with their
fragrance sweetening the moist air. The immense trees assert a vital
presence, their woodlands framing long sweeps of lawn.

Back on the Beara Peninsula, the road between Glengarriff—an oasis of palm trees warmed by the Gulf Stream—and CASTLETOWNBERE
passes beneath the jagged Caha Mountains. On your right, between
the road and the bare mountains, stretch green fields radiant under
twilight and dotted white with grazing sheep. On your left, high fuchsia

hedges block the view of Bantry Bay. Like the cycle of life and death the hag laments so fiercely, the Beara is at once lovely and ominous, a peninsula of greening and graying. West of Ardrigole, you pass along-side HUNGRY HILL, the highest peak on the peninsula, a dramatic mound with a fine waterfall on its slopes. (Daphne du Maurier named a novel after Hungry Hill. Joss Lynam's *Best Irish Walks* describes three separate hikes to the summit.) This area also has hundreds of archaeological ruins of the pre-Christian and early Christian eras.

In the cozy little fishing town of Castletownbere, you can stop at LYNCH'S PUB on Main Street, where middle-aged Sheila Lynch, publican, chef, and mother, is the self-possessed woman in charge, a living counter-text to the raging Hag. Mrs. Lynch also makes fantastic fresh seafood sandwiches. In her friendly pub you can listen to the local people talk about what Ireland's membership in the EU has meant to the town's fishing industry. The opinions mix positive and negative with conviction. Just next to the harbor as you enter the town, on the wall of John Murphy's cheerful blue and yellow café (with bed-and-breakfast), there's a photograph of the hands of an old man, the Beara's last cobbler—a visual testament to the embodied beauty of the people of the southwest.

Rounding the tip of the peninsula, you can follow the coast north-east—looking across at the Kerry mountains of the Iveragh Peninsula—from Allihies to Eyeries, to Ardgroom, to Kenmare. The walking route of the BEARA WAY is splendid along this shoreline. (The Beara Way Map Guide is available at local tourist offices. Also useful are *The Waymarket Trails of Ireland*, by Michael Fewer, and the Ordnance Survey Discovery Series maps 78, 84, and 85.) Just beyond Eyeries Point and the village of Eyeries, around the shoreline in a deep harbor of Coulagh Bay, you will find a tiny island marked on the walking map as AN CHAILLEACH BEARA, or "the Hag of Beara," the specific place with which the hag's name is associated on the Beara Peninsula, beneath the northern flanks of the SLIEVE MISHKISH MOUNTAINS.

To get a sense from on high of the Beara's thirty-mile long rock-ribbed spine, cross it on either the spectacular HEALY PASS (at the summit is the Cork/Kerry border and sometimes sudden fog rolling in from the Atlantic) or, for a less scary but also stunning route, on the GLENGARRIFF/KENMARE ROAD (N71)—the "Tunnel Road," "one of Ireland's most scenic roads," according to one travel writer. As you climb and twist higher and higher for seventeen miles, passing through tunnels carved out of the rock, emerging as if onto the roof of the world, the Hag's pitiless scrutiny of love's body comes to mind against the background of this severe, almost intimidating landscape. Yet there in the distance, far below the dry mountain ridges, are the green valleys and blue lakes of her springtime and the ocean beating against the ragged coasts. After rain, you may see a rainbow arcing the Beara's body, nature punctuating herself with glad colors.

# Liam Dall O'hlfearnáin

## c. 1720–1803

*Kathleen Ní Houlihan, the most famous of the names personifying Ireland as a beautiful woman, might be imagined as the presiding presence of the Iveragh Peninsula, the largest of Ireland's southwest peninsulas jutting into the Atlantic. As described in the poem that follows here, Kathleen is a beauty in captivity, waiting to be liberated by her lover. Whereas the old crone to the south, the Hag of Beara, cries out in anger against the tyranny of time, lovely Kathleen is all patient expectancy. Kerry's Iveragh Peninsula, ringed by the sea and gorgeously bathed in an astonishing luminosity, is a believable landscape in which to locate this personification of mythic Ireland as a radiant queen of the Gael. According to folklore, Kathleen Ní Houlihan—Caitlin Ní Uallachain in Irish—is usually figured as waiting on the seashore for her true spouse. In historical terms he's the Catholic Stuart king who would come from France to help the Irish dethrone the English usurpers, and in fact, many times over the centuries, Catholic Europe, arriving on ships from Spain, France, Portugal, and Italy, tried—and failed—to land their armies along the western shores of Kerry. Not until the rebels of 1916 took action in*

*Dublin did Kathleen become more than the idealized feminine land-scape dreamed of by poets and playwrights. Then she became the muse of revolution. (Yeats worried that* Cathleen Ní Houlihan, *the nationalistic play he wrote with Lady Gregory, had so fired up Dublin audiences in 1902 that fourteen years later they grabbed their guns and marched on the GPO: "Did that play of mine send out / Certain men the English shot?") Contemporary Kerry poet Nuala Ní Dhomhnaill (see p. 249) revises the idealized Kathleen. In her poem "Cathleen," she makes the silent muse open her mouth to pronounce her role as an idealized Mother Ireland "as truly over."*

### KATHALEEN NY-HOULAHAN
#### TRANSLATED BY JAMES CLARENCE MANGAN

*This Jacobite poem, written in Irish by Liam Dall O'hlfearnain, reflects the politics of all the eighteenth-century Jacobite poets after the defeat and exile of the Gaelic aristocracy and the Catholic Stuart king, James II (in Latin Jacobus, thus Jacobite) by William III of Orange ("King Billy") after the Battle of the Boyne in the Williamite Wars (1689–91). Oppressed and hu-miliated by the Penal Laws enacted after the war to exclude Catholics from every function of power, they cried out in long-ing for James's return. Like a messiah, he would redeem Ire-land from the Protestant scourge. Often the Jacobite poets told of an encounter with or vision of a beautiful woman in an un-earthly setting of mountain or glen who reveals herself to be Ireland in waiting. Rescue by her true king or lover, she tells the poet, will free her from the slavery of occupation.*

Long they pine in weary woe, the nobles of our land,
Long they wander to and fro, proscribed, alas! and banned;
Feastless, houseless, altarless, they bear the exile's brand;
    But their hope is in the coming-to of Kathleen Ny-Houlahan!

Think her not a ghastly hag, too hideous to be seen,
Call her not unseemly names, our matchless Kathleen;
Young she is, and fair she is, and would be crowned queen,
    Were the king's son at home here with Kathleen Ny-Houlahan!

*Sweet and mild would look her face, O none so sweet and mild,*
*Could she crush the foes by whom her beauty is reviled;*
*Woollen plaids would grace herself, and robes of silk her child,*
    *If the king's son were living here with Kathaleen Ny-Houlahan!*

*Sore disgrace it is to see the Arbitress of thrones,*
*Vassal to a Saxoneen of cold and sapless bones!*
*Bitter anguish wrings our souls—with heavy sighs and groans*
    *We wait the young Deliverer of Kathaleen Ny-Houlahan!*

*Let us pray to Him who holds life's issues in His hands—*
*Him who formed the mighty globe, with all its thousand lands;*
*Girdling them with seas and mountains, rivers deep, and strands,*
    *To cast a look of pity upon Kathaleen Ny-Houlahan!*

*He who over sands and waves led Israel along—*
*He who fed, with heavenly bread, that chosen tribe and throng—*
*He who stood by Moses, when his foes were fierce and strong—*
    *May He show forth His might in saving Kathaleen Ny-Houlahan!*

## For the Literary Traveler

THE RING OF KERRY, the 110-mile coast road around the IVERAGH PENIN-
SULA, deserves its reputation as the equal of the most beautiful drives
on the Continent. Because the Ring's splendors are of world renown,
in summer you'll find yourself among throngs of her admirers. It's
worth taking the extra time to look for her most alluring places off the
main Ring route, along the small roads and walking trails. And by twilight time, when the Ring's vistas are most radiant, the coach tours
have usually called it quits.

The introduction, coming from Killarney to Kenmare on the N71,
offers steep narrow scenic highs (especially at LADIES VIEW) until you hit
the flat, unmemorable stretch (N70) out along the peninsula's south
coast on the Kenmare River, passing through Sneem. At the south-

west tip, the Atlantic rolls in at CASTLECOVE, and the Iveragh's seductive powers enter full play. There are small, beautifully sited beaches in the cove itself. Around the bend of the main road and two and a half miles up a narrow, potholed road (buses wouldn't dare), the fierce world of the Gaelic past rises high over a sweeping valley and the sea: STAIGUE FORT, a prehistoric ring fort twenty-five hundred years old and once the residence and coronation site of the kings of Munster, stands eighteen feet tall and ninety feet in diameter with walls thirteen feet thick, similar in structure to Dun Aengus on the Aran Islands and Greenan Fort (*Grianan Aileach*) in Donegal. From its proud, remote heights (accessible by stairways that run inside the walls up to narrow lookout platforms), its defenders, Kerry warriors and their warrior queens, commanded long, strategic views of approaching cattle raiders, rival clans, and foreign invaders. It's a good place to imagine the embattled heroic past, before the sovereignty of the Gael was replaced by an English king, forcing Kathleen Ní Houlihan's submission beneath a Saxon overlord. (Historians contradict the poets' image of a passive Kathleen. English visitors during the sixteenth-century Tudor conquest, according to Peter Neville, were shocked to encounter "sensual" and "volatile" Irish women, "who greeted them with a kiss, drank alcohol, and presided at feasts.")

Four miles beyond Staigue Fort, just outside Caherdaniel, tucked between the Ring road and the sea, is DERRYNANE, the ancestral home of the ancient Gaelic O'Connell family. (Open May-Sept., Mon.-Sat. 9–6, Sun. 11–7; Oct.-Apr., Tues.-Sun. 1–5.) The passionate poet, Eileen Dhubh ("Black-haired") O'Connell, who married Art O'Leary (see p. 212), was the daughter of Donal *Mor* ("Big") O'Connell of Derrynane; her nephew Daniel O'Connell (1775–1847), the "Great Liberator," lived here and inherited the property in 1825. O'Connell was not the royal messiah from across the water the Jacobite poets dreamed about. A Munster lawyer, he plotted the emancipation of the Catholic majority (successfully) and the restoration of Home Rule (unsuccessfully) by holding "Monster Rallies" all over Ireland, becoming the first Catholic Irishman to sit in Britain's Parliament. Acknowledged as one of history's most eloquent orators (Gladstone called him "the greatest popular leader the world has ever known"), dubbed "King of the Beggars" by his enemies (also the title of Sean O'Faolain's biography), he revived the pride of a crushed people. Because constitutional politics and nonviolent mass action were his chosen instruments, he was eventually replaced by the more militant "Young Irelanders" under Thomas Davis. Daniel O'Connell's shrewdness was bred in his Kerry bones. In the dark days of the British occupation and monopoly of trade, the O'Connells of Derrynane recognized that their only economic opportunity lay in smuggling: embargoed goods in, Irishmen out to fill the ranks of Continental armies. ("A forerunner of Shannon Airport's Duty Free," as Marianne Heron puts it in *The Hidden Houses of Ireland*.) DERRYNANE NATIONAL PARK, open year round, provides a nature trail along white sandy beaches and dunes, a peaceful wildflowered stretch where outlaws in boats and pragmatic politics seem unreal against the sunset glow of Kathleen Ní Houlihan's secluded southwestern reaches. Irish poet Glen Delanty (1958– )—*Cast in the Fire, American Wake, The Hellbox*—born in Cork, now teaching in Vermont, sees a connection between this fertile landscape and the voluble sensibility of the Irish southwest of Kerry and Cork:

> The landscape and sense of language must be considered. The west and southwest have a somewhat different landscape, fauna and flora. The seascape of, say, Derrynane in South Kerry looks a bit like some places in the Mediterranean. There you can find lizards and an abundance of tropical flowers that the Gulf Stream makes possible. And what about the type of fuchsia that grows all down the west coast, Fuchsia Magallencia? It's a fuchsia that came from Magallanes in Chile, and the soil and climate here particularly suited it. There are plenty examples of this southern, Latin phenomenon. Landscape obviously somehow forms the character of the people who live there.... People here are far more open and tend to be more tempestuous than people in the North where the dictum is: "Whatever you say, say nothing." In the part of the country I come from, it's more: "Whatever you say, say everything."

It's true: as Irish and Irish-Americans go, the more chatty they are, the more you're likely to find they've got Kerry—splashed with Cork—in the blood.

The glory of the Iveragh intensifies between Caherdaniel and Waterville as you ascend the COOMAKISTA PASS and maybe stop to take the forty-five-minute walk along its rugged trail (signposted at the summit) to HOG'S HEAD: up here you look down on Derrynane Park and SCARIFF ISLAND out in the sea, like Kathleen herself on her mythic pedestal, waiting for deliverance.

Just south of Cahirsiveen, there's a twenty-two-mile ocean drive—SKELLIG LOOP—tailing off from the Ring of Kerry that Synge describes in *In West Kerry*:

> I have been out to BOLUS HEAD, one of the finest places I have met with. A little beyond BALLINSKELLIGS the road turns up the side of a steep mountainy hill where one sees a brilliant stretch of sea, with many rocks and islands—DEENISH, SCARIFF, HOG'S HEAD, and DURSEY far away.

Near Portmagee, where you turn for Valentia Island, the SKELLIG HERITAGE CENTRE (Apr.–Sept., daily 10–6) introduces the history of the stone pyramid you see rising 714 feet high out of the Atlantic about eight miles off the western tip of the Iveragh Peninsula: GREAT SKELLIG MICHAEL, once the chosen home of sixth-century hermits. "No experience," said George Bernard Shaw, "that the conventional tourist travel can bring you will stick in your memory so strangely; for Skellig Michael is not after the fashion of this world." (The boat ride out to the Rock, an hour and a half into the Atlantic from Portmagee, Waterville, and Ballinskelligs, weather permitting, passes the bird sanctuary on LITTLE SKELLIG. Reserve a day in advance.) Before the hermits landed, druids may have studied the movement of the stars from these dizzying heights. Like Monte Sant'Angelo in Italy, Mont Saint-Michel in France, and St. Michael's Mount in Cornwall, Skellig Michael is dedicated to St. Michael the Archangel, patron saint of high places. You ascend, as if heading toward heaven, on open stone stairs—544 of them—cut into a cliff, climbing above the ruins of beehive huts, oratories, and crosses, all enclosed on the edge of a precipice, and near the summit, you find what penitents on pilgrimage to Skellig Michael saw before the Vikings raided it in 823: a final oratory and small hermitage near the peak. The descent is equally challenging, especially if you're nervous about missing the return boat. (Eyes front, ignore the drop to the ocean—all the way down. Stiletto heels not recommended.)

The Ring's western fringe, which winds northeast between CAHER-SIVEEN, KELLS, and GLENBEIGH, borders Dingle Bay, with the humpy Blasket Islands and the mountains of Dingle in the blue distance. Sunsets seen from this stretch of the Iveragh have the color of rosy amethyst; the bay turns a shimmering royal blue. This is why people come to Kerry: it's hard to believe these views from her shores are real and not a dream of a blissed-out otherworld.

   Just beyond Glenbeigh (near Mountain Stage, where Synge stayed in Philly Harris's cottage), there's another detour from the main Ring road that for some travelers leads to the Iveragh Peninsula's most impressive mountains, their sides gashed with moody sweeps of light and shadow. Turn right at the sign for CARAGH LAKE (Lough Caragh), go straight, and then wind around the lake, bearing southwest beneath steep mountainsides, until GLENCAR. Here, in what's called "the Highlands of Kerry," you're likely to find yourself alone at the foot of CAR-RANTUOHILL ("the Left-handed Reaping Hook"), at 3,414 feet the highest peak of the MACGILLYCUDDY'S REEKS, Ireland's highest mountain range. Standing on the bridge over the Caragh River, you hear only the rushing water and the wind in the trees of LICKEEN WOOD.

   John Montague's "Windharp" captures this music that nature plays all over Ireland:

> The sounds of Ireland,
> that restless whispering
> you never get away from, seeping out of
> low bushes and grass,
> heatherbells and fern,
> wrinkling bog pools,
> scraping tree branches,
> light hunting cloud,
> sound hounding sight,
> a hand ceaselessly
> combing and stroking

*the landscape, till*
*the valley gleams*
*like the pile upon*
*a mountain pony's coat.*

Continue along through forests of holly trees, beneath the jagged peaks of the Reeks: you're crossing the long spine of the Iveragh, along the lonely and awesome BALLAGHISHEEN PASS, between the mountains of Knocknacusha and Knocknagapple. At LISSATINNIG BRIDGE, the road divides. If you bear left, you descend the pass along the Inny River to Waterville; bearing right, you ascend along a narrow, steep road—with each sharp turn, your only choice is to slow down (and laugh like a maniac, as there's no turning back)—and then drop down into Caher-siveen. This is the Kerry road less traveled, and, on the map of thrills and hills, one of the best.

About an hour back along the Pass, toward Killorglin and Killarney, Caragh Lodge (listed in *Ireland's Blue Book: Irish Country Houses and Restaurants*) is set in an award-winning garden of azaleas, magnolias, rhododendrons, and camellias on the shores of Caragh Lake, looking toward the MacGillycuddy's Reeks. (Open Apr.–Oct., tel. (800) 323-5436 from the United States or (066) 976-9115 in Ireland.) It's no budget hideaway, but the matchless topography of the Iveragh's inland middle section makes splurging feel right. (And if the Irish weather has gotten to you or if you have a cold, proprietor Mary Gaunt's hot toddy is about the best remedy you're likely to find in the four provinces.) Caragh Lodge is also a convenient base if you're exploring the Iveragh by walking THE KERRY WAY. (Contact Cork/Kerry Tourism, Killarney Tourist Office, Beech Road, Killarney, for its Kerry Way Map Guide and for *Walk Guide—The South West of Ireland* by Sean O' Sullivan, published by Gill & Macmillan. Use the Ordnance Survey Discovery Series maps 70, 78, 83, 84, and 85.) Though this long-distance path does not climb very high, it's still higher than the N70 road and so improves on what is already extraordinary scenery. It's easy to imagine that in the years when "matchless" Kathleen was waiting for her savior, this was the route most traveled by the Kerry rebels who subverted her humilating occupation along the Iveragh's hidden arteries.

It's less than fifteen minutes from Caragh Lake to KILLORGLIN, a plain mountain town (with a good octagonal Tourist Office in the center), renowned for its annual Puck Fair. Puck, the heftiest male goat to be found on Carrantuohill, is hauled into town on Gathering Day (August 10) to wild musical accompaniment, and hoisted and crowned above the market square to preside as king over the trading of animals and the carnivalesque merrymaking until Scattering Day (August 12), when Puck is escorted back to his mountain. (Puck Fair turns up in American poet Muriel Rukeyser's novel *The Orgy*.)

From Killorglin it's a short hop south on the N72 to KILLARNEY, Blarney's rival for tourist helltown. But not to worry; it's more of a gateway than a destination, where many tourists begin their circuit of the Ring. (The Tourist Office in Beech Street has a large supply of Kerry maps and information as well as, across the street, a civic work of mercy: a parking lot for a town where traffic stays jammed.)

In College Street, across from the Franciscan friary and away from the crowds of Main Street, you encounter again a visual image of Ireland's persona (and muse) as a woman's body. The SKY-WOMAN OF KERRY *(speirbhean)*, sculptor Seamus Murphy's statue, stands tall on her pedestal—and awfully stiff for a representation of a womanhood once perceived as "volatile" and "sensual," her left hand over her heart, her right gripping a harp. (Maybe idealizations of women always look a bit petrified.) Beneath her feet are inscribed the names of Mother Kerry's four best-known Gaelic poets of the seventeenth and eighteenth centuries: Pierce Ferriter of Dingle, Geoffrey O'Donoghue of the Glens, Aogan O'Rahillly of Scrahanaveale, and Eoghan Rua O'Sullivan of Meentogues. They expressed their rebellious and romantic hearts in Irish, faithful to their visions of Ireland as a beautiful woman, the Hag of Beara grown young again, prophesying and promising the resurrection of the glorious Gaelic past. Favored by the Kerry poets, the vision poem *(aisling* in Irish) is the Gaelic literary genre associated with this political message of restoration.

A mile east of town in the beautiful MUCKROSS ABBEY (c. 1340) in KILLARNEY NATIONAL PARK, some of the Kerry poets are buried along with the chieftains of the Kerry clans who were their patrons—the MacCarthys, MacGillycuddys, O'Donoghues, and O'Sullivans—and whose overthrow by the English the poets cursed. (Open daily 9–6.) This twenty-five-thousand-acre woodland on the borders of LOUGH LEANE (Lower Lake), a favorite holiday spot of Victorians such as Thackeray and Tennyson, is still a bounty of flowers, waterfalls, the three lakes (Upper, Middle, and Lower), and mountains. Joss Lynam's *Best Irish Walks* simplifies a six-mile hike up TORC MOUNTAIN, accessible just down the main road from Muckross Abbey from the carpark on the N71/T65 at the bottom of TORC WATERFALL. At the top of Torc, all three Killarney lakes are in view.

Another magnificent site dear to Victorians and to today's visitors, especially from Germany and Switzerland, is the GAP OF DUNLOE (signposted, with Kate Kearney's Cottage, about five miles north of town on the Killarney/Tralee road, N22). The beautiful seven-mile walk through the Gap between the stark wall of Purple Mountain, on the left, and the MacGillycuddy's Reeks, on the right, both sides thick with fuschia, myrtle, and quince, leads to the shore of the Upper Lake at Gearhameen.

For another view (right out of the song "By Killarney's Lakes and Fells"), two miles north of the town, a right turn off the Killarney/Tralee road (N22) followed by another right brings you up to AGHA-DOE HILL. (Don't be deterred by the golf course and suburban houses.) Here in a broad meadow, with benches, you look down upon the most comprehensive view of the entire Killarney district. The panorama of the MacGillycuddy's Reeks suggests every anatomical feature and position: recumbent bodies facing up to the sky, bold profiles, a perfect nose, nice thighs. Light and clouds cavort in every crevice, changing the mountains' shapes, sweeping across the island-studded Lough Leane below. Shelley found such views of Killarney more dramatic than Switzerland.

"Aghadoe" by John Todhunter (1839–1916), a dramatist and friend of Yeats, sounds both the lyricism and the danger that filled the glens of Kerry, for centuries the hideouts of rebels. (Resistance went with the territory of Lord Headley of Aghadoe, a notoriously cruel landlord.)

AGHADOE

*There's a glade in Aghadoe, Aghadoe, Aghadoe,*
*There's a green and silent glade in Aghadoe,*

Where we met, my love and I, love's fair planet in the sky,
O'er that sweet and silent glade in Aghadoe.

There's a glen in Aghadoe, Aghadoe, Aghadoe,
There's a deep and secret glen in Aghadoe,
Where I hid him from the eyes of the red-coats and their spies,
That year the trouble came to Aghadoe.

Oh! my curse on one black heart in Aghadoe, Aghadoe,
On Shaun Dhuv, my mother's son, in Aghadoe!
When your throat fries in hell's drouth, salt the flame
    be in your mouth,
For the treachery you did in Aghadoe!

For they tracked me to that glen in Aghadoe, Aghadoe,
When the price was on his head in Aghadoe,
O'er the mountain, by the wood, as I stole to him with food,
Where in hiding lone he lay in Aghadoe.

But they never took him living in Aghadoe, Aghadoe,
With the bullets in his heart in Aghadoe,
There he lay—the head my breast feels the warmth of,
    where 'twould rest,
Gone, to win the traitor's gold, from Aghadoe!

I walked to Mallow town from Aghadoe, Aghadoe,
Brought his head from the gaol's gate to Aghadoe,
Then I covered him with fern, and I piled him on the cairn,*
Like an Irish king he sleeps in Aghadoe.

Oh! to creep into that cairn in Aghadoe, Aghadoe!
There to rest upon his breast in Aghadoe,
Sure your dog for you could die with no truer heart than I,
Your own love, cold on your cairn, in Aghadoe.

*A heap of stones

# John Millington Synge

## 1871–1909

### IN WEST KERRY

At Tralee station—I was on my way to a village many miles beyond Dingle—I found a boy who carried my bag some way
along the road to an open yard where the light railway starts for the
west. . . .

Then, when the carriage was closely packed, we moved slowly
out of the station. At my side there was an old man who explained
the Irish names of the places that we came to, and pointed out the
Seven Pigs, a group of islands in the bay; Kerry Head, further off;
and many distant mountains. Beyond him a dozen big women in
shawls were crowded together; and just opposite me there was a
young woman wearing a wedding ring, who was one of the peculiarly refined women of Kerry, with supreme charm in every movement and expression. The big woman talked to her about some
elderly man who had been sick—her husband, it was likely—and
some young man who had gone away to England, and was breaking his heart with loneliness.

'Ah, poor fellow!' she said; 'I suppose he will get used to it like
another; and wouldn't he be worse off if he was beyond the seas in
Saint Louis, or the towns of America?'

This woman seemed to unite the healthiness of the country people with the greatest sensitiveness, and whenever there was any little stir or joke in the carriage, her face and neck flushed with
pleasure and amusement. As we went on there were superb

sights—first on the north, towards Loop Head, and then when we reached the top of the ridge, to the south also, to Drung Hill, Macgillicuddy's Reeks, and other mountains of South Kerry. A little further on, nearly all the people got out at a small station; and the young woman I had admired, gathered up most of the household goods and got down also, lifting heavy boxes with the power of a man. Then two returned American girls got in, fine, stout-looking women, with distress in their expression, and we started again. Dingle Bay could now be seen through narrow valleys on our left, and had extraordinary beauty in the evening light. In the carriage next to ours a number of herds and jobbers were travelling, and for the last hour they kept up a furious altercation that seemed always on the verge of breaking into a dangerous quarrel, but no blows were given.

At the end of the line an old blue side-car was waiting to take me to the village where I was going. I was some time fastening on my goods, with the raggedy boy who was to drive me; and then we set off, passing through the usual streets of a Kerry town, with public-houses at the corners, till we left the town by a narrow quay with a few sailing boats and a small steamer with coal. . . .

◊   ◊

Just as the twilight was beginning to deepen we reached the top of the ridge and came out through a gap into sight of Smerwick Harbour, a wild bay with magnificent headlands beyond it, and a long stretch of the Atlantic. We drove on towards the west, sometimes very quickly, where the slope was gradual, and then slowly again when the road seemed to fall away under us, like the wall of a house. As the night fell the sea became like a piece of white silver on our right; and the mountains got black on our left, and heavy night smells began to come up out of the bogs. Once or twice I noticed a blue cloud over the edge of the road, and then I saw that we were nearly against the gables of a little village, where the houses were so closely packed together there was no light from any of them. It was now quite dark, and the boy got cautious in his driving, pulling the car almost into the ditch once or twice to avoid an enormous cavity where the middle of the road had settled down into the bogs. At last we came to another river and a public-house, and went up a hill, from which we could see the outline of a chapel; then the boy turned to me: 'Is it ten o'clock yet?' he said; 'for we're mostly now in the village.'

◊   ◊

This morning, a Sunday, rain was threatening; but I went out west after my breakfast under Croagh Martin, in the direction of the Atlantic. At one of the first villages I came to I had a long talk with a man who was sitting on the ditch waiting till it was time for Mass. Before long we began talking about the Irish language.

'A few years ago,' he said, 'they were all for stopping it off; and when I was a boy they tied a gobban into my mouth for the whole afternoon because I was heard speaking Irish. Wasn't that great cruelty? And now when I hear the same busybodies coming around and telling us for the love of God to speak nothing but Irish, I've a good mind to tell them to go to hell. There was a priest out here a while since who was telling us to stay always where we are, and to speak nothing but Irish; but, I suppose, although the priests are learned men, and great scholars, they don't understand the life of the people the same as another man would. In this place the land is poor—you can see that for yourself—and the people have little else to live on; so that when there is a long family, one son will stay at home and keep on the farm, and the others will go away because they must go. Then when they once pass out of the Dingle station in Tralee they won't hear a word of Irish, or meet anyone who'd understand it; so what good, I ask you, is a man who hasn't got the English, and plenty of it?'

After I left him I went on towards Dunquin, and lay for a long time on the side of a magnificently wild road under Croagh Martin, where I could see the Blasket Islands and the end of Dunmore Head, the most westerly point of Europe. It was a grey day with a curious silence on the sea and sky and no sign of life anywhere, except the sail of one curagh—or niavogue, as they are called here—that was sailing in from the islands. Now and then a cart passed me filled with old people and children, who saluted me in Irish; then I turned back myself. I got on a long road running through a bog, with a smooth mountain on one side and the sea on the other, and Brandon in front of me, partly covered with clouds. As far as I could see there were little groups of people on their way to the chapel in Ballyferriter, the men in homespun and the women wearing blue cloaks, or, more often, black shawls twisted over their heads. This procession along the olive bogs, between the mountains and the sea, on this grey day of autumn seemed to wring me with the pang of emotion one meets everywhere in Ireland—an emotion that is partly local and patriotic, and partly a share of the desolation that is mixed everywhere with the supreme beauty of the world. . . .

◊      ◊

Often, when one comes back to a place that one's memory and imagination have been busy with, there is a feeling of smallness and disappointment, and it is a day or two before one can renew all one's enjoyment. This morning, however, when I went up the gap between Croagh Martin and then back to Slea Head, and saw Innishtooskert and Inishvickillaun and the Great Blasket Island itself, they seemed ten times more grey and wild and magnificent than anything I had kept in my memory. The cold sea and surf, and the feeling of winter in the clouds, and the blackness of the rocks, and the red fern everywhere, were a continual surprise and excitement.

Here and there on my way I met old men with tailcoats of frieze, that are becoming so uncommon. When I spoke to them in English they shook their heads and muttered something I could not hear; but when I tried Irish they made me long speeches about the weather and the clearness of the day.

In the evening, as I was coming home, I got a glimpse that seemed to have the whole character of Corkaguiney*—a little line of low cottages with yellow roofs, and an elder tree without leaves beside them, standing out against a high mountain that seemed far away, yet was near enough to be dense and rich and wonderful in its colour.

Then I wandered round the wonderful forts of Fahan. The

*Another name for the Dingle Peninsula

blueness of the sea and the hills from Carrantuohill to the Skelligs, the singular loneliness of the hillside I was on, with a few choughs and gulls in sight only, had a splendour that was almost a grief in the mind.

## For the Literary Traveler

Synge had what he called "West Kerry"—both the IVERAGH and DIN-GLE peninsulas—blissfully to himself during his visits of 1903, 1904, and 1905. These days the circuit of West Kerry is required riding by tourist coaches in high season. On Dingle's INCH STRAND, only twenty-five years ago a shining white beach fit for hermits, there's now a café. If you walk out onto the strand, though, the café at your back, Inch is still pristine, unfurled beneath the high violet altars of the Kerry mountains against the blue arc of Dingle Bay. It may take time to find, but Synge's Dingle still lives: nature, untamed and severely beautiful, is everywhere. *National Geographic Traveler* calls this landscape "the most beautiful place on earth."

Approaching from Tralee (the Tralee / Dingle train Synge took no longer runs), the main road (N86) parallels Tralee Bay on the right and on the left the old railway line. (This is the Dingle Way / Pilgrim's Route marked on the Dingle Way Map Guide and in O'Callaghan's *The Dingle Way Companion*.) Near the intersection of N86 at Camp and R560 to Castlegregory, the road passes P. J. Fitzgerald's pub, also known as the Junction Bar. With its wonderful old photographs of local people in the days of the railroad—Synge's time—this pub makes Synge's impressions of the people of West Kerry, especially the women, seem immediate. The place has a life of its own.

From the pub's outdoor picnic area you can look across Tralee Bay to the long whiteness of BANNA STRAND: there Roger Casement (1864–1916), an Anglo-Irishman who converted to Irish nationalism, landed with the German arms he hoped to route through Kerry to support Dublin's Easter Rising; he was arrested on Good Friday 1916 at a nearby ring fort, and though he was a knight of the British Empire, he was executed without any chance of a pardon because of the evidence of homosexuality in his *Black Diaries*. "Sure my grandfather was there. He said he [Casement] and the other lads were thrown in the barracks down the road—it's now a fast-food joint—and no one knew who they were for a few days. They could've walked out!" a Kerryman fresh from a swim on a frigid afternoon in May told me. There's a monument to Casement behind the dunes of Banna Strand—and there's this last testament that he wrote to his sister before his execution:

When I landed in Ireland, swamped and swimming ashore on an unknown strand, I was happy for the first time for over a year. Although I knew that this fate waited on me, I was for one brief spell happy and smiling once more. I cannot tell you what I felt. The sandhills were full of skylarks rising in the dawn, the first I had heard for years—the first sound I heard through the surf was their song, as I waded through the breakers, and they kept rising all the time up to the old rath at Currsahone, where I stayed and sent the others on, and all around were primroses and wild violets and the singing of the skylarks in the air, and I was back in Ireland again.

You can cross the high mountainous back of Dingle on the N86 to Anascaul, detouring for the fun of it down unmarked mountain roads to Inch Strand, or you can take the spectacular CONOR PASS, the highest mountain pass in Ireland—Paul Theroux found it scarier than the Khyber Pass—which climbs for four and a half miles along the mass of Mount Brandon, named for St. Brendan the Navigator, born near Tralee (d. 577).

DINGLE TOWN is an exhilarating walk, especially up Green Street, with a stop into the excellent Dingle Bookshop. At the end of it, a right turn into Main Street brings you past Benner's Hotel, a restored 250-year-old inn with an open fire in the pub, The Lord Baker, and further along in John Street are Doyle's Seafood and The Half Door, both good places to eat and drink. There are fifty-two pubs in town for its fifteen hundred people, and traditional music is heard all over the place. The Dingle Storytelling Pub Crawl (tel. 064-52161) offers a literary tour of Dingle's pubs and "other sacred sights" (July–Aug., Thurs.–Mon. 7–8:30 outside the post office on Main Street).

Synge's Kerry continues west of town. The strand at VENTRY is rich in natural beauty, mythology, and literature. According to *The Book of Invasions*, the great medieval chronicle of Ireland's legendary history, it was on Ventry's *Fionn Tragha* (white strand) that the sons of Mil (the Milesians) came ashore from Spain in 1268 B.C. to colonize Ireland, conquering its pagan divinities, the Tuatha De Danann. Amergin, one of those conquering sons and the chief bard of the invaders, sang a cosmic hymn as he came ashore, identifying himself with the whole of creation. According to tradition, these verses (entitled "The Mystery" by some editors) are the first to have been composed in Ireland:

> I am the wind which breathes upon the sea,
> I am the wave of the ocean,
> I am the murmur of the billows,
> I am the ox of the seven combats,
> I am the vulture upon the rocks,
> I am a beam of the sun,
> I am the fairest of plants,
> I am the wild boar in valour,
> I am a salmon in the water,
> I am a lake in the plain,
> I am a word of science,
> I am the point of the lance of battle,
> I am the God who created in the head the fire.
> Who is it who throws light into the meeting on the mountain?
> Who announces the ages of the moon?
> Who teaches the place where couches the sun?
>
>                                                   (If not I)

In *The White Goddess*, Robert Graves devotes a chapter to "The Song of Amergin," a pantheistic chant about the godhead that is everywhere in nature. It became a liturgical hymn in ancient Ireland that some say had "as wide a currency as, say, the opening chapters of the *Koran*, or the Apostles' Creed." Amergin was cherished as the first poet of the Gaels, the prototype of all Irish poets, according to Kuno

Meyer, who have "mixed their souls with Ireland's mountains and waters, her woods, and her tribal hostings on the hilly places. To seek out and watch and love Nature, in its tiniest phenomena as in its grandest, was given to no people so early and so fully as to the Celt."

Synge, according to this description, was pure Celt, Amergin's soul brother. Continuing along his route, from VENTRY you proceed (slowly!) around SLEA HEAD. (Of Dingle and Slea Head, Irish-American actor Bill Murray says in Cinderella Story: My Life in Golf (1999), "[T]he where there is beyond compare. You can only call it laughingly beautiful. You just keep turning—turning to see this vista, then that vista, walking the course, turning around in its beauty until you're drunk.") The road around Slea Head hairpins narrowly between the sea and the high slopes of MOUNT EAGLE. (You must go on foot to find the FAHAN clochans, the beehive-shaped cells of the hermits.) At DUNQUIN, there's a lay-by that looks out on the six BLASKET ISLANDS: Beginish, Tearaght, Inishnabro, Inishvickillane, Inishtooskert, and (is it a whale?) the Great Blasket. "Seen from above you think them sea-monsters of an antique world languidly lifting time-worn backs above the restless and transitory waves," wrote Robin Flower in The Western Island. In August 1905, Synge visited the largest of the Blaskets, the most westerly lands in Europe and also the legendary setting of TIR-NA-NOG, the Celtic Otherworld—the Land of the Forever Young: "Youth does not give way to age there," the poet tells us in the ancient poem, The Voyage of Bran. Kruger's in Dunquin, the most westerly pub in Europe, is a well-known live music stop. Dunquin Pottery Café, up the hill from the lookout on the Blaskets, has a bookshop in the back room and magnificent views of the sunsets over Tir-na-nOg as well as of the raging, lashing rainstorms Bill Murray plays golf in: "Ireland," says he, "my favorite place to golf."

Along the small roads out of BALLYFERRITER, you'll find the headland where Synge liked to watch the flights of the birds over the Blaskets. Here, dwarfed by the stern slopes of CROAGH MARTIN, above Ferriter's Cove (recent excavations here found the earliest settlement in Kerry, dated c. 4,000 B.C.), are the remains of FERRITER'S CASTLE, the birthplace and family home of Kerry poet Pierce Ferriter, a leader of the Munster resistance to Cromwell. Near the castle, the ghost of his beloved Sybil

Lynch is said to walk; the two had lived here together after they ran away from her family, and when her kinsmen came to bring her home, Ferriter hid Sybil in a cave by the sea, only to find later that she'd been drowned by the rising tide.

From the castle, the climb to the top of SYBIL HEAD is bracing, windswept, and glorious. You look out over the adjoining peaks of the THREE SISTERS and northeast to Ireland's second highest mountain, MOUNT BRANDON, a mighty throne of rock and clouds set high over SMERWICK HARBOR, where in 1580 Walter Raleigh and Edmund Spenser, secretary to Arthur Grey, the viceroy of Ireland, watched Lord Grey's army massacre Kathleen Ní Houlihan's Catholic deliverers—700 Irish, Spanish, and Italian soldiers—after they had surrendered in DUN AN OIR (the Fort of Gold). For this and other atrocities committed on behalf of Queen Elizabeth's conquest of Ireland, Lord Grey was recalled two years later for "cruel and dishonourable conduct." Spenser, though he later sang the idyll of the Irish countryside in *The Fairie Queen*, "never wavered," according to *The Oxford Companion to Irish Literature*, in his support for the methods used by the queen's soldiers to suppress the rebellion in West Kerry.

Modern Irish poet (and Princeton University professor) Paul Muldoon memorializes the Renaissance men of Smerwick Harbor in these verses from *Kerry Slides* (1996):

> *Earl Grey of Wilton*
> *gnaws at a Stilton*
> *and knocks back some port*
> *as his men poniard*
> *six hundred Spaniards*
> *in the Golden Fort.*

> *Nor can Ed Spenser*
> *be above censure*
> *since he keeps tally,*
> *while the greatest fan*
> *of this scorched earth plan*
> *is Walter Raleigh.*

Going counterclockwise around Smerwick Harbor from Ballyferriter, you will reach the field of GALLARUS ORATORY (signposted), the most perfectly preserved of the upturned boat-shaped oratories in Kerry. Its unmortared stones still watertight after twelve hundred years, Gallarus is an image of the early Irish Church before it was overwhelmed by the marauding Vikings. Organized tourism threatens the place these days; once set off by itself, small and alone beneath the shadow of Brandon, its people free to worship the God they saw everywhere in nature and in every living creature, today Gallarus Oratory faces a complex of gift shop and toilets, with cashiers ringing up the cost of admission. Even here the Celtic Tiger slouches, in these Kerry wilds loved by monks and that self-described "old tramp," John Synge.

# Nuala Ní Dhomhnaill

## 1952–

*The most widely translated poet in Irish of this century, Nuala Ní Dhomhnaill grew up in the Dingle Gaeltacht, west of Ventry, in Kerry. The convergence in her work of Gaelic tradition and folklore with a modern woman's experience of sex, pregnancy, and child-birth have won her a large audience in Ireland and a growing reputation in America. Her collections, best-sellers in Ireland—*An Dealg Droighin *(1981), about the* Munster fertility goddess Mor; Pharaoh's Daughter *(1990);* The Astrakhan Cloak *(1991), and* The Water Horse *(1999)—include many love poems in the voice of a woman taking delight in the male body. A visiting scholar at Boston College in 1998–99 and Villanova in 2001, Ní Dhomhnaill lives with her family in Cabinteely, County Dublin.*

## OILEÁN*

*Translated by John Montague*

*Your nude body is an island
asprawl on the ocean bed. How
beautiful your limbs, spread-
eagled under seagulls' wings!*

*Spring wells, your temples,
deeps of blood, honey crests.
A cooling fountain you furnish
in the furious, sweltering heat
and a healing drink
when feverish.*

*Your two eyes gleam
like mountain lakes
on a bright Lammas day
when the sky sparkles
in dark waters.
Your eyelashes are reeds
rustling along the fringe.*

*And if I had a tiny boat
to waft me towards you,
a boat of findrinny,
not a stitch out of place
from top to bottom
but a single plume
of reddish brown
to play me on board,
To hoist the large white
billowing sails; thrust
through foaming seas
and come beside you
where you lie back,
wistful, emerald,
islanded.*

* Island

◻◊◻

## *For the Literary Traveler*

Travelers who came to visit and couldn't make themselves go home again are not unknown on the tip of Dingle, the gorgeous and harrowing landscape of Nuala Ní Dhomhnaill's poetry. (Use Discovery Series Kerry map 70.) You won't find her places on ordinary road maps; they're off up the bohreens (small roads) west of VENTRY, their names written in Irish, the language of Corca Dhuibhne, Dingle's GAELTACHT, the Irish word for a geographical area where the Irish language is spoken. Used today mostly in rural pockets along the western seaboard, among 2 percent of the population—about sixty thousand people—the language is a controversial issue, a tangle of Gaelic pride, pragmatic globalism, and historical memory, each arguing for or against its preservation. Nuala Ní Dhomhnaill is all in favor: "Irish is a language of enormous elasticity and emotional sensitivity ... an instrument of imaginative depth and scope, which has been tempered by the community for generations until it can pick up and sing out every hint of emotional modulation that can occur between people." She has also called Irish "the language of the Mothers": after the collapse of Gaelic Ireland at the end of the seventeenth century, the native language lost its status, and it has shared a legacy of voicelessness with Ireland's women, on whom (with few exceptions) silence in the public arena was imposed.

The poem "Oileán," in which the body of the poet's lover is the destination of her desire, has as its geographical inspiration OILEÁN BAN, a small island you can spot from the northwest tip of the GREAT BLASKET (near where the Dunquin ferry drops you off); Ní Dhomhnaill knows the beaches and bracken trail across the Great Blasket well. (Beware the drops over the cliffs on the north side.) From its southwest tip are good views of the islands of Inishabro and Inishvickillane. Ní Dhomhnaill's play on John Donne's "No man is an island" exemplifies the humor of her poetry as well as her unbounded delight in the living world of the flesh. Earth's bodies are multiple and navigable, animal and vegetable, floral and mineral, male and female—their modulations, as she says of the Irish language, are endless. (In good weather, boats go out to the Blaskets from Dunquin from May to Sept., daily every half hour from 10 to 3.) The BLASKET CENTER, between Dunquin and Ballyferriter, features exhibits on the Blasket memoirists: Maurice O'Sullivan *(Twenty Years a-Growing)*, Thomas O'Crohan *(The Islandman)*, and Peig Sayers *(Peig)*. (Sayers's reputation as a writer and storyteller, damaged by her translators, is now being reclaimed by the scholarship of Margaret McCurtain and Irish folklorists).

# Mary Carbery

## 1867–1949

*On a visit to Ireland, the English-born Mary Toulmin fell in love with Lord Carbery of Castlefreke, County Cork. She also loved his Irish world, which, as his wife, she explored with the zeal of a cultural anthropologist. In* The Farm by Lough Gur *(recently reissued), she wove together the memories of an old woman, Mary Fogarty (Sissy O'Brien in her youth), who had grown up on a nineteenth-century hillside farm overlooking the enchanted lake of Limerick. According to Irish writer Shane Leslie (1885–1971) (a favorite of F. Scott Fitzgerald), the memoir "carries all the mists and memories, all the scent and sting of the Irish countryside." At its center, Lough Gur "lies like a mirror," neither reservoir nor fishing preserve, but rather a living creature.*

## FROM *THE FARM BY LOUGH GUR*

There is a hill in the county Limerick called Knockfennel whose southern slopes fall steeply into Lough Gur. On a green ridge above the lake stands an old farmhouse where I was born on the twenty-ninth of May, 1858. . . .

By and by my playmates came, three little sisters, Janie, Bessie, and Annie who I believed was brought in a bag by the fat, kind woman who nursed my mother. I was six when this baby came, and although I was timid by nature and unassertive, I felt a superiority over my sisters because I was the eldest daughter and could remember farther back than they could.


### THE MAGIC LAKE

When I think of home I see first Lough Gur, lying in summer sunshine like a bright mirror in which are reflected blue sky, bare hills, precipitous grey rocks and green pastures dotted with cattle and sheep; then a small, white house, half-hiding the fine farm buildings behind it, and four little girls playing ring-o'-roses before the door of their home, or touch-wood on the lawn, darting from the old oak before the house to the copper-beech, from the weeping-ash to the two rings of trees planted by our mother when she came to the farm as a bride.

Lough Gur dominates the scene. It was to us a personality loved, but also feared. Every seven years, so it is said, Gur demands the heart of a human being. Drownings were not infrequent and, as the bodies of the drowned were sometimes not recovered, Gur was said by some to be a bottomless lough.

In the lake is Knockadoon hill, joined to the land by a causeway built on the isthmus, once guarded by two fortresses where now only one, the ruined Black Castle, remains. Sometimes we children climbed by a steep and stony way to the summit of Knockadoon, where, when father was a boy, eagles made their nests and flew about the hills searching for leverets and newborn lambs to feed their young. From the top of Knockadoon we could see Garret Island, interesting for its prehistoric remains which were visited from time to time by antiquaries who gave my mother curious implements of the stone age in return for her hospitality.

Lough Gur has been called the Enchanted Lake; some say that in ancient days there was a city where the lake is now, before an earthquake threw up the hills and filled the hollow with water so that the city was submerged. Even now, the peasants say, when the surface of the lake is smooth one may see from a boat, far down and down again, the drowned city, its walls and castle, houses and church, perfect and intact, waiting for the Day of Resurrection. And on Christmas eve, a dark night without moon and stars, if one looks down and down again, one may see lights in the windows, and listening with the ears of the mind, hear the muffled chiming of church bells.

◊ ◊

The hills round Gur are bare of trees, but once they were covered with forest. Great giants, who were among Ireland's first people, hunted in the woods; they hunted deer, wild pigs and wild horses. The bones they picked and gnawed with their strong teeth are brought up from the floor of the lake to this day, with the fossil bones of polar bears and some say of rhinoceros.

On Baile-na-Cailleach hill one of these giants lies buried in a stone coffin with a long gold sword beside him. The stones of a cromlech stand over the grave, which is called the Pig's Bed or Leaba-na-muice.

Old people who lived on the shore believed that giants built the stone circles which stand near the lake, for who but giants could move such great stones? They were heathen, these giants. Their god was Bel, and a mighty one he was, as the god of giants should be. Wasn't the curse of Bel a dread and a danger to this day? Wasn't it to please Bel, to get on the right side of him, that the people lit Bel-fires on the hills? Bel could be kind; his blessing was good and lucky, but his brother, the Thunder God, was a Fright and a Spit-Fire—if he spared you to-day he would take you to-morrow. So the old people said. They knew little more than we children did of the gentle moon-worshippers of old who burnt the fire of Samhuin on the night of November the first, and on the sixth night of every moon brought their sick into the moonlight to be healed. The old folk had heard that night called All-Heal. They knew that if a sick person was not better by the eighth or ninth day of the moon he would hear *Ceolsidhe*, the fairy music with which Ainë the Banshee, Spirit of Lough Gur, comforts the dying. He would fall asleep to *Suantraighe*, the whispering song of sleep which Fer Fi* plays on a three-stringed harp.

No wonder that they who travelled the roads, the wandering beggars, pipers and harpers, story-tellers, Poor Scholars, drovers and tinkers, all feared to be benighted within a mile of Gur's enchanted waters, feared even to fall asleep in broad daylight, so great was the magic in the air.

We children knew nothing of this dread. The only story we half-believed was of one of the Desmonds, Garret the Earl,** who was doomed to gallop once in seven years over the surface of the water and around the lake. He rides on a milk-white horse, shod with silver shoes, and must ride until the silver shoes are worn out. Then he will be loosed from the enchantment which binds him and will live, a man among men, for he has never died.

We were afraid to go near the lake alone at twilight lest we should meet him; we wondered why he was cursed and what he sought on his wild ride. Often we prayed that he might find peace.

My father's land came down to the lake on the slope of the hill called the Carrigeen, which lay at the foot of Knockfennel. The Carrigeen was well fenced to keep in the yearling bulls which grazed there. Within this enclosure was a smaller one with high stone walls on three sides where dwelt our great bull; on the fourth side was the lake. We were thankful that father kept him safely shut up, for at that time many farmers let their bulls range the fields with other cattle and many were the stories we heard of people being chased and gored.

The road to our house led past the orchard which father let to old Malachy for a very small rent. We bought all the apples, and it

---

*Fer Fi is Ainë's brother, a kindly red-haired dwarf who plays only three tunes, Wail, Sleep, Laughter. It is lucky to hear Fer Fi laughing.
**Garret FitzGerald, Earl of Desmond, was the unfortunate leader who fought against the forces of Elizabeth.

would have been cheaper to keep the orchard, but when one day someone who thought himself very clever, suggested that to mother, father answered, 'You may be right; it would be cheaper for us, but for Malachy it would be starvation.'

Malachy was deaf, his sight was getting scattered, and he relied on his old dog to tell him when thieving boys were climbing into the orchard. 'Bite 'em, good fella, bite 'em,' he shouted, waving his blackthorn. If they weren't quick in escaping, old Barker gave them a nip.

Beyond the orchard was a place we called the alley, where there was a small cowshed and a haystack within the crumbled walls of a ruin. When we had passed that and the dangerous sandpit and mother's trees, we arrived at our house.

⊏◇⊐

## For the Literary Traveler

LOUGH GUR, about thirteen miles south of Limerick City (on the R512), is a pretty lake shaped like a horseshoe between the two hills of KNOCKADOON and KNOCKFENNELL. Archaeologists, vivid comic characters in Carbery's memoir, have discovered a vast number of habitats and artifacts of the Neolithic community that lived and farmed on these lakeside hills four thousand years ago. The Lough Gur interpretive center (on the northeastern lakeshore) sorts out—and directs you along the walking trail to—Gur's archaeological treasure: house and hut sites, ring forts, the largest stone circle in Ireland (at Grange), standing stones, crannogs (man-made islands in the lake), cairns, a chamber tomb, and gallery graves in which human skeletons and such grave goods as Neolithic decorated pottery and farm implements were found. The farm where Sissy O'Brien and her sisters grew up watching the intrigues of the ubiquitous archaeologists is still occupied (by O'Briens in 1999), just up the hill of Knockfennell from the interpretive center, beyond the hut sites called the "Spectacles." On a fine day the view from the top of Knockfennell is the same one Sissy saw and Mary Carbery describes: the hills of Clare to the north, the Slievefelim and Keeper hills to the northeast, and the Galtees to the southeast.

Though not a regular stop on foreign tourists' itinerary, Lough Gur is popular with the Irish. "It's a place where you can sit for hours and let the world go by," a friend of mine from Clare told me, and as I found out, she has the place just right. And so does the book, which describes the flow of affection in an Irish family of four girls as one enlivening current, like the underground spring that feeds the lake.

# Kate O'Brien

## 1897–1974

*Ahead of her time, Kate O'Brien, Limerick native and exile, wrote about sexual love as well as relationships between women in nine superbly readable novels. Her first,* Without My Cloak *(1931), won the Hawthornden Prize, became a best-seller, and established her literary reputation. The Censorship Board banned* Mary Lavelle *(1936), whose heroine chooses sex over abstinence, and* The Land of Spices *(1941), about a nun's growing capacity for compassion, with muted homosexual content. O'Brien lived in Spain, England, and Roundstone, County Galway, finally moving back to England, where she died. Her idiosyncratic travel book* My Ireland *(1962) has the cranky tone of an insider who sees that her native place is not all it could be. (She goes after Irish cooking, in particular, in the days before Irish chefs learned new skills in France.) But she loves Ireland, she says, with a "fidgety" kind of love. And in her hometown, "I learnt the world."*

FROM *MY IRELAND*

### CHAPTER ONE: LIMERICK

As my life began at Limerick and has often brought me back there, so these memories and reflections about Irish travel seem naturally to start there too and to weave and wind from that

first focus. And now from Shannon Airport it must often be the
first Irish city that a stranger will set foot in. It may not be a radiant
starting point; but first impression need not dazzle; and a slow approach is wise where true acquaintance is expected. . . .

It seems to me that a sensitive stranger, crossing one of Limerick's bridges, having looked up and down the Shannon and along
any one of the wide, grey streets, might feel detached awhile . . . and
inclined to postpone the sending-off of first-impression postcards.

◊    ◊

The Shannon is a formidable water; nothing parochial about it,
nothing of prattle or girlish dream. It sweeps in and out of the
ocean and the world according to the rules of far-out tides, and in
association with dangerous distances. So its harbour has been long
accustomed to news and trouble in and out, and in the general
movement of time Limerick has been shaped as much by invasions
and sieges as by acts of God and the usual weatherings. It is for Ireland therefore a representative city: whatever happened to Ireland
happened also here—and some things happened to Ireland because
of things that happened here. . . .

◊    ◊

The stranger passing by from far away, and bent on present pleasure, does not seek a history lesson. Perhaps least of all from Ireland will he want history, since he may likely have the impression,
erroneous maybe, that he has heard it all and that enough's enough.
But in Limerick he will see in souvenir form of some kind, or on
postcards, or in its unprepossessing actuality, an object called the
Treaty Stone. This undressed lump of limestone sits on a squat,
small pedestal; when I was a child I thought it partook in some degree of the sacred, the supernatural, but I did not find it endearing.
No one could indeed. Yet oddly enough, seated obscurely there on
the western end of Thomond Bridge the Treaty Stone commemorates unheeded two pieces of European history, each of a peculiarly
brilliant poignancy: (a) the end for all practical purposes, in 1691,
of the Jacobite cause and: (b) the gift to the terrible advancing

battlefields of eighteenth-century Europe of the Irish Brigade. That is all the imagination needs to know about the awkward piece of stone that Sarsfield and the Williamite used as writing table.

Walking back from the Stone along the North Strand which is leafy and residential and in County Clare, one can take a good stare at Limerick's best façade. . . . The old town rises mainly in grey from here, its dominant being the stained and shadowed limestone of St. Mary's Cathedral and King John's Castle on their dark, lichened rocks: Limerick's chief Norman remains, and specimens with merit. But as for the still grim and strong Castle, now made to look silly by the ugly tops of little mean cement houses built within and staring stupidly over its parapets—I for one am allergic to fortifications, and find them boring wherever I go. . . .

◊     ◊

But if I do find my imagination naturally and always bored by turrets, keeps, dungeons and, onward from them, by architectural expressions of defensiveness of any kind, and so of extreme functionalism—that baulk may come from a weak non-combativeness in me, an innate dislike of side-taking, a shrinking from passionate convictions—a condition of all-round uncertainty that bedevils me. But it also comes, less feebly, out of humanism; and out of aesthetic boredom before the unsubtle and brutal principles upon which the expressions of defence and functionalism must stand.

◊     ◊

City walls, in short, displease the eye; as do Norman forts and keeps, and nineteenth-century gaols, and twentieth-century barracks, oil tankers, hotels, spaceships, garages, warheads and space-war emplacements. All are conceived in defensiveness and ruthlessly; egotism and 'I'm All Right, Jack' always come out on their strong features.

This dislike has often saddened my contemplation of the scene of Ireland. Our plains and hills are over-richly marked by broken keeps and towers, square-face, efficient structures which in their day of pride existed for one function only: for a man to defend himself and kill the man outside. Ivy, weather, and the beholder's awareness of the desolating centuries that were to follow on the dereliction of all this stony arrogance, these give pathos now, and that is all; there was never beauty in these buildings, and where beauty has not been in at birth it does not visit. . . .

◊    ◊

I have gone a long way round merely to say that I care not at all for King John's Castle in Limerick, while always gratefully admiring of gentle St Mary's. Square-towered and grey, never of first-flight inspiration, and often patchily restored, it is nevertheless of stalwart Norman bearing and the city's only extant reminder now of the saints and scholars.

The stranger should visit St Mary's. If he climbs the tower on a summer's day, as I did long ago, he may think himself rewarded, for the view thence on any side is at once lively and tranquillising; beyond the intricacies of roofs, trees, streets and people, the landscape spreads, if the sun is shining, in a Persian weave of colours broken by serpentine flashes of waters, to blue hills, mainly blue, and a high, transparent sky. . . .

Myself when I am in a new city, I think it a fair plan to begin by walking round its places of worship. Not, at first, to examine them—no, not if they are Chartres itself, or La Sainte Chapelle. (All the more *no* indeed, if they are such as these.) The idea is much lazier than anything like study or examination. By merely strolling about in quiet aisles you can catch on to a place without much effort. You get the local names off the walls and floor; you take in something of history, and can guess at past and present status; and quite without reference to your own faith or non-faith, you can—or anyway, I can—find out sometimes whether you are going to like or dislike a town—quite secularly I mean this—by walking round its churches. Not all of them, of course. Indeed, such a plan in Limerick would be downright exhausting. . . .

You can easily get into discreet conversation in a church—and even if with a too-loquacious sexton, or a sycophantic, would-be guide, such encounters it is often wise to accept with grace, as they can be oddly fruitful. But the really casual exchange of talk is best—with some individual who has dropped in to say a prayer, or who is polishing the brasses, or waiting for confession. People are gratified as a rule if one seeks information from them, and to ask for a simple piece of advice is to give pleasure almost infallibly.

## For the Literary Traveler

Kate O'Brien's frankness about her LIMERICK'S "grave" personality rings dully true as you walk in search of the city where "she learnt the world." Though her impressions date from more than half a century ago, and she didn't write them down until 1962, they still feel right: compared to, say, Galway, there's something contained about the city on the Shannon. It's no longer the "poor" place O'Brien remembers, however, with traffic, shoppers, and construction projects visibly in play in each of the city's three sections: Englishtown (across Matthew's Bridge on the Abbey River, the location of the medieval SAINT MARY'S CATHEDRAL and KING JOHN'S CASTLE), Irishtown (southeast of the city center, an area of low-income flats), and Newtown Pery (up O'Connell Street, the main thoroughfare, the area around the Georgian CRESCENT). Walking-tour maps are available at the Tourist Office, on a cement island across from the ARTHUR'S QUAY MALL, a good place to observe knots of talkers deep in a gab. These are people who stop in their tracks to say more than hello. They pick up a joke or some gossip for their time. Used to the determined pace of American cities, you envy this rhythm that has time for human beings.

The river city's cruel weather (rain with a biting wind seems a daily event) makes literary sense. The Shannon is named after a young woman, Sinann, one of the legendary tribe of the Tuatha de Danann, who was killed at the Shannon Pot, the name of the river's source up in County Cavan. She'd come to the well as a seeker of its wisdom. The well answered her quest with a flooding that drowned her. The story of how the Shannon got its name is a warning to curious maidens that it's safer to stay at home and not ask questions, a lesson the uppity girls in Kate O'Brien's novels—like their author—chose to ignore. O'Brien herself was a travel addict. Her fictional theme is the individual (usually female) conscience in conflict with the conformist tribe and despotic power.

The seaport city's factual history also floods over with stories of the slaughter of innocents and their fierce resistance. The Vikings, the Normans, the English as represented by Oliver Cromwell in an especially bad mood and then King William III in 1691—all sailed up the Shannon, conquered the city (which, after the Normans, was entirely walled), usually by burning it to the ground, then moving on when the defeated but not beaten O'Briens and MacNamaras intermittently came in from Irishtown or from across the Shannon in Clare to send them packing. Though Catholic (or Jacobite) Limerick, led by the brave Patrick Sarsfield (the namesake of the SARSFIELD BRIDGE, which leads to the Ennis/Shannon airport road) mounted a final heroic defense in 1691, the English won again, though this time they agreed to the Treaty of Limerick, which promised to restore the Catholics' religious freedom and the right to hold property. Within a few weeks, however, the English broke the treaty (and came up instead with the Penal Laws), leaving Limerick with the permanent conviction that you could trust an Englishman about as far as you could throw the TREATY STONE, the "table" on which King Billy and Sarsfield supposedly signed the agreement. (Limerick is called "the City of the Violated Treaty.") Today the Stone stands on a pedestal on the west side of THOMOND BRIDGE, within walking distance of King John's Castle (c. 1200), which O'Brien dislikes. At the other end of Nicholas Street, ST. MARY'S CATHEDRAL, founded by Donal Mor O'Brien, king of Thomond (1168–94)—Thomond, the name for North Munster (distinct from Desmond, or South Munster), included Clare, Limerick, Tipperary, and North Kerry—is, along with its surrounding wildflower garden and graveyard, the quietest haven in the city. The stained-glass window over the altar tells the story of the Good Samaritan. In the choir are the renowned misericords (mercy seats), choir stalls with oak panels on the underside of each seat, decorated with carved figures of angels, griffins, humans, and beasts. These choir stools (under restoration in 1999) enabled the clergy, who had to stand during long, elaborate liturgies, to rest their backsides on the stalls' mercifully tipped-up seats. (The steeple is no longer open to visitors, which doesn't matter since the view over Limerick is now one vast sprawl of houses and gas stations.)

Leaving St. Mary's Cathedral in English Town, you walk back across Matthew's Bridge toward Patrick's Street. (You're headed in the direction of Frank McCourt's Limerick—see below.) Attuned to the cultural legacy of Catholicism (she wrote a protofeminist biography of Teresa of Avila), O'Brien would no doubt stop to admire the extraordinary collection of medieval religious art (and the Leonardo da Vinci and Picasso) in the HUNT MUSEUM (Tues.-Sat. 10–5; Sun. 2–5), located in the fine Palladian CUSTOM HOUSE (1765), to your left on Charlotte's Quay.

◘

# Frank McCourt

## 1931–

*Born in Brooklyn to Irish immigrant parents who brought their family back to Ireland when he was "four going on five," Frank McCourt grew up in the poor lanes of Limerick on the river Shannon, where "from October to April the walls [of the city] glistened with the damp." Thirteen years later, he returned alone to New York. In 1996, retired after twenty-seven years as a New York City schoolteacher, he published his memoir about his Irish childhood, the best-selling and every-prize-under-the-sun-winning* Angela's Ashes. *Its power, according to* The Nation, *lies in "its account of an emerging consciousness— a universal experience that is rarely articulated well. It's also about poverty and childhood, survival and laughter, and to an extent the long tragedy of the Irish." Though some Limerick natives found it too harsh (a few Long Island Limerick immigrants threatened to burn it in honor of St. Patrick's Day 2000), many more have called the portrait of his childhood city far too kind. Beyond Ireland, millions of readers—it's been translated into thirty languages—have loved the*

book for how it tells its story. In the guileless voice of a child, it con-
jures a horrific cast of bullies, hypocrites, and sourpusses, nailing in
precise and vivid detail their habits of cruelty. But there's also a desperate tenderness at the heart of the story, especially when McCourt
remembers his family and the neighbors who showed them some
kindness. And in the following pages, there is gratitude for the schoolmaster, Mr. Hoppy O'Halloran, the humanist-in-residence at Leamy's
National School, who spotted young McCourt's potential and inspired
him to somehow break free from the dead end that was Limerick in
the forties.

FROM *ANGELA'S ASHES*

> Frank has been hospitalized for two months with typhoid fever.
> Now he returns to Leamy's National School.

I can't stay at home forever and Mam takes me back to Leamy's
School in November. The new headmaster, Mr. O'Halloran, says
he's sorry, I've missed over two months of school and I have to be
put back in fifth class. Mam says surely I'm ready for sixth class.
After all, she says, he's missed only a few weeks. Mr. O'Halloran
says he's sorry, take the boy next door to Mr. O'Dea.

We walk along the hallway and I tell Mam I don't want to be in
fifth class. Malachy is in that class and I don't want to be in a class
with my brother who is a year younger. I made my Confirmation
last year. He didn't. I'm older. I'm not bigger anymore because of
the typhoid but I'm older.

Mam says, It won't kill you.

She doesn't care and I'm put into that class with Malachy and I
know all his friends are there sneering at me because I was put
back. Mr. O'Dea makes me sit in the front and tells me get that
sour look off my puss or I'll feel the end of his ash plant.

Then a miracle happens and it's all because of St. Francis of Assisi, my favorite saint, and Our Lord Himself. I find a penny in the
street that first day back at school and I want to run to Kathleen
O'Connell's for a big square of Cleeves' toffee but I can't run because my legs are still weak from the typhoid and sometimes I have

to hold on to a wall. I'm desperate for the Cleeves' toffee but I'm also desperate to get out of fifth class.

I know I have to go to the statue of St. Francis of Assisi. He's the only one who will listen but he's at the other end of Limerick and it takes me an hour to walk there, sitting on steps, holding on to walls. It's a penny to light a candle and I wonder if I should just light the candle and keep the penny. No, St. Francis would know. He loves the bird in the air and the fish in the stream but he's not a fool. I light the candle, I kneel at his statue and beg him to get me out of fifth class where I'm stuck with my brother, who is probably going around the lane now bragging that his big brother was kept back. St. Francis doesn't say a word but I know he's listening and I know he'll get me out of that class. It's the least he could do after all my trouble coming to his statue, sitting on steps, holding on to walls, when I could have gone to St. Joseph's Church and lit a candle to the Little Flower or the Sacred Heart of Jesus Himself. What's the use of being named after him if he's going to desert me in my hour of need?

I have to sit in Mr. O'Dea's class listening to the catechism and all the other stuff he taught last year. I'd like to raise my hand and give the answers but he says, Be quiet, let your brother answer. He gives them tests in arithmetic and makes me sit there and correct them. He dictates to them in Irish and makes me correct what they've written. Then he gives me special compositions to write and makes me read them to the class because of all I learned from him last year. He tells the class, Frank McCourt is going to show you how well he learned to write in this class last year. He's going to write a composition on Our Lord, aren't you, McCourt? He's going to tell us what it would be like if Our Lord had grown up in Limerick which has the Arch Confraternity of the Holy Family and is the holiest city in Ireland. We know that if Our Lord had grown up in Limerick He would never have been crucified because the people of Limerick were always good Catholics and not given to crucifixion. So, McCourt, you are to go home and write that composition and bring it in tomorrow.

Dad says Mr. O'Dea has a great imagination but didn't Our Lord suffer enough on the cross without sticking Him in Limerick on top of it with the damp from the River Shannon. He puts on his cap and goes for a long walk and I have to think about Our Lord by myself and wonder what I'm going to write tomorrow.

The next day Mr. O'Dea says, All right, McCourt, read your composition to the class.

The name of my composition is—

The title, McCourt, the title.

The title of my composition is, "Jesus and the Weather."

What?

"Jesus and the Weather."

All right, read it.

This is my composition. I don't think Jesus Who is Our Lord would have liked the weather in Limerick because it's always raining and the Shannon keeps the whole city damp. My father says the Shannon is a killer river because it killed my two brothers. When you look at pictures of Jesus He's always wandering around ancient Israel in a sheet. It never rains there and you never hear of anyone coughing or getting consumption or anything like that and no one has a job there because all they do is stand around and eat manna and shake their fists and go to crucifixions.

Anytime Jesus got hungry all He had to do was walk up the road to a fig tree or an orange tree and have His fill. If He wanted a pint He could wave His hand over a big glass and there was the pint. Or He could visit Mary Magdalene and her sister, Martha, and they'd give Him His dinner no questions asked and He'd get his feet washed and dried with Mary Magdalene's hair while Martha washed the dishes, which I don't think is fair. Why should she have to wash the dishes while her sister sits out there chatting away with Our Lord? It's a good thing Jesus decided to be born Jewish in that warm place because if he was born in Limerick he'd catch the consumption and be dead in a month and there wouldn't be any Catholic Church and there wouldn't be any Communion or Confirmation and we wouldn't have to learn the catechism and write compositions about Him. The End.

Mr. O'Dea is quiet and gives me a strange look and I'm worried because when he's quiet like that it means someone is going to suffer. He says, McCourt, who wrote that composition?

I did, sir.

Did your father write that composition?

He didn't, sir.

Come here, McCourt.

I follow him out the door, along the hall to the headmaster's room. Mr. O'Dea shows him my composition and Mr. O'Halloran gives me the strange look, too. Did you write this composition?

I did, sir.

I'm taken out of the fifth class and put into Mr. O'Halloran's sixth class with all the boys I know, Paddy Clohessy, Fintan Slattery, The Question Quigley, and when school is over that day I have to go back down to the statue of St. Francis of Assisi to thank him even if my legs are still weak from the typhoid and I have to sit on steps and hold on to walls and I wonder was it something good I said in that composition or something bad.

Mr. Thomas L. O'Halloran teaches three classes in one room, sixth, seventh, eighth. He has a head like President Roosevelt and he wears gold glasses. He wears suits, navy blue or gray, and there's a gold watch chain that hangs across his belly from pocket to pocket in his waistcoat. We call him Hoppy because he has a short leg and hops when he walks. He knows what we call him and he says, Yes, I'm Hoppy and I'll hop on you. He carries a long stick, a pointer, and if you don't pay attention or give a stupid answer he gives you three slaps on each hand or whacks you across the backs of your legs. He makes you learn everything by heart, everything, and that makes him the hardest master in the school. He loves America and makes us know all the American states in alphabetical order. He makes charts of Irish grammar, Irish history and algebra at home, hangs them on an easel and we have to chant our way through the cases, conjugations and declensions of Irish, famous names and battles, proportions, ratios, equations. We have to know all the important dates in Irish history. He tells us what is important and why. No master ever told us why before. If you asked why you'd be hit on the head. Hoppy doesn't call us idiots and if you ask a question he doesn't go into a rage. He's the only master who stops and says, Do ye understand what I'm talking about? Do ye want to ask a question?

It's a shock to everyone when he says, the Battle of Kinsale in sixteen nought one was the saddest moment in Irish history, a close battle with cruelty and atrocities on both sides.

Cruelty on both sides? The Irish side? How could that be? All the other masters told us the Irish always fought nobly, they always fought the fair fight. He recites and makes us remember,

> They went forth to battle, but they always fell,
> Their eyes were fixed above the sullen shields.
> Nobly they fought and bravely, but not well,
> And sank heart-wounded by a subtle spell.

If they lost it was because of traitors and informers. But I want to know about these Irish atrocities.

Sir, did the Irish commit atrocities at the Battle of Kinsale?

They did, indeed. It is recorded that they killed prisoners but they were no better nor worse than the English.

Mr. O'Halloran can't lie. He's the headmaster. All these years we were told the Irish were always noble and they made brave speeches before the English hanged them. Now Hoppy O'Halloran is saying the Irish did bad things. Next thing he'll be saying the English did good things. He says, You have to study and learn so that you can make up your own mind about history and everything else but you can't make up an empty mind. Stock your mind, stock your mind. It is your house of treasure and no one in the world can interfere with it. If you won the Irish Sweepstakes and bought a house that needed furniture would you fill it with bits and pieces of rubbish? Your mind is your house and if you fill it with rubbish from the cinemas it will rot in your head. You might be poor, your shoes might be broken, but your mind is a palace. . . .

◊     ◊

In seventh class he hands out a small book, a poem that goes on for pages and pages, *The Deserted Village,* by Oliver Goldsmith. He says that this seems to be a poem about England but it is a lament for the poet's native land, our own native land, Ireland.* We are to

---

*Goldsmith's "Sweet Auburn" refers to Lissoy in County Westmeath, the boyhood Irish home he called "the most pleasing horizon of nature."

get this poem by heart, twenty lines a night to be recited every morning. Six boys are called to the front of the room for reciting and if you miss a line you are slapped twice on each hand. He tells us put the books under the desks and the whole class chants the passage on the schoolmaster in the village.

> *Beside yon straggling fence that skirts the way,*
> *With blossomed furze unprofitably gay,*
> *There, in his noisy mansion, skilled to rule*
> *The village master taught his little school.*
> *A man severe he was and stern to view,*
> *I knew him well, and every truant knew.*
> *Full well the boding tremblers learned to trace*
> *The day's disaster in his morning face.*
> *Full well they laughed with counterfeited glee*
> *At all his jokes for many a joke had he.*
> *Full well the busy whisper circling round*
> *Conveyed the dismal tidings when he frowned.*

He always closes his eyes and smiles when we reach the last lines of the passage,

> *Yet he was kind, or, if severe in aught,*
> *The love he bore to learning was in fault.*
> *The village all declared how much he knew.*
> *'Twas certain he could write, and cipher too.*
> *Lands he could measure, terms and tides presage,*
> *And even the story ran that he could gauge.*
> *In arguing, too, the parson owned his skill,*
> *For, even though vanquished, he could argue still,*
> *While words of learned length and thundering sound*
> *Amazed the gazing rustics ranged around.*
> *And still they gazed, and still the wonder grew,*
> *That one small head could carry all he knew.*

We know he loves these lines because they're about a schoolmaster, about him, and he's right because we wonder how one small head could carry all he knows and we will remember him in these lines. He says, Ah, boys, boys, You can make up your own minds but first stock them. Are you listening to me? Stock your minds and you can move through the world resplendent. Clarke, define resplendent. . . .

◊     ◊

I'm thirteen going on fourteen and it's June, the last month of school forever. Mam takes me to see the priest, Dr. Cowpar, about getting a job as telegram boy. The supervisor in the post office, Mrs. O'Connell, says, Do you know how to cycle, and I lie that I do. She says I can't start till I'm fourteen so come back in August.

Mr. O'Halloran tells the class it's a disgrace that boys like McCourt, Clarke, Kennedy, have to hew wood and draw water. He is disgusted by this free and independent Ireland that keeps a class system foisted on us by the English, that we are throwing our talented children on the dungheap.

You must get out of this country, boys. Go to America, McCourt. Do you hear me?

I do, sir.

## For the Literary Traveler

You can walk the world of *Angela's Ashes* solo or in the company of a walking tour that, according to the Web site "The Limerick of Angela's Ashes," (www.iol.ie/~smidp/) "commences daily at 2:30 P.M. from St. Mary's Action Centre, 44 Nicholas St." Except when it doesn't. The day I showed up in Nicholas Street (behind St. Mary's Cathedral), the Action Centre was locked up tight. "There's been a death," a man informed me in a mysterious voice. "Wednesday week."

Unless the dead awaken, it's just as easy to be off on your own, with the memoir in hand, as well as the Tourist Office's map of Limerick, or better yet, the excellent map of McCourt's "city of gray miseries" available at the Web site called "The Club of Angela's Ashes," created by the Ireland-Japan Friendly Club (www.asahi-net.or.jp). McCourt Country lies mostly in the opposite direction from St. Mary's Cathedral and the other main tourist sites of Englishtown, Irishtown, and the new riverside walkways around Arthur's Quay and City Hall. (The infested old houses on Arthur's Quay where McCourt's friend Paddy Clohessy lived with his tubercular father are gone.)

Heading up O'Connell Street in the direction of the Georgian CRESCENT, you pass on your left EASON'S BOOKSELLERS, where Frank worked, and further along on the right—the river side of the street—O'MAHONY'S BOOKSTORE. It's a good place to duck into, out of the inevitable rain: "Above all," as McCourt could never forget, "we were wet." According to owner David O'Mahony, Angela's Ashes has been their biggest-selling title "of all time," solid evidence, in his opinion, that there's more affection than hostility in Limerick toward McCourt's portrait of the "gray place with a river that kills." For the walker in search of the book's settings, one useful title (among a good stock of books about Limerick) is Through Irish Eyes: A Visual Companion to Angela McCourt's Ireland, a book of photographs of Limerick in the 1930s and 1940s—the years Frank grew up here—with captions identifying what's left and what's gone the way of the bulldozer. The graphics show the former whereabouts of the now demolished "Lanes," for instance, the huddled, squalid alleys such as Windmill Street (where Oliver died) and Roden Lane on Barrack Hill, where the McCourts settled into "Ireland and Italy."

As you reach the Crescent at the south end of O'Connell Street, a handsome enclave of Georgian houses under the protective shadow of a statue of Daniel O'Connell (1857), you turn left into HARTSTONGE STREET, where on the right-hand side stands Leamy House, LEAMY'S NATIONAL SCHOOL in McCourt's time, a Tudor Revival building of 1843, with a 1975 plaque to LEAMY'S NATIONAL SCHOOL AND TO THE TEACHERS AND PUPILS OF MANY GENERATIONS WHO ATTENDED HERE. Today the offices of accountants and auditors (the school closed in 1952), there's not a sound coming out of it on an early afternoon in spring, but in the reader's memory, as you stand in the entrance foyer and then climb the old stairs, there are echoes of schoolboys chanting Oliver Goldsmith's "The Deserted Village" punctuated by the thwack of Mr. O'Dea's cane on a bad boy's hands

and the basso profundo of headmaster O'Halloran out in the hallway instructing Angela McCourt on how to help her son Frank avoid
"the messenger boy trap," the dead end awaiting boys who could
not afford to pay for schooling after elementary school. (The Irish
government did not provide free secondary education until 1967.)
Though the Christian Brothers slammed the door on O'Halloran's
plan for Frank's educational future, he eventually made his own way
through university in New York, turning into a scholar and a schoolmaster himself, today as fresh in the memory of many of his old
Stuyvesant High School students (who pop up all over the world at
his readings and signings) as Mr. O'Halloran remains in his.

A few steps beyond Leamy House is the building of the ST. VIN-
CENT DE PAUL SOCIETY, where Angela and Frank stood in line waiting for
used clothes and a Christmas turkey. (Instead, they were given a pig's
head.) At the end of this short block you come into PERY SQUARE, the
heart of Newtown Pery, the Georgian district planned and named for
Sexton Pery (1719–1806), the speaker of the Irish House of Commons from 1771 to 1785. A solid line of Georgian houses faces the
railings and lawns of PEOPLE'S PARK. Here Angela and her friend Nora
sat smoking their Woodbines and Frank and Malachy sucked on
sweets after an afternoon in Hartstonge Street, queuing outside the
Society of St. Vincent de Paul. People's Park, where the McCourt
brothers and their friends played, is still an urban oasis of wide greens
and magnificent trees, dominated by an elegant column in the center,
commemorating Thomas Spring-Rice (1790–1866), politician and
lawyer. Small boys play soccer, women sit on benches smoking and jig-
gling baby carriages, men read the newspaper, ignoring the light drizzle.
Exiting through the arch that leads to Pery Square, you find to your
immediate left the most unambiguously influential place in McCourt's
Limerick: the CARNEGIE LIBRARY, the public sanctuary and temple of language where the scabby-eyed child began to become the literary man.
Though the library is now the Limerick City Gallery of Art—a beautiful exhibition space—you can stand in the old foyer of fine woodwork
and stained glass and read the Latin inscription over the door that
Frankie McCourt often passed through (on his way to impress Miss
O'Riordan with his interest in Butler's *Lives of the Saints*): URBS ANTIQUA
FUIT STUDIIS QUE ASPERRIMA BELLI ("The city was ancient and devoted to

extreme savagery in war"). A reference to Carthage from Book I of the *Aeneid*, the line also captures the violence of Limerick's historical memory.

Turn left as you leave the library. At the end of Pery Square is St. Michael's Protestant Church, where children still play in the yard as they did when Frank and a friend looked on at their games. Bearing right into Barrington Street, at the end of it you're back on O'Connell Street and the Crescent, only a block south of where you turned into Hartstonge Street. To your left is ST. JOSEPH'S CHURCH, where Frank made his First Communion and Confirmation, becoming a true Catholic and "official sinner." It's still a functioning parish church, though empty on a weekday afternoon, decorated with drawings by catechism students and their teachers, whose classes now emphasize a Jesus-is-love approach to religion, a sea change from the predictions of the temperature of hellfire that frightened Francis the First Communicant in the thirties.

Across O'Connell Street from St. Joseph's is the main entrance to SOUTH'S PUB, the repository of Frank's alcoholic father's fantasies and dole money. The back door is around the corner on Newenham Street. Inside, there are signs of a major facelift since the years when a hungry Frank or his younger brother Malachy came looking for their father. The dark wood is polished, the smoky glass gleams, and framed testimonials and McCourt's face needlepointed into a large wall hanging indicate a thriving *Angela's Ashes* industry that is literally part of the woodwork.

Limerick is a transformed place these days, mostly, according to some, because of the presence of the UNIVERSITY OF LIMERICK, three miles from the city center; the university opened in 1972. (As part of his triumphal return to Limerick after the success of *Angela's Ashes*, Frank McCourt was made an honorary doctor of letters by the university.) Others (the afternoon regulars in South's Pub) cite money—"It's as plain as that, it's the pure, filthy money."

Ironically, if Limerick's reputation among travelers as a city to avoid begins to change, it may well be in large measure because of the dark portrait of her most famous emigrant, the New Yorker Frank McCourt. On your way out of town, if you take the Dock Road (coast road) along the south side of the Shannon (N69/Tralee), in about three miles you will come to MUNGRET ABBEY and the ruins of a monastery founded by St. Patrick; the graveyard holds the remains of Angela Sheehan McCourt's family and, since 1985, her own ashes, returned to Ireland by her sons, which is recounted at the end of 'Tis. Off to the right you can see the towers of CARRIGOGUNNELL CASTLE, "the Rock of the O'Connells," a late medieval (1400–1600) Norman fortification built on a crag overlooking the Limerick side of the Shannon "where Dad brought me twice."

The view from Carrigogunnell Castle looks down on the well-worn route of the Irish exile:

> When I'm finished delivering the telegrams there's enough time to go to the ancient monastery graveyard where my mother's relations are buried, the Guilfoyles and the Sheehans, where my mother wants to be buried. I can see from here the high ruins of Carrigogunnell Castle and there's plenty of time to cycle there, sit up on the highest wall, look at the Shannon flowing out to the Atlantic on its way to America and dream of the day I'll be sailing off myself.

# Sean O'Faolain

## 1900–1991

FROM *AN IRISH JOURNEY*

*O'Faolain's 1941 travel memoir aimed to discover the "simpler, more racy Ireland of the people." Here the native Corkman is roaming around Clare and her capital "city" of Ennis.*

[From Limerick] I sailed down the Shannon to Foynes in an old boat laden with Guinness and coal. The traveller should try hard to do this, or to reverse the journey, as I have also done on another occasion. On land one is, to some extent, always entangled in the geography. On river there is a sense of quiet possession. It is as if one possessed a human body by a perfect knowledge of the line of every artery. It is a grand river for a long quiet sail. It soothes like milk. The shores are wide and low. . . .

When they landed me on the tiny pier opposite Foynes, on the Clare side, I looked back with regret at . . . the new buildings recently built to cope with the transatlantic flights which start from there. The Shannon has been, invariably, the boundary of wildness in Irish history. 'The wild Irish across the Shannon' is a common phrase. Then I turned past Cahircon . . . and proceeded to walk along the Fergus to Ennis. It was a grand walk, for the clouds were mounting the air like soapsuds, and this is the finest possible stretch of the Shannon and the noblest and most impressive river-stretch in all Ireland. I once taught school in Ennis for a year, so I enjoyed the prospect of revisiting old haunts. . . .

◊   ◊

As I entered Ennis past Clarecastle I began to recall my first impressions of Ennis. The narrowest streets of any Irish town, I know, and all winding like serpents . . . no library in my time—nowhere at all to get books to read, not even a shop where one could buy a book. . . .

What other impressions did I recall? My little digs opposite the Franciscan church—very cosy, spotlessly clean, with my first and most kind-hearted landlady. I remember she had a great weakness for the *True Story* magazine—an American publication, I think, with real photographs as illustrations, and always a slight suggestion, not too much, just a titillation, of sex in the supposed revelations. *How I married Two Men*—a story of unconscious bigamy. *My First Wedding Night*—a ghost story with a juicy background. I used to amuse myself by stealing her magazine and putting it in the fanlight of the door whenever I thought my friend from the friary across the road, a young priest with a St Anthony face, might be coming to visit me. Once she had a slight haemorrhage. As she was very pious she took her attack as a warning from the skies, and renounced the *True Story* magazine for a whole month after.

Her brother-in-law was my colleague at the Christian Brothers School. His passion was Crosswords, which had just then come into popularity. In this he was joined by all the monks in the school. 'Jezebel in six letters' once stumped them in a £1,000 competition. The next week, when the solutions came out, Brother Paul gave me the answer. 'Harlot,' he said, innocently. 'That's some queer kind of foreign woman, I believe.'

I liked that school, and I liked the brothers, and I liked the boys, and I liked Ennis. I had, I think, a salary of £150 a year. It may have been less—certainly not more. It was my first job as a teacher, and the salary was ample. I saved money on it. But, of course, if I had remained there I should have gone to seed. No books, no plays, no conversation, no stimulus. I'd have taken to drink. I would have become a bad teacher, all my freshness gone. . . .

I had no pastimes but to walk about Clare Abbey, and Quin Abbey, and down by Dromoland, or even as far as Newmarket-on-Fergus and out over the bog, or swim in the river in summer, and study in the winter. . . .

You need money to live in places the size of Ennis—money to be able to . . . have a few drinks, and buy books, and to be able to run out to Kilkee on summer Sundays, or into Limerick to friends, or up to Galway. Above all, one should be able to take a good month's holiday out of Ireland every summer; and two or three times a year, at Easter and Christmas, say, a holiday in some other part of Ireland, such as Dublin. (Or *even* Cork.)

⟨◇⟩

## For the Literary Traveler

The ferry O'Faolain took across the RIVER SHANNON fifty years ago now carries cars and people between Tarbert in Kerry and Killimer in south-west Clare (Apr.-Sept., Mon.-Sat. 7 A.M.-9 P.M., Sun. 9-9; Oct.-Mar., Mon.-Sat. 7-7, Sun. 10-7, every hour; tel. (065) 53124). Though scenic—sometimes there are dolphins to watch—it's no longer the idyllic boat ride he recommends; since 1940, the Shannon Development Corporation has come to town. But his walking route from Cahircon north along the RIVER FERGUS to Clare's chief town of ENNIS is pleasant enough. Weekdays, the shore road is deserted, so you won't risk your life. (At rush hour, however, the roads out of Ennis are jammed.)

Just to the south on this river road, on LABYSHEEDY BAY, an estuary of the Shannon, you'll find the tiny hamlet of LABYSHEEDY (or Labasheeda). Kerry poet Nuala Ní Dhomhnaill (see p. 249) evokes its sweet by-and-by stillness in her poem "Labysheedy, (the Silken Bed)":

> I'd make a bed for you
> in Labysheedy
> in the tall grass
> under the wrestling trees
> where your skin
> would be silk upon silk
> in the darkness
> when the moths are coming down....
>
> And your damp lips
> would be as sweet as sugar
> at evening and we walking
> by the riverside
> with honeyed breezes
> blowing over the Shannon
> and the fuchsias bowing down to you
> one by one....

*O I'd make a bed for you*
*in Labysheedy,*
*in the twilight hour*
*with evening falling slow*
*and what a pleasure it would be*
*to have our limbs entwine*
*wrestling*
*while the moths are coming down.*

Among visitors who know Ireland well, ENNIS, the destination of O'Faolain's eighteen-mile stroll, is a favorite. A smart countrygirl town, her eye is sharp, and the local speech comes across as an unemphatic ripple afloat on quick breathy laughter. What is now true all over Ireland certainly holds true here: these days travelers (or schoolteachers like O'Faolain) with time (and money) on their hands have more choices. For book lovers, there's the fine Ennis Bookshop at 13 Abbey Street; or the book section of the spacious Tourist Information Center, off Abbey Street, behind the new Templegate Hotel; or Spellacy's, the secondhand bookshop at the bottom of Parnell Street. As it was during O'Faolain's captivity, THE POET'S CORNER, the pub/restaurant in the OLD GROUND HOTEL (tel. 065-2817) on O'Connell Street is a warm, snug retreat, especially in the insistent Clare rain. (The entrance to the Old Ground, one of the most unpretentiously comfortable and welcoming hotels in Ireland, is on your right as you approach the town center coming from Quin (R469). The dark walls of the Poet's Corner are covered with prints and photographs of the Ireland of the writers.

The serpentine streets of Ennis, though no narrower than Clonakilty's in Cork, feel more ancient. ENNIS FRIARY, or, as O'Faolain calls it, "the Franciscan Church," in the town's center (May-Sept., 9:30–6:30), was founded in 1242 and by the fourteenth century was the most prestigious educational institution in Ireland for the clergy and the Gaelic aristocracy. The lancet windows, the medieval sculpture, and in particular the relief of St. Francis are well preserved.

Rain or shine—and it does sometimes turn sunny in moody Clare—Ennis has spirit. It's like a big party afternoons when school lets out and kids and their parents overflow the narrow sidewalks, surging past the lordly O'Connell monument at the head of O'Connell/

Abbey/Parnell Streets. You're reminded of the rebel energy Clare was known for in the nineteenth century: it elected Daniel O'Connell as the first Catholic to the British Parliament, though he was barred from taking his seat, and was also, as a center of the Land League ("The Land for the People" was its slogan), a hotbed of anti-landlordism. At night there's music in Brogan's in O'Connell Street and Cruises in Abbey Street. On Thursday nights you have your choice between a singing club, Brandon's in O'Connell Street, and "set dancing" (Irish folk dancing) in the COIS na HABNA ("CUSH-na-Hanna," which means "beside the stream"), a building three-quarters of a mile out of Ennis on the Galway road, on your left, across from Our Lady's Hospital.

Clare resident and Irish novelist Niall Williams *(The Four Letters of Love)*, coauthor with his American wife, Christine Breen, of *O Come Ye Back to Ireland*, offers this glimpse of a set dance in *The Pipes Are Calling: Our Jaunts Through Ireland*:

It was eight o'clock on a Thursday morning in Ennis, County Clare. *Ceili* music was playing on the radio, Chris and I, still clad in our pajamas, were dancing, hop two three, around the kitchen. Our heads jigging up and down, flashing past the window and round again, we were mad Irish clockwork figures, characters of the May morning spinning and wheeling and housing away to the fiddles, pipes, and whistles of the Tulla Ceili Band.

We were mad for dancing.

Every Thursday evening at nine o'clock for three months of the winter we had gathered down at the school with four or five other couples to learn Irish folk dancing, "set dancing." Beside us were the Normoyles, the Reidys, the McMahons, the Cotters, and our great friends the Hartys. Our dancing master was Noel Conway. He taught us, with patience and bemusement, the Clare Set (also known as the Caledonian Set), in much the same way it has been taught and danced in the west of Ireland for a hundred years. Most of the Irish, particularly those reared in the west, have at one time or another danced a set. In country pubs or in wedding halls and in kitchens around the country, set dancing is still a great pastime.

The Clare Set is composed of six figures: three reels, followed by a jig, another reel, and a hornpipe. Four couples make up a set:

They stand in a square and dance in a circle, and if that isn't confusing enough, one couple is "tops," another "tails," and the other two are both known as sides. In olden days, the tops were the couple standing at the kitchen dresser, and opposite them were the tails, standing with their backs to the hearth. The best dancer always won the place of honor at the hearth and when he rose from his seat to dance a set, the host would say to him, "You're for the flag." His dancing, drumming feet, then, keep time on the flagstone before the hearth. His "battering" could be heard throughout the house.

It is unclear from the annals of history when Irish folk dancing began. In fact, in eleventh-century, pre-Norman Ireland, when Irish was the only language, there doesn't appear to have been any word for dancing. The word *leimneach*, its primary meaning being leaping, was used to translate the Latin word *saltare*, to dance, in describing Salome's dance before Herod. But most historians discount the assumption that because no Irish word exists for the activity of dancing that the activity itself was unknown in ancient Ireland.

The Normans introduced "round" dancing in Ireland around the twelfth century, and later, dancing inside "The Pale" (the area in and around mid-sixteenth-century Dublin) was extremely tame in comparison to dancing done "beyond the Pale." The dance names themselves indicate what an exciting amusement was the folk dancing of the pre-Anglo-Irish countryside. "The sword dance," "A dance of ranks with change of music," and "The long dance with the sporting of young maidens" are just a few examples.

The word *"ceili"* in some parts of Ireland means a gathering of neighbors in the evening. In Clare this is known as "making a *cuaird*," or a visit; no musical entertainment or dancing is implied. So using a word *"ceili"* to describe organized dancing is, in fact, a misnomer, but the borrowing of the word is justified by the qualities of sociability and friendliness that are inherent in the *ceilis* of today.

Ironically, the first organized *ceili* was held on October 30, 1897, in London.

The long-awaited night of our own Ceili Mór had been Friday, January 27, at half past eight in Cois na Habna, in Ennis. It was arranged that we would meet the other members of "our set" there, Brendan and Geraldine, Noel and Moira, and Liz and her nondancing husband, Aidan. Michael and Gerry were coming with us but at the last minute Gerry had to stay home with a sick child. That left Michael without his partner. But as the saying goes, *"Is olc an gaoith na seadann le duine eigan,"* or "It's an ill wind that blows nobody good." Michael and Liz teamed up and the Kilmihil set was completed.

Cois na Habna is a wooden decagonal-shaped building ideally suited for *ceilis*. In keeping with the philosophy of Comhaltas Ceoltoiri na hEirinn, the organization of Irish traditional musicians and a body dedicated to the preservation of Irish music and dance, all functions held within Cois na Habna must be strictly involved with the traditional aspects of Irish culture. And on that night, the national chairman of Comhaltas Ceoltoiri na hEirinn, Labhrás O Murchú, came from Dublin to participate in the grand occasion of an evening's meal and a *ceili* dance.

Chris and I were very keyed-up for the night. We had practiced in our kitchen for hours, with little Deirdre sounding the steps with us, "hop two, three, and a two two three, and a three two three, and four two three . . ." We had danced down at the school with the rest of our set, and we had danced over at the Hartys'. We had even shown Mary Breen, our neighbor, our steps one day out on the road when a group of us went walking one Sunday afternoon. She giggled and said, "Oh ye have it, Niall, so you do," and she danced part of a reel herself, lilting the tune and wheeling me around and around on a boreen in Kiltumper.

The air was filled with the quick lively sounds of fiddles. The Kilmihil set met over near the front doors while twenty-five or so other sets established themselves around the room. One of the band members announced that the first set would be a Clare Set and the dancing began. But were we ready? Was the Kilmihil set assembled? No, we weren't. There was a moment of panic when Noel shouted, "Where's my wife? Where is Moira?" But it was too late for a search party, the set had begun. We had rehearsed this so often that when the music began, the dance took over and our feet flew away to the rhythm of the reel. We were holding hands and advancing and retreating in the opening steps of the first figure. Chris and I and Brendan and Geraldine were declared tops and tails and in a flash, we were off halfway around the "house," and advancing and retreating. Fortunately, just then, Chris whispered to me the crucial reminder "own place," which meant that we were to dance a measure in our own place before another advance and retreat and halfway around the house to "their place" before coming home again.

In unison the room bellowed with the excited sounds of 250 people in shared activity. The tops and tails and the sides joined together in one loud burst of exuberance. It was as if we were all members of a team in a contest and our team was winning. All around the room, the tops, tails, and sides of each and every set advanced to the center of their squares and retreated. Smiles abounded.

I have to say that we were beside ourselves with joy. Pure joy.


The environs of Ennis, where O'Faolain found relief from small-town tedium, also sharpen the lasting impression that Clare makes. It's a ten-minute drive to the village of QUIN and QUIN ABBEY, the most complete of all the Franciscan abbeys in the country. (Apr.-Oct., Mon.-Fri. 10–6:30, Sat., Sun. 11:30–5:30.) The Abbey rises in the middle of a field beyond a small bridge over the little River Rine. Except for the birds, you have the place to yourself as you wander through the arcade of cloisters, the artistry of their double piers intricate and full of joy. Climbing up one story, you look down on the cloisters' supporting buttresses. In summer, when the light lasts until almost eleven, Quin Abbey feels like an inspired destination along the back roads of Clare. In the surrounding fields, the cattle, lowing and grazing under the waning green daylight, keep their distance. Quin's pubs, the new Monks Well and the old Abbey, also offer good sanctuary. Three-quarters of a mile from Quin is the signposted MAGH ADHAIR, the inauguration site of the kings of Thomond, including Brian Boru. At night you might have trouble spotting the inaugural mound; it's surrounded by a ditch, and across a stream there's a stone pillar used in the crowning ceremony.

Further away, in southwest Clare (where O'Faolain disembarked and to which he sometimes returned on his holidays), there's KILRUSH, a pretty seaside town across from Scattery Island. At the marina on Cappagh Pier, you can hire a boat out to Scattery and its ancient ruins; they include Ireland's oldest and tallest surviving round tower. Heading down onto Clare's southwest peninsula, you come to CARRIGAHOLT, the setting of Irish-American poet Thomas Lynch's fine memoir, *The Undertaking: Life Studies from the Distant Trade* (1997), "one of the most life-affirming books in a long time," according to *The Nation*. From LOOP HEAD, the peninsula's tip, the views south (of Kerry) and north (of Connemara) are extraordinary. Returning northward, along a coast drenched with light off the ocean, you pass KILKEE, where O'Faolain went swimming on his days off and did not die of hypothermia. At the start of the twenty-first century, Kilkee is overbuilt, and threatened with mega-sized golf courses and hotels to match. (Critics charge the booming and insatiable Irish real-estate industry with turning all of County Clare into an endangered species.) If you continue along this coast (passing through Quilty, which is a great place for music), Spanish Point (where many bodies floated ashore when the Armada sank in 1588), and Lahinch, after turning east you'll come into the charming old town of ENNISTYMON on the River Cullenagh. Here, in the large house that is now the Falls Hotel, Caitlin Macnamara, daughter of Francis "Fireball" Macnamara, spent part of her youth before she married the Welch poet Dylan Thomas. Her memoir, *Double Drink Story: My Life with Dylan Thomas,* expresses her melodramatic love and fear of her native place, a mix of emotions you also find in O'Faolain's response to the West:

W hen I first went back to Ireland as a young green girl (I had been there as a small child but remembered nothing of it), a most extraordinary feeling came over me: I felt I was coming home. I had never any particular feeling, one way or the other, for England, the country I was living in, but when I first went to our home at Ennistymon, County Clare, I felt uplifted; a wild lust for this country surged up in me. I felt that it was mine, that it belonged to me, that the very air of it ran singing in my veins, that it was me. I understood all of a sudden what being patriotic meant. I would have gladly died, then and there, for this green enchanted island that was in all parts of me, that was my spiritual mother. The very air of it, the very smells of it, the very stone walls of it, the very craggy roads that always went over the hill to the sea (they had no-where else to go): they all intoxicated me. . . . Rain outside, beating on the roof of the warm inside; that was delicious manna to the soul. The rain in Ireland was all part of the giant sadness already ly-ing latent in me as a young girl. I was madly in love at first sight with Ireland in the rain. I was infatuated, I was happy. I could not believe it, but I was.

It did not last, of course. I knew, even then, that this unnatural happiness could not last. I knew I would have to plunge back, sooner or late, into real gritty life. I knew it was a glimpse, a tiny taste of paradise that would never come back again. This quickly passing possibility of a paradise on earth happened to me again when I went back to England and met Dylan, in a pub, of course, and knowingly started to drink. . . .

You can approach the section of Clare between Lough Derg and the Atlantic—the county's "most beautiful face," according to O'Faolain—from either Ennistymon or Ennis. In his words,

All this region between Lough Derg and Slieve Aughty and the sea is, physically speaking, lovely in a way that no other part of Ireland is lovely. . . . That is the thing about Clare which gives it such attraction. It is hard, and barren, and windy, and wild, yet its power to enchant comes from the delicacy and lightness and gentleness of its lyrical moods. Clare is now a shaggy-dressed, hairy-faced, dark-eyed, rough-voiced man of the roads—a drover or a travelling man: now a girl whose natural wildness is constantly forgotten in and overlain by the softness of her temperament. (Yeats, I see, felt this double quality too: 'cold Clare rock and Gal-

way rock and thorn. . . . That stern colour and that delicate line.')
This land full of grey rocks, little lakes, large horizons, seeping
dusk, clumped trees, wandering and winding roads, happy green
nooks among the stones, rich deposits among the boglands, is the
west without the savagery of the west, and the midlands without
their sloth and ease. It is amazing that a river could make such a
division.

Moving north from Ennis (on the R476 through COROFIN), you enter
the BURREN, with LOUGH INCHIQUIN to your left and on the right the
huge POULNABRONE DOLMEN, which dominates this Irish moonscape. If
the sun is hiding, these hundred square miles of limestone desert can
feel like a sci-fi Metallica wasteland. But on a bright day, the prehistoric
gray stones glimmer. Bending down, you see wedged deep within the
rocks a world of wildflowers. Irish botanist Robert Lloyd Praeger
names them in his brilliant guide to the flowers, birds, and animals of
Ireland, *The Way that I Went* (1937):

The strangeness of this grey limestone country must be seen to
be realized; it is like nothing else in Ireland or in Britain. . . .
And this brings me to the subject of the flora of Burren, which is so
remarkable, and in spring so beautiful, that it is celebrated far outside the ranks of botanists. . . . To see it at its maximum of profusion and beauty one must go to Burren or to Aran, during the
second half of May. Its interest lies in the presence and frequent
abundance of many plants elsewhere rare; and these plants display
a very remarkable variety of type as regards their normal headquarters. Extremely profuse are several which are usually found on
the mountains or in the far north—such as Mountain Avens, Bear-
berry, Spring Gentian and several Mossy Saxifrages. With these are
others of quite southern range, like the Close-flowered Orchis and
the Maidenhair; and all alike grow mixed together right down to
sea-level. Some of the former group are here found further south,
in view of their lowland habitat, than they are anywhere else, while
some of the latter occur nowhere else so far north. We have, indeed,

a very remarkable mixture of northern and southern species, most
of which, by a happy chance, are also most beautiful plants. With
these are others which are very rare in the British area, like the
Hoary Rock-rose and Pyramidal Bugle: others again are conspicuous by their immense profusion, like Bloody Crane's-bill and Madder, Hart's-tongue and Scale Fern. The result of the luxuriance and
abundance of these is that over miles the grey limestone is converted into a veritable rock-garden in spring, brilliant with blossom. How do these plants attain such profusion on ground that is
mostly bare rock? Many live in chinks and in the rain-widened
joints of the limestone, where humus has collected; and the damp
Atlantic wind, laden with mist and showers, does the rest.

A few miles north of Corofin, you'll come to KILLINABOY or KILNABOY,
with two ruins of early Christian churches. One has a well-preserved
*sheela-na-gig* over the door. (There are others in the National Museum
in Dublin, in Bunratty Castle, in Seirkieran in Offaly, and in Ballylarkin in
Kilkenny.) Celticists argue about the significance of these grotesque
carvings of naked women with their legs wide open to display their distended genitals. Are they witches? Fertility goddesses? Totems against
evil spirits? Irish journalist, drama critic, and biographer of Richard Brinsley Sheridan Fintan O'Toole uses the *sheela-na-gig* as an emblem of a
scandal that rocked Ireland in the early 1990s, leaving the clerical authority of the Catholic Church in the same shape as Kilnaboy. His piece
is called "Annie and the Bishop, Ireland and America," in his collection of
essays *The Lie of the Land*:

There is a ruined old church in Kilnaboy that is, in its way, . . .
powerfully symbolic. Roofless and open to the elements, it has
yet survived the centuries and its grey, hand-cut stones embody the
unadorned endurance of the Irish Catholic Church, its gravity and
its ascetic beauty. Just over the doorway, though, is a sheela-na-gig,
a grotesquely sexual and sternly obscene figure of a woman exposing herself. The same monks who prayed and fasted here placed
this figure of terrifying womanhood at the centre of their church, a
reminder, perhaps, of the flesh they had to fear and shun.

Annie Murphy is the Irish Catholic Church's sheela-na-gig made flesh, an avenging spirit risen up from the dark of the celibate mind to haunt and to terrify, to embody all those dangerous thoughts subdued by prayer and fasting. She is their worst nightmare come true, a figure from the mediaeval witch-hunters' manuals: wild and indiscreet, loose-tongued and lusty. She has written a book* about her love affair with a bishop, a book that is full not just of sex, but of the body itself, of beard rash and high blood pressure, of colitis and groin infections, of cancers and amputations. Of all the ills and sins that flesh is heir to.

In Irish folklore, the priest's mistress is a figure of almost super-natural evil. One old Gaelic proverb tells of 'three who will never see the light of Paradise':

> *The angel of pride,*
> *The unbaptised child,*
> *And a priest's concubine.*

The angel of pride is Satan. The priest's concubine (ceile shagairt) is associated with him. So, too, is the buried child, the forgotten child, the child interred at night in unconsecrated ground. For some true believers, no doubt, Annie Murphy and her son, her long-buried child, will still be associated with the satanic. Her book will be not just an act of personal betrayal, but an act of sacrilege.

Both of these roles—sheela-na-gig to terrify the Irish Church, and desecrator of the faithful's ideas of the sacred—are ones which Annie Murphy is happy to play in her book. They are, after all, starring roles, big parts in a drama that has been played for cen-turies. To describe making love in the bishop's palace in Killarney, to describe distracting the bishop while he is saying Mass, to men-tion his cross and ring in the context of furtive coupling, is to be one of the two main players, not in the kitchen tragedy of Annie and Eamonn, but in the grand opera of the clash of eternal forces. It is to play Body to his Soul, avenging angel to his tarnished saint,

*Forbidden Fruit*

world, flesh and devil to his Father, Son and Holy Ghost. It is a lot more glorious than to be poor, wounded Annie.

Yet the real story, the story that comes through so painfully in her book once you get used to the strange circumstances of this love affair, is ineffably ordinary. Take away the one sensational aspect of the story—that the man involved is a Catholic bishop, sworn to celibacy and preaching a strict code of sexual morality—and what you are left with is a story that life has told over and over, until it is blue in the face.

A younger, more vulnerable woman meets an older, more powerful man. He dazzles her with his power, his confidence, his command of the world. They fall in love and begin a sexual relationship. He promises her nothing but he doesn't need to for, hurt and abused as she is, she is more than capable of making him into a promise to herself. She gives him pleasure, excitement and adoration. He gives her the first two but probably not the third. She thinks of the future, he thinks of the present, floating on the delusion that he can have the best of all worlds. He makes her pregnant. The baby forces choices on her, choices which, because he is a man and a powerful one, he doesn't believe he has to make. He behaves badly, hypocritically, politically. It ends in tears: first hers, then, after many years, his.

Take away the thrill of discovering that bishops as a class are no better than many other men, and what remains is the fact that they are no worse. Little would have to change in Annie Murphy's book if Eamonn Casey were a prominent politician, or a judge, or just an ordinary married man indulging in a passionate but doomed side-affair which he will shake off when it becomes too threatening to his marriage and his settled place in the world. Desecration lies in the treacherous, abusive things that people do to each other, not in the fact that they are done in a bishop's palace rather than a bedsit.

We were promised some shocking revelations: that the affair lasted longer than was previously believed and continued after the birth of their son, Peter; that it was conducted for a period in a car parked in a gravel pit in Dublin; that they slept together again in a New York hotel as recently as early 1991. But given the initial premise—that an Irish bishop had an affair and a child—and the inevitable deceptions and moral contortions that flow from it, these are not shocking at all. They come with the territory, and the territory is a well-worn ground of deceit and double-dealing, a landscape that is there whether bishops choose to tread on it or not.

What is actually much more striking in Annie Murphy's story is the shock of the familiar. The view from the bishop's bed is a new angle on the sumptuousness and luxury of life at the top of the clerical ladder. There is nothing shocking in the notion that some bishops live in palaces, eat like kings and behave like princelings, that they are often waited on, flattered and pampered. But this is seldom described, because outsiders do not get close enough to do so. Annie Murphy is one outsider who did, who became privy to a world whose sensual delights may exclude sex but include the best food and drink, the finest places to live, the swankiest cars, clothes bought straight from Harrods. She is a privileged reporter, and the value of her testimony lies at least as much in its description of things that are taken for granted by the faithful, as of things that will shock and horrify them.

If there is an extraordinary dimension to this story of ordinary things, it is not the clash of sacred and secular, but the clash of Ireland and Irish-America. Annie Murphy's family could have been invented by Eugene O'Neill, such is its archetypal drama of lace curtain Irish respectability riddled with alcoholism, subdued violence and the hard bitterness of exile. John Steinbeck looked at the Irish-Americans and said that they 'do have a despairing gaiety, but they also have a dour and brooding ghost that rides on their shoulders and peers in on their thoughts': Annie Murphy embodies both the despairing gaiety and the brooding ghost, with a view of the world that is often wildly comic and often haunted by nameless forebodings.

Her love for Eamonn Casey seems inextricable from her love for Ireland, an exile's love of the dream homeland. She is in love with the place as much as with the man. The sea, the mountains, the flowers are characters in her love affair. She brings to that affair both the illusory longing and the driven ambition of Irish-America, both the rosy view of Ireland and the all-American drive to make the world conform to her view of it.

In many ways Eamonn Casey is as typically Irish as she is Irish-American. Energetic, garrulous, at home with the world, but also full of evasions and denials. In certain ways she is more ambitious than he is, for she wants the world to change, wants a clerical princeling to come down off his throne and take charge of her messy life, while he wants things to be the same only more so. He wants everything he has and something else as well—the joy of sex, maybe the comfort of being loved rather than adored. He just has to make room in his busy life for another pleasure. She has to re-invent the world, make it conform to her desires. It is a clash of mother country and restless exile as much as it is a clash of Mother Church and restless desire.

As in a Greek play, the clash of these incompatible but in-eluctable forces can produce only tragedy. The directness which the Irish learned in America cannot communicate with the evasions of life at home. The elaborate cathedral of airy self-justifications which he builds on the restless foundations of his desire is demol-ished by her impatience. The ambition of her desire, the vision of a future in which she and Eamonn and Peter will live happily ever af-ter, is thwarted by his ability to live with all his contradictions in a never-ending present rather than have to face the hard choices for the future.

The tragedy, strangely, is at its sharpest when the story is most comic. The awful events—the abandonment of a son and the hu-miliation of an important public man—are awful only because there is a glimmer that things might have been otherwise. What is most wretched about the abandonment of Peter is that there are times when there is another sort of abandonment, times when An-nie and Eamonn seem to have abandoned themselves to a kind of exuberant madness in which their laughter mingled into one wild cascade.

There are episodes in their story during which the absurdity of their situation is funny instead of sordid, during which they seem to have been able to stand back and look at themselves and col-lapse in a helpless laughter.

That kind of removal from oneself, that release into a zone where nothing matters, is what lovers call love and saints call a state of grace. Though the faithful may think it blasphemous, it is never-theless possible that in those moments of wild laughter Eamonn Casey and Annie Murphy were in love and in a state of grace at the same time.

If that is so, then it is also possible that the real sacrilege in relation to Annie Murphy's story would be not to allow for those moments when the sacred and the secular, the soul and the body, the monk and the sheela-na-gig, sex and holiness, were, how-ever fleetingly, one and the same thing. Because the story is so pub-lic, so symbolic, it is easy to overlook this precious intimacy at its core, the sacred humanity without which there would be no tragedy.

Tragedies are supposed to teach us something, and what is to be learned from the tragedy of these hurt people is that a world which insists on neat divisions between the holy and the unholy, between men and women, between courage and hypocrisy, is one which cre-ates tragedies.

Brecht replied to the adage 'unhappy the land that has no he-roes' with the correction 'unhappy the land that needs heroes'. Equally, unhappy the Church that needs heroes, that is so threat-ened and terrified by the revelation that within its upper ranks there exist ordinary human desires and ordinary human hypocrisies. All Annie Murphy has really done is to state the obvious. That she can gain so much notice from doing so is the fault of those who have denied the obvious for too long.

William Butler Yeats stated the obvious more elegantly many years ago in a poem called *Crazy Jane Talks With the Bishop*:

> *A woman can be proud and stiff*
> *When on love intent;*
> *But Love has pitched his mansion in*
> *The place of excrement;*
> *For nothing can be sole or whole*
> *That has not been rent.*

Whether the bishop listened to Crazy Jane or not, Yeats does not tell us. It would be nice to think, though, that some bishops might listen to the strange, abandoned laughter of Annie Murphy and Eamonn Casey before they became hateful and afraid.

In today's Ireland, writers like O'Toole have their say about institutional meltdown as a matter of course. But when Sean O'Faolain published *An Irish Journey*, the bishop of Galway, one of Eamonn Casey's predecessors, disliking O'Faolain's portrait of Galway City, threatened to sue if the book was not with withdrawn from publication. It was.

North of Kilnaboy, the Burren road descends into spiffy Bally-vaughan on Galway Bay. (The best descent—and view of Clare—is from CORKSCREW HILL, the curviest road in Ireland, between Lisdoon-varna and Ballyvaughan.) Six miles east (on the way to Kinvara) is the twelfth-century CORCOMROE ABBEY, originally named St. Mary of the Fertile Rock because it stands in a lush green cavity between two lime-stone mountains. In these stony hills Yeats set his play *The Dreaming of the Bones*: a modern revolutionary encounters the ghosts of the twelfth-century lovers Dervorgilla O'Rourke and Dermot MacMur-rough, whose adultery and elopement led to the Norman invasion.

From Ballyvaughan, you can approach THE CLIFFS OF MOHER—Clare's grand finale—from the circuitous north coast of Black Head and Fanore. (The seafood and music at Ballyvaughan's The Monk's Kitchen on the pier of Galway Bay are wonderful; so are the views from Bally-vaughan's Whitethorn restaurant, open 10–6 daily.) Stopping to hike up to the high places along this coast—or down to O'Lochlan's Castle at the edge of the sea—you'll come upon unnamed stone forts (there are hundreds of Stone Age, Iron Age, and early Christian ruins in the Burren) as well as a wind sweeping in from the ocean that, as O'Fao-lain puts it, makes "thorn-trees grow at right angles to their trunks." This coast is a perfect overture to the massive symphonic climax of the cliffs themselves, rising sheer from the sea to a height of eight hun-dred feet, stretching for a distance of almost five miles. American poet Wallace Stevens felt their primordial alien power in his poem "The Irish Cliffs of Moher":

*Who is my father in this world, in this house,*
*At the spirit's base?*

*My father's father, his father's father, his—*
*Shadows like winds*

*Go back to a parent before thought, before speech,*
*At the head of the past.*

*They go to the cliffs of Moher rising out of the mist,*
*Above the real,*

*Rising out of present time and place, above*
*The wet, green grass.*

*This is not landscape, full of the somnambulations*
*Of poetry*

*And the sea. This is my father or, maybe,*
*It is as he was,*

*A likeness, one of the race of fathers: earth*
*And sea and air.*

If you time it right (before and after the many tourist buses), you can walk these cliffs, which Stevens saw only with the eyes of his imagination. A longtime resident of and insurance executive in Hartford, Connecticut, he was no traveler. By way of metaphor, however, and his correspondence with Tom MacGreevy, Irish poet and friend of Beckett, he made a kinship with Ireland's landscape. MacGreevy inspired Stevens's poem "Our Stars Come from Ireland":

*The stars are washing up from Ireland . . .*
*the ashes of fiery weather,*
*Of nights full of the green stars from Ireland . . .*
*These Gaeled and fitful-fangled darknesses.*

# Brian Merriman

## 1745?–1805

*In his off hours, schoolteacher and farmer Brian Merriman of East Clare produced the only work of Gaelic verse ever to have been banned in Ireland, when it was translated into English in 1945. His eighteenth-century poem* The Midnight Court, *a long piece of sexual politics, turns the poetic convention of the* aisling *(dream or vision poem) upside down. Instead of the poet having a vision of Ireland in the form of a beautiful woman—*speirbhean *or "sky-woman" (see p. 237), he falls asleep on the shore of Lough Graney (after an opening bucolic reverie) and has a harrowing dream: a "hellish" and "hairy" female orders him to stand trial in the court of Aeval (Aoibheall), the Queen of the Fairies, for the crime of Irish bachelorhood. He wakes up just as he about to be punished—tied up and spanked—by the court-appointed frustrated girls.*

## FROM *THE MIDNIGHT COURT*

*Translated by Frank O'Connor*

I
*I liked to walk in the river meadows
In the thick of the dew and the morning shadows,
At the edge of the woods in a deep defile
At peace with myself in the first sunshine.
When I looked at Lough Graney my heart grew bright,
Ploughed lands and green in the morning light,
Mountains in rows with crimson borders*

*Peering above their neighbours' shoulders.*
*The heart that never had known relief*
*In a lonesome old man distraught with grief,*
*Without money or home or friends or ease,*
*Would quicken to glimpse beyond the trees*
*The ducks sail by on a mistless bay*
*And a swan before them lead the way;*
*A speckled trout that in their track*
*Splashed in the air with arching back;*
*The grey of the lake and the waves around*
*That foamed at its edge with a hollow sound. . . .*

*Yesterday morning the sky was clear,*
*The sun fell hot on river and mere, . . .*
*Longing for sleep bore down my head,*
*And in the grass I scooped a bed*
*With a hollow behind to house my back,*
*A prop for my head and my limbs stretched slack.*
*What more could one ask? I covered my face*
*To avert the flies as I dozed a space,*
*But my mind in dreams was filled with grief*
*And I tossed and groaned as I sought relief.*

*I had only begun when I felt a shock,*
*And all the landscape seemed to rock;*
*A north wind made my senses tingle*
*And thunder crackled along the shingle.*
*As I looked up—as I thought, awake—*
*I seemed to see at the edge of the lake*
*As ugly a brute as man could see*
*In the shape of woman approaching me . . .*

*She cried in a voice with a brassy ring:*
*'Get up out of that, you lazy thing!*
*That a man like you could think 'tis fitting*
*To lie in a ditch while the court is sitting!*
*A decenter court than e'er you knew,*
*And far too good for the likes of you.*

*Justice and Mercy hand in hand*
*Sit in the courts of Fairyland. . . .*

The dreaming poet is now dragged off to court, where he
must face the music for his crime of perpetual virginity.

*I stared at it all, the lighted hall,*
*Crammed with faces from wall to wall,*
*And a young woman with downcast eye,*
*Attractive, good-looking and shy,*
*With long and sweeping golden locks*
*Who was standing alone in the witness box.*
*The cut of her spoke of some disgrace;*
*I saw misfortune in her face . . .*
*And bit by bit she mastered her sorrows,*
*And dried her eyes, and spoke as follows—*
*'Yourself is the woman we're glad to see,*
*Eevul, Queen of Carriglee,*
*Our moon at night, our morning light,*
*Our comfort in the teeth of spite;*
*Mistress of the host of delight,*
*Munster and Ireland stand in your sight.*
*My chief complaint and principal grief,*
*The thing that gives me no relief,*
*Sweeps me from harbour in my mind*
*And blows me like smoke on every wind*
*Is all the girls whose charms miscarry*
*Throughout the land and who'll never marry;*
*Bitter old maids without house or home,*
*Put on one side through no fault of their own.*
*I know myself from the things I've seen*
*Enough and to spare of the sort I mean,*
*And to give an example, here am I*
*While the tide is flowing, left high and dry.*
*Wouldn't you think I must be a fright,*
*To be shelved before I get started right;*
*Heartsick, bitter, dour and wan,*

*Unable to sleep for the want of a man? . . .*
*Couldn't some man love me as well?*
*Amn't I plump and sound as a bell?*
*Lips for kissing and teeth for smiling,*
*Blossomy skin and forehead shining?*
*My eyes are blue and my hair is thick*
*And coils in streams about my neck—*
*A man who's looking for a wife,*
*Here's a face that will keep for life!*
*Hand and arm and neck and breast,*
*Each is better than the rest.*
*Look at that waist! My legs are long,*
*Limber as willows and light and strong.*
*There's bottom and belly that claim attention,*
*And the best concealed that I needn't mention.*
*I'm the sort a natural man desires,*
*Not a freak or a death-on-wires,*
*A sloven that comes to life in flashes,*
*A creature of moods with her heels in the ashes,*
*Or a sluggard stewing in her own grease,*
*But a good-looking girl that's bound to please. . . .*

The woman now attacks the rule of celibacy that the
Catholic Church imposes on its well-fed clergy.

*'But oye, my heart will grow grey hairs*
*Brooding forever on idle cares,*
*Has the Catholic Church a glimmer of sense*
*That the priests won't come to the girls' defence?*
*Is it any wonder the way I moan,*
*Out of my mind for a man of my own*
*While there's men around can afford one well*
*But shun a girl as they shun Hell.*
*The full of a fair of primest beef,*
*Warranted to afford relief;*
*Cherry-red cheeks and bull-like voices*
*And bellies dripping with fat in slices;*

*Backs erect and huge hind-quarters,*
*Hot-blooded men, the best of partners,*
*Freshness and charm, youth and good looks*
*And nothing to ease their mind but books!*
*The best-fed men that travel the country,*
*With beef and mutton, game and poultry,*
*Whiskey and wine forever in stock,*
*Sides of bacon and beds of flock.*
*Mostly they're hardy under the hood,*
*And we know like ourselves they're flesh and blood. . . .*
*A pardon and a job for life*
*To every priest that takes a wife! . . .*
*And though some as we know were always savage,*
*Gnashing their teeth at the thought of marriage,*
*And, modest beyond the needs of merit,*
*Invoked hell-fire on girls of spirit,*
*Yet some who took to their pastoral labours*
*Made very good priests and the best of neighbours.*
*Many a girl filled byre and stall*
*And furnished her house through a clerical call. . . .'*

IV

*The day crept in and the lights grew pale,*
*The girl sat down as she ended her tale;*
*The princess rose with face aglow*
*And her voice when she spoke was grave and slow.*
*'My child,' she said, 'I will not deny*
*That you've reason enough to scold and cry,*
*And, as a woman, I can't but grieve*
*To see girls like you, and Moll and Maeve,*
*With your dues diminished and favours gone,*
*And none to enjoy a likely man*
*But misers sucking a lonely bone*
*Or hairy old harpies living alone.*
*I do enact according then*
*That all the present unmarried men*

Shall be arrested by the guard,
Detained inside the chapel yard
And stripped and tied beside the gate
Until you decide upon their fate. . . .
Those that you find whom the years have thwarted
With masculine parts that were never exerted
To the palpable loss of some woman's employment,
The thrill of the milk and their own enjoyment;
Who, having the chance of wife and home
Went wild and took to the hills to roam,
Are only a burden on the earth
So give it to them for all you're worth. . . .'

Then the bailiff strode along the aisle
And reached for me with an ugly smile;
She nipped my ear as if in sport
And dragged me up before the court.
Then the girl who'd complained of how she was slighted,
Spotted my face and sprang up, excited.
'Is it you?' says she. 'Of all the old crocks!
I'm waiting for years to comb your locks.
You had your chance and you missed your shot,
And devil's cure to you now you're caught! . . .
I'll never believe there's truth in a name:
A wonder the Merrymans stand the shame!
The doggedest devil that tramps the hill
With grey in his hair and a virgin still! . . .
Hand me the rope till I give him a crack;
I'll earth it up in the small of his back.
That, young man, is the place to hurt you;
I'll teach you to respect your virtue!
Steady now, till we give him a sample!
Women alive, he's a grand example!
Set to it now and we'll nourish him well!
One good clout and ye'll hear him yell!
Tan him the more the more he'll yell. . . .'

*And while I stood there, stripped and crazy,*
*Knowing that nothing could save my skin,*
*She opened her book, immersed her pen,*
*And wrote it down with careful art,*
*As the girls all sighed for the fun to start.*
*And then I shivered and gave a shake,*
*Opened my eyes, and was wide awake.*

## For the Literary Traveler

East Clare on a cloudy, wet day looks as lonesome as the beds the women of the poem lament. Start looking for Merriman and his abandoned world, appropriately enough, in the graveyard at FEAKLE. His grave is unmarked, but there's a marker beside the entrance (opposite the Feakle post office/Pepper's Bar): "Honor to the Poet Brian Merriman who composed *The Midnight Court* in this area." Eight miles from Feakle, bearing left as you leave tiny CAHER, in a short distance you come to a bridge at Hanlon's Wood and then a lay-by on the southeastern shore of LOUGH GRANEY, where "in the river meadows / In the thick of the dew and the morning shadows," *The Midnight Court* begins. A large rock next to the water is inscribed with the poem's first twenty lines or so, in Irish—schoolchildren memorize this part—as well as the information that Merriman wrote his twelve-hundred-line poem here, where he also lived, played the violin, and taught school for thirty years. Said to have been illegitimate, Merriman bore a name that's evidence of his birth history: the bastard sons of priests were often surnamed "Merryman." (As he puts it in the poem, "Many a girl filled byre and stall / And furnished her house through a clerical call.")

The poet's pastoral idyll ends abruptly as he is removed to the harsh scrutiny of the fairy goddess's high court: drive on, bearing right over the SLIEVE AUGHTY MOUNTAINS above the bleak valley of LOUGH ATORICK on your left. (This is the Woodford/Lough Derg road.) This mountain "back o' beyond" is what the women in the poem are raging about. With only a few cabins and boarded-up National Schools, it's a paradise up here for the bachelors and clerical celibates Merriman portrays as Ireland's criminal element. Merriman's poet, a comic stand-in for the traditional (pre-EEC) Irish male, is afflicted with a fear of sex, marriage, and, if Merriman's landscape is to be believed, any likelihood of cohabitation. (Edna O'Brien, also of East Clare, catalogs "a variety of fears" in the Irish psyche: "fear of church, fear of gombeenism, fear of phantoms, fear of ridicule, fear of hunger, fear of annihilation, and fear of their own deeply ingrained aggression.") The marriage drought, however, is probably more attributable to the ancient fear of property loss through impoverishing alliances than to Irish Jansenism and Victorian prudery. As many Irish short stories tell it, when marriages do take place, the talk is of the bride's heifers and fields, not her personal charms. But Merriman lets the rejected women have their day in court: as infertile as his local landscape may look, the poem's language casts the plaintiffs as hot-tempered and eager sports. Lough Graney shimmers under an occasional sun.

Merriman locates the turf of the fairy goddess on the southeastern slope of the SLIEVE BERNAGH mountains, on the picturesque hill of CRA-GLEA (Aoibheall, or Eevul, is "queen of Carriglee") overlooking Lough Derg and the Shannon. This take-no-prisoners deity presides on a hill with a view (accessible only on foot from the East Clare Way or the R463/Killaloe road). Aoibheall's Rock—Carrickeeval—is just north of the hilltop.

Every August in a seaside Clare town, fans of *The Midnight Court*, including guest speakers such as Seamus Heaney and academics from Dublin, Edinburgh, and the University of Limerick (where Merriman died), celebrate through three nights and three long days of merry Merriman "studies." Information about the Merriman School is available on the "Cultural Courses in Ireland" list, from the Tourist Board at Baggot Street Bridge in Dublin.

# Edna O'Brien

## 1932–

*Edna O'Brien is still reviled in some back o' beyonds as the bold, brazen runaway who shacked up with an older man at the age of nineteen and lived to write bestsellers about her wickedness. In Europe, America, and the new Ireland, however, she is admired as a first-rate writer of fiction: "The most gifted woman now writing fiction in English" in the opinion of Philip Roth; to her "the great Colette's mantle has fallen." In 1995 she was awarded the European Prize for Literature in recognition of her life's work: eighteen works of fiction, of which the best known is the Country Girls Trilogy:* The Country Girls *(1960);* The Lonely Girl *(1962), reprinted as* The Girl with Green Eyes; *and* Girls in Their Married Bliss *(1963). For the sexual candor of her country-girl narrators, these and subsequent books were banned in Ireland. In* Mother Ireland *(1976), a memoir and travelogue written before the "new" Ireland took root, she blends her own youth on a farm in East Clare with her version of Ireland's history and ethos. It's a harsh book. And yet, like all the other self-exiled Irish writers, O'Brien is also ardent about the place she carries with her. In her own words, "Ireland may have cost me a few sleepless nights, but it has given me a lot as well. [Am I] Irish? In truth I would not want to be anything else. . . . At least it does not leave one pusillanimous."*

FROM *MOTHER IRELAND*

Countries are either mothers or fathers, and engender the emotional bristle secretly reserved for either sire. Ireland has always been a woman, a womb, a cave, a cow, a Rosaleen, a sow, a bride, a harlot, and, of course, the gaunt Hag of Beare. Originally a land of woods and thickets, such as Orpheus had seen when prescribing the voyage of Jason, through a misted atmosphere. She is thought to have known invasion from the time when the Ice Age ended and the improving climate allowed deer to throng her dense forests.

These infiltrations have been told and fabricated by men and by mediums who described the violation of her body and soul. Ireland has always been Godridden. St Patrick, her patron saint (uncanonized!) fled as a slave from Antrim in answer to a voice that told him to join a ship and go to the Continent. He travelled with a consignment of Irish wolfhounds and got off in France, where at Auxerre, he studied to be a cleric. Again a voice accompanied by a vision summoned him back to Ireland and in the fifth century he began to convert the North, then the lowlands, so that the speech and thinking of men changed as they fell under Patrick's rule and the yoke of the Scriptures. Patrick's forbears, the Romans, did not invade Ireland, but Tacitus records how a Roman general gazed across the sea from Scotland and reckoned that a single legion could have subdued her. He was possibly mistaken, for despite the many other legions that tried to subdue her, Ireland was never fully taken, though most thoroughly dispossessed. . . .

◊        ◊

People fall in love with Ireland. They go there and are smitten, see the white cottages nestling so to speak beneath the hills, the ranges of brooding blue mountain, the haze above them, the fuchsia hedges in Kerry, the barking dogs, the chalky limestone steppes of west Clare, a phenomenon so unyielding it is as if Wuthering Heights were transmitted from paper to landscape. The visitors talk and are talked at, they fish, they fowl, they eat brown bread, dip into holy wells, kiss wishing stones, are bowled over but have no desire to stay. There must be something secretly catastrophic about a country from which so many people go, escape, and that something alongside the economic exigencies that sent over a million people in coffin ships when a blight hit the potato crops in 1847 and has been sending them in considerable numbers ever since.

Loneliness, the longing for adventure, the Roman Catholic Church, or the family tie that is more umbilical than among any other race on earth? The martyred Irish mother and the raving rollicking Irish father is not peculiar to the works of exorcized writers but common to families throughout the land. The children inherit a trinity of guilts (a Shamrock): the guilt for Christ's Passion and Crucifixion, the guilt for the plundered land, and the furtive guilt for the mother frequently defiled by the insatiable father. All that scenery, all those undercurrents are too much. There is a hopelessness that a glut of natural beauty can create when there is a cultural and intellectual morass. The question is not where have all the fairies gone but where are all the thinkers now.

But the writers and the poets always speak with a more natural feeling for a place and, if you want to feel Ireland's many guises you can feel it, say, in Somerville and Ross, a description of a day's hunt when "frost and sunshine combined and went to one's head like iced champagne, and the hunting field (being) none other than long stretches of unfenced moorland and bog". You get the showers of rain, the harriers in tumult, the riders, the onlookers in traps or bicycles or on foot, the lanes full of stones and furze bushes and the insurmountable stubborn grass banks. You read Frank O'Connor's description of a cycle through Cavan—blue lakes, little hills continuous and rolling, crabbed, stunted country which as he said "was for a draughtsman and not a painter." Uncloying country that produced in him a sense of gentle animation. J. M. Synge said he regretted every hour spent away from her and every night lived in a city. Elizabeth Bowen knew the landscape and mood of north-east Cork when in her story "Summer Night" she wrote:

> Released from the glare of noon, the haycocks now seemed to
> float on the aftergrass: their freshness penetrated the air. In

the not far distance hills with woods up their flanks lay in
light like hills in another world—it would be a pleasure of
heaven to stand up there, where no foot ever seemed to have
trodden, on the spaces between the woods soft as powder
dusted over with gold. Against those hills, the burning red
rambler roses in cottage gardens along the roadside looked
earthy—they were too near the eye. The road was in Ireland.

In a country so passionately dedicated to the banning of books it
is amazing and maybe relevant that literature is still revered and
any ploughman anywhere might recite to you about the "Siege of
Limerick", or the flight of wild geese, or those soldiers in their
tents before the "Battle of Fontenoy" invoking their native Clare:

> *The whole night long we dream of you and*
> *waking think we're there.*
> *Brave dream and foolish waking we never shall see Clare.*

That was my territory. A few miles from my birthplace was the
seat of Brian Boru's former palace—Kincora—of which we used to
chant "Oh where, Kincora, is Brian the Great and where is the
beauty that once was thine?" The road near there was dark and
shielded by a dense vault of interlocking trees. There was a ball alley, green and lichened from saturations of rain, the trees rustled,
the leaves rustled, and a man who lived in a nearby estate was a
bird watcher and reputed to have always a fresh feather in his
check hat. In the adjoining estate lived two ladies who did their
own bottling and preserving, and both fortresses were flanked with
great gates and ornamental limestone piers. Then inside were
the low hunched fairy-story little gate-lodges with the windows
diamond-paned and the chimneys perpetually smoking. Driving
there on one of those long-promised, never-to-be-forgotten, childhood outings we were told to look out for Kincora and suddenly a
dizziness possessed me, seeing became impossible, what with the
excitement, the speed of the car, what with the darkness, the ball
alley. The eyes lost the power to focus and I missed seeing it. The

car headed for Killaloe where we were going to see a bridge on which four local boys were shot, and a new houseboat owned by an Englishman. I thought of the poem, the beautiful lament that celebrated the place, and the poem became more a living thing than the actual bypassed landmark:

> *I am Mac Liag, and my home is on the lake.*
> *Thither often, to that palace whose beauty is fled,*
> *Came Brian to ask me, and I went for his sake*
> *Oh, my grief! That I should live, and Brian be dead!*\*

━◇━

## For the Literary Traveler

At a quick glance, TUAMGRANEY in EAST CLARE, where Edna O'Brien was born and grew up on a small farm, seems like a place only a writer on the payroll of the Irish Tourist Board could like. But if you take some time here, it's possible to feel this moody countryside that she evokes with a passionate precision. And "feeling," in her words, "is the nub and fulcrum of all literature."

How her birthplace got its name sounds like one of her plots. The ancient annalists called Tuamgraney *Tuam Greine*, "the tomb (or mound or altar) of Grian." According to the legend, in prehistoric times a beautiful woman called Gile Greine—her name means "the Brightness of the Sun"—lived in these parts and in a fit of depression threw herself into the lake that bears her name, Lough Graney (see p. 300). Carried by the River Graney, which flows southeasterly out of the lake, her body was found by her friends. They raised over her grave a mound that they named Tuam Greine. In the emotional pain of the country girls and women who are O'Brien's main characters, there are echoes of Grian's story. It's ironic that a writer who so deplores the

---

\*The poem that O'Brien loved and memorized as a child is attributed to Mac Liag (c. 1015), its many verses translated from the Irish by James Clarence Mangan.

"Godridden" side of Irish life has the fascinating Tuamgraney church—
St. Cronan's—as the historic center of her hometown: it's the oldest
place of Christian worship still in use in Ireland and England. Built on
the site of a seventh-century monastery, the church (c. 930), though
much altered, still preserved its original western portion, visited by
Brian Boru. (The church and its on-site East Clare Heritage Centre are
open daily June-Sept., 9-6).

Tuamgraney was also a pagan ceremonial site in pre-Christian Ireland, a background invoked in the title of O'Brien's dark novel *A Pagan
Place*. The druids worshiped in sacred oak groves, and the many towns
with the prefix or suffix "Derry" (*doire* in Irish, which means "oak grove
or wood") testify to the large number of druidic spaces. The largest
primeval oak wood in Munster until 1700 was on the southern slopes
of the Slieve Aughty mountains, a few miles northwest, in Brian Merriman Country. A remnant of that great wood can still be visited just
outside of Tuamgraney village (turn left off the road O'Brien traveled
as a child, the 463 to Killaloe) into RAHEEN OAK WOOD, where there's a
nature walk and the Brian Boru Oak, at one thousand years of age
"the oldest living tree in Ireland.")

Readers of O'Brien will recognize the name SCARRIFF, two miles
north of Tuamgraney, where she attended the National School. From
Scarriff or from nearby MOUNTSHANNON (an annual winner of the
West of Ireland's Tidy Towns contest), you can hire a boat out to the
seventh-century monastic ruins on HOLY ISLAND (Inis Cealtra) in LOUGH
DERG, a symbolic setting in many of O'Brien's fictions. There, in the
shadow of the round "tall tower as grim and admonishing as some
elongated monk," Bugler and Breege Brennan, the star-crossed lovers
of O'Brien's most recent novel, *Wild Decembers,* consummate their
adulterous love.

The drive south from Mountshannon to KILLALOE (pronounced "kill-
a-LOO"), remembered as a childhood treat by O'Brien, follows the
western shore of Lough Derg; across the lake you see the Arra Mountains of County Tipperary. It's a lovely, dreamy half-hour ride, passing a
pretty riverside park at RINNAMEN POINT. In the story "Irish Revel," the
beauty of Lough Derg is the young girl's only relief from the bleakness
of the boulder-strewn mountain farms: "the lake ... was noted for its

colors. It changed color rapidly—it was blue and green and black, all within an hour. At sunset it was often a strange burgundy, not like a lake at all, but like wine."

These days East Clare feels friendlier than the landscape of O'Brien's fiction. But one thing is exactly the same as she remembers it in *Mother Ireland*: along this road, it's easy to miss the turnoff for KIN-CORA, celebrated seat of the kings of Thomond, if you're driving too fast. (It's about two miles south of the slope of Brian Merriman's CRAGLEA—see p. 294.) Signposted on the left side of the road as BEAL BORU ("Pass of the Tributes"), from which King Brian Boru (926–1014) took his title, this tree-planted earthern ring fort about a mile and a half north of Killaloe is thought to be the site of Brian Boru's command post; the palace of Kincora was nearby. This is the territory of the heroic verses O'Brien memorized as a child. Wear boots if you stop to look at Beal Boru, because the overgrown path that leads from the road into the site is muddy.

Brian Boru, as king of Munster, aspired to be High King *(Ard-Ri)* of Ireland. His holy cause (like his family's, the O'Briens of Thomond) was the defeat of the Vikings, who had been looting and murdering since their first invasion of Dublin in 795. Brian saw the key to final victory in the control of the River Shannon and its tributaries; Lough Derg is the Shannon's largest lake. Brian the warrior (he picked up loot and hostages on his many campaigns, thus his title, "Brian of the Tributes") is also remembered as a patron and protector of poets, craftsmen, and the monastic cities where the arts flourished. Royal Kincora was known in Europe as a center of civilization, a haven for artists.

Today Killaloe feels like a vacation town. Lough Derg is full of boats. The steep, narrow streets around St. Flannan's Cathedral belong to the ancient past of King Brian Boru's household of poets, soldiers, and wives. His fourth wife, Gormfhlaith—Gormley in English—turned testy (and traitorous) when she learned after their marriage that Brian had another wife still in residence at Kincora. (In mid-July, Killaloe honors the memory of its polygamous royal ancestor with a four-day-long festival of music and boat races, the Féile Brian Ború.)

On the Ballina side of the Killaloe bridge that O'Brien was taken to see in her childhood (you're now in Tipperary), there's an old pub/restaurant called Goosers. In late afternoon there is perfection in its salmon plate and the views of Killaloe across the wine-tinged lake. O'Brien, you think, would like this place, the rhythm of friends on holiday and of couples, young and old, looking beautiful in one another's eyes. In *Wild Decembers* she describes a Clare twilight: "the sky all pageant, clouds of every denomination, their pink-frilled edges overlapping, like the waves of the sea. Sunset like a monstrance, spokes of light forking out from it, white white gold." You can imagine her here, raising a glass to love, unthwarted in the new Ireland—which, as she told an interviewer, has begun at last to talk about sex. Toasted herself by one London critic for having "the soul of Molly Bloom and the gifts of Virginia Woolf," O'Brien deserves some credit.

# THE
## PROVINCE OF
# CONNACHT

---

GALWAY

MAYO

SLIGO

---

*Lady Augusta Gregory*

*William Butler Yeats* • *James Joyce*

*Rita Ann Higgins* • *John Millington Synge*

*Maria Edgeworth* • *Michael Longley*

# Lady Augusta Gregory

## 1852–1932

*Isabella Augusta Persse grew up one of thirteen children in a wealthy Anglo-Irish family on Roxborough estate in famine-ravaged County Galway in the West of Ireland. When she married William Gregory in 1880, she moved eight miles south to his estate at Coole Park. It was in the years following her husband's death in 1892, as she began to see the injustices of landlordism and felt herself becoming an Irish nationalist, that she met Yeats and with him planned the Abbey Theatre. At Coole she welcomed the writers of the Irish Literary Revival, who included Sean O'Casey, a manual laborer whose playwriting she encouraged. A woman of great energy, Gregory traveled around Galway, Clare, and the Aran Islands, visiting with local people, writing down their stories and legends in dialect. Eventually she earned recognition as one of the first great modern folklorists: her* Visions and Beliefs in the West of Ireland *(2 vols., 1920), collected over many years, is considered a masterpiece of folkloric literature. She also wrote the dialogue and provided the Irish material for some of Yeats's plays. The more than forty plays she wrote or collaborated on for the Abbey Theatre, including* Cathleen ní Houlihan, Spreading the News, The Rising of the Moon, The Workhouse Ward, *and three tragedies about powerful heroines—Gormfhlaith of Kincora, Dervorgilla, and Grania—are grounded in her face-to-face visits in the cottages of the West of Ireland. Lady Gregory, according to recent scholarship, also had a personal life. Her passionate love poems to the British poet Wilfrid Blunt, her affair with the American lawyer and patron of Irish art John Quinn, and the publication of her diaries and*

313

*letters show a woman of larger humanity than was first acknowl-
edged in histories of Irish literature.*

## THE RISING OF THE MOON

*First produced at the Abbey Theatre, March 9, 1907, Lady
Gregory's most famous one-act play portrays the subtle psy-
chology of the Irish colony's resistance: a hunted rebel, disguised
as a ballad singer, stirs the latent patriotism of a policeman, who
lets him escape to a waiting boat below the Kinvara pier.*

PERSONS:
   Sergeant.
   Policeman X.
   Policeman B.
   A Ragged Man.
SCENE: *Side of a quay in a seaport town. Some posts and chains. A
   large barrel. Enter three policemen. Moonlight.*

*(Sergeant, who is older than the others, crosses the stage to right and
   looks down steps. The others put down a paste-pot and unroll a
   bundle of placards.)*
POLICEMAN B: I think this would be a good place to put up a no-
   tice. *(He points to barrel.)*
POLICEMAN X: Better ask him. *(Calls to Sergt.)* Will this be a good
   place for a placard?
*(No answer.)*
POLICEMAN B: Will we put up a notice here on the barrel?
*(No answer.)*
SERGEANT: There's a flight of steps here that leads to the water.
   This is a place that should be minded well. If he got down here,
   his friends might have a boat to meet him; they might send it in
   here from outside.
POLICEMAN B: Would the barrel be a good place to put a notice up?
SERGEANT: It might; you can put it there.
*(They paste the notice up.)*

SERGEANT: *(Reading it.)* Dark hair—dark eyes, smooth face, height five feet five—there's not much to take hold of in that—It's a pity I had no chance of seeing him before he broke out of gaol. They say he's a wonder, that it's he makes all the plans for the whole organization. There isn't another man in Ireland would have broken gaol the way he did. He must have some friends among the gaolers.

POLICEMAN B: A hundred pounds is little enough for the Government to offer for him. You may be sure any man in the force that takes him will get promotion.

SERGEANT: I'll mind this place myself. I wouldn't wonder at all if he came this way. He might come slipping along there *(points to side of quay)*, and his friends might be waiting for him there *(points down steps)*, and once he got away it's little chance we'd have of finding him; it's maybe under a load of kelp he'd be in a fishing boat, and not one to help a married man that wants it to the reward.

POLICEMAN X: And if we get him itself, nothing but abuse on our heads for it from the people, and maybe from our own relations.

SERGEANT: Well, we have to do our duty in the force. Haven't we the whole country depending on us to keep law and order? It's those that are down would be up and those that are up would be down, if it wasn't for us. Well, hurry on, you have plenty of other places to placard yet, and come back here then to me. You can take the lantern. Don't be too long now. It's very lonesome here with nothing but the moon.

POLICEMAN B: It's a pity we can't stop with you. The Government should have brought more police into the town, with *him* in gaol, and at assize time too. Well, good luck to your watch.

*(They go out.)*

SERGEANT: *(Walks up and down once or twice and looks at placard.)* A hundred pounds and promotion sure. There must be a great deal of spending in a hundred pounds. It's a pity some honest man not to be the better of that.

*(A ragged man appears at left and tries to slip past. Sergeant suddenly turns.)*

SERGEANT: Where are you going?

MAN: I'm a poor ballad-singer, your honour. I thought to sell some of these *(holds out bundle of ballads)* to the sailors. *(He goes on.)*

SERGEANT: Stop! Didn't I tell you to stop? You can't go on there.

MAN: Oh, very well. It's a hard thing to be poor. All the world's against the poor!

SERGEANT: Who are you?

MAN: You'd be as wise as myself if I told you, but I don't mind. I'm one Jimmy Walsh, a ballad-singer.

SERGEANT: Jimmy Walsh? I don't know that name.

MAN: Ah, sure, they know it well enough in Ennis. Were you ever in Ennis, sergeant?

SERGEANT: What brought you here?

MAN: Sure, it's to the assizes I came, thinking I might make a few shillings here or there. It's in the one train with the judges I came.

SERGEANT: Well, if you came so far, you may as well go farther, for you'll walk out of this.

MAN: I will, I will; I'll just go on where I was going.

*(Goes towards steps.)*

SERGEANT: Come back from those steps; no one has leave to pass down them to-night.

MAN: I'll just sit on the top of the steps till I see will some sailor buy a ballad off me that would give me my supper. They do be late going back to the ship. It's often I saw them in Cork carried down the quay in a hand-cart.

SERGEANT: Move on, I tell you. I won't have any one lingering about the quay to-night.

MAN: Well, I'll go. It's the poor have the hard life! Maybe yourself might like one, sergeant. Here's a good sheet now. *(Turns one over.)* "Content and a pipe"—that's not much. "The Peeler and the goat"—you wouldn't like that. "Johnny Hart"—that's a lovely song.

SERGEANT: Move on.

MAN: Ah, wait till you hear it. *(Sings:)*

> There was a rich farmer's daughter lived near the town
> of Ross;
> She courted a Highland soldier, his name was Johnny Hart;
> Says the mother to her daughter, "I'll go distracted mad
> If you marry that Highland soldier dressed up in Highland
> plaid."

SERGEANT: Stop that noise.

*(Man wraps up his ballads and shuffles towards the steps.)*

SERGEANT: Where are you going?

MAN: Sure you told me to be going, and I am going.

SERGEANT: Don't be a fool. I didn't tell you to go that way; I told
you to go back to the town.

MAN: Back to the town, is it?

SERGEANT: *(Taking him by the shoulder and shoving him before
him.)* Here, I'll show you the way. Be off with you. What are you
stopping for?

MAN: *(Who has been keeping his eye on the notice, points to it.)* I
think I know what you're waiting for, sergeant.

SERGEANT: What's that to you?

MAN: And I know well the man you're waiting for—I know him
well—I'll be going.

*(He shuffles on.)*

SERGEANT: You know him? Come back here. What sort is he?

MAN: Come back is it, sergeant? Do you want to have me killed?

SERGEANT: Why do you say that?

MAN: Never mind. I'm going. I wouldn't be in your shoes if the reward was ten times as much. *(Goes on off stage to left.)* Not if it
was ten times as much.

SERGEANT: *(Rushing after him.)* Come back here, come back.
*(Drags him back.)* What sort is he? Where did you see him?

MAN: I saw him in my own place, in the County Clare. I tell you
you wouldn't like to be looking at him. You'd be afraid to be in
the one place with him. There isn't a weapon he doesn't know
the use of, and as to strength, his muscles are as hard as that
board *(slaps barrel).*

SERGEANT: Is he as bad as that?

MAN: He is then.

SERGEANT: Do you tell me so?

MAN: There was a poor man in our place, a sergeant from Ballyvaughan.—It was with a lump of stone he did it.

SERGEANT: I never heard of that.

MAN: And you wouldn't, sergeant. It's not everything that happens gets into the papers. And there was a policeman in plain clothes, too . . . It is in Limerick he was. . . . It was after the time of the attack on the police barrack at Kilmallock. . . . Moonlight . . . just like this . . . waterside. . . . Nothing was known for certain.

SERGEANT: Do you say so? It's a terrible county to belong to.

MAN: That's so, indeed! You might be standing there, looking out that way, thinking you saw him coming up this side of the quay (*points*), and he might be coming up this other side (*points*), and he'd be on you before you knew where you were.

SERGEANT: It's a whole troop of police they ought to put here to stop a man like that.

MAN: But if you'd like me to stop with you, I could be looking down this side. I could be sitting up here on this barrel.

SERGEANT: And you know him well, too?

MAN: I'd know him a mile off, sergeant.

SERGEANT: But you wouldn't want to share the reward?

MAN: Is it a poor man like me, that has to be going the roads and singing in fairs, to have the name on him that he took a reward? But you don't want me. I'll be safer in the town.

SERGEANT: Well, you can stop.

MAN: (*Getting up on barrel.*) All right, sergeant. I wonder, now, you're not tired out, sergeant, walking up and down the way you are.

SERGEANT: If I'm tired I'm used to it.

MAN: You might have hard work before you to-night yet. Take it easy while you can. There's plenty of room up here on the barrel, and you see farther when you're higher up.

SERGEANT: Maybe so. (*Gets up beside him on barrel, facing right. They sit back to back, looking different ways.*) You made me feel a bit queer with the way you talked.

MAN: Give me a match, sergeant (*he gives it and man lights pipe*);

take a draw yourself? It'll quiet you. Wait now till I give you a light, but you needn't turn round. Don't take your eye off the quay for the life of you.

SERGEANT: Never fear, I won't. *(Lights pipe. They both smoke.)* Indeed it's a hard thing to be in the force, out at night and no thanks for it, for all the danger we're in. And it's little we get but abuse from the people, and no choice but to obey our orders, and never asked when a man is sent into danger, if you are a married man with a family.

MAN: *(Sings)*—

> As through the hills I walked to view the hills and shamrock plain,
> I stood awhile where nature smiles to view the rocks and streams,
> On a matron fair I fixed my eyes beneath a fertile vale,
> As she sang her song it was on the wrong of poor old Granuaile.*

SERGEANT: Stop that; that's no song to be singing in these times.

MAN: Ah, sergeant, I was only singing to keep my heart up. It sinks when I think of him. To think of us two sitting here, and he creeping up the quay, maybe, to get to us.

SERGEANT: Are you keeping a good lookout?

MAN: I am; and for no reward too. Amn't I the foolish man? But when I saw a man in trouble, I never could help trying to get him out of it. What's that? Did something hit me? *(Rubs his heart.)*

SERGEANT: *(Patting him on the shoulder.)* You will get your reward in heaven.

MAN: I know that, I know that, sergeant, but life is precious.

SERGEANT: Well, you can sing if it gives you more courage.

MAN: *(Sings)*—

> Her head was bare, her hands and feet with iron bands were bound,

---

* Pronounced "gron-yuh-whale"; in English, Grace O'Malley, the Irish Pirate Queen (see p. 373)

Her pensive strain and plaintive wail mingles with the eve-
ning gale,
And the song she sang with mournful air, I am old Granuaile.
Her lips so sweet that monarchs kissed . . .

SERGEANT: That's not it. . . . "Her gown she wore was stained with
gore." . . . That's it—you missed that.

MAN: You're right, sergeant, so it is; I missed it. *(Repeats line.)* But
to think of a man like you knowing a song like that.

SERGEANT: There's many a thing a man might know and might not
have any wish for.

MAN: Now, I daresay, sergeant, in your youth, you used to be sitting
up on a wall, the way you are sitting up on this barrel now, and
the other lads beside you, and you singing "Granuaile"? . . .

SERGEANT: I did then.

MAN: And the "Shan Bhean Bhocht"?*. . .

SERGEANT: I did then.

MAN: And the "Green on the Cape"?

SERGEANT: That was one of them.

MAN: And maybe the man you are watching for to-night used to be
sitting on the wall, when he was young, and singing those same
songs. . . . It's a queer world. . . .

SERGEANT: Whisht! . . . I think I see something coming. . . . It's
only a dog.

MAN: And isn't it a queer world? . . . Maybe it's one of the boys you
used to be singing with that time you will be arresting to-day or
to-morrow, and sending into the dock. . . .

SERGEANT: That's true indeed.

MAN: And maybe one night, after you had been singing, if the other
boys had told you some plan they had, some plan to free the
country, you might have joined with them . . . and maybe it is
you might be in trouble now.

SERGEANT: Well, who knows but I might? I had a great spirit in
those days.

---

*A phrase in Irish meaning "The Poor Old Woman," a traditional name for Ire-
land and the title of a patriotic folk song.

MAN: It's a queer world, sergeant, and it's little any mother knows when she sees her child creeping on the floor what might happen to it before it has gone through its life, or who will be who in the end.

SERGEANT: That's a queer thought now, and a true thought. Wait now till I think it out. . . . If it wasn't for the sense I have, and for my wife and family, and for me joining the force the time I did, it might be myself now would be after breaking gaol and hiding in the dark, and it might be him that's hiding in the dark and that got out of gaol would be sitting up where I am on this barrel. . . . And it might be myself would be creeping up trying to make my escape from himself, and it might be himself would be keeping the law, and myself would be breaking it, and myself would be trying maybe to put a bullet in his head, or to take up a lump of a stone the way you said he did . . . no, that myself did. . . . Oh! *(Gasps. After a pause.)* What's that? *(Grasps man's arm.)*

MAN: *(Jumps off barrel and listens, looking out over water.)* It's nothing, sergeant.

SERGEANT: I thought it might be a boat. I had a notion there might be friends of his coming about the quays with a boat.

MAN: Sergeant, I am thinking it was with the people you were, and not with the law you were, when you were a young man.

SERGEANT: Well, if I was foolish then, that time's gone.

MAN: Maybe, sergeant, it comes into your head sometimes, in spite of your belt and your tunic, that it might have been as well for you to have followed Granuaile.

SERGEANT: It's no business of yours what I think.

MAN: Maybe, sergeant, you'll be on the side of the country yet.

SERGEANT: *(Gets off barrel.)* Don't talk to me like that. I have my duties and I know them. *(Looks round.)* That was a boat; I hear the oars.

*(Goes to the steps and looks down.)*

MAN: *(Sings)*—

    O, then, tell me, Shawn O'Farrell,
      Where the gathering is to be.
    In the old spot by the river
      Right well known to you and me!

SERGEANT: Stop that! Stop that, I tell you!

MAN: *(Sings louder)*—

> One word more, for signal token,
>> Whistle up the marching tune,
> With your pike upon your shoulder,
>> At the Rising of the Moon.

SERGEANT: If you don't stop that, I'll arrest you.

*(A whistle from below answers, repeating the air.)*

SERGEANT: That's a signal. *(Stands between him and steps.)* You must not pass this way. . . . Step farther back. . . . Who are you? You are no ballad-singer.

MAN: You needn't ask who I am; that placard will tell you. *(Points to placard.)*

SERGEANT: You are the man I am looking for.

MAN: *(Takes off hat and wig. Sergeant seizes them.)* I am. There's a hundred pounds on my head. There is a friend of mine below in a boat. He knows a safe place to bring me to.

SERGEANT: *(Looking still at hat and wig.)* It's a pity! It's a pity. You deceived me. You deceived me well.

MAN: I am a friend of Granuaile. There is a hundred pounds on my head.

SERGEANT: It's a pity, it's a pity!

MAN: Will you let me pass, or must I make you let me?

SERGEANT: I am in the force. I will not let you pass.

MAN: I thought to do it with my tongue. *(Puts hand in breast.)* What is that?

*(Voice of Policeman X outside:)* Here, this is where we left him.

SERGEANT: It's my comrades coming.

MAN: You won't betray me . . . the friend of Granuaile. *(Slips behind barrel.)*

*(Voice of Policeman B:)* That was the last of the placards.

POLICEMAN X: *(As they come in.)* If he makes his escape it won't be unknown he'll make it.

*(Sergeant puts hat and wig behind his back.)*

POLICEMAN B: Did any one come this way?

SERGEANT: *(After a pause.)* No one.

POLICEMAN B: No one at all?

SERGEANT: No one at all.

POLICEMAN B: We had no orders to go back to the station; we can stop along with you.

SERGEANT: I don't want you. There is nothing for you to do here.

POLICEMAN B: You bade us to come back here and keep watch with you.

SERGEANT: I'd sooner be alone. Would any man come this way and you making all that talk? It is better the place to be quiet.

POLICEMAN B: Well, we'll leave you the lantern anyhow. *(Hands it to him.)*

SERGEANT: I don't want it. Bring it with you.

POLICEMAN B: You might want it. There are clouds coming up and you have the darkness of the night before you yet. I'll leave it over here on the barrel. *(Goes to barrel.)*

SERGEANT: Bring it with you I tell you. No more talk.

POLICEMAN B: Well, I thought it might be a comfort to you. I often think when I have it in my hand and can be flashing it about into every dark corner *(doing so)* that it's the same as being beside the fire at home, and the bits of bogwood blazing up now and again.

*(Flashes it about, now on the barrel, now on Sergeant.)*

SERGEANT: *(Furious.)* Be off the two of you, yourselves and your lantern!

*(They go out. Man comes from behind barrel. He and Sergeant stand looking at one another.)*

SERGEANT: What are you waiting for?

MAN: For my hat, of course, and my wig. You wouldn't wish me to get my death of cold?

*(Sergeant gives them.)*

MAN: *(Going towards steps.)* Well, good-night, comrade, and thank you. You did me a good turn to-night, and I'm obliged to you. Maybe I'll be able to do as much for you when the small rise up and the big fall down . . . when we all change places at the Rising *(waves his hand and disappears)* of the Moon.

SERGEANT: *(Turning his back to audience and reading placard.)* A

hundred pounds reward! A hundred pounds! *(Turns towards audience.)* I wonder, now, am I as great a fool as I think I am?
*Curtain.*

FROM *THE COLLECTED POEMS OF WILLIAM BUTLER YEATS*

*Inspired by Lady Gregory's "Coole Park"*

IN THE SEVEN WOODS

*I have heard the pigeons of the Seven Woods*
*Make their faint thunder, and the garden bees*
*Hum in the lime-tree flowers; and put away*
*The unavailing outcries and the old bitterness*
*That empty the heart. I have forgot awhile*
*Tara uprooted, and new commonness*
*Upon the throne and crying about the streets*
*And hanging its paper flowers from post to post,*
*Because it is alone of all things happy.*
*I am contented, for I know that Quiet*
*Wanders laughing and eating her wild heart*
*Among pigeons and bees, while that Great Archer,*
*Who but awaits His hour to shoot, still hangs*
*A cloudy quiver over Pairc-na-lee.*

THE WILD SWANS AT COOLE

*The trees are in their autumn beauty,*
*The woodland paths are dry,*
*Under the October twilight the water*
*Mirrors a still sky;*
*Upon the brimming water among the stones*
*Are nine-and-fifty swans.*

*The nineteenth autumn has come upon me*
*Since I first made my count;*
*I saw, before I had well finished,*

*All suddenly mount*
*And scatter wheeling in great broken rings*
*Upon their clamorous wings.*

*I have looked upon those brilliant creatures,*
*And now my heart is sore.*
*All's changed since I, hearing at twilight,*
*The first time on this shore,*
*The bell-beat of their wings above my head,*
*Trod with a lighter tread.*

*Unwearied still, lover by lover,*
*They paddle in the cold*
*Companionable streams or climb the air;*
*Their hearts have not grown old;*
*Passion or conquest, wander where they will,*
*Attend upon them still.*
*But now they drift on the still water,*
*Mysterious, beautiful;*
*Among what rushes will they build,*
*By what lake's edge or pool*
*Delight men's eyes when I awake some day*
*To find they have flown away?*

## For the Literary Traveler

Lady Gregory's childhood at ROXBOROUGH seems to have matched the surrounding bleakness of Clare-Galway (the most godforsaken region in Ireland, according to Sean O'Faolain). (The demesne is on the left about four miles north of Yeats's THOOR BALLYLEE on the N66, the Gort/Loughrea road.) Like Edith Wharton, another daughter of privilege, Augusta had a cold mother who preferred her sons and discouraged her daughter's education. Yet in her autobiography, Gregory finds some brightness in her early years: she remembers the mother's milk of imagination she took from her Catholic nanny, Mary Sheridan, who told her wild Irish tales of monsters and fairies, a subversively delicious taste in an evangelical mother's Bible-fed Big House dominated by an impersonal father who was a notoriously oppressive landlord. Outings to GORT—still a pleasant market town—and to LOUGHREA, where as a child–Irish-nationalist, she bought her Fenian comic books, also count among her good first memories. Never the whole story, bleak appearances, especially in Ireland, deceive.

When she married William Gregory (her mother, who harped on Augusta's plainness, said he'd only proposed as a compliment to her), she moved to COOLE PARK: a seventeenth-century house at the end of a long avenue of ilex trees, with miles of woods, a river, and a lake just out the front door. The entrance gates are two miles north of Gort, on the left, off the Galway road (N18). The house was demolished in 1941, a brutal act that still feels like a vengeful strike of the Catholic Free State against the Anglo-Irish Big House and its cultural revival, resented from its inception as a pagan and Protestant thing.

Coole Park's new visitors' center (mid-June through Aug., daily 9:30–6:30; mid Apr. through mid-June and Sept., Tues.–Sun. 10–5) provides an excellent audiovisual show about Augusta's life here and the botanical diversity of the ancient grounds, now a nature preserve. (You can also buy the map of Gregory's Kiltartan Country.) The park is open year round.

To enter the heart of this place is to walk in COOLE WOODS for as long as you can. There are few tourists. Birds claim the air, calling, diving through the still forest of oak, poplar, and elm rooted in a mossy floor thick with wildflowers. More than the house, Augusta Gregory loved these woods, spending hours here and in the walled garden, alone and with Yeats, other guests, and her grandchildren. (Lines from a poem that George Bernard Shaw wrote for her grandchildren, Anne and Catherine, are inscribed on stones bedded in a path near the visitors' center.)

The high points of the park are signposted: the AUTOGRAPH TREE, the great copper beech (now within a railing) on whose trunk the famous visitors carved their initials—JMS, SO'C, WBY, JBY (the painter Jack Yeats), AE (in a triangle), VM (Violet Martin, the "Ross" of Somerville and Ross), AG and RG (Lady Gregory and her only son, Robert, who died in the First World War), and, in a glad sweep, GBS.

A path to the west leads to COOLE LAKE and stream, with swans in season. These waters run underground, connecting Ballylee, where Yeats's Tower is, with Coole, to which Ballylee once belonged, a detail of nature repeated in the profound friendship between the owners of the two houses. The waters run into the sea about ten miles north-west of Coole at KINVARA, a quiet fishing village on an inlet of Galway Bay. You can stand on the pier where Gregory set her nationalist play *The Rising of the Moon* or look out on it and the boats on Kinvara Bay from a window seat in the Pier Head restaurant. Kinvara holds an annual boat race (the *Crumniú na mBád*) the second weekend in August: in addition to the race of Galway hookers (fishing boats), there's lots of singing and dancing in the local pubs (Keogh's in Main Street, the Ould Plaid Shawl, and Linnane's, three miles off a signposted road from Kinvara) which are renowned year-round for their traditional and folk music sessions. Lady Gregory understood the political power of this music: its subversive rebel spirit drives the energy of her play.

Just north of the village, looming over the bay for more than four hundred years, is the moated DUN GUAIRE CASTLE. Named for King Guaire, the legendary King of Connacht (who set up Saint Colman in the nearby monastery of KILMACDUAGH), the castle hosts a medieval banquet with entertainment, May through October. Eight miles north, at Kilcolgan, Moran's-on-the-Weir (follow the signs to the west) serves Galway's finest oysters and salmon in a remote waterside setting. Like Kinvara's low-key pubs, it feels like a good hideout for Lady Gregory's ballad-singing man on the run.

# William Butler Yeats

## 1865–1939

*Yeats first saw the tower at Ballylee—Thoor Ballylee—during his first visit to Lady Gregory's Coole Park in 1896. He bought it in 1916 for thirty-five pounds and, after restoring it and the adjoining cottage, moved in with his wife, George Hyde-Lees, and infant daughter, Anne, in 1919. In the words of Seamus Heaney, "by dwelling in a Norman tower conjoined with a thatched cabin, Yeats intended to open and complicate the meaning of Irishness." Yeats's "house," in its antiquity and severity, served him well as a many-layered symbol of his art. (Ezra Pound called the tower "Ballyphallus.") Summering here off and on during the 1920s, when he became a celebrated public man, appointed to the senate of the new Irish Free State in 1922, and awarded the Nobel Prize for Literature in 1923, Yeats produced some of his most powerful writing: The Tower (1928), his first bestseller, includes "Sailing to Byzantium," "Meditations in Time of Civil War" (in 1922 the tower was occupied by anti-Treaty Republican soldiers), "Nineteen Hundred and Nineteen," Among School Children," and "Leda and the Swan." (To a friend he wrote, somewhat fancifully, "If I had had this tower when Joyce began I might have been of use, have got him to meet those who might have helped him.") Eventually the Yeatses gave up Thoor Ballylee—the damp and lack of running water had never charmed George, and Yeats was more often away from Ireland than at home—but the countryside, immortalized as "cold Clare rock and Galway rock and thorn" in his eulogy for Lady Gregory's son, "In Memory of Major Robert Gregory," stayed strong in his imagination. The Irish Tourist Board and the Kiltartan*

*Society opened the tower as a museum in 1965, the centenary of his birth.*

## TO BE CARVED ON A STONE
## AT THOOR BALLYLEE

*I, the poet William Yeats,*
*With old mill boards and sea-green slates,*
*And smithy work from the Gort forge,*
*Restored this tower for my wife George;*
*And may these characters remain*
*When all is ruin once again.*

## A PRAYER FOR MY DAUGHTER

*Once more the storm is howling, and half hid*
*Under this cradle-hood and coverlid*
*My child sleeps on. There is no obstacle*
*But Gregory's wood and one bare hill*
*Whereby the haystack- and roof-levelling wind,*
*Bred on the Atlantic, can be stayed;*
*And for an hour I have walked and prayed*
*Because of the great gloom that is in my mind.*

*I have walked and prayed for this young child an hour,*
*And heard the sea-wind scream upon the tower,*
*And under the arches of the bridge, and scream*
*In the elms above the flooded stream;*
*Imagining in excited reverie*
*That the future years had come,*
*Dancing to a frenzied drum,*
*Out of the murderous innocence of the sea.*

*May she be granted beauty and yet not*
*Beauty to make a stranger's eye distraught,*
*Or hers before a looking-glass, for such,*

Being made beautiful overmuch,
Consider beauty a sufficient end,
Lose natural kindness and maybe
The heart-revealing intimacy
That chooses right, and never find a friend. . . .

An intellectual hatred is the worst,
So let her think opinions are accursed.
Have I not seen the loveliest woman born
Out of the mouth of Plenty's horn,
Because of her opinionated mind
Barter that horn and every good
By quiet natures understood
For an old bellows full of angry wind?

Considering that, all hatred driven hence,
The soul recovers radical innocence
And learns at last that it is self-delighting,
Self-appeasing, self-affrighting,
And that its own sweet will is Heaven's will;
She can, though every face should scowl
And every windy quarter howl
Or every bellows burst, be happy still.

And may her bridegroom bring her to a house
Where all's accustomed, ceremonious;
For arrogance and hatred are the wares
Peddled in the thoroughfares.
How but in custom and in ceremony
Are innocence and beauty born?
Ceremony's a name for the rich horn,
And custom for the spreading laurel tree.

## *For the Literary Traveler*

Signposted two miles northeast of Coole Park (off the N18), Yeats's sixteenth-century THOOR BALLYLEE (Easter–Sept., daily 10–6) stands magisterially on a narrow back road beside a small bridge over the RIVER CLOON. The setting is peace incarnate. Inside, however, a tour of the four-story tower demands the concentration of a monk: the place has been stocked with blaring speakers to within an inch of its ancestral life. (Galway, meet Broadway.) Whether the Irish academic establishment or the Tourist Board is responsible, you can't hear yourself think, much less savor a few syllables of Yeats's poetry, what with the roar of taped professorial voices reciting the poems and then—no kidding—explaining them louder and louder as you ascend the spiral stone staircase built into the tower's walls. As you pass into the bedchamber on the third floor, looking up to admire the gold stars George Yeats painted on the ceiling, the barrage of audio from the first and second floors grabs the air, clashing with the poetry that the curators have taped to play in the bedchamber. The visiting tourists are dutifully pressing the play buttons in the doorway of each room, releasing an unrelenting thunder of recitations that rises as you do. (And the booming commentary played out in the bedchamber about Yeats's contented married love—serene at last at fifty-two—is misleading; Yeats's extramarital affections are well documented by now.) Escape to the roof, where you can hear and see Yeats's inspiration as he paced upon the battlements: the "assault and battery of the wind," "Gregory's wood" in the distance, "the elms above the flooded stream" of the River Cloon twinkling beneath the arches of the bridge below. Down on the ground, the tower's gift shop stocks many good books (and the useful map and walker's guide Kiltartan Country: South Galway). Browsing, however, is also accompanied by the echoing audio thunder from on high.

Outside, you hear the music of silence that was for Yeats an ecstasy.

*At the grey round of the hill*
*Music of a lost kingdom*
*Runs, runs and is suddenly still.*
*The winds out of Clare-Galway*
*Carry it: suddenly it is still.*

◘

# James Joyce

## 1882–1941

*"The Dead," the last and greatest short story in Joyce's* Dubliners, *and his poem "She Weeps over Rahoon" were both inspired by a story that Galway-born Nora Barnacle told him. In 1903, the year before she moved from Galway City to Dublin and met Joyce, she had been courted by Michael "Sonny" Bodkin. Though sick with tuberculosis, he left his house on the rainy night before Nora left Galway to sing beneath her window a song of sorrow and farewell. He died from exposure a short time later and was buried in Rahoon cemetery. In "The Dead," Gretta Conroy, hearing "The Lass of Aughrim" sung at a Dublin Christmas party, remembers Michael Furey (Nora's Michael Bodkin) and tells her husband about the Galway boy who died of love for her. Gabriel Conroy, a cosmopolitan and bookish man who denies any bond with the primitive West of Ireland (his mother dismisses his wife as "country cute"), knows the time has come to set out on his own "journey westward," into the passionate Ireland of Gretta and her dead sweetheart.*

*Joyce visited Galway and Nora's family during two of his three visits back to Ireland in 1909 and 1912. He loved the ancient port city, ruled in the Middle Ages by fourteen "Tribes"—aristocratic merchant families of Anglo-Norman or English extraction—among whom were the Joyces. The Tribes had hereditary traits: the Joyces, whose coat of arms he always kept in his home, were merry. He spent long afternoons in Nora's mother's kitchen, listening to her sing "The Lass of Aughrim" and, with Nora, visiting Sonny Bodkin's grave and the Aran Islands.*

### SHE WEEPS OVER RAHOON

*Rain on Rahoon falls softly, softly falling,*
*Where my dark lover lies.*
*Sad is his voice that calls me, sadly calling,*
*At grey moonrise.*

*Love, hear thou*
*How soft, how sad his voice is ever calling,*
*Ever unanswered, and the dark rain falling,*
*Then as now.*

*Dark too our hearts, O love, shall lie and cold*
*As his sad heart has lain*
*Under the moongrey nettles, the black mould*
*And muttering rain.*

## For the Literary Traveler

Galway is the crackling capital city of the West of Ireland, the gateway to Connemara and the Aran Islands. It's a university town, at night full of students' high spirits, tourists speaking many languages, and visitors to the arts and music festivals. The Galway Poetry and Literature Festival, in the last week of April, and the mid-July Galway Arts Festival, Ireland's largest, pack the city tight: reserve accommodations in advance. (There are lots of bed-and-breakfasts out along College Road.) To find the Galway Joyce and Nora saw together, you can take the Tourist Office's walking tour or make your own way with the help of the "Galway City Map and Information Sheet," available in hotel lobbies and the Tourist Information Office near the south side of Eyre Square at Victoria Place and Merchant's Road.

Nora Barnacle, Joyce's muse, the model for Gretta Conroy, Molly Bloom, and Anna Livia Plurabelle, was born at 8 BOWLING GREEN, a small bungalow with a red door and a brass knocker, to the right of Bridge Street, near the River Corrib. It's now a museum (mid-May to mid-Sept., Mon.-Sat. 10–1, 2–5) with letters, photographs, and a table on which Joyce wrote to Nora; according to neighborhood women having a chat outside on a Sunday morning, "There's nothin' in it a-tall." It's around the corner from the fourteenth-century CHURCH OF ST. NICHOLAS, where Galwegians claim Columbus prayed before sailing to America. (Joyce insisted St. Brendan crossed the Atlantic centuries before Cristofero.) At the top of Bowling Green are LYNCH'S WINDOW and LYNCH'S CASTLE, memorials of Galway's Mayor Lynch, who in 1493 executed his own son, a convicted murderer, and thus launched the verb *lynch*; in his fiction, Joyce gives the name Lynch to a character based on a treacherous "friend" of his university years, Vincent Cosgrave.

At the age of five, Nora was sent to live with her grandmother and uncles at 5 NUNS' ISLAND in a small three-story house with eight windows and a black door. Two bridges access Nuns' Island: the lovely SALMON WEIR BRIDGE—Nora met a boyfriend here—on the River Corrib (in front of St. Nicholas's Cathedral, where a good choir sings the 11 A.M. Sunday Mass in Latin), and the Wolfe Tone Bridge, from which you bear right and walk along Corrib's canals onto Nuns' Island.

It's a ten-minute drive out to RAHOON CEMETERY, to which Joyce bicycled. Follow University Road behind the modern cathedral, turn left onto Newcastle Road, and then go right onto Shantalla Road, which leads to a main highway, Rahoon Road; turn right and then take the first left up the hill past the Rock Park development, where the entrance to the much-enlarged cemetery will be on your right. The cemetery overlooks hills and dales crammed with Galway's many new housing developments. The grave of Michael Maria Bodkin, in the Bodkin family vault, is to your left from the new entrance gates, up the hill and then, as you turn right, against the stone wall, just at the end of a line of yew trees and the green spear-shaped bars of the old entrance gate. In the surrounding fields thorn trees lean into the wind. Joyce remembered these details in the last paragraph of "The Dead":

> Snow was general all over Ireland. It was falling on every part of the dark central plain, on the treeless hills, falling softly upon the Bog of Allen and, farther westward, softly falling into the dark mutinous Shannon waves. It was falling, too, upon every part of the lonely churchyard on the hill where Michael Furey lay buried. It lay thickly drifted on the crooked crosses and headstones, on the spears of the little gate, on the barren thorns.

Later, as biographer Richard Ellmann tells it, Joyce compared this scene with that of Shelley's grave in Rome, equating Rahoon and Bodkin's grave with Nora's "buried life, her past." The connection between Rome and Rahoon seems a stretch, one only Joyce would dare.

⬛◇⬛

# Rita Ann Higgins

## 1955 –

*Poet Paul Durcan wrote, "There are not many books of poems of which I can say that I can remember the day, the month, the year when I read them. Higgins's* Goddess on the Mervue Bus *was such a book." A native of Galway, Rita Ann Higgins received immediate recognition for that first volume of 1986; her subsequent* Witch in the Bushes *(1988),* Philomena's Revenge *(1992), and* Sunnyside Plucked *(1996) have received many awards in England and Ireland. A poet of the working-class world of women, children, and the poor, she grew up one of eleven children, left school at fourteen, began writing poetry in her twenties, and is now writer in residence at*

*University College Galway and a teacher of poetry workshops in Irish and English prisons.*

## ODE TO RAHOON FLATS

*O Rahoon, who made you
to break the hearts
of young girls with
pregnant dreams*

*of an end terrace,
crisp white clothes
lines and hire purchase
personalities?*

*You don't care if her
children crawl into her
curved spine,
distort her thinking.*

*You put Valium on a
velvet cushion
in the form of a
juicy red apple.*

*Rahoon, why are you
so cruel to young
husbands, hooked on
your butter voucher*

*bribes? If you crumbled
would it take three days
or would the ground swallow
you up, payment for your sins?*

## THE DID-YOU-COME-YETS
## OF THE WESTERN WORLD

When he says to you:
You look so beautiful
you smell so nice—
how I've missed you—
and did you come yet?

It means nothing,
and he is smaller
than a mouse's fart.

Don't listen to him . . .
Go to Annaghdown Pier
with your father's rod.
Don't necessarily hold out
for the biggest one;
oftentimes the biggest ones
are the smallest in the end.

Bring them all home,
but not together.
One by one is the trick;
avoid red herrings and scandal.

Maybe you could take two
on the shortest day of the year.
Time is the cheater here
not you, so don't worry.

Many will bite the usual bait;
they will talk their slippery way
through fine clothes and expensive perfume,
fishing up your independence.

These are
the did-you-come-yets of the western world,
the feather and fin rufflers.
Pity for them they have no wisdom.

*Others will bite at any bait.*
*Maggot, suspender, or dead worm.*
*Throw them to the sharks.*

*In time one will crawl*
*out from under thigh-land.*
*Although drowning he will say,*

*'Woman I am terrified, why is this house shaking?'*

*And you'll know he's the one.*


## For the Literary Traveler

There's nothing romantic about the RAHOON Higgins knows: take a close look at the Shantalla Road (a reference in several of her poems) and the Rahoon housing flats on your way out to the Rahoon cemetery of Joyce's Galway (see p. 334). In her world, the Celtic Tiger economy has not been kind to the working poor.

The tourists' Galway City and the city of poet and playwright Higgins intersect as you move southwest of EYRE SQUARE (a great place to watch performance art) and along William Street, winding up at the Wolfe Tone Bridge. Along the way, SHOP STREET, HIGH STREET, and QUAY STREET are a cobblestoned pedestrian walkway: in the excellent KENNY'S BOOKSHOP in High Street you can join Kenny's mail-order book club and receive books by Irish writers not available in the United States (or e-mail Kenny's at desi@kennys.ie or niamh@kennys.ie). Left off Quay Street in CHAPEL LANE is the DRUID THEATRE COMPANY (tel. (091) 568617), where Martin McDonagh's prize-winning *The Beauty Queen of Leenane* was first produced. (Reserve tickets in advance; the acclaimed troupe is often away on tour.) To the right off Quay Street (at 22 Quay Street, McDonagh's Seafood Bar is good enough but jammed), in Kirwan's Lane are the exhibitions of pottery, jewelry, and furniture of DESIGN CONCOURSE IRELAND. Further along, down by the quays in Quay Lane, is THE PUNCHBAG THEATRE COMPANY (tel.

(091) 565422), where two of Higgins's three plays have been produced. If you take a shortcut across Nuns' Island, around the cathedral, and back across the Salmon Weir Bridge, you come out at the impressive new TOWN HALL THEATRE in Courthouse Square (tel. (091) 569777), where productions of opera, film, and theater (daily in summer at 8 P.M.) are well attended and well reviewed.

Higgin's second poem looks across Galway Bay to the Aran Islands, where Synge first heard the story about the patricidal son on which he based his play *The Playboy of the Western World*, but Higgins takes a woman's sardonic view of playboy rhetoric. Romantic love is not dead and gone in the new Ireland—it's just different, and more fun for everybody. For the schedule of daily ferries to Aran from the Galway City docks, visit the Tourist Office, (tel. 091 563081, a block southeast of Eyre Square, open daily 9–5:45. You'll find the poem's ANNAGH-DOWN ("Marsh of the Fort") PIER north of Galway City on the eastern shore of Lough Corrib, five miles west off the main (N84) road to Headford.

# John Millington Synge
## 1871–1909

FROM *THE ARAN ISLANDS*

*After Yeats urged him to go to Aran to "express a life which has never found expression," Synge visited the islands several times between 1898 and 1902, later on working the stories he heard there into the plots of his plays. The Aran Islands, written in 1901, published in 1907, is an account and defense of the primitive culture he found on Inishmore, the largest and*

*northernmost island; Inishmaan, the middle island; and In-*
*isheer, the smallest (two miles across).*

PART I

I am in Aranmor, sitting over a turf fire, listening to a murmur of
Gaelic that is rising from a little public-house under my room.

The steamer which comes to Aran sails according to the tide,
and it was six o'clock this morning when we left the quay of Galway in a dense shroud of mist.

A low line of shore was visible at first on the right between the
movement of the waves and fog, but when we came further it was
lost sight of, and nothing could be seen but the mist curling in the
rigging, and a small circle of foam.

There were few passengers; a couple of men going out with
young pigs tied loosely in sacking, three or four young girls who sat
in the cabin with their heads completely twisted in their shawls, and
a builder, on his way to repair the pier at Kilronan, who walked up
and down and talked with me.

In about three hours Aran came in sight. A dreary rock appeared at first sloping up from the sea into the fog; then, as we
drew nearer, a coastguard station and the village.

A little later I was wandering out along the one good roadway of
the island, looking over low walls on either side into small flat fields
of naked rock. I have seen nothing so desolate. Grey floods of water were sweeping everywhere upon the limestone, making at times
a wild torrent of the road, which twined continually over low hills
and cavities in the rock or passed between a few small fields of
potatoes or grass hidden away in corners that had shelter. Whenever the cloud lifted I could see the edge of the sea below me on
the right, and the naked ridge of the island above me on the other
side. Occasionally I passed a lonely chapel or schoolhouse, or a line
of stone pillars with crosses above them and inscriptions asking a
prayer for the soul of the person they commemorated. . . .

◊     ◊

The rain has cleared off, and I have had my first real introduction to the island and its people.

I went out through Killeany—the poorest village in Aranmor—to a long neck of sandhill that runs out into the sea towards the south-west. As I lay there on the grass the clouds lifted from the Connemara mountains and, for a moment, the green undulating foreground, backed in the distance by a mass of hills, reminded me of the country near Rome. Then the dun top-sail of a hooker swept above the edge of the sandhill and revealed the presence of the sea.

As I moved on a boy and a man came down from the next village to talk to me, and I found that here, at least, English was imperfectly understood. When I asked them if there were any trees in the island they held a hurried consultation in Gaelic, and then the man asked if 'tree' meant the same thing as 'bush', for if so there were a few in sheltered hollows to the east.

They walked on with me to the sound which separates this island from Inishmaan—the middle island of the group—and showed me the roll from the Atlantic running up between two walls of cliff. . . . The intense insular clearness one sees only in Ireland, and after rain, was throwing out every ripple in the sea and sky, and every crevice in the hills beyond the bay.

◊    ◊

Another old man, the oldest on the island, is fond of telling me anecdotes—not folk-tales—of things that have happened here in his lifetime.

He often tells me about a Connaught man who killed his father with the blow of a spade when he was in passion, and then fled to this island and threw himself on the mercy of some of the natives with whom he was said to be related. They hid him in a hole—which the old man has shown me—and kept him safe for weeks, though the police came and searched for him, and he could hear their boots grinding on the stones over his head. In spite of a reward which was offered, the island was incorruptible, and after much trouble the man was safely shipped to America.

This impulse to protect the criminal is universal in the west. It seems partly due to the association between justice and the hated English jurisdiction, but more directly to the primitive feeling of these people, who are never criminals yet always capable of crime, that a man will not do wrong unless he is under the influence of a passion which is as irresponsible as a storm on the sea. If a man has killed his father, and is already sick and broken with remorse, they can see no reason why he should be dragged away and killed by the law.

Such a man, they say, will be quiet all the rest of his life, and if you suggest that punishment is needed as an example, they ask, 'Would any one kill his father if he was able to help it?'

Some time ago, before the introduction of police, all the people of the islands were as innocent as the people here remain to this day. I have heard that at that time the ruling proprietor and magistrate of the north island used to give any man who had done wrong a letter to a jailer in Galway, and send him off by himself to serve a term of imprisonment.

As there was no steamer, the ill-doer was given a passage in some chance hooker to the nearest point on the mainland. Then he walked for many miles along a desolate shore till he reached the town. When his time had been put through, he crawled back along the same route, feeble and emaciated, and had often to wait many weeks before he could regain the island. Such at least is the story.

It seems absurd to apply the same laws to these people and to the criminal classes of a city. The most intelligent man on Inishmaan has often spoken to me of his contempt of the law, and of the increase of crime the police have brought to Aranmor. On this island, he says, if men have a little difference, or a little fight, their friends take care it does not go too far, and in a little time it is forgotten. In Kilronan there is a band of men paid to make out cases for themselves; the moment a blow is struck they come down and arrest the man who gave it. The other man he quarrelled with has to give evidence against him; whole families come down to the court and swear against each other till they become bitter enemies. If there is a conviction the man who is convicted never forgives. He waits his time, and before the year is out there is a cross summons, which the other man in turn never forgives. The feud continues to grow, till a dispute about the colour of a man's hair may end in a murder, after a year's forcing by the law. The mere fact that it is impossible to get reliable evidence in the island—not because the people are dishonest, but because they think the claim of kinship more sacred than the claims of abstract truth—turns the whole system of sworn evidence into a demoralizing farce, and it is easy to believe that law dealings on this false basis must lead to every sort of injustice.

While I am discussing these questions with the old men the curaghs begin to come in with cargoes of salt, and flour, and porter.

## For the Literary Traveler

Natives of Aran claim there's no resemblance between the islands Synge knew and the place day-trippers now invade in summer, renting bikes, minivans, and pony traps. (There's also a biennial Aran Islands International Poetry and Prose Festival in August.) But with Synge in hand—especially *Riders to the Sea* (1904), the tragedy of Maurya, the old island woman who has lost her husband and five sons to the sea and begs her last son not to go out on what turns out to be another fatal trip—travelers can head out on foot—or better, on a bicycle—and decide for themselves. For all the changes, stony Aran is still wrapped in silence, especially at night in the off-season. And it's always ringed by the sea and wheeling seabirds—gannets, razorbills, and cormorants.

On INISHMORE (Inis Mor, or "Big Island"; in Synge's time, Aranmor), the Aran Heritage Centre (Apr.-Oct., daily 10–7) in Kilronan, where the Galway ferry docks (County Clare's Doolin ferry goes to Inishsheer), offers a good introduction and regular showings of Robert Flaherty's film *Man of Aran*. Out the KILRONAN/KILMURVEY road, beside the HOLY WELL at the Church of the Four Beautiful Persons (Ceathair Aluinn), an old man told Synge the story of the miraculous well, which became the play *The Well of the Saints*. (There's nothing folksy about this Aran play—Beckett's favorite—which expresses one of the grimmest visions of the human condition in modern drama.) Near Kilmurvey in the small fishing village of Gort na gCapall, Liam O'Flaherty (1897–1984) was born a year before Synge's first visit. He grew up on Inishmore and wrote superb short stories about his native place in the collections *Spring Sowing* and *The Tent*; his novels include *The Informer* (1925), *Famine* (1937), and *Skerrett* (1932), a story portraying Aran religion with a heart of stone. Here is a portion of "Going into Exile," his story about an Aran family whose two oldest children must emigrate.

### THE AMERICAN WAKE

At last everything was ready. Mrs. Feeney had exhausted all excuses for moving about, engaged on trivial tasks. She had to go into the big bedroom where Mary was putting on her new hat. The mother sat on a chair by the window, her face contorting on account of the flood of tears she was keeping back. Michael moved about the room uneasily, his two hands knotting a big red handkerchief behind his back. Mary twisted about in front of the mirror that hung over the black wooden mantelpiece. She was spending a long time with the hat. It was the first one she had ever worn, but it fitted her beautifully, and it was in excellent taste. It was given to her by the school-mistress, who was very fond of her, and she herself had taken it in a little. She had an instinct for beauty in dress and deportment.

But the mother, looking at how well her daughter wore the cheap navy blue costume and the white frilled blouse, and the little round black hat with a fat, fluffy, glossy curl covering each ear, and the black silk stockings with blue clocks in them, and the little black shoes that had laces of three colours in them, got suddenly enraged with . . . She didn't know with what she got enraged. But for the moment she hated her daughter's beauty, and she remembered all the anguish of giving birth to her and nursing her and toiling for her, for no other purpose than to lose her now and let her go away, maybe to be ravished wantonly because of her beauty and her love of gaiety. A cloud of mad jealousy and hatred against

this impersonal beauty that she saw in her daughter almost suffo-
cated the mother, and she stretched out her hands in front of her
unconsciously and then just as suddenly her anger vanished like a
puff of smoke, and she burst into wild tears, wailing: "My children,
oh, my children, far over the sea you will be carried from me, your
mother." And she began to rock herself and she threw her apron
over her head.

Immediately the cabin was full of the sound of bitter wailing. A
dismal cry rose from the women gathered in the kitchen. "Far over
the sea they will be carried," began woman after woman, and they
all rocked themselves and hid their heads in their aprons. Michael's
mongrel dog began to howl on the hearth. Little Thomas sat down
on the hearth beside the dog and, putting his arms around him, he
began to cry, although he didn't know exactly why he was crying,
but he felt melancholy on account of the dog howling and so many
people being about.

In the bedroom the son and daughter, on their knees, clung to
their mother, who held their heads between her hands and rained
kisses on both heads ravenously. After the first wave of tears she
had stopped weeping. The tears still ran down her cheeks, but her
eyes gleamed and they were dry. There was a fierce look in them as
she searched all over the heads of her two children with them, with
her brows contracted, searching with a fierce terror-stricken expression, as if by the intensity of her stare she hoped to keep a living photograph of them before her mind. With her quivering lips
she made a queer sound like "im-m-m-m" and she kept kissing.
Her right hand clutched at Mary's left shoulder and with her
left she fondled the back of Michael's neck. The two children
were sobbing freely. They must have stayed that way a quarter of
an hour.

Then the father came into the room, dressed in his best clothes.
He wore a new frieze waistcoat, with a grey and black front and a
white back. He held his soft black felt hat in one hand and in the
other hand he had a bottle of holy water. He coughed and said in a
weak gentle voice that was strange to him, as he touched his son:
"Come now, it is time."

Mary and Michael got to their feet. The father sprinkled them with holy water and they crossed themselves. Then, without looking at their mother, who lay in the chair with her hands clasped on her lap, looking at the ground in a silent tearless stupor, they left the room. Each hurriedly kissed little Thomas, who was not going to Kilmurrage, and then, hand in hand, they left the house. As Michael was going out the door he picked a piece of loose whitewash from the wall and put it in his pocket. The people filed out after them, down the yard and on to the road, like a funeral procession. The mother was left in the house with little Thomas and two old peasant women from the village. Nobody spoke in the cabin for a long time.

The emotional wrench of forced emigration was all too familiar to Irish families, especially in the West. The exodus started during and after the Famine. From the 1850s to the 1960s, Ireland's population dropped from more than 8 million before the Famine to 2.8 million in 1961. The ruined, unroofed cabins you still see on Aran and all over rural Ireland stand as the sad evidence of a process that turned into a national hemorrhage. (These days, the recent Irish emigrants of the 1970s and 1980s are being encouraged to come home, since there are plenty of jobs available in the Celtic Tiger economy.)

South of Kilmurvey, about five miles west of Kilronan, a short climb up a rock-strewn slope brings you to what some consider the most magnificent barbaric monument in Europe, the four-thousand-year-old DUN AENGUS, a stone fort—its walls are eighteen feet thick—perched spectacularly on a three hundred-foot cliff overlooking the Atlantic. Nearby, the prehistoric islanders—perhaps the pre-Celtic Fir Bolg—passed their domestic lives in dwellings such as CLOCHAN NA CARRAIGE, a beehive hut in perfect condition midway between Kilmurvey and THE SEVEN CHURCHES, a litter of monastic ruins near TEMPLE BREANCAN. Synge saw in all these antiquities the mingling of paganism and Christianity that he felt everywhere in Aran culture.

On INISHMAAN (Inis Meain, or "Middle Island"), Patrick McDonagh's cottage, where Synge lived, is no longer thatched: it's a Synge museum. With the help of the "Inishmaan Way" guide, available at the Galway and Inishmore Tourist Offices, you can find SYNGE'S CHAIR (Cathaoir Synge) carved into a rock near TRA LEITREACH, the island's best beach.

Inishmaan is greener than the Burren-like big island, and while the islanders were at Sunday mass or out in their curraghs—the tar-and-hide-covered fishing boats still in use—Synge spent many hours here, loafing and writing in his notebooks the stories of Pat Dirane he later made into *In the Shadow of the Glen* (see p. 122) and *The Playboy of the Western World* (see p. 365).

On tiny INISHEER (Inis Oirr, or "Eastern Island"), a rock confined to the ocean (and crowded with day-trippers off the Doolin ferry), it's easy to imagine the despairing perspective toward island life felt in "A Young Matron Dances Free of the Island," a poem by Mary O'Malley (b. 1954), a prize-winning poet from Connemara with a long association with the people of Inishmore, where she conducts a writing workshop:

> One Tuesday in November she finished the wash-up,
> Mounted a white horse
> And rode into the force nine waves
> Out beyond the lighthouse.
> Feck it, she said, startling the neighbours,
> It's go now or be stuck here forever
> Chained to this rock like that Greek,
> With the gannets tearing at my liver.
> She rode bareback out the roads. The horse reared
> But climbed the foothills of the breakers.
> When she heard her children calling
> Mama, mama, she turned, praying
> Jesus, let me make shore
> And I will never desert them again,
> Nor be ungrateful. When she got in
> Half drowned, there was no-one there.
>
> For weeks in the psychiatric all she could see
> Were graveyards, men laid out in coffins,
> The little satin curtains
> They would have shunned in life, of palest ivory
> About to be drawn. It was the long winters
> They say, drove her out again

To where there was no going back.
She loved parties, was a beautiful dancer—

There is no other explanation.
The husband was good to her, by all accounts.
Does it matter? There should be a moment,
A shard of glass to hold against the light,
A checkpoint to pass before the end.
He has nothing, though people are kind.
They say her hair caught the sun
As she waltzed over the cliff, haloing beautifully down.

⊏◇⊐

# Maria Edgeworth

## 1767–1849

*According to Yeats, "The one serious novelist coming from the upper classes in Ireland, and the most finished and famous produced by any class there, is undoubtedly Miss Edgeworth." The author of* Castle Rackrent *(1800), the first regional novel in English, Maria Edgeworth lived most of her life in Ireland on her family's Edgeworthstown estate in County Longford. As the eldest daughter of a father who married four times and sired twenty-two children, she spent her life as a friend to his wives and a live-in domestic on behalf of his brood, managing also to write prolifically. Her father both encouraged and edited her writing. On a visit to her friend Walter Scott, who said she inspired his novels of Scotland—"I felt that something might be attempted for my own country of the same kind with that which Miss Edgeworth so fortunately achieved for Ireland"—she was described as a "little, impudent, fearless, outspoken, unchristian, good-tempered, kindly, ultra-Irish body." (She was four feet seven inches tall, "a monster dwarf of an authoress" in her own words.) She*

*based many of her characters on the Irish people, whom she knew
and liked, expressing her agreement with a friend who said, "How ig-
norant the English still are of Ireland, and how positive in their ignorance." Because the native Irish considered the Edgeworths fair
landlords, the rebels of the Rising of 1798 spared the family's home
in Longford.*

FROM *ADVENTURES IN CONNEMARA*

*In this letter to her youngest brother, Michael Pakenham,
Edgeworth sketches her tour of the wilds of County Galway before there were roads. After her horse-drawn carriage sank in
the mud, she continued on foot to Ballynahinch Castle near
Clifden.*

March 8, 1833

Ever since I finished my last to you I have had my head so immersed in accounts that I have never been able till this moment to
fulfill my intention of giving you my travels in Connemara.

I traveled with Sir Culling and Lady Smith (Isabella Carr).

My curiosity had been raised even when I first came to Ireland
fifty years ago, by hearing my father talk of the King of Connemara,
and his immense territory, and his ways of ruling over his people
with almost absolute power, with laws of his own, and setting all
other laws at defiance. Smugglers, and caves, and murders, and
mermaids, and duels, and banshees, and fairies, were all mingled
together in my early associations with Connemara and Dick Martin,—
"Hair-trigger Dick,"* who cared so little for his own life or the life
of man, and so much for the life of animals, who fought more duels
than any man of even his "Blue-blaze-devil" day, and who brought
the bill into Parliament for preventing cruelty to animals; thence-
forward changing his cognomen from "Hair-trigger Dick" to "Humanity Martin." He was my father's contemporary, and he knew a
number of anecdotes of him. . . .

* Hair-trigger Dick's ancestral home is Ballynahinch Castle, near Clifden

*After a night in Oughterard, she heads into Connemara by
the long way round of Lough Corrib.*

Next day, sun shining and a good breakfast, our spirit of traveling adventure up within us, we determined that, before proceeding
on our main adventure into Connemara, we would make a little
episode to see a wonderful cave in the neighborhood. Our curiosity
to see it had been excited by the story of the lady and the white
trout in "Lovers' Legends." It is called the Pigeon-hole; not the
least like a pigeon-hole, but it is a subterraneous passage, where a
stream flows which joins the waters of Lough Corrib and Lough
Mask. Outerard is on the borders of Lough Corrib, and we devoted this day to boating across Lough Corrib, to see this famous
cavern, which is on the opposite side of the lake, and also to see a
certain ruined monastery.* We passed over the lake, admiring its
beauty and its many islands—little bits of islands, of which the
boatmen tell there are three hundred and sixty-five; be the same
more or less, one for every day in the year at least. We saw the ruins, which are very fine; but I have not time to say more about
them. We crossed the churchyard and a field or two, and all was as
flat, and bare, and stony as can be imagined; and as we were going
and going farther from the shore of the lake, I wondered how and
when we were to come to this cavern. The guide called me to stop,
and I stopped; and well I did: I was on the brink of the Pigeon-
hole—just like an unfenced entrance to a deep, deep well. The
guide went down before us, and was very welcome! Down and
down and down steps almost perpendicular, and as much as my little legs could do to reach from one to the other; darker and darker,
and there were forty of them I am sure, well counted—though certainly I never counted them, but was right glad when I felt my feet
at the bottom, on *terra firma* again, even in darkness, and was told
to look up, and that I had come down sixty feet and more. I looked
up and saw glimmering light at the top, and as my eyes recovered,
more and more light through the large fern leaves which hung over

* Cong Abbey

the opening at top, and the whole height above looked like the inside of a lime-kiln, magnified to gigantic dimensions, with lady-fern—it must be lady-fern, because of the fairies—and lichens, names unknown, hanging from its sides. The light of the sun now streaming in I saw plainly, and felt why the guide held me fast by the arm—I was on the brink of the very narrow dark stream of water, which flowed quite silently from one side of the cavern to the other! To that other side, my eye following the stream as it flowed, I now looked, and saw that the cavern opened under a high archway in the rock. How high that was, or how spacious, I had not yet light enough to discern. But now there appeared from the steps down which we had descended an old woman with a light in her hand. Our boy guide hailed her by the name of Madgy Burke. She scrambled on a high jut of rock in the cavern; she had a bundle of straw under one arm, and a light flickering in the other, her grizzled locks streaming, her garments loose and tattered, all which became suddenly visible as she set fire to a great wisp of straw, and another and another she plucked from her bundle and lighted, and waved the light above and underneath. It was like a scene in a melodrama of Cavern and Witch—the best cavern scene I ever beheld. . . .

Meanwhile we were to cross Lough Corrib; and well for us that we had the prudence to declare, early in the morning, that we would not take a sailboat, for a sailboat is dangerous in the sudden squalls which rise in these mountain regions and on these lakes, very like the Swiss lakes for that matter. . . .

Our day had changed, and very rough was the lake; and the boatmen, to comfort us and no doubt amuse themselves, as we rose up and down on the billows, told us stories of boats that had been lost in these storms, and of young Mr. Brown last year, that was drowned in a boat within view of his brother standing on that island, which we were just then to pass. "And when so near he could almost have reached him, you'd have thought."

"And why did n't he, then?" said I.

"Oh, bless you, ma'am, he could n't; for," said the boatman, dropping his oar, which I did not like at all, "for, mind you, ma'am, it was all done in the clap of one's hand," and he clapped his hands.

"Well, take up your oar," cried I; which he did, and rowed

amain, and we cleared Brown's Island, and I have no more dangers, fancied or other, to tell you; and after two hours' hard rowing, which may give you the measure of the width of Lough Corrib at this place, we landed. . . .

◊     ◊

The morning came, and a fine morning still it was; and we set out. Invigorated and sanguine, we were ready to get into the carriage again, purposing to reach Clifden this evening—it was now three o'clock; we had got through half our thirty-six miles; no doubt we could easily, Sir Culling argued, manage the other half before dark. But our wary Scotch host shook his head and observed that if his late master Mr. Nimmo's road was but open so we might readily, but Mr. Nimmo's new road was not opened, and why, because it was not finished. Only one mile or so remained unfinished, and as that one mile of unmade unfinished road was impassable by man, boy, or Connemara pony, what availed the new road for our heavy carriage and four horses? There was no possibility of *going round*, as I proposed; we must go the old road, if road it could be called, all bog and bog-holes, as our host explained to us: "It would be wonderful if we could get over it, for no carriage had ever passed, nor ever thought of attempting to pass, nothing but a common car these two years at least, except the Marquis of Anglesea and suite, *and* his Excellency was on horseback." As for such a carriage as Sir Culling's, the like, as men and boys at the door told us, had never been seen in these parts.

Sir Culling stood a little daunted. We inquired—I particularly—how far it was to Ballinahinch Castle, where the Martins live, and which I knew was some miles on this side of Clifden. . . .

The Scotchman could not describe exactly how many *bad steps* there were, but he forewarned us that they were bad enough, and as he sometimes changed the words *bad steps* into *sloughs*, our Galway postilions looked graver and graver, hoped they should get their horses over, but did not know; they had never been this road, never farther than Outerard, but they would do all that men and beasts could do.

The first bad step we came to was indeed a slough, but only a couple of yards wide across the road. The horses, the moment they set their feet upon it, sank up to their knees, and were whipped and spurred, and they struggled and floundered, and the carriage, as we inside passengers felt, sank and sank. Sir Culling was very brave and got down to help. The postilions leaped off, and bridles in hand gained the *shore*, and by dint of tugging, and whipping, and hallooing, and dragging of men and boys, who followed from Corrib Lodge, we were got out and were on the other side.

Farther on we might fare worse, from what we could learn, so in some commotion we got out and said we would rather walk. And when we came to the next bad step, the horses, seeing it was a slough like the first, put back their ears and absolutely refused to set foot upon it, and they were, the postilions agreed, quite right; so they were taken off and left to look on, while by force of arms the carriage was to be got over by men and boys, who, shouting, gathered from all sides, from mountain-paths down which they poured, and from fields where they had been at work or loitering; at the sight of the strangers they flocked to help—such a carriage had never been seen before—to help common cars, or jaunting-cars over these bad steps they had been used. "This heavy carriage! sure it was impossible, but sure they might do it." And they talked and screamed together in English and Irish equally unintelligible to us, and in spite of all remonstrance about breaking the pole—pole, and wheels, and axle, and body, they seized of the carriage, and standing and jumping from stone to stone, or any tuft of bog that could bear them, as their practiced eyes saw; they, I cannot tell you how, dragged, pushed, and *screamed* the carriage over. And Sir Culling got over his way, and Lady Smith would not be carried, but leaping and assisted by men's arms and shouts, she got to the other side. And a great giant, of the name of Ulick Burke, took me up in his arms as he might a child or a doll, and proceeded to carry me over—while I, exceedingly frightened and exceedingly civil, . . . kept alternately flattering my giant, and praying, "Sir, sir, pray set me down; do let me down now, sir, pray."

"Be asy; be *quite*, can't you, dear, and I'll carry you over to the other side safely, all in good time," floundering as he went.

"Thank you, sir, thank you. Now, sir, now set me down, if you will be so very good, on the bank."

Just as we reached the bank he stumbled and sank knee-deep, but threw me, as he would a sack, to shore, and the moment I felt myself on *terra firma*, I got up and ran off, and never looked back, trusting that my giant knew his own business; and so he did, and, all dirt and bog-water, was beside me again in a trice. "Did not I carry you over well, my lady? Oh, it's I am used to it, and helped the Lord Anglesea when he was in it."

So as we walked on, while the horses were coming over, I don't know how, Ulick and a tribe of wild Connemara men and boys followed us, all talking at once, and telling us there were twenty or thirty such bad steps, one worse than another, farther and farther on. . . . I confess, Pakenham, I was frightened nearly out of my wits. . . .

But I know I was very angry with a boy for laughing in the midst of it: a little dare-devil of a fellow, as my giant Ulick called him; I could with pleasure have seen him ducked in bog water! but forgot my anger in the pleasure of safe landing, and now I vowed I could and would walk the whole ten miles farther, and would a thousand times rather. . . .

We walked on, and Ulick, who was a professional wit as well as a giant, told us the long-ago tale of Lord Anglesea's visit to Connemara, and how as he walked beside his horse this gentleman-lord, as he was, had axed him which of his legs he liked best.

Now Ulick knew right well that one was a cork leg, but he never let on, as he told us, and pretended the one leg was just the same as t' other, and he saw no differ in life, "which pleased my lord-liftenant greatly, and then his lordship fell to explaining to me why it was cork, and how he lost it in battle, which I knew before as well as he did, for I had larned all about it from our Mr. Martin, who was expecting him at the castle, but still I never let on, and handled the legs one side of the horse and t' other and asy found out, and tould him, touching the cork, 'Sure this is the more *honorable.'* "

Which observation surely deserved, and I hope obtained, half a crown. Our way thus beguiled by Ulick's Irish wit, we did not for some time feel that we could not walk forever.

◊     ◊

It grew dark, [but] the next bad step, we were told, was the last but one before Ballinahinch Castle. . . .

◊     ◊

*Edgeworth stayed at Ballynahinch Castle for three weeks after one of her companions collapsed from the rigors of the journey. Then they hit the Connemara "road" again.*

At the end of three weeks she was pronounced out of danger, and in spite of the kind remonstrances of our hospitable hosts, not tired of the sick or the well, on a very wet odious day away we went. As there are no inns or place where an invalid could pass the night, I wrote to beg a night's lodging at Renvyle, Mr. Blake's. . . .

Captain Bushby, of the Water Guard—married to a niece of Joanna Baillie's—was very kind in accompanying us on our first day's journey. "I must see you *safe out*," said he. "Safe out" is the common elision for safe out of Connemara. And really it was no easy matter to get us safe out; but I spare you a repetition of sloughs; we safely reached Renvyle, where the agent received us in a most comfortable, well-furnished, well-carpeted, well-lighted library, filled with books. . . .

Next day we got into *Joyce's Country* and had hot potatoes and cold milk, and Renvyle cold fowl at The Lodge, as it is styled, of Big Jacky Joyce—one of the descendants of the ancient proprietors, and quite an original Irish character. He had heard my name often, he said, from Mr. Nimmo, and knew I was a writing-lady, and a friend to Ireland, and he was civil to me, and I was civil to him. . . .

There was an end of our perils by gullies, sloughs, and bog-holes. . . .

That night we reached Westport, . . . a beautiful place, with a town, a port, industrious people all happy, and made so by the sense and energy of a good landlord and a good agent. . . .

Now that it is all over, and I can balance pains and pleasures, I declare that, upon the whole, I had more pleasure than pain from this journey; the perils of the road were far overbalanced by the diversion of seeing the people, and the seeing so many to me perfectly new characters and modes of living.

### For the Literary Traveler

Among lovers of the West of Ireland, Connemara is its beauty queen. On a clear day (don't count on it—Connemara has 255 official rain days a year), the mountain ranges towering over an endless brown-black bog make a stunning impression: the gray-purple crags of the TWELVE BENS (or TWELVE PINS) and the MAUMTURK MOUNTAINS, with the great glaciated valley of GLEN INAGH between them. Thackeray's *Irish Sketchbook* piled on the superlatives at first sight. Up to her knees in muck and bog water, Maria Edgeworth noted the men and boys who came to her rescue.

Forget about Edgeworthstown, where her tour started and ended. (Her house is now a hospital and the town is a blank.) From Galway City, leave the sprawling Galway suburbs behind and go to CONG (where *The Quiet Man* was filmed). LOUGH CORRIB, where Sir William Wilde and his son Oscar fished from their nearby holiday cottage at Moytura, is said to have the best fishing in Ireland and Great Britain. The boat rides on the lake are no longer rowed by Irish storytellers trying to put the fear of God into little old ladies like Miss Edgeworth. Today's travelers see the lake's 365 islands from a motor launch. (For Corrib Cruises, tel. (092) 46029 in Cong, (091) 552644 in Oughterard.) Surrounding the village of Cong (near the twelfth-century Cong Abbey and thirteenth-century Ashford Castle, now a hotel) are many caves, stone circles, and tumuli. The PIGEON HOLE CAVE, into which Edgeworth descended so intrepidly, is a mile out of town on the road to

Clonbur. (Cong's Tourist Office, open Mar.–Sept., 10–6 daily, offers the helpful brochure Cong: Sights, Walks, Stories.) You can also reach the Pigeon Hole Cave on foot from Cong Abbey by crossing a bridge over the River Cong; at the Monk's Fishing House, turn right and follow the footpath to the caves and the four-thousand-year-old Giant's Grave. Trailing Edgeworth to the Pigeon Hole requires a flashlight if it's overcast, waterproof clothing, and a dash of her willpower.

Along the main road (N59)—scenic after MAAM CROSS—going west toward CLIFDEN, you can imagine the sheer determination of these nineteenth-century travelers as they carried on along the N59 when it was just a muddy path through the bog. The comforts of their Connemara adventure are not far distant, however. Turning left at the sign for ROUNDSTONE, you head south for about two miles, when you reach BALLYNAHINCH CASTLE HOTEL, located on a beautifully landscaped island in BALLYNAHINCH LAKE. The castle was originally the home of the O'Flaherty clan, one of Galway's Fourteen Tribes and the powerful Kings of Connaught Maria Edgeworth's father had told her about. The woman of the castle was once Grace O'Malley, an O'Flaherty wife before she became the Pirate Queen of the Irish seas. (See p. 363.)

Since Ballynahinch is a stop for coach tours and group walking tours, you must reserve ahead for a room, or a meal in the dining room facing the lake and gardens (tel. (095) 31006); there are also luxury self-catering apartments in the Old Manor. Ballynahinch's lounge bar, with its open log fire, infectious conviviality, and intriguing portraits, is as relaxing a detour as you could find in rainy Connemara. In no time the boom-box voices of the fishermen-tourists fade into the fine dark woodwork. None of Maria Edgeworth's books are shelved in the castle's large parlor and library, though volumes of Walter Scott and Catherine Cookson abound. (And there's the odd copy of Barbara Grizzuti Harrison.) If you spend time around Ballynahinch, use Discovery Series map 44 to explore the roads going south to Roundstone on the bay, where Kate O'Brien (see p. 257) lived from 1950 to 1961 in a Victorian villa reputed to be haunted.

From Ballynahinch, Edgeworth went next to RENVYLE HOUSE on the magnificent RENVYLE PENINSULA, facing both the Atlantic and Mayo's Mweelrea Mountains. (It's beyond CLIFDEN, which holds concerts in the town hall next to the Alcock and Brown Hotel and has a good bookshop that stocks Edgeworth's *Castle Rackrent*. The Connemara Walking Centre on Market Street (tel. (353) 952-1379) leads tours out to Connemara's deserted offshore islands.) Renvyle House (northwest of Letterfrack; the informative Connemara National Park Visitor Centre is open May-Sept., daily 9:30–6:30, as is the lovely lakeside Kylemore Abbey) is now a luxury hotel and resort (tel. (095) 43511), but Edgeworth knew it as the elegant home of the Blakes, yet another of the original Fourteen Tribes of Galway. Oliver St. John Gogarty, the model for the cruel Buck Mulligan in Joyce's *Ulysses*, later made Renvyle House—in "the faery land of Connemara at the extreme end of Europe"—his home, which he described in his autobiography, *As I Was Walking down Sackville Street*. He hosted literary gatherings and seances here, where the Yeatses, at the height of their paranormal enthusiams, found evidence the place was haunted: fourteen-year-old Athelstone Blake, they said, who'd committed suicide at Renvyle, roamed his old first-floor room at night. More recently, a chambermaid claimed to have spotted Yeats's shade drifting through a rear hallway.

From Renvyle, Edgeworth and her companions moved east through the splendid JOYCE COUNTRY (the lands of James Joyce's declared ancestral Galway Tribe as well as Joyce Cary's), and finally north to Westport House in County Mayo.

Her route out of Galway and into Mayo (N59) passes through tiny LEENANE, where Martin McDonagh (1971– ), the London playwright of Irish background, spent childhood summers with his grandparents. His prize-winning Leenane Trilogy (1997)—*The Beauty Queen of Leenane* (1995), *A Skull in Connemara*, and *The Lonesome West*—is set in this village, which is tucked appropriately under the overpowering flanks of DEVILSMOTHER in the Partry Mountains. High, long, and dark, they wall in KILLARY HARBOR, in the lower valley of the Erriff River. The harrowing topography of Leenane suits well the dark comedy about its native "Beauty Queen," a mother and daughter (Mag and Maureen Folan) at once empowered and destroyed by their lifetime of mutual murderous emotional cruelty. (Just north of town, on the Louisburgh road/R335, another murder scene, that of *The Field*, based on John B. Keane's play, was shot at ASHLEY (Aasleagh) FALLS on the Erriff River, a landmark of cinematic homicide people here like to talk about and visit. Mention of *The Beauty Queen* is met with silence.) The LEENANE CULTURAL CENTRE (open Apr.–Sept.) shows a video about local life and a moving exhibit, "The Politics of the Woollen Industry in Ireland," that clarifies the economic context of McDonagh's view of this place as a dead-end trap of emotional starvation and bitterness.

For scholar Declan Kiberd *(Inventing Ireland),* in the Leenane Trilogy "J. M. Synge Meets Sam Shepard":

> More than three centuries ago, the rampaging armies of Oliver Cromwell told natives to go "to hell—or to Connaught." The western province—including the wild, stony, mountainous region of Connemara in the county of Galway where Leenane can be found—was so bleak and infertile that the [Protestant] planters willingly ceded most of its badlands to the [Catholic] Irish. Ever after it became a byword for all that was primitive and undeveloped. The word "culchie" (pronounced KUL-chee) … is Dublin slang to denote what in America would be called a redneck.
>
> There is, of course, another view. It was summed up at the start of this century by the poet W. B. Yeats, who said: "Connaught for me *is* Ireland." To him, it was the repository of an essential national identity embodied in folklore, poetry, the Irish tongue. It was the landscape of dreams and imagination.… [McDonagh] seems to have turned "to hell—or to Connaught" and "Connaught *is* Ireland" into a syllogism whose conclusion might possibly be "Ireland is hell." But his plays capture also the lyricism of Yeats and Gregory, as well as the bleakness picked up on by Synge and Joyce. Not all Irish audiences approve the ensuing blend. Some accuse the playwright of being a "plastic Paddy" from London who traduces rather than represents western people.… Synge, as a gentleman from Dublin, faced similar charges, and answered by claiming to depict "the psychic state of the locality." … He found the richness of the people's nature "a thing priceless beyond words."

◊    ◊

In the last month of her life, Maria Edgeworth, perhaps having in mind her "dear giant," the witty Ulick Burke, her deliverer from the Connemara bog, wrote these lines to her sister:

> Ireland, with all thy faults, thy follies, too,
> I love thee still, still with a candid eye must view
> Thy wit too quick, still blundering into sense,
> Thy reckless humor, and improvidence,
> And even what sober judges follies call ...
> I, looking at the Heart, forget them all.

Edgeworth and Synge, both products of the Protestant landlord class, had in common a feeling for Ireland's wild westerners that still makes sense to the modern traveler. (Oscar Wilde wrote letters to his friends from Illaunroe, his Lough Fee fishing lodge five miles from Leenane, praising the scenery and the abundant salmon in the Connemara lakes, but he didn't mention the people.)

The surreal beauty of Leenane also figures in the biography of the Viennese philosopher Ludwig Wittgenstein (1889–1951). Resigning from his professorship at Cambridge in 1947—like Beckett, he hated academic life—he came to live here, away from the "disintegrating and putrefying English civilization," in a cottage overlooking Killary Harbor, where he wrote much of his *Philosophical Investigations*. His idea that "the aspect of things that are most important to us are hidden because of their simplicity and familiarity" is a theme that runs through Synge, Yeats, Joyce, Lavin, and now the newcomer, Martin McDonagh. Of another idea of Wittgenstein's last years—the ambiguous nature of language—one could imagine his becoming more and more convinced the longer he came and went through the village of Leenane, listening and talking to people who wouldn't blink at the notion that nothing in this life, including language, is certain. "Ah, 'tis and 'tisn't," as the Irish often say. And in *The Beauty Queen of Leenane*, Maureen had no trouble passing off her mother's murder as an accident. Surely, 'twas and 'twasn't.

# Michael Longley

1939–

*A leading poet of his generation, Longley grew up in South Belfast and, like his friend Seamus Heaney, has published many volumes of poetry, including* No Continuing City *(1969),* An Exploded View *(1973),* The Echo Gate *(1979), and* Gorse Fires *(1991). For twenty-five years he and his wife, the writer Edna Longley, have made their home-away-from-home in southwest Mayo, in the remote Mweelrea mountains between Leenane in Galway and Louisburgh in Mayo. In this poem he imagines the Mayo mountainscape and the woman as one grounded and fertile love's body.*

ON MWEELREA

### 1

*I was lowering my body on to yours*
*When I put my ear to the mountain's side*
*And eavesdropped on water washing itself*
*In the locked bath-house of the underground.*

*When I dipped my hand among hidden sounds*
*It was the water's pulse at wrist and groin,*
*It was the water that reminded me*
*To leave all of my jugs and cups behind.*

### 2

*The slopes of the mountain were commonage*
*For me clambering over the low walls*

To look for the rings of autumn mushrooms
That ripple out across the centuries.

I had made myself the worried shepherd
Of snipe twisting the grasses into curls
And tiny thatches where they hid away,
Of the sheep that grazed your maidenhair.


3
September grew to shadows on Mweelrea
Once the lambs had descended from the ridge
With their fleeces dyed, tinges of sunset,
Rowan berries, and the bracken rusting.

Behind my eyelids I could just make out
In a wash of blood and light and water
Your body colouring the mountainside
Like uncut poppies in the stubbly fields.

## For the Literary Traveler

For this traveler, the most haunting road in Ireland—between LEENANE
in Galway and LOUISBURGH in Mayo—snakes beneath Longley's MWEEL-
REA, the highest peak in Mayo. Soaring on its southern flank above
blue-black Killary Harbor, this mountain wall on its eastern side is separated by a deep gorge from the SHEEFRY HILLS; on its northern and
western sides (visible from Renvyle Peninsula), Mweelrea overlooks
CLEW BAY and the Atlantic. Nine miles north of Leenane (on R335),
you pass through DELPHI, so named when a lord of Sligo, a friend of By-
ron and lover of all places Greek, was so overcome by the first sight of
this valley's beauty that he cried out, "Delphi!" Another mile north are
the radical solitudes of DOO LOUGH ("Black Lake") and the DOOLOUGH
PASS: this is fine walking and hiking country where car traffic is almost
nonexistent. (Lonely Planet's *Walking in Ireland* outlines the best trails
on Mweelrea. Also useful is "The Western Way of Mayo": contact

Mayo County Council, The Mall, Castlebar, Co. Mayo, tel. (094) 2444). On the right side of the road above Doo Lough, there's a Famine monument in the shape of a rough cross, inscribed DOOLOUGH TRAGEDY, ERECTED TO THE MEMORY OF THOSE WHO DIED IN THE FAMINE OF 1845–1849. A gift from the Third World peoples of Africa, where Irish Famine Relief agencies are a continuing presence (a work witnessed by former president Mary Robinson in *A Voice for Somalia*, 1992), the stone cross commemorates a local tragedy: during the Famine, six hundred people walked to Doolough Pass from Louisburgh on the strength of a rumor that food was available in this valley. When the rumor proved false, they died from starvation and exposure as they made their way back over the mountains to Louisburgh. A brooding quality fills this Pass, as if it is possessed by dark historical memory.

North of the Mweelrea range in LOUISBURGH, history takes a turn toward triumph and comedy. If you stop into the GRANUAILE (pronounced "GRON-yuh-whale") INTERPRETIVE CENTRE (June.–Sept., Mon.–Sat. 10–6; left off Bridge Street into Church Street), you'll hear the story of Granuaile or Grace O'Malley (1530–1603), the legendary Pirate Queen and the only Irish woman chieftain ever recorded in the Elizabethan State Papers. From CLARE ISLAND, off Louisburgh's coast, with its commanding view of the Atlantic, CLEW BAY, and ROCKFLEET/CARRIGAHOWLEY CASTLE, one of the Pirate Queen's homes, Granuaile controlled the seafaring trade between the port of Galway and Continental Europe; she also imported Scottish mercenaries to help the native Irish resist the Tudor conquest of the West of Ireland. Her memory is most admired, however, for her having had the nerve to insist on her rights as the sea queen of the West in a face-to-face confrontation with Queen Elizabeth. (Grace also outsmarted a few husbands, a talent the Machiavellian queen would have appreciated entirely.) When Elizabeth tried to appease Granuaile with the title of countess, Granuaile replied haughtily that she was already a queen, the queen of Connacht—the equal, not the inferior, of Elizabeth. Granuaile's small CLARE ISLAND (population 150) is a less popular and less historical destination than Synge's Aran Islands, but at Clare's summit—KNOCKMORE MOUNTAIN—this wind-thrashed outpost feels like a pirate's dream hideout. (From Roonah Quay, it's a twenty-minute ride on *The*

*Pirate Queen* ferry across the choppy turquoise bay; it leaves at 9:45 and 5:45 in July and Aug., but the schedule changes with the weather; tel. (098) 28288 or 26307. To reach the signposted quay, drive three miles west of Louisburgh and turn right toward the ocean, watching out for potholes.)

Grace O'Malley's descendant Lord Altamont (the Marquess of Sligo) is the present owner/proprietor of stately WESTPORT HOUSE (just east of Louisburgh, outside the town of WESTPORT), a Georgian mansion supposedly built on the site of one of Grania's castles, where Maria Edgeworth wrapped up her Connemara adventures. The gardens are as beautiful as she found them in 1833. The town of Westport has a friendly personality as you stroll around the Octagon on a weekday morning, and up and down Bridge Street, where Seamus Duffy's "The Bookshop," is excellent. At night Matt Molloy's Bar, owned by the flautist of the Chieftains, comes alive. The Mall-on-the-river is lined with lime trees and at lunchtime with high-spirited students in uniforms. In the public library further down the river, old men read books of poetry and the daily newspapers. St. Mary's Church on the South Mall has a Harry Clarke window of St. Brigid holding a bishop's crozier, a reminder that Brigid, abbess of Kildare in the sixth century, was viewed as a bishop by the medieval Irish.

Struck by its setting on Clew Bay, Thackeray raved about Westport: "It forms an event in one's life to have seen the place, so beautiful is it, and so unlike all other beauties that I know of." He stayed at the Olde Railway Hotel, on the North Mall, built as a coaching inn in 1780 by the Marquess of Sligo: "One of the prettiest, comfortablist Inns in Ireland, in the best part of this pretty little town." Though the industrial revolution hit Westport after he did (these days there's as much traffic and development around Clew Bay as unspoiled nature), you can still retreat to the Olde Railway's lounge and bar, where you're welcome to relax under Thackeray's portrait in the deep plush wing chairs beside the fire for as long as you wish. The food and rooms—everything about the place—are a comfort after you've spent the day outside, a world away in the Mweelrea Mountains of Michael Longley's southwest Mayo or on the Pirate Queen's proud island.

# John Millington Synge

## 1871–1909

### ACT III

*Those who claim Synge as a genius of world drama and one of the twentieth century's great writers see* The Playboy of the Western World *as his masterpiece and Christy Mahon as the modern hero: he unshackles himself from the past. Arriving in Mayo as a stranger, Christy boasts of having killed his father down in Kerry. His "heroic" deed and fine talk—a sample follows—win the heart of the sharp-tongued Pegeen Mike. But when his father shows up, quite alive, the gullible Mayo peasants turn on Christy, whom they've idolized for his act of antipatriarchal liberation. Pegeen loses her man and with him her chance to escape the "fools" of Mayo.*

CHRISTY *[Indignantly]* Starting from you, is it? [He *follows her*] I will not, then, and when the airs is warming, in four months or five, it's then yourself and me should be pacing Neifin in the dews of night, the times sweet smells do be rising, and you'd see a little, shiny new moon, maybe sinking on the hills.

PEGEEN *[Looking at him playfully]* And it's that kind of a poacher's love you'd make, Christy Mahon, on the sides of Neifin, when the night is down?

CHRISTY It's little you'll think if my love's a poacher's, or an earl's itself, when you'll feel my two hands stretched around you, and I squeezing kisses on your puckered lips, till I'd feel a kind of pity for the Lord God is all ages sitting lonesome in His golden chair.

PEGEEN That'll be right fun, Christy Mahon, and any girl would walk her heart out before she'd meet a young man was your like for eloquence, or talk at all.

CHRISTY *[Encouraged]* Let you wait, to hear me talking, till we're astray in Erris, when Good Friday's by, drinking a sup from a well, and making mighty kisses with our wetted mouths, or gaming in a gap of sunshine, with yourself stretched back unto your necklace, in the flowers of the earth.

PEGEEN *[In a low voice, moved by his tone]* I'd be nice so, is it?

CHRISTY *[With rapture]* If the mitred bishops seen you that time, they'd be the like of the holy prophets, I'm thinking, do be straining the bars of paradise to lay eyes on the Lady Helen of Troy, and she abroad, pacing back and forward with a nosegay in her golden shawl.

PEGEEN *[With real tenderness]* And what is it I have, Christy Mahon, to make me fitting entertainment for the like of you, that has such poet's talking, and such bravery of heart?

CHRISTY *[In a low voice]* Isn't there the light of seven heavens in your heart alone, the way you'll be an angel's lamp to me from this out, and I abroad in the darkness, spearing salmons in the Owen or the Carrowmore?

PEGEEN If I was your wife I'd be along with you those nights, Christy Mahon, the way you'd see I was a great hand at coaxing bailiffs, or coining funny nicknames for the stars of night.

CHRISTY You is it? Taking your death in the hailstones, or in the fogs of dawn.

PEGEEN Yourself and me would shelter easy in a narrow bush *[with a qualm of dread]*; but we're only talking, maybe, for this would be a poor, thatched place to hold a fine lad is the like of you.

CHRISTY *[Putting his arm around her]* If I wasn't a good Christian, it's on my naked knees I'd be saying my prayers and paters to every jackstraw you have roofing your head, and every stony pebble is paving the laneway to your door.

PEGEEN *[Radiantly]* If that's the truth I'll be burning candles from this out to the miracles of God that have brought you from the south to-day and I with my gowns bought ready, the way that I can wed you, and not wait at all.

CHRISTY It's miracles, and that's the truth. Me there toiling a long while and walking a long while, not knowing at all I was drawing all times nearer to this holy day.

PEGEEN And myself, a girl, was tempted often to go sailing the seas till I'd marry a Jew-man, with ten kegs of gold, and I not knowing at all there was the like of you drawing nearer, like the stars of God.

CHRISTY And to think I'm long years hearing women talking that talk to all bloody fools, and this the first time I've heard the like of your voice talking sweetly for my own delight.

PEGEEN And to think it's me is talking sweetly, Christy Mahon, and I the fright of seven townlands for my biting tongue. Well, the heart's a wonder; and I'm thinking there won't be our like in Mayo, for gallant lovers, from this hour today.

---

## For the Literary Traveler

Entering northwestern Mayo from Mulrany, the road (N59) cuts through what looks like a bog without end, a vast emptiness that's appropriate backdrop for a play about the imagination- and sex-starved people of Mayo. Yet, on your right, purpling the air, the NEPHIN BEG MOUNTAINS, the haunt of Synge's lovers, loom in the distance. This mountain range also shelters (at least in Synge's imagination) the anonymous lover of "The Brow of Nephin," a poem from the oral Gaelic tradition, which Douglas Hyde translated in *The Love Songs of Connacht*:

> Did I stand on the bald top of Nephin
> And my hundred-times loved one with me,
> We should nestle together as safe in
> Its shade as the birds on a tree....

Synge knew *The Love Songs of Connacht* by heart, and with this poem in mind he made Nephin the setting for Christy's and Pegeen's

romantic fantasies in Act III. When riots broke out in the Abbey Theatre at the first performances of *Playboy* in 1907, the members of the
Gaelic League in the audience were especially furious about this "titil-
lating" love scene. They didn't recognize that Synge had lifted his
lovers' dialogue straight from *The Love Songs*, edited by their own
leader, Gaelic League president Douglas Hyde.

If you follow Synge's antihero through the north Mayo of *Playboy*—
down the lonesome Bangor-Erris/Gweesalia road toward BLACKSOD
BAY and DOOLOUGH STRAND, where Christy shows off as an athlete—
you might wonder how a Kerry man, even in extremis, could settle for
this Mayo bleakness. From BELMULLET, the gateway to the MULLET PENIN-
SULA, where Synge stayed and his family owned property, the ocean
and boulders off the coast look and sound savage. Further north, the
road to Barnatra along the west shore of CARROWMORE LAKE and out
to PORTACLOY (which has good headland walks), by way of Carrowteige, feels, in a cold rain, as sad as the loveless marriage to Shawn
Keogh that Pegeen has a chance to escape, thanks to her Kerry playboy. Yet this is the same landscape where Christy imagines himself sheltered from harm by "the angel's lamp" of Pegeen's loving heart, "and I
abroad in the darkness, spearing salmons in the Owen, or the Carrowmore." He's in love and he's raving. Or sort of. In the tradition of
Wilde, Yeats, and Joyce, he's elevating blarney to a philosophical level:
through the power of a lie, Christy Mahon transforms himself from a
scared boy on the run into a romantic hero. He becomes his own fiction. "Life imitates art" was how Wilde put it; man becomes his mask
or anti-self, said Yeats. (Chekhov wrote that "nature itself had given
man [the] capacity for lying ... to hide the secrets of his nest as the fox
and the wild duck do.")

Landscape, in the words of Ronald Blythe, is "a condition of the
spirit." The road east from GLENAMOY to KILLALA—the NORTH COAST OF
MAYO—evokes the psychic texture of *The Playboy of the Western World*:
the paradoxical and comic coexistence of desire and repression, imagination and dull-wittedness, each force as strong as its opposite. Synge
traveled through the BARONY OF ERRIS—some call it "the loneliest region in Ireland"—the desolate moors between Glenamoy and
BELDERG, with the Nephin Beg range sprawled in the distance on your
right; he also knew the coast to the left, some of the most dramatic

(and unvisited) cliff scenery in the country. (The walk along the DUN CAOCHAIN CLIFFS covers 22 miles between Carrowteige and Belderg.) You can see the cliffs from the road between BELDERG and BALLYCASTLE, with the spectacular DOWNPATRICK HEAD five miles to the north. If you take time to explore here, you'll never forget what you find. For every boggy, monotonous mile, with one turn of the head come vistas of vertical cliff faces and a sky pouring light (or rain) over sea and earth. Moved by the prospect of life lit by love, Pegeen exclaims, "Well, the heart's a wonder." Yet simultaneously, this unpopulated plain expresses what her loss of love feels like. The word *nothing* echoes through the barony of Erris.

Along this road, perched on the edge of the 350-million-year-old Ceide (pronounced "CAY-juh") cliffs, is CEIDE FIELDS, the most extensive excavated Stone Age foundation in the world: twenty-four square miles of a farm settlement that's fifty centuries old. The pyramid-shaped Visitors Centre (June–Sept., Mon.–Sat. 9:30–6:30; mid-Mar. through May plus Oct., Mon.–Sat. 10–5; Nov., Sat.–Sun. 10–4:30) offers informative exhibits, films, and tours. Excavations have found no signs of war in these agrarian settlements; neighbors were peacekeeping. This prehistoric wonder on the edge of time and the land marks the geographic end of Synge's Mayo. But as they did down in Wicklow, his "heroes" keep on moving on. "Man is intellectually a nomad," he wrote in a journal, "and all wanderers have finer intellectual and physical perceptions than men who are condemned to local habitations." As *Playboy* makes clear, Synge (like many modern writers) saw happiness as life on the road.

Continuing along this north Mayo coast toward KILLALA, you're paralleling the route of General Humbert's ships, whose arrival at KILCUMMIN STRAND (turn left at PALMERSTOWN BRIDGE and follow the wayward signs to Humbert's Landing) launches *The Year of the French*, the historical novel by Irish-American Thomas Flanagan about the Rising of 1798— the United Irishmen's version of the French Revolution. ("Possibly the greatest historical novel of our time," said *The Spectator* upon its publication in 1979.) Also in these Mayo hills overlooking Killala Bay, Yeats and Lady Gregory set their play *Cathleen ni Houlihan*. Like Flanagan's novel, it recapitulates what actually happened after Humbert landed:

Irish peasants, armed only with pikes, joined the French troops march-ing inland. Ousting the English from Killala and other towns, they pro-claimed the "Republic of Connacht" at Castlebar. Eventually, crushed by General Cornwallis of Yorktown fame, the French were sent home. But all through Mayo (and Leinster and Munster), humiliated English regiments "mopped up" the Irish rebels, butchering and throwing into mass graves anyone suspected of a part in the Rising. But that was not the end of the Year of the French: invoked in more than fifty novels, many plays, and folk songs such as "The Croppy Boy," "The West's Awake," and "The Men of the West," it took on new life in 1916 in the streets of Dublin. Mayo history buffs still commemorate 1798 by walk-ing (and driving) the route of Humbert's army. The map is available from the friendly staff at the DownHill hotel in BALLINA, hometown of Mary Robinson, Ireland's first woman president (1990–1997).

# William Butler Yeats

## 1865–1939

*Born in Dublin and raised mostly in London, Yeats spent the sum-mers of his childhood (and the years 1870–74) in Sligo, a seaport town between two mountain ranges in Ireland's glorious northwest. His mother, Susan Mary Pollexfen, grew up here, listening to the lo-cals' stories of ghosts and fairies, developing a passionate interest in the invisible world that her oldest son shared and her husband scorned. The oldest son also loved his mother's birthplace: "I remem-ber when we were children how intense our devotion was to all things in Sligo." Maud Gonne, the beautiful woman he worshiped for a lifetime, once corrected the popular misconception that Yeats's de-votion to Ireland started with his love of her: "It did not," said Maud. "He got that from his child days in Sligo and the influence of those mountains and lakes." The legendary heroics surrounding this land-*

*scape also stirred his imagination; so did the sound of their names—
Knocknarea (pronounced "knock-na-RAY"), Ben Bulben, Innisfree—
which, like Yeats's poetry, enchant the ear. Many biographers have
addressed the estrangement between Yeats's parents: his father made
good paintings, great conversation, and no money; his mother, with
good reason, was morose. Many have detailed the mature Yeats's
"silliness": his spiritualism ("Willy the Spooks," jibed the Dublin
wits), his brief interest in fascism (sympathies belonging more to his
fantasy life than to his convictions, according to some critics), the un-
requited love of Maud Gonne and his pursuit into old age of younger
women (he was "sex-mad" to the Dublin gossipmongers). Yeats called
himself one of the "last Romantics." Others (James Joyce, Ezra
Pound, W. H. Auden, T. S. Eliot, Marianne Moore, Seamus Heaney)
have called him "the greatest poet of our time" and one of the greatest
poets of the English language.*

*More than with most writers, to understand Yeats's art it helps
enormously—and is a lasting pleasure—to visit his world. For behind the beauty of his work is a man haunted by a beautiful place.*

Yeats Country rises and falls between its southern entrance over the
OX MOUNTAINS (Slieve Gamph) and its northern border of the DARTRY
MOUNTAINS (with BEN BULBEN at its eastern peak). Between these
ranges you'll find the high points of the SLIGO landscape with which
Yeats, an energetic walker, had a lifelong intimacy: KNOCKNAREA; LOUGH
GILL; and north of Sligo town, ROSSES POINT; GLENCAR; BEN BULBEN; LIS-
SADELL; and DRUMCLIFF. You can follow him with Discovery Maps 24 and
25 and the "Sligo Map of the Yeats Country," which is available in the
Sligo town Tourist Office on Temple Street. There's no substitute for
the companionship of *The Collected Poems*, which abound with local
references.

SLIGO SOUTH:

OX MOUNTAINS, BELTRA, BALLYSADARE, KNOCKNAREA

### WHO GOES WITH FERGUS?

*A song from his play* The Countess Cathleen. *Fergus, poet and one of the proud Red Branch kings of ancient Ireland, gave up his throne to live in peace and hunt in the woods. Another story says he gave it up for love. (Joyce set this poem to music, calling it the finest lyric in the world. He sang it to both his brother and his mother on their deathbeds.)*

> *Who will go drive with Fergus now,*
> *And pierce the deep wood's woven shade,*
> *And dance upon the level shore?*
> *Young man, lift up your russet brow,*
> *And lift your tender eyelids, maid,*
> *And brood on hopes and fear no more.*
>
> *And no more turn aside and brood*
> *Upon love's bitter mystery;*
> *For Fergus rules the brazen cars,*
> *And rules the shadows of the wood,*
> *And the white breast of the dim sea*
> *And all dishevelled wandering stars.*

## DOWN BY THE SALLEY GARDENS

*Down by the salley gardens my love and I did meet;*
*She passed the salley gardens with little snow-white feet.*
*She bid me take love easy, as the leaves grow on the tree;*
*But I, being young and foolish, with her would not agree.*

*In a field by the river my love and I did stand,*
*And on my leaning shoulder she laid her snow-white hand.*
*She bid me take life easy, as the grass grows on the weirs;*
*But I was young and foolish, and now am full of tears.*

## THE HOSTING OF THE SIDHE

*Yeats's note reads, "The gods of ancient Ireland, the Tuatha de Danaan, . . . or the Sidhe . . . the people of the Faery Hills . . . still ride the country as of old. Sidhe is also Gaelic for wind."*

The host is riding from Knocknarea
And over the grave of Clooth-na-Bare;
Caoilte tossing his burning hair,
And Niamh calling *Away, come away:*
*Empty your heart of its mortal dream.*
*The winds awaken, the leaves whirl round,*
*Our cheeks are pale, our hair is unbound,*
*Our breasts are heaving, our eyes are agleam,*
*Our arms are waving, our lips are apart;*
*And if any gaze on our rushing band,*
*We come between him and the deed of his hand,*
*We come between him and the hope of his heart.*
The host is rushing 'twixt night and day,
And where is there hope or deed as fair?
Caoilte tossing his burning hair,
And Niamh calling *Away, come away.*

### For the Literary Traveler

Approaching Yeats Country from the south, along the scenic coast road from Mayo (N59), beyond Dromore West at Templeboy, above Aughris Head, you'll see a hillside picnic area on the right with a good large map of Sligo. From here you can look down over BELTRA STRAND on the south shore of BALLYSADARE BAY, an inlet of Sligo Bay. Views of Fergus's "level shore" and "the white breast of the dim sea" are superb from the Beach Bar down at Aughris Head, especially if you go late in the day. Atlantic sunsets are a feature of the entire Sligo coast. Further on, at SKREEN, enter the drive across the OX MOUNTAINS—they look like their name—ascending toward a gorse-golden mountain drenched with waterfalls into the pass called LADIES BRAE. A regular hiker here, Yeats wrote this terrain into many plays and poems (*At the Hawk's Well*, "The Host of the Air"). Beyond COOLANEY crossroads, at the bottom of the mountains, you'll join the Dublin/Sligo road (N4), which passes through BALLYSADARE. Yeats often visited his grand-uncle William Middleton of Avena House (the house is still occupied) in the center of the village (next to the post office), listened raptly to the gardener Paddy Flynn's long stories about fairies and Celtic folklore, and later sat on a rock in the Owenmore River—an inlet of Ballysadare Bay, where the Pollexfens' mills were located—looking across at the garden of willows, or salleys. (To walk this riverbank, follow the sign for Knockeen Church or Abbey.)

Continuing north and left off the N4 at Strandhill (R292), the (signposted) road to KNOCKNAREA winds around the peninsula, past CARROWMORE, the second largest Stone Age cemetery in Europe, to the foot of the mountain. In "The Wanderings of Oisin," Yeats has Oisin, the ancient Celtic pagan hero, meet Saint Patrick here: Oisin laments the loss of the lusty pagan Ireland—"those merry couples dancing in tune"—while the croziered Patrick defends the new Christian order Oisin finds so dull. (Yeats loved the technique of setting opposites at each other's throats, neither side listening to a word the other says.) A path leads to the summit; the climb takes about forty-five minutes. (On weekdays, mountain-bike clubs use the trail for practice.) Passionate Maeve, the Celtic warrior queen of Connacht, who dominated his imagination as a boy, is said to lie under the great cairn, a mound of stones thirty-five feet high and two hundred feet in diameter. On these heights, whipped bare with winds off the ocean (or the wild Sidhe), Niamh, the seductive "pearl-pale" beauty with whom Oisin rode off to Tir-na-nOg, the Land of the Forever Young beyond the sea, beckons the reader to "come away." The panorama up here offers a transport of its own: to the south rises the round hill of KNOCKNASHEE in the Ox Mountains, the fairies' headquarters, where their "hostings" over Knocknarea begin and end; to the north you see the bold, noble face of Ben Bulben and the Donegal mountains. It's easy to see how in such a setting the young, daydreamy Yeats could conceive a theme of otherworldly escape from the dullness of the everyday amidst mythic Celtic presences the local folk believed were real.

A mile west of the Knocknarea carpark on the left, a black gate (obscured by bushes) opens onto a muddy path leading to KNOCKNAREA GLEN or ALT. This chasm of mossy trees and high walls of rock, faintly lit with a greenish light, is the setting of one of the most beautiful poems of Yeats's old age, "The Man and the Echo."

## SLIGO EAST: LOUGH GILL

FROM *AUTOBIOGRAPHIES:*
 *REVERIES OVER CHILDHOOD AND YOUTH*

When I said to [my uncle], echoing some book I had read, that one never knew a countryside till one knew it at night he was pleased. . . . And he approved . . . when I told him I was going to walk round Lough Gill and sleep in a wood. I did not tell him all my object, for I was nursing a new ambition. My father had read to me some passage out of *Walden*, and I planned to live some day in a cottage on a little island called Innisfree, and Innisfree was opposite Slish Wood where I meant to sleep. . . .

I set out from Sligo about six in the evening, walking slowly, for it was an evening of great beauty; but though I was well into Slish Wood by bedtime, I could not sleep, not from the discomfort of the dry rock I had chosen for my bed, but from my fear of the wood-ranger. Somebody had told me, though I do not think it could have been true, that he went his round at some unknown hour. I kept going over what I should say if found and could not think of anything he would believe. However, I could watch my island in the early dawn and notice the order of the cries of the birds.

### THE LAKE ISLE OF INNISFREE

*I will arise and go now, and go to Innisfree,*
*And a small cabin build there, of clay and wattles made:*

*Nine bean-rows will I have there, a hive for the honeybee,*
*And live alone in the bee-loud glade.*

*And I shall have some peace there, for peace comes dropping slow,*
*Dropping from the veils of the morning to where the cricket sings;*
*There midnight's all a glimmer, and noon a purple glow,*
*And evening full of the linnet's wings.*

*I will arise and go now, for always night and day*
*I hear lake water lapping with low sounds by the shore;*
*While I stand on the roadway, or on the pavements grey,*
*I hear it in the deep heart's core.*

## THE FIDDLER OF DOONEY

*When I play on my fiddle in Dooney,*
*Folk dance like a wave of the sea;*
*My cousin is priest in Kilvarnet,*
*My brother in Mocharabuiee.**

*I passed my brother and cousin:*
*They read in their books of prayer;*
*I read in my book of songs*
*I bought at the Sligo fair.*

*When we come at the end of time*
*To Peter sitting in state,*
*He will smile on the three old spirits,*
*But call me first through the gate;*

*For the good are always the merry,*
*Save by an evil chance,*
*And the merry love the fiddle,*
*And the merry love to dance:*

*And when the folk there spy me,*
*They will all come up to me,*

* Pronounced "mock-ra-bwee"

*With 'Here is the fiddler of Dooney!'*
*And dance like a wave of the sea.*

## THE SONG OF WANDERING AENGUS

*I went out to the hazel wood,*
*Because a fire was in my head,*
*And cut and peeled a hazel wand,*
*And hooked a berry to a thread;*
*And when white moths were on the wing,*
*And moth-like stars were flickering out,*
*I dropped the berry in a stream*
*And caught a little silver trout.*

*When I had laid it on the floor*
*I went to blow the fire aflame,*
*But something rustled on the floor,*
*And some one called me by my name:*
*It had become a glimmering girl*
*With apple blossom in her hair*
*Who called me by my name and ran*
*And faded through the brightening air.*

*Though I am old with wandering*
*Through hollow lands and hilly lands,*
*I will find out where she has gone,*
*And kiss her lips and take her hands;*
*And walk among long dappled grass,*
*And pluck till time and times are done*
*The silver apples of the moon,*
*The golden apples of the sun.*

⊏◇⊐

## *For the Literary Traveler*

Whether you walk or ride out to LOUGH GILL—following the brown
YEATS COUNTRY signs—a stop at Cairns Hill Forest Park, about two
miles southeast of town, makes a delightful introduction to the twenty-
four-mile circuit of the lake and its islands. (A "Waterbus"—from the
jetty at Doorly Park or from Parkes Castle on the lake's north shore—
visits the islands.) Only a few minutes along Lough Gill's wooded south
shore you come to DOONEY ROCK, in Yeats's youth the meeting place
for Sunday night dances accompanied by a blind fiddler from
Ballysadare. From the top of the Rock, you can see the Dartry Mountains and the prow of Ben Bulben to the north; below them are the
Garavogue River and Lough Gill. Further east is SLISH WOOD, where
Yeats—no Henry David Thoreau—could not fall asleep. In an early
poem, "The Stolen Child," he calls this place "Sleuth Wood":

> *Where dips the rocky highland*
> *Of Sleuth Wood in the lake,*
> *There lies a leafy island*
> *Where flapping herons wake*
> *The drowsy water-rats;*
> *There we've hid our faery vats,*
> *Full of berries*
> *And of reddest stolen cherries.*
> *Come away, O human child!*
> *To the waters and the wild*
> *With a faery, hand in hand,*
> *For the world's more full of weeping than you*
>     *can understand.*

Yeats's biographers find the origin of "The Stolen Child" in the sudden
death of Yeats's younger brother Robert. Seven-year-old Willie was
told only that God had taken Robert home; his mother said she'd
heard the wail of the banshee the night her little boy was taken. In the

poem, fairies kidnap the child (a common folkloric theme in the West of Ireland), hiding and entertaining him all over Sligo, here in Slish Wood, in later stanzas at Glencar and the Rosses.

Leaving the main road, you wind around to a carpark at the (signposted) edge of Lough Gill, where rowboats are tied and the wildflowers and birds are profuse. If the weather's fine, you can swim across to the ISLE OF INNISFREE. Yeats wrote his best-known poem while staring into a shop window in London and daydreaming of Sligo. As his sister Lily recalls,

> [O]ne evening ... Lolly painting and I there sewing—Willy bursting in having just written, or not even written down but just having brought forth 'Innisfree', he repeated it with all the fire of creation & his youth—he was I suppose 23. I felt a thrill all through me and saw Sligo beauty, heard lake water lapping.

The tranquility of Innisfree is no young dreamer's fantasy. It's the noisy modern world that feels unreal here. (Though Ireland's remotenesses often create such a mood.)

Along the lake's north shore (after a detour to pretty DROMAHAIR), you'll find wider views of Lough Gill and its islands against their mountain backdrop. The circuit ends close to town in the shadowy HAZELWOOD, a peninsula of Lough Gill between ANNAGH BAY and HALF MOON BAY. (Turn left at a sign for Saehan Media Ireland.) Here Yeats imagined the wandering Aengus, the ancient Celtic master of love and the god of youth, beauty, and poetry, now grown old and pitiable. The nature walk through the Hazelwood, on a bay with swans, is marked by ghostly wooden figures of mythical creatures. Ireland's first sculpture trail reflects the imagination of her most famous poet.

## SLIGO NORTH:
## ROSSES POINT, GLENCAR AND BEN BULBEN, LISSADELL, DRUMCLIFF

### Rosses Point

FROM *AUTOBIOGRAPHIES: REVERIES OVER
CHILDHOOD AND YOUTH*

A poignant memory came upon me the other day while I was passing the drinking-fountain near Holland Park, for there I and my
sister had spoken together of our longing for Sligo and our hatred
of London. I know we were both very close to tears and remember
with wonder, for I had never known any one that cared for such
mementoes, that I longed for a sod of earth from some field I knew,
something of Sligo to hold in my hand. It was some old race instinct like that of a savage, for we had been brought up to laugh at
all display of emotion. Yet it was our mother, who would have
thought its display a vulgarity, who kept alive that love. She would
spend hours listening to stories or telling stories of the pilots and
fishing-people of Rosses Point, or of her own Sligo girlhood, and it
was always assumed between her and us that Sligo was more beautiful than other places. . . .

◊     ◊

So many stories did I hear from sailors along the wharf, or round
the fo'castle fire of the little steamer that ran between Sligo and
Rosses, or from boys out fishing that the world seemed full of monsters and marvels. The foreign sailors wearing earrings did not tell
me stories, but like the fishing-boys I gazed at them in wonder and
admiration.

When I look at my brother's picture, *Memory Harbour*—houses
and anchored ship and distant lighthouse all set close together as in
some old map—I recognize in the blue-coated man with the mass
of white shirt the pilot I went fishing with, and I am full of disquiet
and of excitement, and I am melancholy because I have not made
more and better verses.

⊏◇⊐

## For the Literary Traveler

Standing above the Atlantic on DEADMAN'S POINT, the western tip of ROSSES POINT, and looking from left to right, first there's Sligo Harbor with the METAL MAN statue and OYSTER ISLAND (images from Jack Yeats's painting "Memory Harbor"). Knocknarea and Maeve's grave are lumped high across the bay. Ben Bulben's slanting wall is at your back. You see all that Yeats loved here and why he longed for this portion of earth's beauty when he was away. The caravans, the golf links you pass on your way out here from town (a signposted five-mile ride)—none of it matters. The sea cliffs are overgrown with thyme, seabirds and sailboats move over the blue-green water, the dunes are high and private. (It was on one of Sligo's shores that Yeats's hero, the Gaelic warrior Cuchulain, died fighting "the horses of the sea.") Walking north, you cross the GREENLANDS, a grassy sand hill with small lakes, ending at RINN POINT, the Rosses' northern tip, "the mournful haunted place" of the stories in Yeats's *The Celtic Twilight* (1893). Here he imagined the Fianna, the divine warriors of pre-Christian Ireland, riding at night between Ben Bulben and Knocknarea, beating it across this peninsula called Rosses: "From mountain to mountain ride the fierce horsemen."

In his autobiography, Yeats names the strand at Rosses Point as the location of his first sexual awakening. After the dreamy otherworldliness of the early poems, the later ones ring with his down-to-earth conviction that "the sexual principle lies at the heart of all behavior as well as history." The imagery of several poems about the erotic pulse of the imagination, its climaxes and failures (the "crawling tide," "the gong-tormented" and "mackerel-crowded seas")—"Sailing to Byzantium" is a well-known example—comes from the pounding ocean rhythm rolling in at Rosses Point.

From Moorings, a friendly seafood restaurant (on the right coming from town), you can watch the harbor where Yeats as a boy often went out on the fishing boats, watching the tides and seabirds, listening to the fishermen's ghost stories. They scared the wits out of him, and they raised his lifelong yearning to know the people of the spirit world.

## Glencar Ben Bulben

### TOWARDS BREAK OF DAY

*Was it the double of my dream*
*The woman that by me lay*
*Dreamed, or did we halve a dream*
*Under the first cold gleam of day?*

*I thought: 'There is a waterfall*
*Upon Ben Bulben side*
*That all my childhood counted dear;*
*Were I to travel far and wide*
*I could not find a thing so dear.'*
*My memories had magnified*
*So many times childish delight.*

*I would have touched it like a child*
*But knew my finger could but have touched*
*Cold stone and water. I grew wild,*
*Even accusing Heaven because*
*It had set down among its laws:*
*Nothing that we love over-much*
*Is ponderable to our touch.*

*I dreamed towards break of day,*
*The cold blown spray in my nostril.*
*But she that beside me lay*
*Had watched in bitterer sleep*
*The marvellous stag of Arthur,*
*That lofty white stag, leap*
*From mountain steep to steep.*

⊂◇⊃

## For the Literary Traveler

The easiest way into GLENCAR (Ireland's "Swiss Valley," at the eastern end of Glencar Lake) is from the Sligo/Enniskillen road (N16). About three miles northeast of town, take the first left—signposted for GLEN-CAR LOUGH. Less than a mile down a narrow road that winds beneath the massive sides of Kings Mountain, Glencar Lake appears on your right. (This is now County Leitrim.) A path to the left, across from the carpark, leads up the mountain (it's about a five–ten minute walk) to GLENCAR WATERFALL, the "waterfall/Upon Ben Bulben's side/That all my childhood counted dear." In Irish its name is *Stuth in Aghaidh an Airde*—"the Stream Against the Cliff"—after the way the water, in a strong wind, blows backward against the cliff like a veil. From up here, you can join the hikers' trail, west across King's Mountain, past the Pinnacle Gully, winding up out on the promontory of BEN BULBEN, the most fa-mous image of Yeats Country. To quote Brenda Maddox: "[Its] massive brooding outcrop deserves to be ranked as one of the world's magic mountains; like Popocatepetl, Fuji, and Vesuvius, it casts its spell over the human settlements beneath." But it looks more spectacular from below, the perspective of Yeats's belief that there's a white door in Ben Bulben's limestone head: "In the middle of the night it swings open and those wild unchristian riders rush forth upon the fields," crossing the Rosses, mounting Knocknarea, paying homage to Maeve. Both Lonely Planet's *Walking in Ireland* and Joss Lynam's *Best Irish Walks* detail safe hikes west from Glencar to Ben Bulben and east to the adjoining spec-tacular horseshoe-shaped GLENADE valley. Ocean fog rolls in fast over these cliffs, the forests turn spooky, the Irish poet's imagination goes wild. Yeats named "the hills above Glen-car" as another of the haunts of the kidnapping fairies in "The Stolen Child."

## Lissadell

IN MEMORY OF EVA GORE-BOOTH
AND CON MARKIEWICZ

*Yeats sees the Gore-Booth sisters of Lissadell as emblems of the ethereal and privileged Anglo-Irish feminine. Both sisters, however, rejected fixed notions of class and gender, which disappointed him. Eva, a poet, became an organizer of factory girls in England and a lesbian. Constance, who married a Polish count, was second in command in the G.P.O. in 1916, sentenced to death, and then pardoned because she was a woman.*

> *The light of evening, Lissadell,*
> *Great windows open to the south,*
> *Two girls in silk kimonos, both*
> *Beautiful, one a gazelle.*
> *But a raving autumn shears*
> *Blossom from the summer's wreath;*
> *The older is condemned to death,*
> *Pardoned, drags out lonely years*
> *Conspiring among the ignorant.*
> *I know not what the younger dreams—*
> *Some vague Utopia—and she seems,*
> *When withered old and skeleton-gaunt,*
> *An image of such politics.*
> *Many a time I think to seek*
> *One or the other out and speak*
> *Of that old Georgian mansion, mix*
> *Pictures of the mind, recall*
> *That table and the talk of youth,*
> *Two girls in silk kimonos, both*
> *Beautiful, one a gazelle. . . .*

## For the Literary Traveler

From RAGHLY PENINSULA (nine miles west of Drumcliff) you get a grand view of the mountains ringing Sligo Bay: in this countryside Yeats watched the elegant Constance Gore-Booth riding her horse in the carefree years of her youth. Four miles inland, LISSADELL HOUSE—Ben Bulben at its back, Drumcliff Bay beneath its sloping front lawn—is also magical in the marine light of day, though time has ravaged the Georgian mansion's interior since his visits of 1894. (Open June through mid-Sept., Mon.–Sat. 10:30–12:30 and 2–4:30.) From the Sligo/Bundoran road (N15), turn left at the signpost for Lissadell and continue west to the house where Yeats found "a very pleasant kindly inflammable family ... ever ready to take up new ideas and new things." Both Eva and Constance were enthusiastic about Irish folklore; Yeats provided them with books of Celtic mythology. When the Celtic fires made nationalists out of them, inspiring a conversion to radical and violent politics, their mentor felt grief and remorse. As it was for Yeats, Lissadell Forest on Drumcliff Bay is great walking country.

### Drumcliff

UNDER BEN BULBEN

V

*Irish poets, learn your trade,*
*Sing whatever is well made,*
*Scorn the sort now growing up*
*All out of shape from toe to top,*
*Their unremembering hearts and heads*
*Base-born products of base beds.*
*Sing the peasantry, and then*

*Hard-riding country gentlemen,*
*The holiness of monks, and after*
*Porter-drinkers' randy laughter;*
*Sing the lords and ladies gay*
*That were beaten into the clay*
*Through seven heroic centuries;*
*Cast your mind on other days*
*That we in coming days may be*
*Still the indomitable Irishry.*

VI

*Under bare Ben Bulben's head*
*In Drumcliff churchyard Yeats is laid.*
*An ancestor was rector there*
*Long years ago, a church stands near,*
*By the road an ancient cross.*
*No marble, no conventional phrase;*
*On limestone quarried near the spot*
*By his command these words are cut:*

Cast a cold eye
On life, on death.
Horseman, pass by!

### For the Literary Traveler

Yeats died in Roquebrune, Cap Martin, in the south of France, in January 1939, having written his imperious epitaph and told his wife that after the publicity died down, in about a year, he wanted his body shipped back to Sligo and buried in the graveyard of Drumcliff church, where his great-grandfather John Yeats had been rector. He did not want a large funeral. Instead, World War II broke out in September,

and the reinterment did not take place until 1948. Bands, flags, politicians, flashbulbs, and huge crowds converged on DRUMCLIFF, at the foot
of BEN BULBEN and at the mouth of the GLENCAR VALLEY. In his chosen
graveyard, as in his life and art, Yeats insisted on his identification with
the dual tradition that suffuses the ancestry of the "indomitable
Irishry": his Christian ancestor's Anglican rectory is across the road; the
pagan Queen Maeve's horsemen reside in the mountain of Ben Bulben, descending to "ride the wintry dawn/Where Ben Bulben sets the
scene" across the Rosses and up the sides of Knocknarea. In a letter to
a friend, Yeats said, "To me all things are made of the conflict of two
states of consciousness." Out of Ireland's—and life's—paradoxes he
made an art for the world as mysterious and enduring as the countryside that inspired it.

Drumcliff, a major tourist attraction crowded with buses in high
season, is about four miles north of Sligo Town on the Sligo/Bundoran
road (N15).


## SLIGO TOWN

Yeats's legacy thrives in this seaport on the Garavogue River. You can
find it on foot in the narrow streets (not built for cars) he knew by
heart: In Stephen Street, there's the MUNICIPAL ART/NILAND GALLERY of
modern Irish art, the SLIGO COUNTY MUSEUM, and the YEATS MEMORIAL
MUSEUM (Mon.–Fri. 10–5, Sat. 10–1). THE WINDING STAIR bookstore
stocks Yeats Country titles, and, like Dublin's Winding Stair on the Liffey,
has a wonderful second-floor café overlooking the Garavogue. YEATS
INTERNATIONAL SUMMER SCHOOL (tel. (071) 42693, fax (071) 42780, e-
mail kavanaghj@s4.rtc-sligo.ie), whose first-rate writers and scholars
offer a good time and most unstuffy scholarship to all, is at Hyde
Bridge. (Across the Garavogue, Hargadon's Pub on O'Connell Street is
a dark old place, fine for conversation; up High Street, McGlynn's on
Old Market Street is, on Friday nights, the best there is for music.) KEO-
HANE'S BOOKSHOP on Castle Street carries every in- and out-of-print
Yeatsian title you can name. You can also pick up Bram (Abraham)
Stoker's *Dracula* (1897), inspired by Stoker's Sligo-born-and-raised
mother, who told him stories of the legendary Irish vampires Boban

Sith and Dearg Dubh as well as of the banshee, the female fairy whose wail in the night means imminent death; she described, too, the walking corpses seen in Sligo during the cholera epidemic of the early 1800s and the Famine. The walk from Keohane's or the town center to Temple Street (home of the helpful Northwest Tourism offices and the HAWK'S WELL THEATRE, named for Yeats's play) passes through narrow back streets lined with small bungalows, the Close of St. John's Cathedral on Church Street, and the Lungy: this is the neighborhood of the brilliant Irish novel, *The Whereabouts of Eneas McNulty* (1998) by playwright Sebastian Barry *(The Steward of Christendom, Our Lady of Sligo)*. (The Sligo of Barry's novel and play and the Sligo of Yeats's poetry are two different universes.) West of Temple Street, on the Dublin road, stands MERVILLE, once the home of the Pollexfen family and now Nazareth House, a residence for the elderly. Here Yeats lived as a shy child and began to love and seek the company of the landscape that became the living body of his poetry.

# THE
# PROVINCE OF
# ULSTER

---

DONEGAL

DERRY

ANTRIM

---

*Brian Friel • Éilís Ní Dhuibhne*

*Joyce Cary • Seamus Deane*

*Seamus Heaney • Brian Moore •*

*Medbh McGuckian*

# Brian Friel

## 1929–

*According to Frank Rich,* New York Times *columnist and former theater critic (and a self-described "Friel fanatic"), Brian Friel is "a great playwright . . . among the very best playwrights of our time but strangely, for all the acclaim, somewhat underappreciated. I still fear that the non-Irish layman in the United States tends to generalize about Irish writing and doesn't quite get him. He's more in the tradition of Chekhov, who can elude American audiences. . . . He captures that Chekhovian heartbreak." Since the 1964 production of* Philadelphia, Here I Come, *Ireland's foremost contemporary dramatist has held a devoted audience among American theatergoers for plays including* The Loves of Cass Maguire *(1966);* The Freedom of the City *(1973), about Bloody Sunday in Derry City where Friel grew up;* Faith Healer *(1979);* Translations *(1980), a favorite with Irish audiences; the Tony-award-winning* Dancing at Lughnasa *(1990), pronounced "LOO-na-suh"; and* Molly Sweeney *(1994). Though some plays have a strong sense of place—his childhood was spent between his mother's rural Donegal and his father's Derry City—Friel's most penetrating eye, especially in his best-known play* Dancing at Lughnasa, *is on the interior landscape of memory and loss.*

FROM *DANCING AT LUGHNASA,* ACT I

> *The play about the Mundy sisters of Ballybeg, who are all unmarried, is based on Friel's mother's family, the MacLoones of Glenties in southwest Donegal, who lived just outside the village. Lughnasa is the name of the games and harvest*

*festival held in honor of the pagan sun god Lugh on August 1.
In this scene we see the time the music from the radio—they've
named it "Marconi"—got the women dancing, releasing for a
few minutes their buried passions.*

KATE: Is it working now, Christina?
CHRIS: What's that?
KATE: Marconi.
CHRIS: Marconi? Yes, yes . . . should be . . .
*(She switches the set on and returns to her ironing. The music, at
first scarcely audible, is Irish dance music—'The Mason's Apron',
played by a ceili band. Very fast; very heavy beat; a raucous sound.
At first we are aware of the beat only. Then, as the volume increases slowly, we hear the melody. For about ten seconds—until
the sound has established itself—the women continue with their
tasks. Then* MAGGIE *turns round. Her head is cocked to the beat,
to the music. She is breathing deeply, rapidly. Now her features become animated by a look of defiance, of aggression; a crude mask
of happiness. For a few seconds she stands still, listening, absorb-
ing the rhythm, surveying her sisters with her defiant grimace.
Now she spreads her fingers (which are covered with flour), pushes
her hair back from her face, pulls her hands down her cheeks and
patterns her face with an instant mask. At the same time she
opens her mouth and emits a wild, raucous 'Yaaaah!'—and immediately begins to dance, arms, legs, hair, long bootlaces flying. And
as she dances she lilts—sings—shouts and calls, 'Come on and
join me! Come on! Come on!' For about ten seconds she dances
alone—a white-faced, frantic dervish. Her sisters watch her.
Then* ROSE's *face lights up. Suddenly she flings away her knitting,
leaps to her feet, shouts, grabs* MAGGIE's *hand. They dance and
sing—shout together; Rose's wellingtons pounding out their own
erratic rhythm. Now after another five seconds* AGNES *looks
around, leaps up, joins* MAGGIE *and* ROSE. *Of all the sisters she
moves most gracefully, most sensuously. Then after the same interval* CHRIS, *who has been folding Jack's surplice, tosses it quickly
over her head and joins in the dance. The moment she tosses the
vestment over her head* KATE *cries out in remonstration, 'Oh,*

*Christina—!' But her protest is drowned.* AGNES *and* ROSE, CHRIS *and* MAGGIE, *are now all doing a dance that is almost recognizable. They meet—they retreat. They form a circle and wheel round and round. But the movements seem caricatured; and the sound is too loud; and the beat is too fast; and the almost recognizable dance is made grotesque because—for example—instead of holding hands, they have their arms tightly around one another's neck, one another's waist. Finally* KATE, *who has been watching the scene with unease, with alarm, suddenly leaps to her feet, flings her head back, and emits a loud 'Yaaaah!'*

KATE *dances alone, totally concentrated, totally private; a movement that is simultaneously controlled and frantic; a weave of complex steps that takes her quickly round the kitchen, past her sisters, out to the garden, round the summer seat, back to the kitchen; a pattern of action that is out of character and at the same time ominous of some deep and true emotion. Throughout the dance* ROSE, AGNES, MAGGIE *and* CHRIS *shout—call—sing to each other.* KATE *makes no sound.*

*With this too loud music, this pounding beat, this shouting— calling—singing, this parodic reel, there is a sense of order being consciously subverted, of the women consciously and crudely caricaturing themselves, indeed of near-hysteria being induced. The music stops abruptly in mid-phrase. But because of the noise they are making the sisters do not notice and continue dancing for a few seconds. Then* KATE. *notices—and stops. Then* AGNES. *Then* CHRIS *and* MAGGIE. *Now only* ROSE *is dancing her graceless dance by herself. Then finally she, too, notices and stops. Silence. For some time they stand where they have stopped. There is no sound but their gasping for breath and short bursts of static from the radio. They look at each other obliquely; avoid looking at each other; half smile in embarrassment; feel and look slightly ashamed and slightly defiant.* CHRIS *moves first. She goes to the radio.)*

CHRIS: It's away again, that aul thing. Sometimes you're good with it, Aggie.

AGNES: Feel the top. Is it warm?

CHRIS: Roasting.

AGNES: Turn it off till it cools down. (CHRIS *turns it off—and slaps it.)*

CHRIS: Bloody useless set, that.
KATE: No need for corner-boy language, Christina.
AGNES: There must be some reason why it overheats.
CHRIS: Because it's a goddamn, bloody useless set—that's why.
ROSE: Goddamn bloody useless.

⊂◊⊃

## For the Literary Traveler

In late fall, when everybody's indoors, DONEGAL, its fierce mountains and two hundred miles of rocky seacoast, can feel ominous. Again, however, appearances in Ireland deceive. Where you find people up here in the northwest, there's usually music close by. All shall be well. Approaching Friel's GLENTIES from Donegal town, you head north off the N56 onto R262, straight on toward the lurch of the BLUE STACK MOUNTAINS and the white cottages daubed along the top of their western ridge. To find his aunts' cottage, go to the end of Glenties' main street, bear right at the Marian grotto onto the R250/FINTOWN Road, and take the first left after crossing a small bridge: it leads down a hill to the cottage, which is now a Friel museum of sorts. Meryl Streep, who played Kate in the shot-on-location movie version of the play, presided over its opening in 1999, a time of great merriment that Glenties people are happy to talk about. You'll find lots of them in the HIGHLANDS HOTEL (tel. (075) 51111, on the left corner at the bottom of the main street as you come into Glenties), just past the new Catholic church by Derry architect Liam McCormack, set like a jewel deep in a garden of rhododendron. If you're lucky enough to walk in on what seems like the whole town's celebration of a First Communion late on a Saturday afternoon in spring, you'll feel swept away by the high spirits, people reveling with their rosy children, who tear through the lounges as if they own the place; as the fun soars, you think about coming back for the harvest festival, held annually on September 12: Glenties likes to party. At the Heritage Centre (on the crossroads across from the Highlands Hotel) are signposts for many fine walks you can take into the mountains. In an hour you can find

LOUGH ANNEY, the Lough Anna where the "simple" sister, Rose, went with Danny Bradley, reporting back, "It's very peaceful up there." For an overview of the town as it nestles into the valley between two converging glens, follow the N56 a few miles north, bearing right at the sign BOTHAR NA RADHARC (scenic drive) along the GWEEBARA RIVER in the direction of DOOCHARRY, turning right off the river road to ascend and cross the hill of CROAGHLEHEEN (keeping an eye out for potholes and oncoming farm carts). The high roads over Glenties (along with the Donegal pages of Lonely Planet's *Walking in Ireland*) could persuade you that hiking Ireland's northwest is what you'd like to do for the rest of your life. There'd be virtue in it, too, since visitors help the economy. Unemployment, which devastated the world of *Dancing at Lughnasa*, is still a fact in Donegal. As the Mundy sisters knew every minute of their hand-to-mouth lives, poverty is a problem beautiful scenery can't solve.

These days the people of Glenties have more sources of music available to them than their radios: all over Donegal, especially in the Gaeltacht, you can find fantastic traditional music, the kind the sisters danced to. In this area there's the Glen Inn, three miles out on the R253/BALLYBOFEY Road, with Saturday night sessions. On the N56/DUN-GLOE Road, the Limelight is the largest disco in the northwest, with performances by traditional dancers in some of its five bars. In his joyful book *Last Night's Fun* (1996), Belfast poet Ciaran Carson (b. 1948) celebrates Irish music, and in this passage he connects the wildness of its sound with the wild landscape of southwest Donegal:

## HALLOWE'EN 1982:
### TEELIN, COUNTY DONEGAL

It is the morning after the night before and snatches of the night before—fiddle tunes, hubbub, the clink of glasses—keep filtering through from the memory-bank. We are driving out to the coast to clear our heads—or rather, *up* to the coast, towards Slieve League, the highest sea-cliff in Western Europe, following this precipitous erratic mountain road that winds between stone walls, potato drills, stone-littered patchy fields, one man idling over a spade who raises his hand in an understated rhetoric of hail or farewell, and the clouds piled high between mountains, while these fiddle tunes keep coming back insistently, hectic, passionate and melancholic; half-remembered fragments. The bits and pieces of the landscape sidle into place, accommodated by the loops and spirals of the road, its meditated salients and inclines: and now, as at other times, I wonder if the disciplined wildness of Donegal music has anything to do with this terrain. For nature, here, is never wholly pristine or untouched: the land is possessed and repossessed, named, forgotten, lost and rediscovered; it is under constant dispute; even in its dereliction, it implies a human history. A line of a sentimental song comes back to me: 'Sure your hearts are like your mountains, in the homes of Donegal'. Presumably, the writer intended that we read 'big' for 'mountains'; yet mountains are also hard and stony; they are barriers to be circumvented or defeated. In Donegal fiddle music, this unconscious irony is transformed into purposeful energy. It is a music of driving, relentless rhythm that teeters on the edge of falling over itself; it seems to almost overtake itself, yet reins in at the brink. A jagged melodic line is nagging at me as we arrive at a high promontory. The sea appears from nowhere. On the right, the immense absurd precipice of Slieve League falls into a tiny silent line of foam, some rocks. How far away is it? The eye has nothing to scale: a human figure, if you could imagine it against this, would be lost; that seagull hovering over there is either miles away, or just within reach. Turning back to the sea again, you can hear it, if you listen very closely: a vast lonesome whispering that stretches all the way to North America.

This harsh terrain, which Carson hears evoked in the ruthlessly unsentimental traditional music (such as the Mundy sisters dance to), rises over the southwest coast road from KILCAR around CARRICK on beautiful TEELIN BAY. To the west are the SLIEVE LEAGUE CLIFFS, at two thousand feet the highest sea cliffs in Europe. The signs for AMHARC MOR will guide you to the summit—in Carson's words, "the immense absurd precipice of Slieve League." Two months after Lughnasa, in October, the Slieve League pub in Carrick hosts a traditional music festival.

# Éilís Ní Dhuibhne

### 1954–

*Until recently the fiction of Éilís Ní Dhuibhne (pronounced "AY-lish ni-DOO"), though popular in Ireland, was, like the work of most Irish women writers, not available in America. Now, however, Ní Dhuibhne is receiving more attention outside Dublin (where she lives): a novel,* The Bray House *(1990), was well reviewed in* The New York Times, *and stories from three collections,* Blood and Water *(1989),* Eating Women Is Not Recommended *(1991), and* Inland Ice *(1997), have been included in* The Vintage Book of Contemporary Irish Fiction, Territories of the Voice: Contemporary Stories by Irish Women Writers, *and* The Anchor Book of New Irish Writing. *Also represented in* Ladies Night at Finbars Hotel, *her writing is the subject of a critical overview in Christina Hunt Mahony's* Contemporary Irish Literature *(1998).*

## BLOOD AND WATER

I have an aunt who is not the full shilling. 'The Mad Aunt' was how my sister and I referred to her when we were children, but that was just a euphemism, designed to shelter us from the truth which we couldn't stomach: she was mentally retarded. Very mildly so: perhaps she was just a slow learner. She survived very successfully as a lone farm woman, letting land, keeping a cow and a few hens and ducks, listening to the local gossip from the neighbours who were kind enough to drop in regularly in the evenings. Quite a few of them were: her house was a popular place for callers, and perhaps that was part of the secret of her survival. She did not participate in the neighbours' conversation to any extent, however. She was articulate only on a very concrete level, and all abstract topics were beyond her.

Had she been born in the fifties or sixties, my aunt would have been scientifically labelled, given special treatment at a special school, taught special skills and eventually employed in a special workshop to carry out a special job, certainly a much duller job than the one she pursued in reality. Luckily for her she was born in 1925 and had been reared as a normal child. Her family had failed to recognize that she was different from others and had not sought medical attention for her. She had merely been considered 'delicate'. The term 'mentally retarded' would have been meaningless in those days, anyway, in the part of Donegal where she and my mother originated, where Irish was the common, if not the only, language. As she grew up, it must have been silently conceded that she was a little odd. But people seemed to have no difficulty in suppressing this fact, and they judged my aunt by the standards which they applied to humanity at large: sometimes lenient and sometimes not.

She lived in a farmhouse in Ballytra on Inishowen, and once a year we visited her. Our annual holiday was spent under her roof. And had it not been for the lodging she provided, we could not have afforded to get away at all. But we did not consider this aspect of the affair.

On the first Saturday of August we always set out, laden with clothes in cardboard boxes and groceries from the cheap city shops, from the street markets: enough to see us through the fortnight. The journey north lasted nearly twelve hours in our ancient battered cars: a Morris Eight, dark green with fragrant leather seats, and a Ford Anglia are two of the models I remember from a long series of fourth-hand crocks. Sometimes they broke down *en route* and caused us long delays in nauseating garages, where I stood around with my father, while the mechanic tinkered, or went, with my sister and mother, for walks down country lanes, or along the wide melancholy street of small market towns.

Apart from such occasional hitches, however, the trips were delightful odysseys through various flavours of Ireland: the dusty rich flatlands outside Dublin, the drumlins of Monaghan with their hint of secrets and better things to come, the luxuriant slopes, rushing rivers and expensive villas of Tyrone, and finally, the ultimate reward: the furze and heather, the dog-roses, the fuchsia, of Donegal.

Donegal was different in those days. Different from what it is now, different then from the eastern urban parts of Ireland. It was rural in a thorough, elemental way. People were old-fashioned in their dress and manners, even in their physiques: weather-beaten faces were highlighted by black or grey suits, shiny with age; broad hips stretched the cotton of navy-blue, flower-sprigged overalls, a kind of uniform for country women which their city sisters had long eschewed, if they ever had it. Residences were thatched cottages ... 'The Irish peasant house' ... or spare grey farmhouses. There was only a single bungalow in the parish where my aunt lived, an area which is now littered with them.

All these things accentuated the rusticity of the place, its strangeness, its uniqueness.

My aunt's house was of the slated, two-storey variety, and it stood, surrounded by a seemingly arbitrary selection of outhouses, in a large yard called 'the street'. Usually we turned into this street at about nine o'clock at night, having been on the road all day. My aunt would be waiting for us, leaning over the half-door. Even though she was deaf, she would have heard the car while it was still a few hundred yards away, chugging along the dirt lane: it was always that kind of car. She would stand up as soon as we appeared, and twist her hands shyly, until we emerged from the car. Then she would walk slowly over to us, and shake hands carefully with each of us in turn, starting with my mother. Care, formality: these were characteristics which were most obvious in her. Slowness.

Greetings over, we would troop into the house, under a low portal apparently designed for a smaller race of people. Then we would sit in front of the hot fire, and my mother would talk, in a loud cheery voice, telling my aunt the news from Dublin and asking for local gossip. My aunt would sometimes try to reply, more often not. After five minutes or so of this, she would indicate, a bit resentfully, that she had expected us earlier, that she had been listening for the car for over two days. And my mother, still, at this early stage of the holiday, in a diplomatic mood, would explain patiently, slowly, loudly, that no, we had been due today. We always came on the first Saturday, didn't we? John only got off on the Friday, sure. But somehow my mother would never have written to my aunt to let her know when we were coming. It was not owing to the fact that the latter was illiterate that she didn't write. Any neighbour would have read a letter for her. It was, rather, the result of a strange convention which my parents, especially my mother, always adhered to: they never wrote to anyone, about anything, except one subject. Death.

While this courteous ritual of fireside conversation was being enacted by my parents (although in fact my father never bothered to take part), my sister and I would sit silently on our hardbacked chairs, fidgeting and looking at the familiar objects in the room: the Sacred Heart, the Little Flower, the calendar from Bells of Buncrana depicting a blond laughing child, the red arc for layers' mash. We answered promptly, monosyllabically, the few questions my aunt put to us, all concerning school. Subdued by the immense boredom of the day, we tolerated a further boredom.

After a long time, my mother would get up, stretch, and prepare a meal of rashers and sausages, from Russells of Camden Street. To this my aunt would add a few provisions she had laid in for us: eggs, butter she had churned herself, and soda bread which she baked in a pot oven, in enormous golden balls. I always refused to eat this bread, because I found the taste repellent and because I didn't think my aunt washed her hands properly. My sister, however, ate no other kind of bread while we were on holiday at that house, and I used to tease her about it, trying to force her to see my point of view. She never did.

After tea, although by that time it was usually late, we would run outside and play. We would visit each of the outhouses in turn, hoping to see an owl in the barn and then we'd run across the road to a stream which flowed behind the back garden. There was a stone bridge over the stream and on our first night we invariably played the same game: we threw sticks into the stream at one side of the bridge, and then ran as fast as we could to the other side in order to catch them as they sailed out. This activity, undertaken at night in the shadow of the black hills, had a magical effect: it plummeted me headlong into the atmosphere of the holidays. At that stream, on that first night, I would suddenly discover within myself a feeling of happiness and freedom that I was normally unaware I possessed. It seemed to emerge from some hidden part of me, like the sticks emerging from underneath the bridge, and it counteracted the faint claustrophobia, the nervousness, which I always had initially in my aunt's house.

Refreshed and elated, we would go to bed in unlit upstairs rooms. These bedrooms were panelled in wood which had been white once, but had faded to the colour of butter, and they had windows less than two feet square which had to be propped up with a stick if you wanted them to remain open: the windows were so small, my mother liked to tell us, because they had been made at a time when there was a tax on glass. I wondered about this: the doors were tiny, too.

When I woke up in the morning, I would lie and count the boards on the ceiling, and then the knots on the boards, until eventually a clattering of footsteps on the uncarpeted stairs and a banging about of pots and pans would announce that my mother was up and that breakfast would soon be available. I would run downstairs to the scullery, which served as a bathroom, and wash. The basin stood on a deal table, the water was in a white enamel bucket on the dresser. A piece of soap was stuck to a saucer on the windowsill, in front of the basin: through the window, you could see a bit of an elm tree, and a purple hill, as you washed.

In a way it was pleasant, but on the whole it worried me, washing in that place. It was so public. There was a constant danger that someone would rush in, and find you there, half undressed, scrubbing your armpits. I liked my ablutions to be private and unobserved.

The scullery worried me for another reason. On its wall, just beside the dresser, was a big splodge of a dirty yellow substance, unlike anything I had ever encountered. I took it to be some sort of fungus. God knows why, since the house was unusually clean. This thing so repelled me that I never even dared to ask what it was, and simply did my very best to avoid looking at it while I was in its vicinity, washing or bringing back the bucket of water from the well, or doing anything else. Years later, when I was taking a course in ethnology at the university, I realized that the stuff was nothing other than butter, daubed on the wall after every churning, for luck. But to me it symbolized something quite other than good fortune, something unthinkably horrible.

After dressing, breakfast. Rashers and sausages again, fried over the fire by my mother, who did all the cooking while we were on holiday. For that fortnight my aunt, usually a skilful frier of rashers, baker of bread, abdicated domestic responsibility to her, and adopted the role of child in her own house, like a displaced rural mother-in-law. She spent her time fiddling around in the henhouse, feeding the cat, or more often she simply sat, like a man, and stared out of the window while my mother worked. After about three days of this, my mother would grow resentful, would begin to mutter, gently but persistently, 'It's no holiday!' And my sister and I, even though we understood the reasons for our aunt's behaviour, as, indeed, did our mother, would nod in agreement. Because we had to share in the housework. We set the table, we did the washing up in an enamel basin, and I had personal responsibility for going to the well to draw water. For this, my sister envied me. She imagined it to be a privileged task, much more fun than sweeping or making beds. And of course it was more exotic than these chores, for the first day or so, which was why I insisted on doing it. But soon enough the novelty palled, and it was really hard work, and boring. Water is heavy, and we seemed to require a great deal of it.

◊    ◊

Unlike our mother, we spent much time away from the kitchen, my sister and I. Most of every morning we passed on the beach. There was an old boathouse there, its roof almost caved in, in which no boat had been kept for many many years. It had a stale smell, faintly disgusting, as if animals, or worse, had used it as a lavatory at some stage in the past. Even though the odour dismayed us, and even though the beach was always quite deserted, we liked to undress in private, both of us together, and therefore going to great lengths with towels to conceal our bodies from one another, until such a time as we should emerge from the yawning door of the building, and run down the golden quartz slip into the sea.

Lough Swilly. Also known as 'The Lake of Shadows', my sister often informed me, this being the type of fact of which she was very fond. One of the only two fiords in Ireland, she might also add. That meant nothing to me, its being a fiord, and as for shadows, I was quite unaware of them. What I remember most about that water is its crystal clarity. It was greenish, to look at it from a slight distance. Or, if you looked at it from my aunt's house, on a fine day, it was a brilliant turquoise colour, it looked like a great jewel, set in the hills. But when you were in that water, bathing, it was as clear as glass: I would swim along with my face just below the lapping surface, and I would open my eyes and look right down to the sandy floor, at the occasional starfish, the tiny crabs that scuttled there, at the shoals of minnows that scudded from place to place, guided by some mysterious mob instinct. I always stayed in for ages, even on the coldest days, even when rain was falling in soft curtains around the rocks. It had a definite benign quality, that water. And I always emerged from it cleansed in both body and soul. When I remember it now, I can understand why rivers are sometimes believed to be holy. Lough Swilly was, for me, a blessed water.

The afternoons we spent *en famille*, going on trips in the car to view distant wonders, Portsalon or the Downings. And the evenings we would spend 'raking', dropping in on our innumerable friends and drinking tea and playing with them.

This pattern continued for the entire holiday, with two exceptions: on one Sunday we would go on a pilgrimage to Doon Well, and on one weekday we would go to Derry, thirty miles away, to shop.

◊    ◊

Doon Well was my aunt's treat. It was the one occasion, apart from Mass, on which she accompanied us on a drive, even though we all realized that she would have liked to be with us every day. But the only outing she insisted upon was Doon Well. She would begin to hint about it gently soon after we arrived. 'The Gallaghers were at Doon Well on Sunday,' she might say. 'Not a great crowd at it!' Then on Sunday she would not change her clothes after Mass, but would don a special elegant apron and perform the morning tasks in a particular and ladylike way: tiptoe into the byre, flutter at the hens.

At two we would set out, and she would sit with me and my sister in the back of the car. My sense of mortification, at being seen in public with my aunt, was mixed with another shame, that of ostentatious religious practices. I couldn't bear processions, missions, concelebrated Masses: display. At heart, I was Protestant, and indeed it would have suited me, in more ways than one, to belong to that faith. But I didn't. So I was going to Doon Well, with my aunt and my unctuous parents, and my embarrassed sister.

You could spot the well from quite a distance: it was dressed. In rags. A large assembly of sticks, to which brightly coloured scraps of cloth were tied, advertised its presence and lent it a somewhat flippant, pagan air. But it was not flippant, it was all too serious. As soon as we left the safety of the car, we had to remove our shoes. The pain! Not only of going barefoot on the stony ground, but of having to witness feet, adult feet, our parents' and our aunt's, so shamelessly revealed to the world. Like all adults then, their feet were horrible: big and yellow, horny with corns and ingrown toenails, twisted and tortured by years of ill-fitting boots, no boots at all. To crown it, both my mother and aunt had varicose veins, purple knots bulging hideously through the yellow skin. As humiliated as anyone could be, and as we were meant to be, no doubt, we had to circle the well some specified number of times, probably three, and we had to say the Rosary, out loud, in the open air. And then my mother had a long litany to Colmcille, to which we had to listen and respond, in about a thousand agonies of shame, 'Pray for us!' The only tolerable part of the expedition occurred immediately after this, when we bought souvenirs at a stall, with a gay striped awning more appropriate to Bray or Bundoran than to this grim place. There we stood and scrutinized the wares on display: beads, statuettes, medals, snowstorms. Reverting to our consumerist role, we . . . do I mean I? I assume my sister felt the same about it all . . . felt almost content, for a few minutes, and we always selected the same souvenirs, namely snowstorms. I have one still: it has a painted blue backdrop, now peeling a little, and figures of elves and mushrooms under the glass, and, painted in black letters on its wooden base, 'I have prayed for you at Doon Well.' I bought that as a present for my best friend, Ann Byrne, but when I returned to Dublin I hadn't the courage to give it to her so it stayed in my bedroom for years, until I moved to Germany to study, and then I brought it with me. As a souvenir, not of Doon Well, I think, but of something.

◊     ◊

We went to Derry without my aunt. We shopped and ate sausages and beans for lunch, in Woolworths. I enjoyed the trip to Derry. It was the highlight of the holiday, for me.

◊     ◊

At the end of the fortnight, we would shake hands with my aunt in the street, and say goodbye. On these occasions her face would grow long and sad, she would always, at the moment when we climbed into the car, actually cry quietly to herself. My mother would say: 'Sure, we won't feel it now till it's Christmas! And then the summer will be here in no time at all!' And this would make everything much more poignant for my aunt, for me, for everyone. I would squirm on the seat, and, although I often wanted to cry myself, not because I was leaving my aunt but because I didn't want to give up the countryside, and the stream, and the clean clear water, I wouldn't think of my own unhappiness, but instead divert all my energy into despising my aunt for breaking yet another taboo: grown-ups do not cry.

My sister was tolerant. She'd laugh kindly as we turned out of the street on to the lane. 'Poor old Annie!' she'd say. But I couldn't laugh, I couldn't forgive her at all, for crying, for being herself, for not being the full shilling.

There was one simple reason for my hatred, so simple that I understood it myself, even when I was eight or nine years old. I resembled my aunt physically. 'You're the image of your aunt Annie!' people, relations, would beam at me as soon as I met them, in the valley. Now I know, looking at photos of her, looking in the glass, that this was not such a very bad thing. She had a reasonable enough face, as faces go. But I could not see this when I was a child, much less when a teenager. All I knew then was that she looked wrong. For one thing, she had straight unpermed hair, cut short across the nape of the neck, unlike the hair of any woman I knew then (but quite like mine as it is today). For another, she had thick unplucked eyebrows, and no lipstick or powder, even on Sunday, even for Doon Well. Although at that time it was unacceptable to be unmade up, it was outrageous to wear straight hair and laced shoes. Even in a place which was decidedly old-fashioned, she looked uniquely outmoded. She looked, to my city-conditioned eyes, like a freak. So when people would say to me, 'God, aren't you the image of your auntie!' I would cringe and wrinkle up in horror. Unable to change my own face, and unable to see that it resembled hers in the slightest ... and how does a face that is ten resemble one that is fifty? ... I grew to hate my physique. And I transferred that hatred, easily and inevitably, to my aunt.

◊　◊

When I was eleven, and almost finished with family holidays, I visited Ballytra alone, not to stay with my aunt, but to attend an Irish college which had just been established in that district. I did not stay with any of my many relatives, on purpose: I wanted to steer clear of all unnecessary contact with my past, and lived with a family I had never seen before.

Even though I loved the rigorous jolly ambience of the college, it posed problems for me. On the one hand, I was the child of one of the natives of the parish, I was almost a native myself. On the other hand, I was what was known there as a 'scholar', one of the kids from Dublin or Derry who descended on Ballytra like a shower of fireworks in July, who acted as if they owned the place, who more or less shunned the native population.

If I'd wanted to, it would have been very difficult for me to steer a median course between my part as a 'scholar' and my other role, as a cousin of the little native 'culchies' who, if they had been my playmates in former years, were now too shabby, too rustic, too outlandish, to tempt me at all. In the event, I made no effort to play to both factions: I managed by ignoring my relations entirely, and throwing myself into the more appealing life of the 'scholar'. My relations, I might add, seemed not to notice this, or care, if they did, and no doubt they were as bound by their own snobberies and conventions as I was by mine.

When the weather was suitable, that is, when it did not rain heavily, afternoons were spent on the beach, the same beach upon which my sister and I had always played. Those who wanted to swim walked there, from the school, in a long straggling crocodile. I love to swim and never missed an opportunity to go to the shore.

The snag about this was that it meant passing by my aunt's house, which was on the road down to the lough: we had to pass through her street to get there. For the first week, she didn't bother me, probably assuming that I would drop in soon. But, even though my mother had warned me to pay an early visit and had given me a head scarf to give her, I procrastinated. So after a week had gone by she began to lie in wait for me: she began to sit on her stone seat, in front of the door, and to look at me dolefully as I passed. And I would give a little casual nod, such as I did to everyone I met, and pass on.

One afternoon, the teacher who supervised the group was walking beside me and some of my friends, much to my pride and discomfiture. When we came to the street, she called, softly, as I passed, 'Mary, Mary.' I nodded and continued on my way. The teacher gave me a funny look and said: 'Is she talking to you, Mary? Does she want to talk to you?' 'I don't know her,' I said, melting in shame. 'Who is she?' 'Annie, that's Annie Bonner.' He didn't let on to know anything more about it, but I bet he did: everyone who had spent more than a day in Ballytra knew everything there was to know about it, everyone, that is who wasn't as egocentric as the 'scholars'.

◊   ◊

My aunt is still alive, but I haven't seen her in many years. I never go to Inishowen now. I don't like it since it became modern and littered with bungalows. Instead I go to Barcelona with my husband, who is a native Catalonian. He teaches Spanish here, part-time, at the university, and runs a school for Spanish students in Ireland during the summers. I help him in the tedious search for digs for all of them, and really we don't have much time to holiday at all.

My aunt is not altogether well. She had a heart attack just before Christmas and had to have a major operation at the Donegal Regional. I meant to pay her a visit, but never got around to it. Then, just before she was discharged, I learned that she was going home for Christmas. Home? To her own empty house, on the lane down to the lough? I was, to my surprise, horrified. God knows why, I've seen people in direr straits. But something gave. I phoned my mother and wondered angrily why she wouldn't have her, just for a few weeks. But my mother is getting on, she has gout, she can hardly walk herself. So I said, 'All right, she can come here!' But Julio was unenthusiastic. Christmas is the only time of the year he manages to relax: in January, the bookings start, the planning, the endless meetings and telephone calls. Besides, he was expecting a guest from home: his sister, Montserrat, who is tiny and dark and lively as a sparrow. The children adore her. In the end, my sister, unmarried and a lecturer in Latin at Trinity, went to stay for a few weeks in Ballytra until my aunt was better. She has very flexible holidays, my sister, and no real ties.

I was relieved, after all, not to have aunt Annie in my home. What would my prim suburban neighbours have thought? How would Julio, who has rather aristocratic blood, have coped? I am still ashamed, you see, of my aunt. I am still ashamed of myself. Perhaps, I suspect, I do resemble her, and not just facially. Perhaps there is some mental likeness too. Are my wide education, my brilliant husband, my posh accent, just attempts at camouflage? Am I really all that bright? Sometimes, as I sit and read in my glass-fronted bungalow, looking out over the clear sheet of the Irish Sea, and try to learn something, the grammar of some foreign language, the names of Hittite gods, something like that, I find the facts running away from me, like sticks escaping downstream on the current. And more often than that, much more often, I feel in my mind a splodge of something that won't allow any knowledge to sink in. A block of some terrible substance, soft and thick and opaque. Like butter.

## For the Literary Traveler

Trust the tale: the INISHOWEN PENINSULA is dotted these days with holiday bungalows. Rusticity still exists, but the busy beaches of Buncrana, Fahan, and Ballymagan on the west coast—the area of the story's Ballytra—are not where to look for it. (See p. 412 for the paradisial Inishowen—Annish—of Joyce Cary's childhood.)

Heading off in the direction of Ní Dhuibhne's story—"The afternoons we spent en famille, going on trips in the car to view distant wonders, PORTSALON or the DOWNINGS ... Sunday we would go on a pilgrimage to DOON WELL"—means going west of Inishowen to some of Donegal's finest and least populated destinations. Once you get out of—or avoid altogether—the traffic snarls of Letterkenny, make your way up the east coast of the FANAD PENINSULA toward Portsalon.

Halfway along, the HERITAGE CENTRE in a martello tower at RATH-MULLEN (June-Sept., Mon.-Sat. 10–6, Sun. 10–5:30; tel. (074) 58178) displays impressive multimedia historical and literary exhibits about the "Flight of the Earls" to the Continent on September 14, 1607. On a ship anchored here, Hugh O'Neill, the Earl of Tyrone (the Great O'Neill of Sean O'Faolain's biography), and Rory O'Donnell, the Earl of Tyrconnell (the ancient name for Donegal), who knew that further resistance to Queen Elizabeth's conquest was futile—they risked death in the Tower of London—sailed away at midnight from Rathmullen with their families and one hundred Ulster leaders. Their departure from Ireland, up the twenty-five-mile-long fjordlike Lough Swilly, marked the end of the Gaelic order in its last stronghold of Ulster and cleared the way for England's final confiscation of Irish property—four million acres—and the Plantation of Ulster. (The infertile land went to the native Irish, the good stuff to English and Scots Protestant land-lords or "planters.") "The Flight of the Earls," a dirge written by the bard of the Tyrconnell clan, captured Ulster's desolation:

> *Away in one frail bark goes all our pride.*
> *Now stolen is the soul from Eire's breast,*
> *And all her coasts and islands mourn oppressed.*
> *The great twin eagles of the flock of Conn*
> *In perilous flight are in one vessel gone.*

Also on Lough Swilly, in 1798, Wolfe Tone, arriving with backup to help the French army in Mayo, was captured on his ship.

Across the road (R24) from the martello tower, in the evenings the lounge in the PIER HOTEL is as cheerful as Rathmullen's history is not. The stranger is welcomed. "From America, is it? Now why would someone like yourself come to this place on your holidays when you have Disneyland, or is it Disney World, and all that sunshine at home?" a nice lawyer from Belfast began. His brother, he told me, makes an annual pilgrimage to Disneywhateverits, wouldn't miss it. No one in the lounge bats an eye at the gorgeous children toddling over a carpet of cabbage roses, swigging their bottles, sampling their parents' chips.

As you continue up the coast, it's clear why Dubliners—"Dubs"—beat it up to Donegal over their bank holiday weekends. On your right, between Fanad and Inishowen, beneath the cliff road that winds higher and narrower out to Fanad's northern head, flows LOUGH SWILLY, the "Lake of Shadows" where in "Blood and Water" Mary swims (on its eastern shore): "It was a brilliant turquoise colour, it looked like a great jewel, set in the hills . . . a blessed water." As you de-scend toward Portsalon, around BALLYMASTOCKER BAY, the story's tone of reverence about Swilly—as well as Donegal as "the ultimate re-ward"—seems like a visionary's good sense. (At a lay-by dug into a hairpin turn at the start of the descent, three weekending Dubs took pictures of themselves, howling as a mighty wind off the cliffs of Knockalla mountain whipped their faces with their hair.) Portsalon (under restoration in 1999) can't match this magnificent opening vista: rounding the cliffs, heading straight down toward the bright blue crescent of Balllymastocker Bay, you swallow hard as you shift gears.

One narrow peninsula west of Fanad, the ROSGUILL, is the location of the THE DOWNINGS, a holiday center still popular with families, and the entrance to one of the most scenic roads in Donegal: the ATLANTIC DRIVE. Rosguill's beaches are sublime.

The only excursion, as Mary says, for which "the Mad Aunt" joined the family is to DOON WELL, a site of religious pilgrimage since the times of the Penal Laws; it's south of Rosguill (through Milford on the R246) at KILMACRENAN (and signposted down a small road that ends at a parking lot). On Sunday afternoons, visitors come to Doon Well, some praying silently and unselfconsciously for healing, some saying the rosary and filling bottles with holy water (though I saw no one leave anything on the small tree decorated with pilgrims' offerings). It's clear that Ní Dhuibhne's self-conscious adolescent narrator is making a connection between her pious and "weak-minded" aunt Annie and the custom of pilgrimage to holy shrines, but the pilgrims struck me as ordinary people out for a Sunday ride, not a nut among them. Most folks moved on from the well to climb up to the nearby DOON ROCK, the ancient hill of coronation where the chieftains of the clan O'Donnell were inaugurated by a presider named O'Friel. It's a respectable scramble, done with gusto by several generations of the same family. Grandchildren give grannies a hand over the rocks; everyone looks out for the physically disabled member of the family for whom prayers have been said down at the well. Once at the top, if the sun is not hiding, you look down on a ring of Donegal hills, thick with gorse, gleaming in every shade of green, not a bungalow in sight.

The religious culture of Donegal has another, far more remote and pastoral setting about seven miles southwest of Doon Rock at LOUGH GARTEN and CHURCH HILL, the birthplace of St. Columcille (or Columba, b. 521), founder of the monastery at Iona and, along with Patrick and Brigid, one of Ireland's three favorite saints. ("I have loved the land of Ireland almost beyond speech," he wrote in one of the many poems attributed to him.)

The signposts around Garten swing in every direction, but with perseverance you'll find the informative ST. COLMCILLE HERITAGE CENTRE on the quiet lake's deserted northeastern shore (open Mon.-Sat. 10:30–6, Sun. 1–6, unless they close early, which they sometimes do) and the other places associated with the saint's early years.

You understand Colmcille's homesickness for Ireland—Iona was a place of exile—exploring this part of Donegal. Beyond Church Hill, skirting Lough Garten, climbing the Bullaba River valley to Glendowan mountain pass, coming upon the pass of Glenveagh—the landscape seems swept with a mystical power. So does majestic Mount Errigal, shadowing Barnesmore Gap.

# Joyce Cary

## 1888–1957

*Named for the Joyce tribe of Galway, from whom his mother claimed descent, novelist Joyce Cary was born in Derry into an Anglo-Irish family that came to Ireland as part of the seventeenth-century Ulster Plantation. Growing up, he spent many summers at his grandparents' houses on Donegal's Inishowen Peninsula, Ireland's northernmost body of land, touching on three sides the Atlantic, Lough Swilly, and Lough Foyle. This is the setting he calls Annish in his autobiographical novel of childhood, A House of Children (1941). A celebration of the beauty of Inishowen (before the bungalows of Éilís Ní Dhuibhne's story—see p. 397), the novel also exalts the ecstatic freedom of the child's Donegal summers, a theme that turns up in his brilliant novel The Horse's Mouth (1944): Cary's characterization of fiction's best-loved artist, the painter Gulley Jimson, connects the child's capacity for joy with the adult's capacity for creativity. The Northern Ireland of his youth (as well as England, where he went to school and lived, and Africa, where he served during World War I) became the dominant landscapes of Cary's imagination, inspiring his*

*fictional themes of freedom, beauty, and violence as well as his politi-
cal belief in the right of colonies to self-determination. Mendacity as
a form of self-creation also reflects his Irish background; there's an
echo of Synge's* Playboy *in Cary's belief that "People lie to each
other and to themselves and the lies they tell become their lives."
And in Gulley Jimson's antics there's a lot of the "jocoserious" James
Joyce, whom Cary admired. "Whenever I am idle," says the writer
Paul Theroux, "I choose a Cary novel in the way I might seek a
friend's company."*

FROM *A HOUSE OF CHILDREN*

1

The other day, in an inland town, I saw through an open window, a branch of fuchsia waving stiffly up and down in the
breeze; and at once I smelt the breeze salty, and had a picture of a
bright curtain flapping inwards and, beyond the curtain, dazzling
sunlight on miles of crinkling water. I felt, too, expectancy so keen
that it was like a physical tightening of the nerves; the very sense of
childhood. I was waiting for a sail, probably my first sail into the
Atlantic. Somebody or something must have fixed that moment
upon my dreaming senses, so that I still possess it. Small children
are thought happy, but for most of the time they do not even live
consciously, they exist; they drift through sensations as a pan-
tomime fairy passes through coloured veils and changing lights.
That moment was grasped out of the flux; a piece of life, unique
and eternal, and the sail also, is still my living delight. The dinghy
had a shiny new gaff, and the mainsail was wet half-way up so that
the sun behind it made a bright half-moon on the canvas. She rose
to the first swell of the Atlantic, beyond Sandy Point,* with a three-
angled motion, neither roll nor pitch. Then we were leaping from
wave to wave, squattering into rollers that had touched Greenland
in their last landfall, and the thin planks sprang and trembled

* Cary is probably remembering sailing as a child off Inishowen Head, above
Greencastle.

under my body. . . . Tens of thousands of dark blue waves rushed towards me, rising and falling like dolphins and spouting thick triangles of foam.

Up above Dunvil,* in the hills, there was an old graveyard, surrounded by a rough wall of loosely piled stones. A church or chapel stood near this lonely place, long disused, but in the yard itself, close to the back wall, there was an ancient building, all of stone, with a stone roof. From a little distance this seemed like a chapel among its graves, in a large square of yard with a high ashlar wall round it. But as one came near, the chapel, which gave scale to the whole, diminished to less than six foot high, from the peak of its roof to the ground, the wall became a low field wall and the graveyard smaller than a cottage garden. This little stone house was said to be the tomb of a saint. By stooping low and looking through an opening about a foot square, in the thick wall, one could see thigh bones and skulls.

I had seen this place once or twice and peeped at the skulls, which gave me no fear, but only a peculiar feeling of suspense with which I always saw or heard anything reminding me of death. My mind seemed to stop for a moment like a traveller who comes suddenly upon a pool in the road and pauses because he does not know how deep it is.

One night when we children were driving home to Crowcliff** from a mountain picnic, with Cousin Philip, we came near this place. Philip sat with Harry on one side of the car, facing the mountains, Cousin Katherine, Anketel's sister, and I, with Anketel between us, faced the lough. There is no more beautiful view in the world than that great lough,*** seventy square miles of salt water, from the mountains of Annish. We had heard my father call it beautiful, and so we enjoyed it with our minds as well as our feelings; keenly with both together. Wherever we went in Annish we were among the mountains and saw the lough or the ocean; often, from some high place, the whole Annish peninsula, between the

*Moville
**Cary's grandparents' home
***Lough Foyle

two great loughs,* and the Atlantic, high up in the sky, seeming like
a mountain of water higher than the tallest of land. So that my
memories are full of enormous skies, as bright as water, in which
clouds sailed bigger than any others; fleets of monsters moving in
one vast school up from the horizon and over my head, a million
miles up, as it seemed to me, and then down again over the far-off
mountains of Derry. They seemed to follow a curving surface of air
concentric with the curve of the Atlantic which I could see bending
down on either hand, a bow, which, even as a child of three or four,
I knew to be the actual shape of the earth. Some grown-up, perhaps my father, had printed that upon my imagination, so that even
while I was playing some childish game in the heather, red Indians
or Eskimos, if I caught sight of the ocean with the tail of my eye, I
would feel suddenly the roundness and independence of the world
beneath me. I would feel it like a ship under my feet moving
through the air just like a larger stiffer cloud, and this gave me an
extraordinary exhilaration. It was expressed, of course, only in a
shout or perhaps a quarrel; but it was a constant source of pleasure.
I can remember jumping on a piece of hard ground, as one jumps
on a deck, to test its spring, or simply to enjoy the feel of a buoyant
ship beneath me.

In Annish we lived in a world which we realised as a floating
planet, and in a beauty which we had been taught to appreciate, as
greatly as small children are capable of enjoying spectacle. I at least
enjoyed it by deliberate vision, for its sunrises and sunsets remain
with me as pictures as well as a sense of glory and magnificence. I
remember very well the aspect of the lough from the Oldcross road
into Dunvil, a road over which I must have passed hundreds of
times, especially in the spring or summer evenings. From above,
the great lough, lying among its ring of mountains, would seem in
the evening light like a long, low hill of water, following a different
curve from the Atlantic beyond. This was because the sun, setting
behind us, would cast its last greenish light on this side of the lough
and leave the far side in a shadow, except where, if the wind was
westerly, a silver line marked the surf. At this time, just before

*Lough Foyle and Lough Swilly

sunset, the sky would be full of a green radiance, fading gradually over the Derry mountains towards Belfast, into a dark blue-green transparency. . . .

We travelled through this enormous and magnificent scene in tranquil happiness. We were tired from running about in the heather and already growing hungry we felt the nearness of supper, and bed, with that calm faith which belongs only to children and saints devoted to the love of God and sure of the delights of communing with him. In that faith, that certainty of coming joys, we existed in a contentment so profound that it was like a lazy kind of drunkenness. I can't count how many times I enjoyed that sense, riding in a sidecar, whose swaying motion would have put me to sleep if I had not been obliged to hold on; so that while my body and head and legs were all swinging together in a half dream, my hand tightly clutched some other child's body; and the memory of bathing, shouting, tea, the blue smoke of picnic fires, was mixed with the dark evening clouds shaped like flying geese, the tall water stretching up to the top of the world, the mountains sinking into darkness like whales into the ocean and over all a sky so deep that the stars, faint green sparks, seemed lost in it and the very sense of it made the heart light and proud, like a bird.

But on this night when we were just swinging round the sharp corner over the graveyard, so that we saw the green sky between our knees instead of the water, Philip said: "There's the bone house now—look if the ghosts are walking."

Harry's voice, muffled like all voices from the other side of a car, said that there was no such thing as ghosts.

"How do you know?" Philip said, in his soft lazy voice. "I wouldn't be too sure."

There was silence for a minute or two while the car crunched down the steep hill, and then he suddenly called out: "Hold hard, Dan—I think we'll give his old boneship a call," and to me: "Come along and I'll show you something—have you ever seen how a skull shines in the dark?"

Kathy, even at nine, had a sense of responsibility. She said promptly that neither she nor Anketel would stir. "I won't have you playing your tricks on An—he's too little."

But Harry and I were ashamed to refuse. Philip, carrying a rug and a stick, led us across the graves to the little bone house.

"Stoop down," he said, "and look in at this end while I go to the other. I'll light a bunch of grass and push it in and keep out the wind with the rug. Then you'll see the skull, and when the bunch goes out you'll see it shine. But mind you pick the right skull—the saint's skull—you can tell it because it's whiter—all holy men have white skulls because of their pure thought, and that's why the light comes out of them."

Harry murmured to me: "Look out for something—he's codding us."

In fact, we had often had practical jokes played on us. They were common in those days, and people liked especially to frighten children. It is done even now. It is not very long ago that two cousins of mine, then a boy of seven and a girl of six, were told by their own nurse, that if they stared out of a certain window, facing the yard, about ten o'clock on a Sunday night, they would see a ghost. She placed them at the window and left them. Then suddenly an immensely tall figure in white came from behind the stables, moved across the yard, came up to their window, and beckoned to them. They saw the face of a skull, as white as snow, with open nostrils and protruding teeth; the beckoning finger was nothing but bone, probably a chicken bone.

These children, who believed that this creature was a real apparition come from the grave to summon them to die, were so struck with horror that, as they tell me, they were unable to speak or move or cry out. They were hypnotised by fear and by the sense of the creature's nearness to them; the same feeling, I suppose, that petrifies some small creatures at the sudden approach of a snake. After several minutes of this trial, the ghost glided away; and the nurse came rushing in, crying: "The ghost—the ghost—it's after us."

She asked the children if they had seen anything, and the children answered that they had seen the ghost.

"Did it beckon to you?"

"It lifted its finger at us."

"And did you cross yourselves?"

"No, we forgot."

"Oh dear, oh dear—but perhaps it was only a warning."

According to the usual idea these children should have gone mad, or at least, been nervously damaged for life; but apparently they accepted the situation calmly and reasonably. A ghost had come to warn them of approaching death and they were going to die, possibly soon. Meanwhile life went on as before.

I daresay the calmness and resignation of the two children was disappointing to the practical jokers. Cousin Philip had more success with us. He went to the other end of the house and called out:

"Ready now, I'm just going to light the grass and put it in at the drain hole."

We peered into the doorway, until we heard a hollow voice saying: "Your time has come." We jumped and saw a tall black form with fiery eyes and mouth coming towards us over the top of the house. It stooped at us. Both of us at once turned and ran. I was so terrified that I felt lightheaded, as if my brain had turned into air, or at least cork. It seemed to float along with me and to have no connection at all with my rushing body and running legs. I didn't utter a sound even when I ran into the wall, as if blinded by terror, and cut a hole in my forehead. There is a piece of that wall still in my forehead. I bounced back from the wall, got up again, all in silence, climbed over it and ran on as hard as I could go.

❑◇❑

## For the Literary Traveler

The pleasures of A House of Children transpire mostly outdoors, on IN-ISHOWEN'S hills and in the choppy waters of LOUGH FOYLE and the AT-LANTIC, where, breaking their parents' rules, the children go sailing with their anarchic Irish tutor. Though the coasts and high ground of Cary's childhood are more populated now, it's still easy to feel what he loved here. Coming from Derry, the main road up the peninsula's east coast (R238) ends in glory at INISHOWEN HEAD, not far beyond busy Green-castle (Brian Friel's home as well as Kealys fine Seafood Bar, across from the pier); its rocky strand and blue shallows are quite likely the Sandy Point of Cary's paradise. From this northern coast, between Inishowen and Malin (the Lonely Planet guide details a scenic walk along CROCKALOUGH CLIFFS) you can see Scotland's Outer Hebrides and the Antrim coast. The surest way into Cary's sense of adventure on Inishowen is to simply explore where you will, choosing, if there's time, the corkscrew, secondary roads over the rolling heather hills (minding the ruts), stopping along the coast to walk the beaches. Just north of the village of MALIN and close to MALIN HEAD, the northernmost point in Ireland, is HELL'S HOLE, a chasm that fits the description of a cave where the eight-year-old narrator (Cary himself) came close to drowning.

Inishowen is also rich in prehistoric and early Christian ruins, especially east of CARDONAGH. Cary describes one such ancient site as a landmark of delicious terror on a hill above Lough Foyle: it stands between COOLEY (and CARROWNAFF) and his family's lakeside house at Dunvil, his name for the area around MOVILLE (before World War II, a port for transatlantic liners, where the McCourts of Angela's Ashes docked on their return to Ireland from New York). Outside the graveyard at Cooley is a cross with a hole in its head; the remains of a church (attributed to St. Patrick); and the SKULL HOUSE, which is possibly the seventh-century tomb of St. Finian. For the children of Cary's novel, it's the macabre that thrills them about the bones strewn around and inside the stone hut; the word relic never crosses their Protestant minds. As they descend from the Skull House toward Dunvil/Moville, Cary's reverence is for the natural beauty of the far-off mountains of Derry in late twilight (close to midnight in high summer). If you take the main coast road from Derry to Moville, the Skull House is signposted to the left, just before you reach Moville.

Written memories of summer in Ireland often run to Donegal, its peninsulas, glens, and wild, hidden beaches, the music in the pubs at night. Brian Friel names Glenties to the west (see p. 391) as well as Greencastle on Lough Foyle. Seamus Heaney, Seamus Deane, John Hume, and many Irish people from both the North and the Republic call Inishowen their place apart. Joyce Cary paints it as the birthplace of his artist's soul, a womb of beauty. Another Anglo-Irishman's words about summers in Donegal call to mind Elaine Scarry's point in On

*Beauty and Being Just:* Beauty stops us, she says, transfixes us, fills us with a "surfeit of aliveness"; in so doing it takes us away from our self-preoccupation and prompts us to pay attention outward, toward others, and, ultimately, toward ethical fairness. Speaking in 1998 across an eight-hundred-year-old divide of enmity, Tony Blair, the first British prime minister ever to address the Parliament of the Irish Republic, invoked the memory of Donegal. His mother was born and raised there; he visited every summer "up to when the Troubles really took hold. We would travel the beautiful countryside of Donegal. It was there in the seas off the Irish coast that I first learned to swim, there that my father took me to my first pub, a remote little house in the country."

In this speech urging London and Dublin to work together to rescue the stalled Northern Ireland peace effort, he received an ovation when he said, "So much shared history, so much shared pain." On Inishowen and in the luminous *A House of Children*, it's clear: for not a few English as well as Irish—hybrids, like most of us—Ireland's beauty is at once common ground and a ground for being just.

# Seamus Deane

## 1940–

*Short-listed for the Booker Prize in 1996,* Reading in the Dark *is Deane's celebrated first novel—though it reads like a memoir—of growing up in the Catholic Bogside of Derry City in the forties and fifties. But the Inishowen peninsula in Donegal (where his parents' families come from), five miles west of the city, is the setting of their rare holidays. The amazing prehistoric ring fort, Grianan—the scene of the following selection—overlooks it. The narrator's family is full of secrets, among them its past connections with the IRA and with informers. Since the 1921 signing of the Anglo-Irish Treaty, the IRA had kept up its guerrilla warfare; in big towns such as Derry (and Belfast), where the Catholic minority faced discrimination in housing, jobs, and civil rights, it had no trouble finding recruits. The young narrator, with the determination of a historian—or a poet looking for the precise word—insists on tearing away the webs of secrecy obfuscating his family's past and haunting his mother. The consequences of his ferocious deconstruction, for him and his parents (and filial love has rarely been rendered so powerfully), are scalding. Deane is also a widely published critic and poet, editor of the three-volume* Field Day Anthology of Irish Literature, *and a professor at Notre Dame.*

## FROM *READING IN THE DARK*

### THE FORT

#### June 1950

Lying in the filtered green light of the high fernstalks that shook slightly above our heads, we listened to the sharp birdsong of the hillside. This was border country. Less than a mile beyond, a stream, crossed by a hump-backed bridge, marked part of the red line that wriggled around the city on the map and hemmed it in to the waters of Lough Foyle. Every so often, we would stand up clear of the ferns and survey the heathered hills, the pale white roads winding between high hedgerows. Even when no one could be seen, we felt we were watched. When we went down to the bridge, we liked to cross and re-cross it, half-expecting that something punitive would happen because of these repeated violations.

At one end, just above the stream, there was a clump of thorn bushes where wrens turned and twisted endlessly, hooking and un-hooking their tiny bodies between the close branches in dapper knitting motions. At the other end, the Free State began—a grassy road that ran straight for thirty yards and then swerved away under an oak tree into that territory where there was an isolated shop, a

tin hut thrown up to exploit the post-war food shortages on our side
of the border. There the cigarette packets were different, Sweet
Afton Virginia in yellow and white with a medallion of Robbie Burns
and two lines of the song "Sweet Afton" slanted underneath across a
picture of a stream, a tree, a miniature landscape. The voices of the
people there seemed to us as sleek and soft as the glistening wheels
of butter on the counter that had a print of a swan on their bright
yellow faces. My parents' people came from out there, in Donegal.

## GRIANAN
### September 1950

Grianan was a great stone ring with flights of worn steps on the inside leading to a parapet that overlooked the countryside in one
direction and the coastal sands of the lough in the other. At the base of
one inside wall, there was a secret passage, tight and black as you
crawled in and then briefly higher at the end where there was a wishing-chair of slabbed stone. You sat there and closed your eyes and
wished for what you wanted most, while you listened for the breathing
of the sleeping warriors of the legendary Fianna who lay below. They
were waiting there for the person who would make that one wish that
would rouse them from their thousand-year sleep to make final war on
the English and drive them from our shores forever. That would be a
special person, maybe with fairy eyes, a green one and a brown one, I
thought, or maybe a person with an intent in him, hard and secret as a
gun in his pocket, moving only when he could make everything else
move with him. I was terrified that I might, by accident, make that special wish and feel the ground buckle under me and see the dead faces
rise, indistinct behind their definite axes and spears.

Liam* and I spent a large part of our school holidays there in
the summer. When there were others with us, we would break into
groups and have races to the fort at the top. The winners then defended the fort against the rest, struggling wildly on the parapet,
scaling the walls, our cries lost in the wild heather and rocks of the
reserved landscape.

*Seamus's brother

Once, my friends—Moran, Harkin, Toland—locked me in the secret passage. At first, I hardly reacted at all—just sat there in the stone wishing-chair. Gradually, the dark passageway up which I had just crawled lost its vague roundness and simply became blackness. I sat there, cold, even though it was hot outside and there were larks lost in song on high warm thermals above the old fort. I touched the wet walls and felt the skin of slime sliding in slow motion over their hardness. Even there, it stirred something in me to move my hand up against the wrinkling moss and water. If I were out and on the circular parapet again, I would see Inch Island and the wide flat estuaries of the dark-soiled coast and hear the distant war noise of the sea grumbling beyond. But here, inside the thick-walled secret passage which ended in this chair-shaped niche, there was nothing but the groan of the light breeze in that bronchial space, and the sound of water slitting into rivulets on the sharp rock face. I imagined I could hear the breathing of the sleeping Fianna waiting for the trumpet call that would bring them to life again to fight the last battle which, as the prophecies of St. Columcille told us, would take place somewhere between Derry and Strabane, after which the one remaining English ship would sail out of Lough Foyle and away from Ireland forever. If you concentrated even further, you would scent the herbal perfumes of the Druid spells and you would hear the women sighing in sexual pleasure— yes-esss-yes-esss. If you then made a wish, especially a love-wish, you would always be attractive to women.

My friends had done this. I had been sitting there, in the wishing-chair, wondering how I could concentrate more on the emaciated ghost sounds within the passage, when the little light there was disappeared. I heard the grunt of the stone that covered the entrance being rolled back into place to shut me in. I yelled, but they laughed and ran up the parapet steps above me. The stone could not be moved from inside the passageway; it was too narrow to allow for leverage. So I sat and waited. When I shouted, my voice ricocheted all around me and then vanished. I had never known such blackness. I could hear the wind, or maybe it was the far-off sea. That was the breathing Fianna. I could smell the heather and the gorse tinting the air; that was the Druid spells. I could hear the underground waters whispering; that was the women sighing. The cold was marrow-deep; the chair seemed to shine with it. A scuttling, as of field mice, would come and go; perhaps it was mortar trickling away from the stones. I crawled down to the entrance and shouted again. Eventually, someone came and rolled the stone back and I scrambled out into the sunshine, dazed by the light, unsteady when I walked, as though all my blood had collected around my ankles. Later, when we climbed to the parapet again and scrambled down the wall to the road that took us home, the sky and the hills around seemed so wide and high that the dark passageway felt even worse in retrospect, more chilling and enclosed.

We had crossed the border by more than a field's width and were approaching the road when a car came round a bend and almost caught us in its lights. We ducked into the darkness of the hedgerow. "Water rats," said Brendan Moran, peering up after them. It was the nickname given to customs officers. "Looking for smugglers. My father told me the smugglers caught one of them one night near Grianan and they took his customs jacket off, tied him up and closed him inside the passage. It was nearly two days before they found him, and he was stark, staring mad when they got him out. He's still in the asylum at Gransha and they say he's always cold; never warmed up since. Never will."

As we came over the last rise in the road, the city lay braided in lights below us. We seemed to fall towards it, too tired to talk, into the network of narrow streets on that still Indian summer's night.

## For the Literary Traveler

"Border country" refers to the land either side of the line that scrawls between the six counties of the Ulster Province that fall under the jurisdiction of the Parliament of Northern Ireland/English control (Derry, Down, Antrim, Armagh, Tyrone, and Fermanagh) and the three northern counties of the Ulster Province that are part of the Republic

(Donegal, Cavan, and Monaghan). Journalist and novelist Colm Tóibín (*The Heather Blazing*) describes the daunting confusions of this boundary in his autobiographical *Bad Blood: A Walk Along the Irish Border* (1987). As a child, Seamus Deane—or his alter ego, the unnamed narrator—walks the five miles from his home in Derry City across the border into DONEGAL and up the steep hill to GRIANAN OF AILEACH (pronounced "GREEN-ya of ALL-ya"), the amazing thirty-five-hundred-year-old ring fort that overlooks the INISHOWEN PENINSULA, LOUGH FOYLE, LOUGH SWILLY, and, in the distance (back over the border), the city of Derry. Inside the fort's monumentally thick walls, you can see the openings to the caves where the narrator's friends lock him in, a cruelly symbolic event for the imaginative child, who, troubled by the adults' dark secrecies, is determined to make an opening for light. Grianan, more impressive than Staigue Fort in Kerry—and attracting more visitors and tour buses—was the royal seat and coronation site of the northern O'Neills, the tribe that claimed descent from the legendary hero Niall of the Nine Hostages. But after an O'Neill attacked the royal palace of rival chieftain Brian Boru at Kincora down in Clare (see p. 308), the inevitable revenge was taken by the king of Munster: he ransacked Grianan in the twelfth century, and until the Flight of the Earls in 1607, the inaugurations of the O'Neill chieftains took place in Tyrone. The GRIANAN OF AILEACH INTERPRETIVE CENTER, down the hill on the south side of the Derry/Letterkenny Road (it's inside a stone church), makes the history and legends associated with this place at least fascinating, if not exactly clear. (Upstairs there's a miniature museum, featuring life-sized wax figures of scary Ulster chieftains surrounded by musical waterfalls and stuffed monsters and animals. You can't help liking whoever put this exhibit together—they had a good time.) The Liam McCormack church-in-the-round (St. Aengus) at the bottom of the hill, modeled on the fort above it, is stunning.

The best place to get an overview of DERRY CITY—and "the network of narrow streets" of Deane's Bogside—is from the top of the city walls: the one-mile promenade covers some of the best-preserved defensive walls in Europe. Near Shipquay Gate, you see the cannons contributed by Queen Elizabeth I and pointed directly across at the stately nineteenth-century GUILD HALL and clock tower—the setting of Brian

Friel's electrifying play *The Freedom of the City* (tours every hour, July-Oct., 9:30–4:30). Proceeding around the corner onto Magazine Street and continuing uphill, from this side—at BUTCHER'S GATE—you look down on the valley of THE BOGSIDE, with its Bloody Sunday memorial as well as the YOU ARE NOW ENTERING FREE DERRY wall at Lecky Road, (a slogan painted in 1969 in imitation of a similar slogan in West Berlin); Creggan Hill looks down over the valley. This is also the home turf of the popular *Irish Times* journalist Nell McCafferty, which she recalls in "All Our Yesterdays." Bernadette Devlin, whose life-sized image is in front of you on a wall mural, describes the 1969 Battle of the Bogside—in which citizens defended the neighborhood against the invasion of the police—in her autobiography *The Price of My Soul.*

You'll find an indoor lookout post over Derry that's higher than the walls at THE DIAMOND in the city center: here, from the top-floor restaurant of the elegant old AUSTIN'S DEPARTMENT STORE, in the company of Derry shoppers taking their tea at scenic window seats, you can look down over the serpentine RIVER FOYLE and the dominant spires of the mutually suspicious Catholic and Protestant cathedrals.

Half a block off the Diamond on Bishop's Street, the BOOKWORM BOOKSHOP carries extensive Irish (and other) writers, including Derry-born Joyce Cary (born three doors down from the bookshop), Derry resident and award-winning novelist Jennifer Johnston (1930– ), Derry/Donegal's Brian Friel, and Derry native Nell McCafferty (whose collected columns, *The Best of Nell* (1984), crackle with searing insight into the politics of Derry's civil rights struggle). Martin Lynch, the helpful proprietor, has clearly read the books on his shelves, though this is more typical than not of bookstore personnel in Ireland.

Two monuments representing the plight of Derry's Catholic minority, a theme of Deane's novel (and McCafferty's columns), lie in opposite directions from the Diamond: each is a reminder of a ferocious unemployment driving the dole and forcing the exodus of so many natives. Southeast of the old city, toward the Foyle Road, on the west side of the Craigavon Bridge, is the TILLIE AND HENDERSON'S SHIRT FACTORY. This grandiose emblem of industrial Derry and its miserable working class is where most Catholic girls wound up after elementary school: 90 percent of the workers in this factory, its cruelties singled

out in Karl Marx's *Das Kapital*, were women. In the other direction,
west of the Guild Hall and beneath the walls, on the pedestrian walkways of Waterloo Place and Waterloo Street (where there are many
good musical pubs), is a bronze sculpture group appropriately placed
near the Harbor Museum of this historic port of embarkation: its
name is EMIGRANTS.

# Seamus Heaney

## 1939–

*The most important Irish poet since Yeats and the most recent Irish
recipient of the Nobel Prize for Literature, Heaney grew up in south
County Derry, on a small farm in the townland of Mossbawn—near
the northern shore of Lough Neagh—and in the nearby town of Bellaghy: "The house I lived in was not a literary or a bookish household
at all, but there was respect for books and for education. . . . Our own
house was a farmhouse . . . going about its farm business, but there
was an education of a kind in that too. It was very, very close to the
primal issues of life and death." As a writer, he's taken to heart Carson McCullers's comment that "to know who you are you have to
have a place to come from." In ten volumes of poetry published between 1966 and 1996, he has delved deep into the body of his native
place to shape the particular truths of his always changing perspective
on both himself and Ireland's fractured history. Sex, violence, and
death resonate through his work as insistently as they rend the landscape and the politics of Derry. After studying and teaching English
literature at Queens University in Belfast, in 1970 he left Ulster to
teach at Berkeley, "possibly the most important year of [my] life." Returning home to find the Troubles in full blaze, he moved his family
south, to Wicklow (see p. 117) and later to Dublin, where he lives*

*now. For years a professor of poetry at Harvard and Oxford, Heaney
is rare among contemporary poets for having won a large audience
that's both academic and popular. In this he resembles Robert Frost,
one of the poets he most admires: "I loved [him] for his farmer's
accuracy, and his wily down-to-earthness," he said in his Nobel
lecture.*

DIGGING

*Between my finger and my thumb
The squat pen rests; snug as a gun.*

*Under my window, a clean rasping sound
When the spade sinks into gravelly ground:
My father, digging. I look down*

*Till his straining rump among the flowerbeds
Bends low, comes up twenty years away
Stooping in rhythm through potato drills
Where he was digging.*

*The coarse boot nestled on the lug, the shaft
Against the inside knee was levered firmly.
He rooted out tall tops, buried the bright edge deep
To scatter new potatoes that we picked
Loving their cool hardness in our hands.*

*By God, the old man could handle a spade.
Just like his old man.*

*My grandfather cut more turf in a day
Than any other man on Toner's bog.
Once I carried him milk in a bottle
Corked sloppily with paper. He straightened up
To drink it, then fell to right away*

*Nicking and slicing neatly, heaving sods
Over his shoulder, going down and down
For the good turf. Digging.*

*The cold smell of potato mould, the squelch and slap*
*Of soggy peat, the curt cuts of an edge*
*Through living roots awaken in my head.*
*But I've no spade to follow men like them.*

*Between my finger and my thumb*
*The squat pen rests.*
*I'll dig with it.*

MOSSBAWN

*for Mary Heaney*

SUNLIGHT

*There was a sunlit absence.*
*The helmeted pump in the yard*
*heated its iron,*
*water honeyed*

*in the slung bucket*
*and the sun stood*
*like a griddle cooling*
*against the wall*

*of each long afternoon.*
*So, her hands scuffled*
*over the bakeboard,*
*the reddening stove*

*sent its plaque of heat*
*against her where she stood*
*in a floury apron*
*by the window.*

*Now she dusts the board*
*with a goose's wing,*
*now sits, broad-lapped,*
*with whitened nails*

*and measling shins:*
*here is a space*
*again, the scone rising*
*to the tick of two clocks.*

*And here is love*
*like a tinsmith's scoop*
*sunk past its gleam*
*in the meal-bin.*

## THE STRAND AT LOUGH BEG

*in memory of Colum McCartney*

All round this little island, on the strand
Far down below there, where the breakers strive,
Grow the tall rushes from the oozy sand.
                    —*DANTE*, Purgatorio, I, 100–3

*Leaving the white glow of filling stations*
*And a few lonely streetlamps among fields*
*You climbed the hills towards Newtownhamilton*
*Past the Fews Forest, out beneath the stars—*
*Along that road, a high, bare pilgrim's track*
*Where Sweeney fled before the bloodied heads,*
*Goat-beards and dogs' eyes in a demon pack*
*Blazing out of the ground, snapping and squealing.*
*What blazed ahead of you? A faked roadblock?*
*The red lamp swung, the sudden brakes and stalling*
*Engine, voices, heads hooded and the cold-nosed gun?*
*Or in your driving mirror, tailing headlights*
*That pulled out suddenly and flagged you down*
*Where you weren't known and far from what you knew:*
*The lowland clays and waters of Lough Beg,*
*Church Island's spire, its soft treeline of yew.*

*There you once heard guns fired behind the house*
*Long before rising time, when duck shooters*
*Haunted the marigolds and bulrushes,*
*But still were scared to find spent cartridges,*

*Acrid, brassy, genital, ejected,*
*On your way across the strand to fetch the cows.*
*For you and yours and yours and mine fought shy,*
*Spoke an old language of conspirators*
*And could not crack the whip or seize the day:*
*Big-voiced scullions, herders, feelers round*
*Haycocks and hindquarters, talkers in byres,*
*Slow arbitrators of the burial ground.*

*Across that strand of yours the cattle graze*
*Up to their bellies in an early mist*
*And now they turn their unbewildered gaze*
*To where we work our way through squeaking sedge*
*Drowning in dew. Like a dull blade with its edge*
*Honed bright, Lough Beg half-shines under the haze.*
*I turn because the sweeping of your feet*
*Has stopped behind me, to find you on your knees*
*With blood and roadside muck in your hair and eyes,*
*Then kneel in front of you in brimming grass*
*And gather up cold handfuls of the dew*
*To wash you, cousin. I dab you clean with moss*
*Fine as the drizzle out of a low cloud.*
*I lift you under the arms and lay you flat.*
*With rushes that shoot green again, I plait*
*Green scapulars to wear over your shroud.*

### ANAHORISH

*My 'place of clear water',*
*the first hill in the world*
*where springs washed into*
*the shiny grass*

*and darkened cobbles*
*in the bed of the lane.*
Anahorish, *soft gradient*
*of consonant, vowel-meadow,*

*after-image of lamps*
*swung through the yards*
*on winter evenings.*
*With pails and barrows*

*those mound-dwellers*
*go waist-deep in mist*
*to break the light ice*
*at wells and dunghills.*

## For the Literary Traveler

For some nine thousand years BELLAGHY (pronounced "beh-LA-he") has known the habitations of Mesolithic hunters, Neolithic farmers, Bronze Age warriors, Iron Age Celts, early Christians, Normans, Gaels, and English Planters. As you come into the village, a few miles north of the Derry-Belfast (A6) road, on the B152, on your left is BELLAGHY BAWN, the setting of a prehistoric rath—a Celtic hill fort/farm—and, after its sacking in 1641, a farm of the Ulster Plantation. Today, over these layers of time and cultures rises a reconstructed bawn, a spacious and light-filled exhibition hall in the shape of a ring, where the local backgrounds of Seamus Heaney's multilayered poetry are on display.

"We can all live in two or three places at the same time. The truth is nothing stands still inside or outside," comments Heaney, the narrator on the video about his native place, shown in the Bawn's second-floor Tower Room. On the walls are watercolors and photographs of the local settings of his poems. From the windows of the Tower Room and the Library of Contemporary Writing you can see the meadows and hills that textured his memory in the forties and fifties, when Bellaghy was more medieval "Brueghelesque" than modern. The Bawn (Apr.–Sept., Mon.–Sat. 10–6, Sun. 2–6; Oct.–Mar., Mon.–Sat. 10–5, Sun. 2–6) offers an instructive introduction to HEANEY COUNTRY, parts of which are within a few miles of Bellaghy and is also farther-flung (the Moyola River valley, the Sperrin Mountains, Slemish).

As you leave the Bawn, take your first left (heading back along the B152) onto Ballyscullion Road and then an immediate right onto Drumanee Lane, continuing on for about a mile until you come straight into the approach to CHURCH ISLAND and LOUGH BEG, a remote place that Heaney loved in his youth, but, like many of the hidden retreats around Bellaghy, one that has also figured in the politics of Ulster. This idyllic setting was the scene of his cousin's murder. The poem "The Strand at Lough Beg" is Heaney's anguished elegy for his cousin and for his own memory of "the soft treeline of yew" on Lough Beg's strand. (In *Station Island* he looks at his cousin's death from a different perspective.) On the walk out to the peninsula, you head through marshy grasslands toward the church spire, feeling in the oozy ground beneath your feet the literal truth of Fintan O'Toole's observation that Heaney's poetry and his native County Derry are "saturated with political meaning." On the Church Island peninsula are a walled graveyard, the early Christian ruins of St. Taoide's monastery, and a church said to have been founded by St. Patrick.

LOUGH BEG is part of the vast fish-rich waterways of this part of Derry (it's a tributary of nearby LOUG NEAGH, the biggest lake in Ireland), and Heaney's poems reflect his childhood sense of being surrounded by water—they're drenched with it. "Digging" and "Sunlight," poems about the family farm at Mossbawn, are lit with a watery brightness, and one of the pleasures of exploring the small back roads east of Bellaghy is the feeling you're always heading toward a clearing: in spring the fields look washed, almost bleached clean. Heaney's line "The end of art is peace" captures this quiet world of small streams under cloud-swirls of bright gray sky. On weekday mornings, you're alone back here.

You can see Lough Neagh and its eel fisheries from nearby TOOME-BRIDGE, which figures in several poems—and where after the Rising of 1798 the rebel Roddy McCorley went to die (honored in late-night song by Frank McCourt's father in *Angela's Ashes*). Heaney has written of the sense of doubleness he knew growing up between Toomebridge and CASTLEDAWSON (his birthplace, a few miles southwest of Bellaghy on the A54 and across the A6), one place connected with the native Irish rebel tradition and the other with the power of the Protestant Ascendancy and the English occupation. The town of

Toomebridge feels peaceful if a bit grim these days (at least in the lounge of the O'Neill Arms), but Unionist order is palpable in Castledawson's main streetscape, where in 1999 British flags and posters of Ian Paisley decorated the lampposts. In the poem "Anahorish" (the ANAHORISH primary school that Heaney attended is now modernized but still located just off the A6/B154 crossroads en route to Bellaghy, on the right), addressing the doubleness of his experience, Heaney distinguishes between the soft vowel sounds of Irish place names and the hard consonant sounds of the English Big Houses, a sound difference that attuned travelers can pick up all over Ireland, but especially in Heaney's Ulster. Poem after poem ("A New Song," for instance) suggests that the sound system of a language carries worlds of feeling that are of profound cultural significance; the sounds of Irish and English express the different emotional landscapes of the two populations of Northern Ireland. And with this linguistic/psychic difference in mind, Heaney's chosen vocation of Irish poet in occupied Derry can be interpreted as an act of claiming his own hybrid poetic identity. ("Ulster was British, but with no rights on the English lyric," he says in "The Singing School.")

As a hybrid, Heaney is thoroughly at home in both the English and Irish literary traditions. His translation of the Anglo-Saxon *Beowulf* (2000), English literature's oldest epic, won England's prestigious Whitbread Award (beating out *Harry Potter*) and made the best-seller lists in America. For years he's been translating early Irish poems into modern English. His version of the Irish epic of Mad Sweeney, a pagan king whom St. Ronan cursed into exile, to live like a bird of the air, has the cursed madman trekking from place to place, all over Ireland, screaming his preference for the birdsong that fills the BANN RIVER valley to the "grinding" of holy church bells in the monasteries of his enemies, the Christian monks. In Heaney's "Sweeney in Flight," Mad Sweeney screams from the treetops, for Celtic pagans the nests of living gods and a source of poetic inspiration. In less than an hour by car you can follow Mad Sweeney's flight through the luminous BANN VALLEY (north of Bellaghy) to SLEMISH MOUNTAIN in County Antrim, one of his resting places (and where legend locates the captive St. Patrick—one of Sweeney's enemies—herding swine as the teenage slave of Miluic): follow the A54 north and the A42 east, crossing the Bann at Port-glenone. The PORTGLENONE FOREST is a good setting in which to imag-ine divinely inspired trees exploding with birds cawing as if possessed. SLEMISH is on the other side of Ballymena. (After Broughshane, leave the A42 at Rathnell Road and take the first left onto Buckna Road; the route to Slemish is signposted. The prettiest approach is on Rathkeel Road, the A36, out of Ballymena.)

From the summit (the climb takes about an hour) you see in the green-blue distance the Antrim glens and Scottish coast to the east, Lough Neagh and the brown Sperrin Mountains to the west, and to the north, a bright green patchwork of Bann Valley farmlands criss-crossed by stone walls enclosing pastures of white and black sheep. The distinctive dome shape of Slemish makes it visible for miles: Heaney saw it from Mossbawn and Bellaghy, where, he says, he grew up "in sight of some of Sweeney's places and in earshot of others." Somewhere along the lovely back roads that lead to this beautiful mountain, you can read Heaney's translation of the mad old king's song about the trees he loves.

### FROM *SWEENEY IN FLIGHT*

*Birch tree, smooth and blessed,*
*delicious to the breeze,*
*high twigs plait and crown it*
*the queen of trees.*

*The aspen pales*
*and whispers, hesitates:*
*a thousand frightened scuts*
*race in its leaves.*

*But what disturbs me most*
*in the leafy wood*
*is the to and fro and to and fro*
*of an oak rod.*

*A starry frost will come*
*dropping on the pools*
*and I'll be astray*
*on unsheltered heights:*

*herons calling*
*in cold Glenelly,*
*flocks of birds quickly*
*coming and going.*

*I prefer the elusive*
*rhapsody of blackbirds*
*to the garrulous blather*
*of men and women.*

CXD

# Brian Moore

## 1921–1999

*The assaults of history have changed the Belfast that Brian Moore*
*grew up in—and left in 1943—the Nazi bombs of World War II, tar-*
*geting the famous shipyards (where the* Titanic *was built); the terror-*
*ist bombs of the Troubles, targeting the Other, damn the civilians;*
*and most recently, a massive urban renewal. But the city known*
*throughout the world for religious polarization is starkly preserved in*
*Moore's Belfast/Ulster novels:* The Lonely Passion of Judith Hearne
*(1955), his first book, which made his reputation;* The Feast of Lu-
percal *(1957);* The Emperor of Ice Cream *(1965); and* Lies of Silence *(1990). Eventually settling in Malibu, California, Moore*
*published twenty novels, among them a few masterpieces, admired*
*especially by other writers: William Trevor (see p. 138), Anita*
*Brookner, Mordecai Richeler, Joan Didion, Calvin Trillin, Thomas*

*Flanagan, Irish novelist John Banville, filmmaker Alfred Hitchcock, and Graham Greene, who, claiming Moore as his favorite novelist, said, "Each book of his is dangerous, unpredictable, and amusing. He treats the novel as a trainer treats a wild beast."*

*Except for the fake ending, the film version of* The Lonely Passion of Judith Hearne *(1987), starring Maggie Smith, was, according to Pauline Kael's* New Yorker *review, true to the novel's genius. With a heartbreaking empathy, Moore created an alcoholic spinster who has become one of the most unforgettable women characters in contemporary literature. A casualty of a family and church at once unloving and disapproving (Belfast writ large), Judith Hearne is no match for Moore's hometown, the subject of his final retrospective.*

## GOING HOME

Commissioned by *Granta* in 1998, this is the last piece Moore wrote.

A few years ago on holiday in the west of Ireland I came upon a field which faced a small strand and, beyond it, the Atlantic Ocean. Ahead of me five cows raised their heads and stared at the intruder. And then behind the cows I saw a few stone crosses, irregular, askew as though they had been thrown there in a game of pitch-and-toss. This was not a field but a graveyard. I walked among graves and came to a path which led to the sandy shore below. There, at the edge of this humble burial ground was a headstone unlike the others, a rectangular slab of white marble laid flat on the ground:

BULMER HOBSON
1883–1969

I stared at this name, the name of a man I had never known, yet familiar to me as a member of my family. I had heard it spoken again and again by my father in our house in Clifton Street in Belfast and by my uncle, Eoin MacNeill, when during school holidays I spent summers in his house in Dublin. For my uncle and my father, Bulmer Hobson was both a friend and in some sense a saint. A Quaker, he, like my uncle, devoted much of his life to the cause of Irish independence, becoming in the early years of this century an exemplary patriot whose nonviolent beliefs made our tribal animosities seem brutal and mean. That his body lay here in this small Connemara field, facing the ocean under a simple marker, was somehow emblematic of his life.

Proust says of our past: "It is a labor in vain to try to recapture it: all the efforts of our intellect are useless. The past is hidden somewhere outside its own domain in some material object which we never suspected. And it depends on chance whether or not we come upon it before we die."

I believe now that the "material object" was, for me, that gravestone in Connemara, a part of Ireland which I had never known in my youth. And as I stood staring at Bulmer Hobson's name, my past as a child and adolescent in Belfast surged up, vivid and importunate, bringing back a life which ended forever when I sailed to North Africa on a British troopship in the autumn of 1943.

There are those who choose to leave home vowing never to return and those who, forced to leave for economic reasons, remain in thrall to a dream of the land they left behind. And then there are those stateless wanderers who, finding the larger world into which they have stumbled vast, varied and exciting, become confused in their loyalties and lose their sense of home.

I am one of those wanderers. After the wartime years in North Africa and Italy, I worked in Poland for the United Nations, then emigrated to Canada, where I became a citizen before moving on to New York, and at last to California, where I have spent the greater part of my life.

And yet in all the years I have lived in North America I have never felt that it is my home. Annually, in pilgrimage, I go back to Paris and the French countryside and to London, the city which first welcomed me as a writer. And if I think of re-emigrating it is to France or England, not to the place where I was born.

For I know that I cannot go back. Of course, over the years I have made many return visits to my native Belfast. But Belfast, its configuration changed by the great air raids of the blitz, its inner city covered with a carapace of flyovers, its new notoriety as a theater of violence, armed patrols and hovering helicopters, seems another city, a distant relative to that Belfast which in a graveyard in Connemara filled my mind with a jumbled kaleidoscope of images fond, frightening, surprising and sad.

—My pet canary is singing in its cage above my father's head as he sits reading *The Irish News* in the breakfast room of our house in Belfast—

—A shrill electric bell summons me to Latin class in the damp, hateful corridors of St. Malachy's College. I have forgotten the declension and hear the swish of a rattan cane as I hold out my hand for punishment—

—In Fortstewart, where we spent our summer holidays, I have been all day on the sands, building an elaborate sand sculpture in hopes of winning the Cadbury contest first prize, a box of chocolates—

—Alexandra Park, where, a 7-year-old, I walk beside my sister's pram holding the hand of my nurse Nellie Ritchie, who at that time I secretly believe to be my real mother—

—I hear the terrified squeal of a pig dragged out into the yard for butchery on my uncle's farm in Donegal—

—I stand with my brothers singing a ludicrous Marian hymn in St. Patrick's Church at evening devotions:

> *O Virgin pure, O spotless maid,*
> *We sinners send out prayers to thee*
> *Remind thy Son that He has paid*
> *The price of our iniquity—*

—I hear martial music, as a regimental band of the British Army marches out from the military barracks behind our house. I see the shining brass instruments, the drummers in tiger-skin aprons, the regimental mascot, a large horned goat. Behind that imperial panoply long lines of poor recruits are marched through the streets of our native city to board ship for India, a journey from which many will never return—

—Inattentive and bored, I kneel at the Mass amid the stench of unwashed bodies in our parish church, where 80 percent of the female parishioners have no money to buy overcoats or hats and instead wear black woolen shawls which cover head and shoulders, marking them as "Shawlies," the poorest of the poor—

—We, properly dressed in our middle-class school uniforms, sitting in a crosstown bus, move through the poor streets of Shankill and the Falls, where children without shoes play on the cobbled pavements—

—The front gates of the Mater Infirmorum Hospital, where my father, a surgeon, is medical superintendent. As he drives out of those gates, a man so poor and desperate that he will court minor bodily injury to be given a bed and food for a few days steps in front of my father's car—

—An evening curfew is announced following Orange parades and the clashes which invariably follow them. The curfew, my father says, is less to prevent riots than to stop the looting of shops by both Catholic and Protestant poor—

—Older now, I sit in silent teenage rebellion as I hear my elders talk complacently of the "Irish Free State" and the differences between the Fianna Fail and Fine Gael parties who compete to govern it. Can't they see that this Catholic theocratic "grocer's republic" is narrow-minded, repressive and no real alternative to the miseries and injustices of Protestant Ulster?—

—Unbeknownst to my parents I stand on Royal Avenue hawking copies of a broadsheet called *The Socialist Appeal*, although I have refused to join the Trotskyite party which publishes it. Belfast and my childhood have made me suspicious of faiths, allegiances, certainties. It is time to leave home—

The kaleidoscope blurs. The images disappear.

The past is buried until, in Connemara, the sight of Bulmer Hobson's grave brings back those faces, those scenes, those sounds and smells which now live only in my memory. And in that moment I know that when I die I would like to come home at last to be buried here in this quiet place among the grazing cows.

▢◇▢

## *For the Literary Traveler*

Moore's sense of himself as Belfast exile rings true with what you can't help feeling as you walk this city's streets: this is not a seductive place, you don't want to dig in deeper and stay awhile. Though you might come across many easygoing people, especially among the students, from others you feel a tightness. Maybe it's the tormented history or simply the arthritic weather projecting itself.

It makes sense that the city's most free-spirited neighborhood surrounds the university, a community devoted more to possibility than to past hatreds. This is also, ironically, the neighborhood of Moore's fictional Judith Hearne, another Belfast exile, though she never leaves home and has neither the money nor the confidence to enroll in the university that's diagonally across the road from where she lives (in bed-and-breakfast territory—the narrow streets between Lisburn and University Road/Malone Road, now full of students—on CAMDEN STREET, between Fitzwilliam and Claremont Streets). The handsome main building of QUEENS UNIVERSITY on University Road in South Belfast (south of Shaftesbury Square), a warm red brick with a mock-Tudor facade that's modeled on Oxford's Magdalene College, lifts your spirits at first sight. And the campus is a friendly place to roam. It's easy to strike up a conversation among the nine thousand students, most of them from Northern Ireland; in the summer you can hear lectures by visiting professors. There's a sculpture of Joyce by Mike Hogg outside the main library; another library is named for Seamus Heaney, who was a student and then a teacher here, nurturing a generation of younger poets. The university's new honorary chancellor, former U.S. senator George Mitchell, who forged the alliance between Ulster's Protestant Unionists and Catholic Republicans (known as the Good Friday agreement), recently awarded Edna O'Brien an honorary doctorate from the university: "[She] changed the course of Irish womanhood." (The government censor who banned her first novel called it "a smear on Irish womanhood.")

The street adjoining the quad, UNIVERSITY SQUARE, is an unbroken line of lovely Georgian or early Victorian houses with gardens, now the offices of academic departments. University Square leads to COLLEGE PARK and, inside College Green Park, the UNION THEOLOGICAL COLLEGE, whose fine architecture bears no resemblance to the ugly caricature that passes for theology in the religious wars of Belfast and the Sunday morning sermons Judith Hearne hears in her parish church. (Behind College Green Park, off Rugby Road, is FITZROY AVENUE, a signature song title of Belfast native—and exile—Van Morrison.) Left (north) of College Park, along Botanic Avenue, are students' shops, an art-film theater, and, at the corner of University Street, the Duke Hotel, an amiable place to stay or have a meal (tel. (01232) 236666). In the other direction, south of College Park and the campus, are the BOTANIC GARDENS, where Judith Hearne and the man she fantasizes about as her future husband, the unscrupulous James Madden, walk in mutual misunderstanding. In Moore's city "of gray buildings and black backyards," this is an oasis of greenery, fragrant with rose gardens and the tropical plants in the glass-domed PALM HOUSE.

The ULSTER MUSEUM, next to the Gardens and a good place to take shelter (often in Belfast, in Moore's words, "the rain wept itself into a lashing rage"), has a pleasant rooftop café that overlooks the Gardens. In the museum store you'll find books about Irish painters whose subjects are literary (T. P. Flanagan's contemplative impressions of Lissadell and of Seamus Heaney's settings; the anthology *Irish Poetry and Painting*); and monographs on such first-rate Irish artists as John Lavery, Louis le Brocquy, Henry Moore, Paul Henry, and Roderic O'Conor, whose work is displayed on the top floor.

For more indoor shelter as well as for browsing through the books of the prolific Ulster/Belfast writers of the twentieth century (the esteemed poets Louis MacNeice, John Hewitt, Patrick Fiacc, Michael Longley (see p. 361), Derek Mahon, Ciaran Carson (see p. 395, and look for his poem "Belfast Confetti"), Medbh McGuckian (see p. 445), and Joan Newman), the university bookstore, THE BOOKSHOP AT QUEENS, across a junction of three roads at 91 University Road, though not cozy, is fully stocked. The helpful staff will identify the painted heads of writers with Belfast associations (including Philip Larkin and Dublin-born Iris Murdoch, whose father came from Belfast) that look down from literal high seriousness close to the ceiling. For atmosphere (and food) while you browse, walk a block or so north, along University Road toward the city center, to BOOKFINDERS. Here the gracious owner, Mary Denver, and her friendly young assistants—the absolute opposite of the cold creatures Judith Hearne encounters in her walks around Belfast—have the answers to most questions about the used books crowding the shelves as well as about the local writers from both within and outside the university and the small magazines who publish them. Van the Man Morrison of East Belfast (where you can find the street names of his songs) is the younger staff's favorite local poet. Bookfinders should have a copy of Mary Beckett's devastating collection *A Belfast Woman* (1980): the stories (especially the title story) of this "extraordinary miniaturist," portraying the lives of the women of Northern Ireland, "make us flinch," wrote Brian Moore, "creat[ing] a strange poetry out of the poverty and ugliness of these lives." Bookfinders, a popular student hangout, hosts a weekly Platform for New Poets in the café and jazz nights upstairs in the art gallery.

Leaving the "the gown" of Belfast behind (as Judith Hearne does on her way to the public library and Sunday Mass), you approach the "town" across its signature junctions. Taking the right fork at the junction of SHAFTSBURY SQUARE, head straight down the Dublin Road (for about ten minutes, on foot) toward the CITY CENTER, in its staid Victorian hulkiness resembling Manchester and Leeds in northern England or the old Glasgow in Scotland more than any place in Ireland. For the Catholic-born Brian Moore, the CITY HALL, "a staring white ugliness" dominating DONEGALL SQUARE, represents the prevailing ethos of Northern Ireland's capital city:

There, under the great dome of the building, ringed around by forgotten memorials, bordered by the garrison neatness of a Garden of Remembrance, everything that was Belfast came into focus. The newsvendors calling out the great events of the world in flat, uninterested Ulster voices; the drab facades of the buildings grouped around the Square, proclaiming the virtues of trade, hard dealing and Presbyterian righteousness. The order, the neatness, the floodlit cenotaph, a white respectable phallus planted in sinking Irish bog. The Protestant dearth of gaiety, the Protestant surfeit of order, the dour Ulster burghers walking proudly among these monuments to their mediocrity.

Box-like double-decker buses nosed into the Square, picking up patient queues of people, whirling them off quietly to the outer edges of the city. Like trained soldiers, Mr Madden and Miss Hearne marched to a queue and took their places.

Just north of City Hall, on ROYAL AVENUE (Belfast's Fifth Avenue), Moore as a teenager hawked his socialist newspapers. About five blocks north of CASTLE JUNCTION is the neighborhood where Brian Moore grew up in middle-class security, observing the poverty that is the stale daily bread of Judith Hearne's world (and today's still-embattled West Belfast). In ST. PATRICK'S CHURCH (which has a painting by John Lavery), at the intersection of Upper Donegall Street and York Street, Moore sang "ludicrous hymns." He lived in CLIFTON STREET. Nearby is the Georgian Clifton House, also called the MATER INFIRMORUM, Belfast's oldest public building (1771), built as a home for the sick elderly; Moore's father was medical superintendent here. Further north is ALEXANDRA PARK, a memory of Moore's very earliest years in Belfast. (ST. MALACHY'S COL-LEGE, south of the city, is still in operation.)

In the movie version of *The Lonely Passion of Judith Hearne*, the director changed the setting from Belfast to Dublin. At first that seemed a mistake. Yet there is something about Moore's Belfast and the lonely image of Judith Hearne as she passes through its streets that reminds you of the late-nineteenth-century Dublin Joyce re-creates in *Dubliners*. Both capital cities had a blight in common. Terry Eagleton calls it "anomie" and explains it this way: "[It] is partly the effect of a tyranni-cal clericalism and a stifling patriarchy; but it is also just as plainly the upshot of a colonial condition of political powerlessness and eco-nomic backwardness."

The Antrim bus (number 5, 10, or 45) will take you from the city center six miles into North Belfast and CAVE HILL, the topographical hulk that Belfast people climb on weekends and where Belfast couples can enjoy some privacy. But in both *Judith Hearne* and *The Emperor of Ice Cream*, his novel about the German bombardment of Belfast in World War II, Moore makes Cave Hill a scene of oppressiveness. In *The Emperor*, young Gavin Burke, receiving only a lecture from his girlfriend on this scenic hilltop, comes to see her as "a nun in mufti." Like the young Brian Moore, he goes his own way, into a larger world. Spread out below Cave Hill is Belfast in its beautiful natural setting. Yet for Brian Moore it was the sentiment behind the words of Belfast writer Maurice Craig (1919– ) that hit closer to home:

> O the bricks they will bleed and the rain it will weep,
> And the damp Lagan fog lull the city to sleep;
> It's to hell with the future and live on the past:
> May the Lord in His Mercy be kind to Belfast.

# Medbh McGuckian

## 1950–

*The first woman to be appointed writer in residence at Queens University, Belfast, the poet Medbh McGuckian has been described as "revolutionary" in Peggy O'Brien's* Irish Women's Poetry: 1967–2000, *"the most daring and innovative poet" of her generation. Her latest collection,* Shemalier *(1999), was praised in* The New Yorker *for its "private landscape of striking intensity." Previous volumes—The Flower Master (1982); Venus and the Rain (1984); On Ballycastle Beach (1988); Marconi's Cottage (1991); and Captain Lavender (1995) received recognition in France, America, and England, winning many literary prizes, including Britain's National Poetry Competition. Unlike many of her writing colleagues who have left Northern Ireland, McGuckian still lives in Belfast, where she grew up.*

### THE SOCIETY OF THE BOMB

*The sleep of her lover is her sleep:*
*it warms her and brings her out to people*

*like half-making love or the wider now,*
*exceptionally sunlit spring.*

*Before violence was actually offered*
*to us, we followed a trail of words*
*into the daylight, those palest and clearest*
*blues, and all the snow to come.*

ON BALLYCASTLE BEACH

*for my father*

*If I found you wandering round the edge*
*of a French-born sea, when children*
*should be taken in by their parents,*
*I would read these words to you,*
*like a ship coming in to harbour,*
*as meaningless and full of meaning*
*as the homeless flow of life*
*from room to homesick room.*

*The words and you would fall asleep,*
*sheltering just beyond my reach*
*in a city that has vanished to regain*
*its language. My words are traps*
*through which you pick your way*
*from a damp March to an April date,*
*or a mid-August misstep; until enough winter*
*makes you throw your watch, the heartbeat*
*of everyone present, out into the snow.*

*My forbidden squares and your small circles*
*were a book that formed within you*
*in some pocket, so permanently distended,*
*that what does not face north faces east.*
*Your hand, dark as a cedar lane by nature,*
*grows more and more tired of the skidding light,*
*the hunched-up waves, and all the wet clothing,*
*toys and treasures of a late summer house.*

*Even the Atlantic has begun its breakdown*
*like a heavy mask thinned out scene after scene*
*in a more protected time—like one who has*
*gradually, unnoticed, lengthened her pre-wedding*
*dress. But, staring at the old escape and release*
*of the water's speech, faithless to the end,*
*your voice was the longest I heard in my mind,*
*although I had forgotten there could be such light.*

## For the Literary Traveler

"From a very early age I knew that because of our religion we were as outcast as Jews," McGuckian has said of her childhood in a Catholic ghetto of North Belfast. When the Troubles began in earnest, she was a student at Queens University, where Seamus Heaney was her tutor in honors English. Violence destroyed WEST BELFAST, turning its Protestant community on the Shankill Road and the Catholic one on the Falls Road into "a society of bombs," in the words of her poem's title. To separate the warring tribes, a metal "Peace Line" was built between the two neighborhoods. Visitors can tour West Belfast in taxis or buses departing from Donegall Square and see the famous battleground murals and graffiti of "Little Beirut." Along Sandy Row and Donegall Road (on the way to the M1), both Protestant enclaves, you pass others; you can also see them reproduced as books and postcards, which are sold all over Belfast. Since the cease-fires of the nineties and the popular vote in favor of the Good Friday agreement, murals of peace have appeared on both sides of the divide. Just as the guerrilla war drives the furies of McGuckian's literary contemporaries in Northern Ireland (Eoin McNamee in his novel *Resurrection* and Belfast-born, Belfast-exile Bernard MacLaverty in *Cal* and *Lamb*), so the Troubles also gave two women, the Catholic Mairead Corrigan and the Protestant Betty Williams, the courage to organize the Northern Ireland Peace Movement, for which they received the Nobel Prize for Peace in 1976.

But McGuckian's poetic landscape is larger than a war zone. In her second poem, she takes us away to her personal paradise of NORTH ANTRIM: "I lived only for the summers, which were spent in the fields of my father's childhood by the Atlantic, opposite Rathlin Island on the North Antrim coast. This to me became my Ireland." Northern Ireland's fifty-mile-long North Atlantic shore attracts many tourists and summer residents from Belfast and Scotland, which looks as close as the next parish from the famous, fabulous, and crowded GIANT'S CAUSEWAY. You can also wave at the Scots from the spectacular cliffs of FAIR HEAD, just five miles east of McGuckian's BALLYCASTLE, a popular seaside resort at the junction of the most northerly Antrim glens, GLENTAISE and GLENSHESK. The way up north to McGuckian Country (on the B94/A2) passes through or past the nine green GLENS OF ANTRIM, all sloping down toward the Irish Sea and in their beauty fully deserving of the praise they receive in folk songs and poetry. A vacation town and home to Ireland's oldest fair, the OULD LAMMAS FAIR in August, Ballycastle is named for the castle of the MacDonnells that's long gone. But BALLYCASTLE BEACH, where McGuckian found her only emotional harbor during the Troubles, is wide and peaceful, resonant with her tribute to her father's memory. Ballycastle is also the starting point for the six-mile boat trip out to RATHLIN ISLAND (call Rathlin Ventures, (012657) 63917, or Iona Isle, (012657) 63915), its gory history the subject of poems by McGuckian and Derek Mahon. Five miles west of Ballycastle is the salmon fishermen's rope bridge at CARRICK-A-REDE, where the mother in Lorrie Moore's story "Which Is More than I Can Say About Some People" (see p. 187) comes close to scaring herself to death as she walks, then crawls, the swaying bridge while looking down at the thunderous waves crashing beneath her. If it's self-assertiveness you're after (like Abby's mother), a bit of Outward Bound on the cheap, this bridge, spanning a sixty-foot gap between the coast and Carrick-a-Rede Island, awaits you Apr.-Sept., 10–6 daily; June-Aug., 10–8 daily, weather permitting.

At the end of summer, McGuckian now, as in childhood, leaves Ballycastle, going home to BELFAST (with her husband and four children) and going back to school. In 1995, after the cease-fires, she talked about her teaching job:

I teach poetry classes at two local universities ... to reasonable and intelligent and highly sensitive adults, from both sides of what they call the "divide." There are many new institutional ways in which artificial enemies who have never met, who have been segregated and ostracised from each other, can slowly come together, and poetry's a deeply rewarding, if dangerous way.... This year I have a Derry Unionist cheerfully giving State information to a Crumlin Road nun, and a Free Presbyterian minister denouncing fornication in the most exquisite love poems.... There's a loosening, as of icebergs around the Titanic, there's a respect for the hurt of words as well as bullets, and the hurt of no words. There's a determined search for the right language in which to say what we really mean, to each other and about each other, no longer behind each other's backs in each other's houses.

Transforming the bitter facts of history by the power of their words, Irish continue to perform a kind of magic. This pattern of redemption by language can take root in even the most unpromising circumstances. And, as in the experience of Medbh McGuckian's students, it can change lives. From the beginning, literature, above all other arts, has flourished in Ireland. In this new century, it is still a vital work of peace and beauty.

# For Further Reading

*In addition to the writings mentioned in the text.*

NONFICTION

Aldington, Richard, and Stanley Weintraub, eds. *The Portable Oscar Wilde.* Rev. ed. 1981.

Appel, Alfred. *The Art of Celebration: 20th-Century Painting, Literature, Sculpture, Photography and Jazz.* 1992.

Behan, Brendan. *Borstal Boy.* 1958.

Bell, J. Bowyer. *The Irish Troubles: A Generation of Violence, 1967–1992.* 1993.

Bitel, Lisa M. *Land of Women: Tales of Sex and Gender from Early Ireland.* 1996.

Blythe, Ronald. "An Inherited Perspective." *Characters and Their Landscapes.* 1984.

Boland, Eavan. *Object Lessons.* 1995.

Bourke, Angela. *The Burning of Bridget Cleary.* 1994.

Bowen, Elizabeth. *The Shelburne Hotel.* 1951.

Cahill, Susan, and Thomas Cahill. *A Literary Guide to Ireland.* 1973.

Corkery, Daniel. *The Hidden Ireland.* 1925.

De Paor, Liam. *The Peoples of Ireland.* 1986.

Deane, Seamus, ed. *The Field Day Anthology of Irish Writing.* 3 vols. 1991.

Donoghue, Denis. *Warrenpoint.* 1990.

Donovan, Katie, and Brendan Kennelly, eds. *Dublines.* 1995.

Eagleton, Terry. *The Truth About the Irish.* 1999.

Ellmann, Richard. *Eminent Domain.* 1974.

———. *James Joyce.* Rev. ed. 1983.

Feehan, John M. *The Secret Places of the Burren.* 1987.

Foster, Roy. *W. B. Yeats, a Life.* Vol. 1. 1998.

Gregory, Anne. *Me and Nu: Childhood at Coole.* 1970.

Harbison, Peter. *Guide to the National Monuments of Ireland.* 1970.

Igoe, Vivien. *A Literary Guide to Dublin.* 1999.

Keneally, Thomas. *The Great Shame: And the Triumph of the Irish in the English-Speaking World.* 1998.

Kenner, Hugh. *A Colder Eye: The Modern Irish Writers.* 1983.

Kirby, Sheelah. *The Yeats Country.* 1969.

Krause, David. *Sean O'Casey: The Man and His Work.* 1967.

Jeffares, A. Norman. *A Pocket History of Irish Literature.* 1997.

Leland, Mary. *The Lie of the Land: Journeys Through Literary Cork.* 1999.

Lyons, F. S. L. *Charles Stewart Parnell.* 1977.

McDiarmid, Lucy, and Maureen Waters, eds. *Lady Gregory: Selected Writings.* 1995.

McGarry, James. *Place Names in the Writings of William Butler Yeats.* 1976.

McGlinchey, Charles. *The Last of the Name: Stories of Inishowen, Donegal.* 1986.

MacMahon, Bryan. *The Master.* 1992.

Maddox, Brenda. *Nora: A Biography of Nora Joyce.* 1988.

———. *Yeats's Ghosts: The Secret Life of W. B. Yeats.* 1999.

Mahoney, Rosemary. *Whoredom in Kimmage.* 1993.

Mercier, Vivian. *Beckett/Beckett.* 1977.

———. *The Irish Comic Tradition.* 1962.

Mitchell, Flora H. *Vanishing Dublin.* 1966.

Moreton, Cole. *Hungry for Home.* 2000.

na Gopaleen, Myles. *The Best of Myles na Gopaleen.* 1968.

Neville, Peter. *A Traveller's History of Ireland.* 1997.

Newby, Eric. *Round Ireland in Low Gear.* 1987.

O'Brien, Jacqueline, and Peter Harbison. *Ancient Ireland.* 1996.

O'Connor, Frank. *The Big Fellow.* 1935.

———. *Irish Miles.* 1947.

O'Connor, Joseph. *The Secret World of the Irish Male.* 1995.

O'Mara, Veronica, and Fionnuala O'Reilly. *An Irish Literary Cookbook.* 1991.

O'Toole, Fintan. *The Lie of the Land: Irish Identities.* 1997.

Quinn, John, ed. *My Education: RTE Radio Interviews with Writers.* 1997.

Raymo, Chet. *Honey from Stone.* 1987.

Robinson, Mary. "A New Ireland." Inauguration address. 1990.

Robinson, Tim. "Introduction." In J. M. Synge, *The Aran Islands.* 1992.

Sawyer, Roger, ed. *Roger Casement's Diaries: 1910: The Black and the White.* 1997.

Scheper-Hughes, Nancy. *Saints, Scholars, and Schizophrenics.* 1979.

Seaver, Richard. "Introduction." In *A Samuel Beckett Reader: I Can't Go on, I'll Go On.* 1976.

Skelton, Robin. J. M. *Synge and His World.* 1971.

Smith, Cecil Woodham. *The Great Hunger.* 1962.

Sontag, Susan. *Against Interpretation.* 1966.

Tyers, Padraig, ed. *Blasket Memories.* 1998.

Vendler, Helen. *Seamus Heaney.* 1998.

Waters, John. *Jiving at the Crossroads.* 1991.

Waters, Maureen. *The Comic Irishman.* 1984.


*FICTION*

Boylan, Clare. *Concerning Virgins.* 1989.

———. *Holy Pictures.* 1983.

Daly, Ita. *The Lady with the Red Shoes.* 1980.

Donoghue, Emma. *Hood.* 1988.

Enright, Anne. *What Are You Like?* 2000.

Fitzpatrick, Nina. "In the Company of Frauds." *Fables of the Irish Intelligentsia.* 1991.

Glassie, Henry, ed. *Irish Folktales.* 1985.

Heaney, Marie. *Over Nine Waves: A Book of Irish Legends.* 1994.

Johnston, Jennifer. *The Old Jest.* 1979.

Jordan, Neil. *Night in Tunisia and Other Stories.* 1976.

Kavanagh, Patrick. *Tarry Flynn.* 1948.

Keane, Molly. *Good Behavior.* 1981.

———. *Time After Time.* 1983.

Kiely, Benedict. *Journey to the Seven Streams.* 1963.

McCabe, Patrick. *The Butcher Boy.* 1992.

McGahern, John. *Amongst Women.* 1990.

———. *The Barracks.* 1962.

———. *Collected Stories.* 1992.

———. *The Dark.* 1965.

MacLaverty, Bernard. *Grace Notes.* 1997.

McNamara, Brinsley. *The Valley of the Squinting Windows.* 1918.

Moore, George. *The Untilled Field.* 1903.

Nolan, Christopher. *The Banyan Tree.* 1999.

O'Brien, Edna. *A Fanatic Heart.* 1985.

———. *Lantern Slides.* 1990.

O'Brien, Flann. *At Swim-Two-Birds.* 1939.

O'Faolain, Julia. "Why Should Not Old Men Be Mad?" *Daughters of Passion.* 1982.

Stephens, James. *The Charwoman's Daughter.* 1966.

Toibin, Colm, ed. *The Penguin Book of Irish Fiction.* 2000.


*POETRY*

Allingham, William. "The Winding Banks of Erne." or, "The Emigrant's Adieu to Ballyshannon." 1877.

Anon. "Kilcash." 17th–19th century. Trans. Frank O'Connor.

Colum, Padraic. "She Moved Through the Fair." *Wild Earth.* 1916.

Fitzgerald, Gerald. "Against Blame of Woman." 14th century.

Hartnett, Michael. *Selected and New Poems.* 1994.

Hewitt, John. *The Collected Poems.* 1991.

Kavanagh, Patrick. *Collected Poems.* 1964.

Kennelly, Brendan. "My Dark Fathers." *Collection One.* 1966.

———, ed. *The Penguin Book of Irish Verse.* 1970.

MacNeice, Louis. "Dublin." *The Closing Album.* 1939.

———. *Poems.* 1935.

Mahon, Derek. "Glengormley." *Night Crossing.* 1968

———. "A Disused Shed in County Wexford." *The Snow-Party.* 1975.

Meehan, Paula. *Pillow Talk.* 1994.

Montague, John. "Like Dolmens Round My Childhood, the Old People." *Poisoned Lands.* 1977.

———, ed. "In the Irish Grain." *The Book of Irish Verse.* 1974.

Ní Chuilleanain, Eilean. *Site of Ambush.* 1975.

———. *The Second Voyage.* 1986.

Ní Dhuibhne, Ellis, ed. *Voices on the Wind: Women Poets of the Celtic Twilight.* 1995.

O'Brien, Peggy, ed. *The Wake Forest Book of Irish Women's Poetry: 1967–2000.* 2000.

O'Connor, Frank, trans. *Kings, Lords, and Commons.* 1959.

O'Donnell, Mary. *Unlegendary Heroes.* 2000.

O'Malley, Mary. *Where the Rocks Float.* 1993.

———. *The Knife in the Wave.* 1997.

Raftery, Anthony. 19th century. "Mary Hynes." Trans. Frank O'Connor.

Simmons, James. *Songs for Derry.* 1969.

Wilde, Oscar. *The Poems of Oscar Wilde.* 1908.

*DRAMA*

Carr, Marina. *Portia Coughlan.* 1996.

Leonard, Hugh. *Da.* 1978.

McGuinness, Frank. *Observe the Sons of Ulster Marching Towards the Somme.* 1985.

MacIntyre, Tom. *Good Evening, Mr. Collins.* 1996.

Shaw, George Bernard. *John Bull's Other Island.* 1904.

# Permissions Acknowledgments

Anonymous, "The Hag of Beara," translated by John Montague. Reprinted with the permission of the translator.

Samuel Beckett, "Ding Dong" from *More Pricks Than Kicks.* Copyright 1934 by Samuel Beckett. Excerpt from *Worstward Ho.* Copyright © 1983 by Samuel Beckett. Both reprinted with the permission of Grove/Atlantic, Inc.

Eavan Boland, "Anna Liffey" from *In a Time of Violence.* Copyright © 1994 by Eavan Boland. Reprinted with the permission of W. W. Norton & Company, Inc.

Elizabeth Bowen, excerpt from *Bowen's Court* (New York: Alfred A. Knopf, 1942). Copyright 1942, © 1964 by Elizabeth Bowen. Reprinted with the permission of Curtis Brown, Ltd.

Thomas Cahill, "Patrick's Breastplate" from *How the Irish Saved Civilization.* Copyright © 1995 by Thomas Cahill. Reprinted with the permission of Doubleday, a division of Random House, Inc.

Mary Carbery, excerpt from *The Farm by Lough Gur.* Longman, London, 1937, reissued by The Mercier Press, Cork, Republic of Ireland. Copyright 1937 by Mary Carbery. Reprinted with the permission of Jeremy Sanford on behalf of the Estate of Mary Carbery.

Joyce Cary, excerpt from *A House of Children* (New York: Harper and Brothers, 1941). Copyright 1941 by Joyce Cary. Reprinted with the permission of the estate of the Andrew Lownie Literary Agency.

Seamus Deane, excerpts from *Reading in the Dark.* Copyright © 1996 by Seamus Deane. Reprinted with the permission of Alfred A. Knopf, a division of Random House, Inc.

Roddy Doyle, excerpt from *The Commitments.* Copyright © 1987 by William Heinemann, Ltd. Reprinted with the permission of The Random House Archive & Library and John Sutton.

Brian Friel, excerpt from *Dancing at Lughnasa.* Copyright © 1990 by Brian Friel. Reprinted with the permission of Faber & Faber, Ltd., and the agency (london) Ltd.

Seamus Heaney, excerpt from "Crediting Poetry" (Nobel Lecture). Reprinted with the permission of Faber & Faber, Ltd. "St. Kevin and the Blackbird" from *The*

Brian Moore, "Going Home" [Commissioned by *Granta*, published in *The New York Times* (February 7, 1999), Book Review Bookend. Copyright © 1999 by Brian Moore. Reprinted with the permission of Curtis Brown, Ltd. Excerpts from *The Lonely Passion of Judith Hearne*. Copyright © 1956 and renewed 1984 by Brian Moore. Reprinted with the permission of Little, Brown and Company.

Lorrie Moore, "Which Is More Than I Can Say About Some People" from *Birds of America*. Copyright © 1998 by Lorrie Moore. Reprinted with the permission of Alfred A. Knopf, a division of Random House, Inc.

Marianne Moore, excerpt from "Spenser's Ireland" from *The Collected Poems of Marianne Moore*. Copyright 1941 and renewed © 1969 by Marianne Moore. Reprinted with the permission of Scribner, a division of Simon & Schuster, Inc.

Jan Morris, "The Rock of Cashel" from Jan Morris and Paul Wakefield, *Ireland: Your Only Place*. Copyright © 1990 by Jan Morris. Reprinted with the permission of Clarkson Potter/Publishers, a division of Random House, Inc.

Paul Muldoon, excerpt from *Kerry Slides*. Copyright © 1996 by Paul Muldoon. Reprinted with the permission of The Gallery Press, Loughcrew, Oldcastle, Co Meath, Ireland.

Dervla Murphy, excerpt from *Wheels Within Wheels*. Copyright © 1979 by Dervla Murphy. Reprinted with the permission of John Murray (Publishers), Ltd.

Nuala Ní Dhomhnaill, "Oileán (Island)" from *Pharoah's Daughter*, translated by John Montague. Copyright © 1990 by Nuala Ní Dhomhnaill. Reprinted with the permission of Wake Forest University Press. "Labasheedy (The Silken Bed)" from *Selected Poems*, translated by Nuala Ní Dhomhnaill. Copyright © 1997 by Nuala Ní Dhomhnaill. Reprinted with the permission of New Island Books.

Eilis Ní Dhuibhne, "Blood and Water" from *Blood and Water and Other Stories*. Copyright © 1988 by Eilis Ní Dhuibhne. Reprinted with the permission of the author c/o Attic Press, Crawford Business Park, Crosses Green, Cork, Ireland.

Edna O'Brien, excerpt from *Mother Ireland* (New York: Harcourt Brace Jovanovich, 1976). Copyright © 1976 by Edna O'Brien. Reprinted with the permission of David Godwin Associates.

Kate O'Brien, excerpt from *My Ireland*. Copyright © 1962 by Kate O'Brien. Reprinted with the permission of Chrysalis Books Ltd.

Eileen O'Connell, excerpt from *Lament for Art O'Leary*, translated by Frank O'Connor (Dublin: Cuala Press, 1940). Copyright 1940 by Frank O'Connor. Reprinted with the permission of Joan Davies agency on behalf of the estate of the author.

Frank O'Connor, "The Drunkard" from *Collected Stories*. Copyright 1951 by Frank O'Connor. Reprinted with the permission of Alfred A. Knopf, a division of Random House, Inc. and Joan Davies Agency on behalf of the estate of the author.